TRIBAL LAND SYSTEMS

ABOUT THE AUTHOR

HARSHAD R. TRIVEDI is a veteran Socio- logist and Social Anthropologist. Doing extensive field-work among the Mers of Saurashtra, he became the first Ph.D. Scholar from Sociology Department under M.N. Srinivas in 1955, Faculty of Arts, M.S. University of Baroda.

Dr. Trivedi worked intensively among the Dubla, Naika and Chaudhari tribes of South Gujarat during 1955-56. From 1957 until 1962, he joined an interdisciplinary project in environmental sanitation in rural Delhi and later became the first Social Scientist in the Government of India, Ministry of Health, New Delhi. Subsequently he was appointed Deputy Director of Cultural Anthropology in National Institute of Community Development, Mussoorie.

Finally as freelance researcher, Trivedi held several positions and assignments in New Delhi, Kanpur, Bombay and Ahmedabad working on a wide range of subjects including urbanisation, public administration, scheduled caste women, community development, panchayati raj, tribal land systems, land for cultivation and housing of scheduled castes, kinship and culture, adaptation of TV and Video, and socio-economic status of sensitive areas in Ahmedabad and Baroda, cities.

TRIBAL LAND SYSTEMS

Land Reform Measures and Development of Tribals

HARSHAD R. TRIVEDI
DIRECTOR
INSTITUTE OF CULTURAL
AND URBAN ANTHROPOLOGY
AHMEDABAD

CONCEPT PUBLISHING COMPANY, NEW DELHI-110059

ISBN 81-7022-454-3

First Published 1993

Published and Printed by
Ashok Kumar Mittal
Concept Publishing Company
A/15-16, Commercial Block, Mohan Garden
NEW DELHI-110059 (India)

Lasertypeset by
Microtech Advance Printing Systems (Pvt.) Ltd.
H-13, Bali Nagar
NEW DELHI-110015

DEDICATED TO LATE
DR. G.D. PATEL

ACKNOWLEDGEMENTS

It is my pleasant duty to acknowledge the help of a number of well wishers and resource persons including those from public and private institutions. Well over a hundred of knowledgeable persons including officials and non-officials helped immensely in satisfactorily discharging my duties and responsibilities. I should like to make reference to select persons on account of their more intimate connections and involvement in successful completion of various operations of this project.

Shri Chinubhai Chimanlal Sheth, Chairman of Gujarat Regional Branch of IIPA was kind to evince keen interest in the working of the project right from the beginning until its conclusion. In spite of his onerous responsibilities and manifold public activities, he was kind to go through a few chapters in the initial stages of report writing and to give valuable suggestions. My thanks go to Shri P.N. Mittal and late Shri S.R. Modi, Hon. Secretary and Treasure respectively of the Institute for their kind cooperation and help. Shri Modi was specially helpful in solving practical problems encountered from time to time by the members of the project.

The parent organisation, IIPA, New Delhi played a crucial role in helping the project by giving necessary guidance and suggestions. Our thanks go to the former Directors Shri R.N. Haldipur and to Shri T.N. Chaturvedi, who were kind enough to offer invaluable advice and guidance at the time of revival of the project after the sad demise of Dr. G.D. Patel.

We must thank the senior officers of the Ministry of Home Affairs, Dr. B.D. Sharma and Dr. Bhupinder Singh, formerly Joint Secretaries and Shri P.V. Rao, Deputy Secretary in the Tribal Development Department who were most helpful in providing grant-in-aid and timely guidance. The project operations were routed through the Revenue Department of the Government of Gujarat, Gandhinagar. I am deeply grateful to a number of officers who were kind to give cooperation in making necessary financial provisions until the completion of the extended project work. They are Shri Harihar Das, the then Revenue Secretary, Shri. B.T. Trivedi, Finance Secretary and Shri T.D. Soyantar, Commissioner, Land Reforms, Shri P.V. Bhatt, Secretary, Tribal Development Department and Shri H.K. Khan, Secretary, Agriculture, Forest and Cooperation. They came to our help not only at the initiation of the project, but also at the time when the project was revived. Shri R.M. Shah, the then Deputy Secretary, Revenue Department and Shri V.G. Risbud, Asstt. Commissioner Land Reforms and Section Officer Shri Hasmukh Patel were helpful in solving difficult problems of releasing instalments of grants at different points of time. I am sincerely grateful to all these cooperative officers of Gujarat Government, especially Shri Vrajlal Brahmabatt for their valuable help.

It would have been almost impossible to take care of complete task left on my shoulder without sincere assistance of Shri T.S. Shah and Shri R.J. Bhatt, who were associated with the working of this project from its very inception. They continued to remain devoted and loyal to the work even after they were recalled to help and complete the work of the project. Shri N.A. Trivedi was mainly instrumental in persuading these two research officers to rejoin the revived project for which he deserves special mention. The team of tabulation experts worked under the guidance of Shri Gokulbhai O. Parikh assisted by Dr. Miss Ushaben Sharma and Shri N.S. Gohel. Although the tabulated field survey data have not been put to use in this publication, their contribution needs to be highly appreciated. The content analysis of the in-depth field interview data was done diligently and sincerely by Shri Ashwin B. Solanki that helped preparation of the write-up on dynamics of tribal land situation. Thanks are due to Shri Verghese, Kum. Asha Bharani, Mrs. Pramila A. Kambale and Shri B.B. Mehta for secretarial assistance and for typing various parts of the report. I should make special references to Shri K.R. Bhatt, Shri Sashikant Shah, Shri Bharat H. Shah and Mrs. R.S. Phanse, working in our neighbouring offices of the PWD and Doordarshan for taking sympathetic interest in our work and becoming helpful as and when required. We are grateful to all of them for their cooperation and help.

Prof. Mohanbhai S. Patel, the then President, Institute of Cultural and Urban Anthropology, Ahmedabad, was kind enough to allow me to take up this responsibility although a lot of work was pending to give necessary boost to the activities of the Institute, as its Hon. Secretary and Director. My younger brother, Dr. P.R. Trivedi, extended fraternal cooperation and help so as to enable me devote full time and energy in the interest of the project.

Hon. Shri Harisinha Mahida, the then Revenue Minister and the then Secretary Shri N. Gopalswami were kind to clear permission for publication in 1988 with the help of the then Deputy Secretary Shri Y.A. Anjaria. I am most thankful to them for support and cooperation. My thanks are due to Hon. Secretary and Members of the Executive Council of Gujarat State Regional branch of IIPA for final approval to get the report printed of my own accord. I must thank Dr. Sidhdhraj Solanki for sparing time for giving a close look at the manuscript and for offering valuable suggestions. Km. Sujata B. Rawal deserves special mention for fine drawings of maps.

HARSHAD R. TRIVEDI

CONTENTS

LIST OF TABLES AND MAPS

Maps

PREFACE

The Government of India, Ministry of Home Affairs sponsored in 1977 the research project for the study of Land Systems in the tribal areas in India with special reference to Tribal Areas in Gujarat. The project received cent per cent central assistance from the Union Government with the concurrence of the Government of Gujarat, Revenue Department, Gandhinagar. The Late Dr. G.D. Patel, the then Hon. Secretary of IIPA of Gujarat State Regional Branch was entrusted with the responsibility to direct the Project.

Infact, he was the originator of the research proposal. The project was initiated on October 21, 1977 with the expectation that though the focus of the study would be on the State of Gujarat, it would project national perspective of tribal land systems. Since it was not possible to update information on land systems in all the new and old States and Union Territories, that part of the report has been kept aside from this abridged version. I hope to get it published after necessary revision and additions later on.

Late Dr. Patel remained in-charge of this Tribal Land Systems Study (TLS) Project for about 11 months. Unfortunately, he expired during a field visit at Surat in the morning of September 13, 1978. The project work was immediately closed down. It created a gap of about five months after which I started the project with re-employment of the old staff that was discharged. To be exact, the project was revived in the second half of the month of March 1979. The credit for fruitful revival of the project goes to Shri T.N. Chaturvedi, the then Director, IIPA, New Delhi. His suggestion to entrust the responsibility to me was accepted by the Gujarat Regional Branch. The task called for me the collection of field data, analysis, tabulation and interpretation of data for report writing. The Government of India, Home Department were kind to agree to extend the period of one additional year to enable me to complete the report.

Comming from Revenue Cadru, Dr. Patel had rich knowledge of land systems of Bilingual Bombay State prior to bifurcation into the States of Maharashtra and Gujarat. He had given up the idea of looking at land systems in a straight-jacket manner. While preparing the broad research design and methodology for completion of this study, he had decided to employ a holistic approach for the study. It included (i) documentary research, (ii) survey research, (iii) in-depth field interviews and (iv) case studies. He was fully acquainted with the first method of research all throughout his career as a scholar and officer for land systems in the State of Gujarat. The other three methods of exploring empirical and dynamic human factors were comparatively new to him. He sought the assistance of a special team of quantitative researchers at a later stage to analyse the field survey data and complete tabulation work. The size of sample for collection of data from select villages and households from tribal districts and tribal pockets was rather limited and therefore, they have not been used in this book.

The method of depth interviews in the field was adopted by Dr. Patel quite successfully and on account of which a huge data covering about 800 pages in long hand notes were prepared by him on various related subjects of tribal land systems. The case studies method was also contemplated by him for collecting data in depth, but limitations of the resources and time did not allow him to pursue case studies. However, some material on two cases concerning record of rights and land alienation based on valuable information was received from experienced government officials and are presented in an appendix.

The enormous qualitative data collected and supplemented by other members of the team after revival of the work became profitable in dealing with various dimensions of land alienation and related problems. Inadequate number of trained hands to undertake responsibility of handling specialised tasks of data processing, analysis and report writing was a serious problem to tackle. Thanks to the expertise and dedication of Shri T.S. Shah and Shri R.G. Bhatt, retired Deputy Collectors who worked on the project as Research Officers that almost all difficulties and shortcomings were overcome after the revival of the project.

It is pertinent to explain briefly the use of term "dynamic" in the titles of a few chapters that throw some light on many aspects of land reforms, alienation etc. including the development of tribal life and culture. The term "dynamic" connotes and denotes exposition of a variety of empirical situations throwing light on the manner in which changes took place and values, attitude and behaviour of the tribals were perceived by officials and non-officials. The views and opinions of the officials on various issues either differed or coincided with those of non-officials. The information from live situations tend to be repetitive but serves the purpose of full exposer of social reality in tribal districts and talukas. Such a style of presentation highlight exceptional cases of facts of tribal situation. Through exceptions do not make rules, they portray profiles of micro level social reality to be taken seriously as instruments of planning and implementing strategies of development.

The draft report of the study was presented to Her Excellency Smt. Sharda Mukherjee, the then Governor of Gujarat on April 5, 1980, while inaugurating the Silver Jubilee Celebrations of Indian Institute of Public Administration. A Seminar was also organised on the next day to discuss the findings of the report in the auditorium of the Gujarat Chamber of Commerce and Industries, Ahmedabad.

I am grateful to Km. Sujata B. Rawal for contributing the maps in this book.

HARSHAD R. TRIVEDI

1

GENERAL INTRODUCTION

Prologue

Howsoever, desirable at a point of time, land systems and reforms per say have not been easy to manage. Land is intimately related to territorial instinct of man and his family as a fundamental right of a land-holding. This study shows many historical twists and turns in legal and tenurial systems of land occupation and confirment of land-holding rights. The most recent example is the decision of decentralising collective ownership of land under the impact of perestroika and glasnost, propagated in the Soviet Union.

Many a value loaded assumptions are reflected in the assessment of policy on land reforms by agents of change. Variously, they are rulers, landlords, cultivators and tenants as well as intermediaries and other interested parties harbouring latent and manifest desires to take hold of as much land as possible. This makes the task of egaliterian land reforms for equitable distribution difficult to set right. The wrongs are being done perpetually to tillers of the soil. This becomes more evident when occupation and confirment of tribal land-holdings are examined in context of survey and settlement. Legal-rational norms of land reforms often remain on paper or statute books because the position at the ground level of meaningful occupation remains ever changing and, therefore, highly complex. This can be ascertained from a countless variety of micro and meso level situations where claims and counter-claims over land-holdings, transfers and alienations are reflected in overt and covert desires and actions of individuals and groups. It is, interesting to analyse and understand the legal rational and behavioural process related to occupation of land in bygone days.

In the Pre-Independent India, the land systems of permanent settlement were of three types, namely, *Malguzari* System, *Mahalwari* System and *Ryotwari* system. These systems were the products of political exigencies of the olden times. They evolved out of the urgent need of realising stable land revenue for administrative purpose by the East India Company of the British Raj. Under this Colonial Rule, the financial needs of the politically articulate and economically stronger persons and ethnic groups entrenched in village administration were attended to. The tribals who lived in farflung villages and hilly and forest areas did not matter much to the British rulers, and, therefore, their interests were left unattended and undisturbed. The British attitude and policy towards the tribals was initially hostile but later became protective and paternalistic. This ambivalent situation is reflected in the following observations.

> "In spite of the suspicious and cautious treatment given to the tribals, allowance had to be made to let local conventions impinge on the administration of tribal areas existing under varying geo-political conditions. The administrators at district and taluka levels had to make final decisions on matters of law and order, land rights, etc., as and when necessary. Those working in the interior or tribal areas had greater freedom to conduct the affairs of the tribals, keeping in mind the broad policy framework of the colonial authority. The policy of caution on one side, and lack of communication facilities on the other, made for a policy of non-interference in the affairs of many inaccessible tribal communities. There was no other way than to let tribal administration operate under the protective or exploitative tendencies of lower level administrators from police, revenue and forest departments. In general, the policy of 'let alone' and status-quo towards tribals was the watchword of higher administration, either for good or bad".[1]

The policy of almost non-interference and partial exclusion of tribal areas from developmental activities was the watch word. It reduced economic competition between the tribals and the non-tribals. The geo-political situation and ecological isolation of tribal areas resulted in the creation of special land tenures and levy systems under which the tribals were given limited rights in land and forest.

The tribals were, however, self-assertive and active in their own way. They cleared the forests from time to time and brought extensive areas under cultivation, and continued to cultivate forest land for generations. But the British Government never thought of considering tribals for conferment of occupancy or ownership rights as the original and old settlers of forest land. In the absence of ownership and proprietary rights on land under self-cultivation, tribals were not permitted to alienate land by lease, exchange, gift, transfer, etc. As they had no transferable rights in land, such land could not be hypothecated for obtaining emergency loans from Government, Banks, Co-operative Societies, etc. In the circumstances, they continued mostly as mere tenants at will of the local governments and were, therefore, liable to be evicted at the sweet will of the Government and the landlord in control of the record of rights.

In some cases, tribals acquired permanent lien on the land due to ancestral occupation and cultivation. But their improvidence and ignorance, compelled them to hypothecate land to money-lenders or non-tribals. They finally lost the land on failure to repay the loans and were reduced to poverty and want. In order to prevent unlawful alienations of tribal and poor man's land, restrictive legislations were later enacted, but these laws remained on paper, since they were not implemented effectively. As a result, alienations of tribals land continued unchecked and with impunity.

The Problem

Before Independence, the tribals were generally able to earn livelihood by hunting, cultivation of land as well as by gathering minor forest produce such as honey, *Mahuda* flowers, gum, wood, fruits, timru leaves, etc. They were also given casual periodical works on daily wages by Forest and Public Works Departments. Their economy was considerably based on barter system. They were used to give away their produce and manual labour in lieu of daily subsistance and goods of personal consumption. Many still continue to lead the same type of insecure life style. Consequently, they hardly have had economic surplus to fall back upon, and had no scope to improve their future socio-economic conditions. It was in sum, a subsistance economy during normal seasons but was subject to intense frugality and starvation in times of scarcity and draught. There was, therefore, a great need of improving upon their primitive agricultural methods and of building suitable hutments and houses and educating tribal youth for gainful employment. Their distant habitat in the tribal hinterland, away from developed regions, generally prevented them from economic and social integration with advanced society. Moreover, the land occupation laws, laws for regulating money-lending and prevention of alienation of tribal land alone were not conducive to their well being and growth.

After independence, the State Governments in India undertook several administrative and legislative measures for amelioration of living conditions, education and socio-economic status of the tribals. The Land Revenue Acts and Rules were amended or new ones enacted in order to provide effective protection to the tribal rights in land. The Land Reform measures were under-taken for assuring security of tenure to tribal land-holder and for regulation of rents and conferment of ownership rights. They are given heritable and transferable rights in land which could be hypothecated for obtaining institutional credit from governmental and co-operative agencies. Where land was put under tribal cultivation for generations, they are given occupancy or ownership rights with or without payment of purchase price of land. Besides the tenancy reforms, ceiling and consolidation laws have been enacted and *Inam* and non-*Ryotwari* tenures abolished. Under these laws, the tribals are either allowed the rights of purchase or are conferred with ownership rights on land. Moreover, alienation of tribal lands to non-tribals is prohibited. Under Agricultural Land Ceiling Law, provisions have been made for grant of surplus lands to tribals on priority basis. Laws regarding consolidation of land-holdings and prevention of fragmentation of plots of land are made applicable. Concessions are given to tribals for payment of land price in suitable instalments. Facilities are provided for institutional credit to be taken from Co-operative Societies and Scheduled Banks. Money-lending laws have been enacted in order to put an end to age-old agrestic serfdom of the tribal household

Under the Five-Year Plans, provision has been made for development of tribal areas by special allocation of funds for Scheduled Tribes and Scheduled Areas. In the Fifth Five-Year Plan, the tribal development policy was drastically revised and changed. The concept of integrated development of the Scheduled Tribes and Scheduled Areas was evolved. As a result of this, the Tribal Area Sub-Plans have been formulated by the States for accelerating over-all socio-economic development of most of the tribal areas, and especially of those with concentration of 50 per cent tribal population.

The Significance of the Problem

The Land System anywhere in the world is a complex system of human relationships under which the rights and interests of the ruler and the ruled are regulated from times immemorial. For the grant of certain rights in land to his subjects, the ruler is entitled to a share from the produce of the land in the form of revenue. The amount and crops of the produce depends upon the quality of soil, irrigation facility, inputs and the extent of area covered. For determining the land revenue, survey and settlement operations are undertaken by the Governments. Soil classification is intimately related to the settlement of land revenue payable to a Government. Thus, it is clear that the land systems of any area (including the tribal area) is vitally connected with survey and settlement operations of land by the ruler. The specific objectives of the present study are centred around this and related land reforms and their impact on tribal life. The land reforms include abolition of intermediaries, tenancy reforms prevention of fragmentation and consolidation of holdings, land ceiling, and prevention of land alienation, money-lending and bonded labour. In view of these, the focus of the study was to ascertain as to how far these land reforms and other programmes of amelioration have contributed to allround development of tribals.

The subject of favourable land system in the tribal areas is of special significance because land provides subsistance as well as a sense of security to tribals in several ways. The Report of the Scheduled Areas and Scheduled Tribes Commission (1960-61) under the Chairmanship of Shri U.N. Dhebar has beautifully described economic and emotional attachments of tribal people to land.

> "The tribal people are bound to their land by many and intimate ties. Their feeling for it is something more than mere possessiveness. It is connected with their sense of history, for their legends tell of the great journeys they made over the wild and lonely hills and of the heroic pioneers who made the first clearings in the forests. It is part of their reverence for the dead whose spirits still haunt the country-sides. The land is the mother who provides for them in response to the labours of their hands and who, when supplies run short, feeds them with a hundred natural gifts. It is the setting of adventure, in love, in hunting and

in war which can never be forgotten. The land is the foundation of a sense of security and freedom from fear; its assured possession is a lasting road to peace."[2]

From the above quotation, the importance of land to the tribals will be appreciated. The original research project of this study was called the *Land Systems of Tribal Areas of Gujarat.* But research was not restricted to the land revenue systems only. This is because the term land has got a very wide connotation. *Land* is widely defined as including various benefits that arise out of land and the things attached to it.[3] The term *land* covers animals, trees, minerals and anything attached to the earth. The forests in relation to tribals are also most precious. The tribals and forests are inseparably linked in symbiotic form of ecology and environment. When land problems, land reforms and forests are studied, the question of exploitation by money-lenders, traders, forest contractors, administrators also arise. The major forms of emploitation involve indebtedness, land alienation to non-tribals and bonded labour. Not only these problems are covered by the study, but problems of development, panchayati raj and social change are also looked into.

The Government of India has under taken several development programmes for tribals under Community Development, multi-purpose and intensive Tribals Development Blocks and various schemes under Five-Year Plans. During the last few years, Tribal Area Sub-Plan for Gujarat has been undertaken for integrated development of the tribal areas. All these schemes are being implemented by Government agencies through Panchayati Raj institutions. For implementing the Tribal Area Sub-Plan, a special post of Project Administration has been set-up for the Tribal sub-area at the district level. In view of this, an attempt is made here to study and assess socio-economic changes brought about by a variety of development programmes of the government.

Theoretical Dimensions

For most people on earth, from times immemorial, there is no commodity more valuable than land and tribals are no exception. The urge to possess land, also called "territorial instinct" by biologists in a regional perspective is common to all human beings and primates. But the man who attributes high value to land, sometimes forgets that human capital in any nation-state is basically more valuable than land. This is the main perspective in which we have to look upon the tribals as human capital to be developed and utilised for their own and national development.

Coming down to brass tags, we have to see that the tribals are well nourished, educated and developed as respectable citizens of India. They have to be assisted in utilising the resources at their disposal in land and forest and in the elementary occupations such as farming, poultry dairying, etc. In the recent past, tribal indebtedness and reliance on others was heavy and frequent. It led to their in human exploitation by the non-tribals. A human and considerate approach to rapidly growing tribal consciousness has to be undertaken to assess their present requirements. They have to be helped and developed to participate meaningfully in the nation building activities.

We have been making development policies under the fervour of high idealism, and are trying to translate them into laws, legislative measures and action programmes. After three decades of Independence, we are at a stage of having made many enlightened policies and initiated necessary measures to improve the land-tribal relationships in such a way that neither of them are neglected from becoming positive factors of mutual assets and of national development as a whole.

In principle, planning is concerned with making policies for development, but its purpose is likely to be defeated if the programmes fail to achieve desired results. As G.P. Misra puts it, "The approach of planning to secure growth with social justice is based on the norm of controlling the ownership of material resources of the community and regulating economic systems for the prevention of the concentration of economic power for the attainment of distributive justice".[4] This means that simply economic growth is not enough to achieve desired results of planning in a developing country like ours. In the course of First Five-Year Plan, land reforms in the area of tenancy, prevention of fragmentation of holdings and consolidation of scattered holdings were undertaken with varying degrees of success. As an instrument of planning, these land reforms were geared to changing and restructuring agrarian relationships. However, it was felt that small and marginal holdings need not be encouraged due to high priority given to the economy of scale, which in fact is applicable more to industry than agriculture.

The utopian proposal of evolving a structure of cooperative farming was also based on this type of thinking. Since large farm holdings were highly valued, ceiling on agricultural land-holdings was looked upon as a policy detrimental to *justice through growth.* If this kind of approach was taken too seriously even for tribal areas, most tribals could have easily lost the chance of having advantage to keep even marginal or small holdings for self-cultivation.

The situation, however, changed during the Second Five-Year Plan for which the Planning Commission Panel on Land Reforms had suggested absolute limit to the amount of land to be held by an individual. However, sporadic landhungry movements by the "have-nots" and highly sophisticated and concealed land-grab strategies by the "haves" continued unabated. Land reforms cannot achieve socialistic goals if such conflicting trends on land acquisition persist and impinge adversely upon desired planned changes in the form of equity-oriented agrarian relationships. The tenancy in its undesirable form exists even today. "Many studies report that a large dimension of tenancy exists in disguise of oral tenancy in India".[5] Not only this, the extension of security of tenure to tenants through legislative and administrative efforts have been put to naught because of voluntary surrender of long standing tenancy rights not only by tribals but also by many other illiterate sons of the soil. The reason is not far to seek. The big land-owning class is constantly busy controlling the socio-economic and political power structure in rural India, through control over land.

We are here concerned with the three generic aspects of the *Land Systems of Tribal Areas of Gujarat,* in both historical and contemporary context. These three generic aspects are: (i) Policy formulation, (ii) Legislation, and (iii) Programmes of implementation of schemes. They are dealt with varying degrees of emphasis.

The history of tribal land systems, in the pre- and post-Independence India provides a cut-off point of change in the outlook on the role of tribals in nation-building activities. This will required us to probe into the overall change in values, attitude and behaviour of the tribals at village, taluka or district levels. The analysis, explanation and interpretation of data from various sources, therefore, will be treated at micro, meso- and macro levels of tribal life and culture.

The various Chapters which deal with the problems related to land reforms, including tenancy, alienation of land, money-lending, fragmentation and consolidation of holdings, forestry, institutional finances, development programmes, Panchayati Raj, etc. will try to explore the empirical situation at the above three levels of tribal areas and community structure. These shall be correlated with the emergence of differentiation and discontinuities in the sphere of values, attitude and behaviour of the tribals. They shall be further examined in the light of norms of the family, group, clan and regional tribal community which may cut across administrative boundaries of village, taluka and district. One of the most significant impact of land reforms and development activities on tribals, has been the emergence of class of tribal elites, giving rise to a relatively complex systems of social stratification in the Sub-Plan areas of higher concentration of tribals.

Epilogue

The focus of the study being on the Tribal areas of Gujarat, it became possible to take almost totalistic view of the situation. The study was based largely on empirical knowledge and behavioural dimensions of people associated with land reforms and development programmes leading to social change among tribals in general. Since no totalistic study can afford to ignore historical past of the situation, care was taken to develop the subject in the light of land systems which prevailed from the very dawn of British rule in Gujarat. An attempt has been made in this introduction to present a kind of critical position of tribal land system derived from the present study and those done by a few perceptive writers on this vital subject.

P.C. Joshi has rightly observed, "There was in India hardly any important problem the economic aspect of which could be understood in isolation from, say, the social, the cultural, the psychological, the technological, the political or the geographical aspect."[6] Keeping this broad perspective and general point of view in mind, an attempt is made to identify age old variations and patterns of tribal land systems with socio-economic and cultural significance rather than merely legal, juridical and rational import. We have also thought it appropriate to shift the focus of the study from analysis of land systems as such to analysis of overall changes in tribal areas in the context of development and change in knowledge, methods of work, production technology and social relationships among the tribals and non-tribals.

In brief, we have tried to study the crucial role of land in moulding the values, attitudes and behaviour of tribals and non-tribals in the context of realignment of forces in relation to changing social stratification, and emerging power structure both among the backward and the progressive tribal communities.

The study tries to reveal a general trend in the processes of changes taking place around land, and affecting the tribal society as a whole. This should help us in evaluating the impact of land reforms, technological change, and innovations in agriculture, etc. in successive transformation of the structural relationship in tribal society that remained relatively stagnant in the past.

An assessment of the overall social development spurred by specific planned change in one area of life could be studied both at macro- and micro levels of social system and organisation of tribal communities. In view of this, the present study not only covers the points of view of macro-micro perspective but also tries to explore middle range or meso point of view expressed by official and non-official respondents.[7]

The aforesaid stance as a scientific approach has been fairly reflected in the manner in which we have tried to deal with this complex subject. As Joshi writers, "It should be noted that scientific enquiry into the land problem requires both *analysis* and *synthesis*. The task of analysis is that of exploring in depth specific aspect of this larger problem through the aid of separate disciplines and through questions derived from a preliminary macro view of the problem. The task of synthesis is that of re-examining the preliminary view in this new light and of re-integrating the numerous insights and findings offered by analysis into a broad perspective of the problem under investigation."[8]

It is pertinent now to shift our attention to some theoretical considerations and practical aspects of the problem as discussed and debated among the scholars. In the light of discussions in recent publications on land and agrarian relationships in the context of broad policy formulations by the government, we should like to put forward some hypotheses-cum-suggestions on the subject of land alienation. This is done in the context of some valuable discussions specially by G.P. Misra of the Institute of Social and Economic Change, Bangalore.[9] It may be appropriate to call them broad perspectives of the study in advance.

Presented below are a few interrelated suggestions on tribal land systems in the context of maximum utilisation of land in a tribal district.

(1) It is practically difficult to completely stop tribal land alienations. Therefore it seems reasonable to reserve at least 50 per cent of the tribal land for tribals alone in order to meet *distributive justice* in land. This means that at least half of the agricultural land in a tribal district remain practically in possession of economically poorer and culturally homogeneous tribal landholders falling in the category of small and marginal farmers.

(2) If the suggestion made above is considered useful and practicable, it would be appropriate to allocate from remaining 50 per cent tribal land, at least 25 per cent to satisfy the principle of *justice through growth.* This means that policy-makers should decide on allowing a sections of well-to-do rich tribal farmers to become the holders of agricultural plots of larger size than those occupied by marginal and small farmers.

(3) A decision in favour of the point two above will help plots of best category of tribal land in a district to be utilised by advanced and potentially best tribal farmers. They will be able to take advantage of various kinds of inputs and technological developments in order to increase output per hectare of land and develop multiple cropping pattern leading to higher growth in agricultural output. Most of such farmers are bound to create demonstration effect on small and marginal tribal landholders who are eligible to hold land in view of socialistic goals of *distributive justice* as mentioned earlier.

(4) In continuation of the above points, we may put forward a supplementary suggestions in the long term perspective and in wider interest of tribal development. This concept may be called *justice through alienation,* lease type). It means that the policy-makers should allow marginal and even a section of small farmers to lease for a temporary purpose, their land to better off tribal farmers with a view to see that land is put to better utilisation by those tribals who can improve productivity by using better techniques of agriculture. This can be done by quasi-legal agreements between the two tribal landholdings, for mutual benefit.

(5) The temporary lease type land alienation agreement by a poorer tribal landholder, with a better off tribal landholder should not exceed the limit of more than 5 years. Moreover, a Tribal Area Sub-Plan Project Administrator should remain a standby for such quasi-legal agreements between a poor and a rich tribal. The District Collector, however, need not come in the picture except under conditions of serious dispute between two contending parties, beyond the scope of Project Administrator to tackle.

(6) In conclusion, it may be noted that lease type land alienations for a short period of time between poor and rich tribals are already taking place in certain areas in Gujarat. And, if this mutually beneficial concealed land alienation is authenticated by the tribal developmental administrators, it can certainly play a useful role in rationalising *justice through alienation* wherein the poorer tribal land-holders are likely to be least exploited by the better off tribals.

NOTES

1. Harshad R. Trivedi (Ed.), The Evolution of National Policy for Tribal Development", in *Micro-social Studies in Development and Change,* Harshad R. Trivedi, Chugh Publications, Allahabad, 1977, pp. 93-94.
2. U.N. Dhebar, *Report of Scheduled Areas and Scheduled Tribes Commission* (1960-61), Vol. I.P. 121.
3. *Bombay Land Revenue Code,* Section 3 (4), 1879.
4. *Some Aspects of Change in Agrarian Structure,* G.P. Misra, Sterling Publishers, New Delhi, 1977, p. 49.
5. Misra, *Ibid.,* p. 63-64.
6. P.C. Joshi, *Land Reforms in India,* Allied Publishers, Bombay, 1975, p. 26.
7. *Op. cit.,* p. 86.
8. It may be noted that *macro area* refers to all tribal areas in the state, *miso area* to district level tribal areas and the *micro area* refers to tribal villages and pockets.
9. G.P. Misra, *Ibid.*

2

TRIBAL AREA SUB-PLAN IN GUJARAT

Introduction

As a general policy, the British Administrators declared some tribal areas as "excluded" and others as "partially excluded".[1] They adopted the policy of administering these areas lightly without much concern. The normal administration of the developed regions was not extended to them. In many tribal areas, single-line administration was established, where all authority was vested in one individual, the Chief Representative of the Government. However, the British, honoured the local customs and there was judicious intervention by Government officers in the local affairs, only when it was considered inevitable. This policy in the administration of tribal areas gave considerable discretion and authority to field administrators of tribal areas. The main objective of the administration in these sub-regions was to maintain Law and Order and uphold effective control of the British Raj. The concept of tribal development was not thought of at all. The simple tribal communities had, nevertheless to be protected from more articulate, economically powerful and aggressive caste groups who moved into these areas alongwith gradual extension of communication facilities and establishment of administration there. Thus the attitude of the British towards the tribals, to begin with, was protective and paternalistic.

The tribals in Gujarat mostly live in the eastern hilly and mountainous regions covered with fairly dense forests. The north-eastern tribal area is divided by Arawalli Hills, the Central eastern tribal area by the Vindhya Hills and the south eastern tribal area by the Sahyadri Ranges. Before the British extended their area of administrative control in tribal hinterlands from different centres of power in the country, the outer extensions of their influence were vaguely defined in the hilly and forest regions. Most of the tribal belts were inaccessible. The tribals of these areas were difficult to subdue.

They rose into revolt against the Britishers as and when disturbed. The tribal regions, therefore, came last under the effective administrative control of the British, but it did not last longer. Finally, sub-regional provincial and administrative boundaries had to be determined. From the point of view of administrative control, predominantly tribal regions of the entire Western Zone of India was divided under the jurisdiction of different States such as Rajasthan, Madhya Pradesh, Gujarat, and Maharashtra.

Even after the establishment of British control the tribal people in many areas continued to rise in rebellion for a long period of historical time to assert their rights to self-governance. They were adamant specially in relation to their rights over land and forest. For instance, the Dangi Rajas resisted to the last ditch all attempts of the British rulers to subjugate them. The administrator, Col. Outram tried various ways to subdue the tribals of Dangs from 1821 to 1825 through perfidy and treachery of some local tribals, and succeeded in bringing Dangi tribals under control.

Generally speaking, the tribal population live in the areas formerly under the control of Princely States in Gujarat. The following table presents amalgamation of these areas in district administration.

Districts of Tribal Concentration	Name of former Princely States or jagirs
Banaskantha	Danta and Palanpur
Sabarkantha	Idar and Vijayanagar
Panchmahals	Santrampur, Devgadh Baria and Sanjeli
Bharuch	Rajpipla and Sagbara
Baroda (Vadodara)	Baroda (Vadodara), Chhotaudepur, Pandu Mewas, Sankheda, Naswadi and Ghadboriad
Surat	Vadodara (Part territory)
Valsad	Dharampur, Vansda and Vadodara (Part territory)
Dangs	Dangi Chieftains and Naiks

The rulers in the Princely States, enjoyed autonomy for internal administration within norms approved by the British Government.

These states, excepting Baroda (Vadodara), were generally small in size and did not have a sophisticated administrative system. The old time relationships between the Rulers and the land-holding people were somewhat intimate and personnel. The Land System was simple and mostly based upon Bhagbatai or crop-share pattern.

In the pre-independence days the administration in tribal areas was obviously not formalised. The decision-making pattern both in British India and princely States was near enough to take care of the problems of common man. The system could respond to the needs of each specific situation of scarcity, drought and calamity. The maintenance of Legal-rational norms and protection of land-holders and public from unwanted rowdy elements were the main objectives of administration.

Post-Independence Development

The post-independence period in India brought several land- marks in social development of all the people in general and the scheduled tribes and scheduled castes in particular. Before attention is focused on the method of formulation and implementation of the Tribal Area Sub-Plan, a bird's-eye view of the total situation is presented in the following points.

Merger of Princely States of Indian Union

During British regime, all regions of India were gradually brought under a common system of public administration. The princely states were at varying levels of progress and development of administrative and political reality. This affected the tribals who were accustomed to informal system of administration of the local princes in pre-British times. The most significant change in the general administrative scenario after Independence was caused by the merger of the Princely States to the Indian Union.

Safeguards for Tribals in Constitution

The Constitution of India was framed in 1950. The subject of tribal development and administration of tribal areas was not assigned to any one of the three lists in the Constitution. But these areas were brought under Fifth and Sixth Schedules. The former "excluded

Areas" were put under the Sixth Schedule and the "partially excluded areas" and some of the tribal areas in the erstwhile Princely States were included in the Fifth Schedule. In conformity with the national goal of evolving a socialistic pattern of society, the administration of these areas was made a responsibility of the Union Government. The executive power of the Union Government was, however, extended to giving directives to the States for good administration of the tribal areas and execution of development programmes for tribal communities in general.

The Constitution gave the State Governors almost unlimited powers in the Fifth Schedule to make Regulations for improving the socio-economic conditions in scheduled tribal areas.

The Special Regulations of the Governor can negate and modify any law on tribals, passed by the Parliament or the State legislature, applicable to any part of the Fifth Schedule. Under the Fifth Schedule, a provision is made for setting up a Tribes Advisory Council by the Governor in relation to his regulation making powers. Thus the need to consult the State Legislature is dispensed with in the case of making regulations for these areas.

The provisions of Sixth Schedule for tribal areas are more stringent. Under the Directive Principles of State Policy, the State is directed to promote with special care educational and economic interest of the weaker sections of the people in general and of Schedule Castes and Schedule Tribes in particular. The States are directed to protect tribals from social injustice and all form of exploitation. The Constitution provides an ideal setting for flexible and effective legal-rational administration and its adaptibility and responsiveness to local tribal situation.

Community Development Programmes

In 1951, Five Year Plans were formulated which included special schemes for tribal development. In 1952 Community Development (CD) programmes at block or sub-divisional level in rural areas were initiated. In 1954, Multipurpose Tribal Development Blocks were started in tribal areas. These T.D. Blocks were expected to cover development of all aspects of the community life of tribals. But in course of time, they became circumscribed by the Schematic Budgetory Constrains. The Community Development and Special Tribal Development Schemes turned out to be sectoral programmes similar to any other items akin to the development of agricultural activities in general. The tribals living in areas outside Tribal Development Blocks did not get any benefit except certain educational concessions. In course of time, C.D. and T.D. Blocks remained more or less on paper without effective implementation. The tribal programmes in particular lacked ecological orientation and ignored local variations. This led to somewhat uniform static pattern in tribal development ignoring regional diversities. Another limiting factor was that the T.D. Blocks were established in areas where tribal population was more than two-thirds of the total population. As a consequence of this criterion and partly due to defective lists of scheduled tribes, many deserving tribal groups remained beyond the reach of tribal development programmes.

In the circumstances, it was realised that the T.D. Blocks were not touching the target groups and greater effort was needed to meet basic problems of the tribals. The U.N. Dhebar Commission (1960-61) referred to earlier, observed that the provisions of the Fifth Schedule and other Articles of the Constitution were not adequately utilised to help tribal development. The Commission, therefore, recom- mended that urgent measures should be taken for protection of tribals in relation to land, forest, excise duty and marketing. This did not meet the needs of all tribal who were in varying stages of development. The Shilu Ao Committee (1967-68) found that the T.D. Block financial outlays became exclusive investments and that no benefit accrued to tribals from general schemes.

Panchayati Raj and Tribal Area Sub-plan

The Community Development Block programmes in general and Tribal Development Blocks in particular could not ensure rapid socio-economic change. Special programmes of tribal areas could not enlist the participation specially of unaware tribal communities. Efforts were made to correct the situation when Panchayati Raj was introduced on the recommendations of the Balwantray Mehta Committee on the principle of Democratic Decentralisation. In Gujarat, three tire Panchayati Raj Institutions came in operation with effect from 1st April, 1963. It envisaged better participation of the people in planning process and effective implementation of development programmes. The statutory Panchayati Raj bodies added new administrative dimension along with District Administration. Panchayati Raj institutions have in reality served as the agencies of Government so far as implementation of development schemes are concerned. The tribal development programmes and centrally sponsored schemes are implemented through the agency of the Panchayati Raj institutions in Gujarat.

In view of the urgent needs of tribal development, the Government of India took a major policy-decision that the main thrust on development of tribal areas should be provided by conserted special efforts by state governments. The problems of tribal areas should be given higher priority and divided into two parts:

(1) Areas of tribal concentration, and
(2) Areas of dispersed tribal communities.

This was necessary for clearly defining policy and strategy of the programmes for faster development. In the case of areas of tribal concentration, programmes for infrastructural development in the remote tribal areas can benefit the tribal communities. An applied concept of area planning with focus on the development of physical infrastructure and human resources of tribal communities has been evolved.

In the case of dispersed tribals, no separate scheme of infrastructural development and area planning can be envisaged. In this case, programmes have to be based on peoples' own efforts including those of non-tribals who are in majority. The tribals must involve themselves in the general development schemes in the region. The major problems of long-term and daily employment etc. of special tribal groups have to be taken care of by project administrators within the provision of tribal Sub-Plan.

Under the new strategy, existing scheduled areas of high concentration and other areas with more than 50 per cent tribal population have been identified. A Tribal Development Block is taken as the smallest unit for the purpose of making population profiles and identification of problems. Accordingly, there are 32 Talukas in the main seven Districts of Gujarat surved by tribal area sub-plan. Of these seven Districts, Surat is the largest one, having nine Tribal Talukas. For the administrative purpose, it has been divided into two Tribal Area Sub-Plan Projects (Surat-I and Surat-II) in charge of two Project Administrators.

The names of all the project areas and the clusters of talukas in Gujarat are presented in the following table.

District and Sub-Plan Area	Names and Number of Talukas
Sabarkantha—one	Khedbrahama, Vijayanagar, Bhiloda and Meghraj (4)
Panchmahals—one	Santrampur, Jhalod, Dahod, Limkheda and Devgadh Baria (6)
Vadodara—one	Chhotaudepur, Naswadi, and Tilakwada (3)
Bharuch—one	Nandod, Dediapada, Sagbara, Valia and Jhagadia (5)
Surat—two	*Surat-I:* Uchhal, Vyara, Valod, Songadh and Nizar. *Surat-II:* Mahuva, Mandvi, Mangrol and Bardoli (9)
Valsad—one	Umbergaon, Pardi, Dharampur, Vansada and Chikhali (5)
Dangs—one	Dangs (1)
Total—8-sub-plan areas	Total—33 Tribal Talukas

The total population of the above cluster of Talukas was 38,95,987, of whom 26,82,115 were tribals as per census of 1971. Thus tribals accounted for 68.84 per cent of the population of these areas. In comparison to the whole of Gujarat, approximate tribal population of these areas was 72 per cent of the total tribal population in Gujarat. In terms of physical dimension, these areas constituted 12.21 per cent of the geographical area of the State. According to demographic criterion, every seventh Gujarati is a tribal and every tenth tribal in the country lives in the Gujarat State. This shows the magnitude and importance of the tribal problems in the State.

The Sub-Plan in Gujarat comprise 33 Talukas with 50 per cent and more tribal population. However, Talukas with little less than 50 per cent of the tribal population did not get full benefit of the Sub-Plan. The people of such Talukas moved the Government to declare their areas as tribal pockets and provide the benefits of Tribal Sub-Plan. In view of this, the State Government added the following 15 pockets in 12 Talukas spread over 6 Districts.

No of Villages	Name of the Pockets	Name of the Talukas	Name of the Districts
*54	Amirgadh	— Palanpur	Banaskantha
120	Danta	— Danta	Banaskantha
41	Kathola	— Halol	Panchmahals
32	Mora	Godhra	Panchmahals
53	Vadeli	— Sankheda	Vadodara
51	Bhatpur	— Sankheda	Vadodara
52	Karali	Pavi Jetpur	Vadodara
46	Bhikhapura	Pavi Jetpur	Vadodara
38	Ankleshwar	Ankleshwar	Bharuch
43	Kamrej	Kamrej	Surat
35	Palsana	Palsana	Surat
31	Rahej	Gandevi	Valsad
20	Atgam	Valsad	Valsad
22	Ronvel	Valsad	Valsad
37	Sisodra-Ganesh	— Navsari	Valsad
675			

* The Gujarat Govt. extended its Tribal Area Sub-Plan activities to these 15 pockets from April 1978.

(a) *Broad Objectives of the Sub-Plan*

According to the Planning Commission, the main objects of the Sub-Plan are:

(a) To narrow the gap between the level of development of the tribal and other areas;
(b) To improve the standard of life of the tribal communities; and
(c) To frame the Sub-Plan so as to answer the main issues facing tribal communities in the area.

To these three broad objectives, the Government of Gujarat added the following supporting objectives:[2]

(i) To meet deficiencies of economic and social infrastructure of tribal economy;

(ii) To provide for specific investments needed to build up natural resource potential of land and forest and for promoting, fostering and developing industrial base for the area;
(iii) To provide for adequate promotional and organisational assistance to voluntary agencies to facilitate social and institutional transformation, and for research in tribal sociology; and
(iv) To safeguard against exploitation of tribal people by vested interests in land, trade and industries, and to ensure accrual of benefits of development to tribals to the fullest extent, and to prevent alienations of tribal land.

Thus the Sub-Plan is a broad frame of the general strategy for achieving developmental objectives in tribal areas. Important features of the Sub-Plan are: (1) The Sub-Plan is tailored to meet special needs and requirements of areas having maximum tribal population; (2) It provides for the Integrated Area Development strategy in place of Tribal Development Blocks; and (3) Its resources are not limited to general development programmes and to special allocation of resources for tribal welfare. The strategy comprise aggregate funds of the State Plan for Sub-Plan area, General Sectoral outlays, Special Central Assistance and Institutional Finance.

The financial resources are to be provided as share from allocations of the State Plan to be supplemented from Central Government and financial institutions. The share from outlays of the State Plan has been worked out, having regards to:

(a) Total population,
(b) Geographical area,
(c) Level of development, and
(d) The state of social services.

It may be possible to indicate financial provisions from the State Plan but such an indication is not possible in the case of central assistance and that from financial institutions. However, on the basis of centrally sponsored schemes and the central assistance, tentative provisions are made in the Sub-Plan.

Apart from these financial provisions from different sources, the Tribal Area Sub-Plan provides for certain safeguards against diversion of funds to other programmes. They are as follows:

(i) The provisions included in the Sub-Plan should be utilised for tribal areas exclusively and not diverted to other areas of expenditure;

(ii) The authority charged with the overall responsibility for implementing Sub-Plan should have unified control over expenditure irrespective of the fact that different Administrative Departments would be responsible for execution of the schemes, and

(iii) Administrative approval and sanction for different schemes and works should be accorded for the entire period of the plan.

These checks and balances are provided to ensure that the funds earmarked and allotted for tribal areas are utilised for tribal development only. The budgetting and accounting procedures are devised on the system of Performance Budgetting and, therefore, the expenditure incurred on the schemes in tribal areas can be identified.

(b) *Administrative Structure and Personnel Policy*

As mentioned earlier, the entire administrative hierarchy of Panchayati Raj organisation attends to development administration in Gujarat. To this are added the tribal area Project Administrators and other staff. The formulation and implementation of planned schemes are looked into by the Gujarat Tribal Development Corporation operating between the Government and the Project Administrator. It works closely with the Tribal Development Commission. At state level, there is a Director of Social Welfare who for the reasons best known to the government was not brought into the direct picture for social development of tribals. With all the officers and their supporting staff, there is a danger of proliferation of roles with diffusion of responsibility and unfruitful division of power. Duplication of roles may lead to excessive and over-administration of tribal areas against which Prime Minister Jawaharlal Nehru had expressed righteous indignation.

The Sub-Plan envisages that the Project Administrator shall be in the overall charge of implementation of all plan schemes in the Project area. However, the Collector and the District Development Officer continue to be responsible for the implementation of the Sub-Plan schemes and will be the king-pin in the schemes of the machinery of implementation. The Collector in fact is the Chairman of the District Advisory Committee of which the D.D.O. and district officers of various departments are members. In Surat, two Project Administrators function through the same District Advisory Committee under the Chairmanship of the Collector.

Since the tribal areas in Gujarat are divided into eight Sub-plan projects, as many Project Administrators have been appointed. They come from the Deputy Collectors' cadre. The question is whether they will able to deliver the goods because of the special tasks assigned to them. We shall discuss here whether senior Deputy Collectors may not be the right persons instead of junior cadre persons. It is very difficult to identify and appoint Project Administrators who are devoted and committed to the welfare of tribals. Like other Civil Servants, most of the junior Deputy Collectors are careerists and generalists with a background of administrative knowledge and training to run routine administration. Most of them have experience in Revenue Department. They cannot be expected to have an intimate knowledge and experience of the tribal problems in depth. Therefore, extreme care needs to be taken by the Government in selection and appointment of Project Administrators for implementation of the Tribal Area Sub-Plans.

The Sub-Plan is formulated with an integrated tribal area development approach. The development schemes are earmarked for tribal areas in the Sub-Plan in order to avoid possible danger of imbalance in tribal development. In the formulation of Sub-Plan, care has been taken to ensure that the tribals of an area are likely to accept the schemes on the basis of utility. As their response is very crucial, special emphasis has to be placed on articulated and felt needs of the tribals. Further it may also be ensured that the implementation of Sub-Plan schemes does not result in creation of a special over-bearing class of tribal elites. Reacting on approach to tribals, Verrier Elwin rightly observed that "unintelligent benevolence can be as great a danger as intelligent exploitation."[3]

Characteristics of Tribal Population

The table presented below clearly shows that the State of Gujarat has sizeable population of the Tribal people. As per the census of 1961, the Scheduled Tribes numbered 2,754,446 or 13.35 per cent, while as per 1971 census, they numbered 3,734,422 or 13,99 per cent of the total state population. This amounted to a decennial increase of 0.64 per cent tribal population in Gujarat State.

Population of Scheduled Tribes in 1961 and 1971.*

General population		Scheduled tribe population		Percentage of ST to general population in the State	
1961	1971	1961	1971	1961	1971
20633350	26697475	2754446	3734422	13.35	13.99

* See Tables 1.1 and 1.7 of *Pocket Book of Population Statistics-Census of India*, 1971, Series V, Gujarat, General Administration Department (Planning). It is significant to note that the rate of growth of general population in Gujarat is +29.39 per cent while that of the scheduled tribe population is +35.58 per cent.

In the country as a whole, the proportion of tribal population to the total population is about 7.0 per cent as against 13.99 per cent in Gujarat. Out of 10 Tribals in the country one lives in Gujarat, while every seventh person in Gujarat is a tribal. Gujarat is fourth among all the States in India in respect of tribal population. The other three States where the tribals are numerically larger in comparison to other states are Madhya Pradesh, Orissa and Bihar.

The decennial increase of 0.64 per cent of tribal population in Gujarat can be attributed to several factors such as:

(i) Migration of tribals from neighbouring States of Rajasthan, Madhya Pradesh and Maharashtra in search of employment;
(ii) Greater awareness of the rights and safeguards provided in the Constitution for scheduled tribes among local tribals;
(iii) Refinement in the enumeration of Census data on tribals; and
(iv) Increase in medical and health care facilities under Five Year Plans, leading to reduction in the death rate in tribal population.

(a) *Regional Distribution of Tribals*

The tribal population in Gujarat is concentrated in and near the eastern border of the State adjoining Rajasthan, Madhya Pradesh and Maharashtra. (See Map 2.1). The concentration is spread in the seven out of eight Tribal Districts from North to South beginning from Sabarkantha to Panchmahals, Vadodara, Bharuch, Surat, Valsad and Dangs. About 72 per cent of the total tribal population of the State lives in this area. The remaining 28 per cent is spread over other parts of the State, including the district of Banaskantha as revealed from the following Table 2.1. (See also Map 2.2).

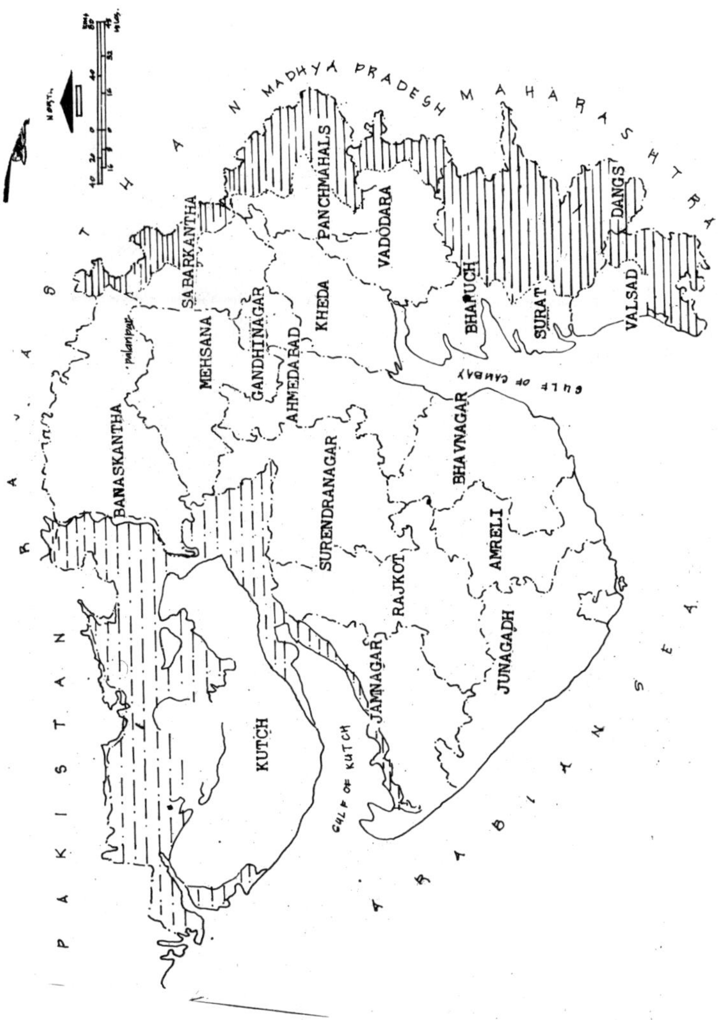

MAP 2.1: Tribal Region in Gujarat

MAP 2.2: Percentage of Scheduled Tribes to Total Population, 1971

TABLE 2.1: Population in eight Tribal Districts of Gujarat in 1961 and 1971*

Name of the districts	Total population		Population of scheduled tribes		Percentage of scheduled tribes to total population	
	1961	1971	1961	1971	1961	1971
Banaskantha**	9,96,144	12,65,383	52,685	77,758	5.29	6.15
Sabarkantha	9,18,587	11,87,637	1,28,085	1,78,804	13.94	15.06
Panchmahals	14,68,946	18,48,804	5,03,214	7,12,713	34.26	38.55
Vadodara	14,27,326	19,80,065	3,27,992	4,73,117	21.47	23.89
Bharuch	8,91,969	11,09,601	3,70,971	4,86,901	41.59	43.88
Surat	13,13,823	17,86,924	6,28,144	8,27,682	47.81	46.32
Valsad	11,37,801	14,28,742	5,96,815	7,76,215	52.45	54.33
Dangs	71,567	94,185	66,233	88,028	92.55	93.46

* See Tables 2.2, 2.4 and 2.17 of *Pocket Book of Population Statistics Census of India*, 1971 Series V, Gujarat General Administration Department, (Planning).

** Tribal area sub-Plan Project does not cover the whole of the Banaskantha District, except two tribal pocket viz. Amirgadh and Danta in one taluka.

It can be seen from the above table that the Dangs, which is a composite taluka-cum-district for administrative purpose is almost entirely tribal (93.46%). Among other tribal districts, Valsad District has the highest i.e. 54.33 per cent tribal population followed by Surat (46.32%), Bharuch (43.88%), Panchmahals (38.55%), Vadodara (23.89%), Sabarkantha (15.06%) and Banaskantha (06.15%).

It should be noted that the Tribal Area Sub-Plan covers seven districts of highest tribal concentration. As stated earlier, the 15 pockets distributed in the districts of Vadodara, Valsad, Panchmahals, Surat, Bharuch and Banaskantha were added in April 1978. The names of the talukas and pockets are presented earlier in this Chapter.

(b) *Talukawise Distribution of Tribals*

It should be pointed out that thirty-two talukas of seven eastern districts in Gujarat constitute the main area of the Tribal Area Sub-Plan. The table 2.2 presented on the next page gives talukawise distribution of tribals for 1961 and 1971 with the percentages of the tribal population to total population in each taluka.

The highest concentration of tribal population is in Uchchal Taluka (96.45%) while the lowest concentration is in Devgadhbaria Taluka (27.54%). Taking an overall view of talukawise situation, one can see that (i) more than 90 per cent tribal concentration is to be found in Uchchal, Dangs, Tilakwada, Dediapada, Sagbara and Dharampur talukas; (ii) more than 80 per cent in Jhalod, Chhotaudepur, Naswadi, Vyara, Mahuva, and Bansda talukas; (iii) more than 70 per cent in Dohad, Valia, Mandvi, Nizar, Songadh, Valod and Vijayanagar talukas, and (iv) more than 60 per cent in Nandod, Jhagadia, Mangrol and Chikhli talukas. Rest of the ten talukas have concentration of population ranging from 58.41 per cent to 27.54 per cent only.

Comparing the differences in decennial percentages of some of the talukas, it is interesting to note that in Songadh taluka of Surat District, there is a considerable decline of nearly 20.00 per cent of tribal population between 1961 and 1971, while Dediapada and Mangrol shows slighter decline. On the other hand, more than 25.00 per cent increase in the comparative percentage of population is to be found in Chhotaudepur taluka and 11.72 per cent in the Naswadi taluka of Vadodara District. Again in the Devgadhbaria taluka of

TABLE 2.2: Talukawise Tribal population covered under Tribal Area Sub-Plan in 1961 and 1971*

Taluka	District	Total population		Population of scheduled tribes		Percentage of scheduled tribes to total population	
		1961	1971	1961	1971	1961	1971
Dangs	Dangs	71,567	94,185	66,233	88,028	92.55	93.46
Jhalod	Panch-Mahals	1,20,996	1,58,860	1,02,131	1,35,038	84.41	85.00
Dohad	Panch-Mahals	1,88,625	2,35,928	1,30,976	1,67,413	69.44	70.96
Santrampur	Panch-Mahals	1,88,734	2,47,300	1,10,038	1,45,678	58.30	58.91
Limkheda	Panch-Mahals	1,26,802	1,63,016	73,185	95,894	57.72	58.82
Devgadh-baria	Panch-Mahals	1,74,706	2,19,373	35,689	60,408	20.42	27.54
Chhotaude-pur	Vadodara	1,45,143	1,88,927	83,247	1,57,197	57.36	83.21
Naswadi	Vadodara	56,952	72,861	38,992	58,259	68.46	80.18
Tilakwada	Vadodara	37,182	43,542	17,987	20,926	48.37	48.06
Dediapada	Bharuch	44,874	67,683	42,464	63,748	94.63	94.19
Sagbara	Bharuch	41,532	52,576	37,944	47,724	89.19	90.77
Valia	Bharuch	64,357	80,927	46,610	61,903	72.42	76.49
Nandod	Bharuch	1,21,397	1,48,294	77,893	98,379	64.16	66.34
Jhagadia	Bharuch	97,928	1,20,000	59,087	73,636	60.34	61.36
Uchchhal	Surat	31,535	44,940	30,329	43,344	96.18	96.45
Vyara	Surat	1,19,100	1,53,536	1,04,041	1,36,297	87.36	88.77
Mahuva	Surat	65,533	82,049	50,933	65,980	77.81	80.41
Nizar	Surat	58,801	71,932	42,034	54,416	71.49	75.63
Mandvi	Surat	93,805	1,19,168	71,509	90,944	76.23	76.31
Songadh	Surat	76,870	1,35,095	71,394	98,429	92.88	72.86
Valod	Surat	42,828	51,999	30,360	37,933	70.89	72.95
Mangrol	Surat	95,367	1,28,904	63,024	85,122	66.09	66.03
Bardoli	Surat	90,608	1,20,120	45,314	62,573	50.01	52.01
Dharampur	Valsad	1,52,669	1,93,711	1,36,534	1,79,181	89.43	92.50
Bansda	Valsad	92,352	1,20,619	81,909	1,08,548	88.69	89.99
Chikhali	Valsad	1,39,986	1,76,089	92,267	1,19,696	65.91	67.97
Pardi	Valsad	1,30,898	1,62,465	75,138	95,059	57.40	58.51
Umbergaon	Valsad	95,973	11,686	51,153	63,884	53.30	54.66
Vijayanagar	Sabar-kantha	30,111	43,378	21,483	31,486	71.35	72.58
Khedbra-hama	Sabar-kantha	74,475	98,559	39,891	55,354	53.56	56.16
Bhiloda	Sabar-kantha	90,766	1,14,190	42,975	56,661	47.34	49.62
Meghraj	Sabar-kantha	50,291	69,095	15,246	22,977	30.31	33.25

******Census of India 1961*, **Vol. V, Gujarat, Part V-B I, Statement III, p. 69. See also** Annexure I of the ***Tribal Area Sub-Plan (Revised 1974-79)*, Gujarat.**

Panch-mahals District one finds nearly 7.0 per cent increase in these percentages of tribal population. Among the rest of the talukas, two have recorded increase in by about 4.0 per cent three about 3.0 per cent and five about 2.0 per cent. Rest of the talukas have shown these increase by 1.0 per cent and less.

(c) *Literacy Among the Tribals*

An account of literacy for 1961 and 1971 among the tribals of Gujarat is presented in the following sections covering (i) general literacy, (ii) literacy in districts, and (iii) literacy by sex in the districts.

(i) *General Literacy*

According to the Census of 1971, the literacy among tribals of Gujarat is only 14.12 per cent as compared to 35.79 per cent among the general population. It reveals considerable backwardness of tribals in the field of literacy. Among the tribals themselves, the percentage of literacy has increased from 11.69 per cent in 1961 to 14.12 per cent in 1971; i.e., rise by 2.43 per cent. On the other hand, the percentage in general population has increased from 30.45 per cent in 1961 to 35.79 per cent in 1971, i.e. by 5.34 per cent. This shows that increase in the percentage of literacy among the tribals during the decade 1961-71 is less than half the increase in percentage of literacy among general population. See the Table 2.3 presented below.

TABLE 2.3: Percentages of literacy among general and Scheduled Tribe Population in 1961 and 1971*

Nature of population	1961 Persons	1961 Males	1961 Females	1971 Persons	1971 Males	1971 Females
General Population	30.45	41.13	19.10	35.79	46.11	24.75
Scheduled Tribe Population	11.69	19.6	4.09	14.12	21.83	6.15

*Source: Tables 1.3, 1.7 of *Pocket Book of Population Statistics — Census of India*, 1971, Series V, Gujarat, General Administration Department (Planning).

(ii) *Literacy in Districts*

The percentage of tribal literacy to that of general population from 1961 to 1971 has increased by about 7.0 per cent in Sabarkantha, 5.0 per cent in Dangs, 4.0 per cent in Vadodara, 3.0 per cent in Surat, Panchmahals and Banaskantha districts respectively. In Bharuch district, the increase is about 1.0 per cent only. The percentage of literacy has increased more in the Dangs and Sabarkantha districts and comparatively less in other districts. This shows that tribals are trying to catch up in literacy with general population, although at a slower pace, as indicated in the following Table 2.4.

TABLE 2.4: **Percentage of literates to total population and that to Scheduled Tribes population in 1961 and 1971***

Name of the District	Percentage of literates to total population		Percentage of literates in S.T. to total S.T. population	
	1961	1971	1961	1971
Banaskantha	12.73	15.76	2.91	4.01
Sabarkantha	24.03	31.14	10.56	16.51
Panchmahals	19.23	22.82	6.67	9.16
Vadodara	35.21	40.67	11.55	11.32
Bharuch	34.26	35.73	13.85	13.83
Surat	35.46	39.39	14.12	17.10
Valsad	N.A.	37.57	N.A.@	18.55
Dangs	9.26	14.16	6.61	11.29

* *Source*: Tables 2.8 and 2.17 of *Pocket Book of Population Statistics — Census of India*, 1971, Series V, Gujarat, General Administration Department (Planning).

@ N.A.: Not available.

(iii) *Literacy by Sex*

The over-all increase in the percentage of literacy among both the sexes of tribals from 1961 to 1971 is about 2.0 per cent. In Sabarkantha and Dangs districts, literacy among males increased by more than 7.0 per cent and among females by 2.0 per cent. In Bharuch and Vadodara these percentages remained almost stationary, while in the case of Banaskantha district, the percentages only in male literacy increased by about 2.0 per cent from 1961 to 1971. See Table 2.5.

TABLE 2.5: Percentages of literacy among Scheduled Tribe population by sex in 1961 and 1971

Name of the district	Percentage of literates in S.T. to total S.T. Population by Sex					
	1961			1971		
	Persons	Males	Females	Persons	Males	Females
Banaskantha	2.51	5.27	0.38	4.01	7.12	0.66
Sabarkantha	10.56	18.79	2.24	16.51	27.03	5.91
Panchmahals	6.67	11.98	1.4	9.16	16.06	2.00
Vadodara	11.55	18.58	4.13	11.32	17.90	4.28
Bharuch	13.85	22.98	4.45	13.83	22.64	4.76
Surat	N.A.	N.A.	N.A.	17.10	25.15	8.87
Valsad	N.A.	N.A.	N.A.	18.55	27.10	9.93
Dangs	6.61	0.80	2.10	11.29	17.55	4.74
Total	11.69	19.6	4.09	14.12	21.83	6.15

Source : Table G 31, Census of India, 1971, *District Hand Books*).
N.A. : Not available.

(d) *Spatial Distribution and Occupations of Tribals*

There are about eighteen major groups and sub-groups of the tribals found in the Tribal Sub-Plan areas in Gujarat. They are, Dungri Garasia, Bhil Garasia, Bhils (of other groups), Patelia, Naikda, Dhanka, Dubla (Halapati), Gamit, Chodhara, Kotwalia, Choudhari, Rathwa, Gamit, Kotwalia, Dhodia, Kokna, Warli and Kolcha. The Table 2.6 presented hereafter gives the distribution of these tribals and also general idea of occupations from which they earn livelihood.

Let us first see their relative concentration in tribal districts. As can be seen from the table (i) Dungri Garasia and Bhil Garasia are found in Sabarkantha district along with other groups of Bhils; (ii) Patelia are found in Panchmahals along with Bhils and Naikdas (iii) Dhanka Gamit and Chodhra are to be found in Bharuch along with Bhil, Dubla, and Kotwalia; (iv) Rathwa are to be found in Vadodara along with Bhil and Naikda; (v) Gamit are to be found in Surat-I along with Chaudhary, Bhil, Kotwalia and Dubla, and (vi) Warli and Kolcha are to be found in Valsad along with Dhodia, Kokra and Dubla.

We may now see the distribution of some of the tribes in more than one district: (i) Bhils are to be found in Sabarkantha,

Panchmahals, Bharuch, Vadodara, Dangs and Surat-I; (ii) Naikda are to be found in Panchmahals and Vadodara; (iii) Dubla (Halpati) are to be found in Bharuch, Surat-I, Surat-II and Valsad; (iv) Chaudhary and Kotwalia are to be found in Surat-I and Surat-II; (v) Dhodia are to be found in Surat-II and Valsad; (vi) Kokna and warli are to be found in Valsad and Dangs districts.

Most of the tribals in Gujarat live by agriculture either as owner-cultivator or as agricultural labourers as can be seen from the Table 2.6. A number of tribals work as paid labourers in forests. They also derive some income from the collection and sale of minor forest produce. In the districts of Surat and Valsad grass-cutting provides employment to the tribals of the area for a few months in the year. Where factories have come up in or around the tribal areas, they get employment as unskilled labourers. They are thus exposed to the forces of urbanisation and industrialisation. Tribals who migrate seasonally for casual labour to towns or otherwise work in factories, face problems of adjustment to the new social and economic environment. There are a number of cases of seasonal migration of tribal labour from Panchmahals, Valsad, Surat and Bharuch districts and elsewhere in search of employment in urban as well as rural areas. Such migrations take place either within the state, district or outside the State.

In order to help alleviate the conditions of most backward and isolated tribal groups, we should know as to how many tribes in a particular district are in minority. Some of these minority tribes may not have total population of more than 100 in the districts concerned. It is most likely that some of these minority tribes are seasonally migratory and, therefore, they have a tendency to leave their habitat for earning livelihood to neighbouring districts. In the case some of minority tribes who may number a little over 100 tribal sub-groups, it is possible that they are migrating to distant districts in hordes of families for a specific period of time. Many forms and systems of group migrations to urban and rural areas in the fields of unorganised sectors have emerged in recent times and it is most urgent that planners look into the matter and see that tribals do not become victims of sophisticated traps of alien exploitation.

Suitability of Sub-Plan Project to Local Tribals

Information of distribution patterns of the tribal groups in absolute and separate numbers has to be collected for serious consideration of the planners so that more backward groups among tribals in a particular sub-area are given special attention. This can be clearly seen from the analysis presented in the following points for each of the areas under tribal sub-plan projects.

TABLE 2.6: Distribution of Tribes and their occupations

Name of the districts	Principal tribal communities	Main occupations
Banaskantha	Bhil, Naikda	Agriculture and Agricultural labour.
Sabarkantha	Dungari Garasia, Bhil-Garasia Bhil	Agriculture and Agricultural labour.
Panchmahals	Bhils, Patelia, Naikda	Agriculture, wage labour and unskilled work during off seasons in adjoining districts, labour work in forest and farms, and collection of timru leaves.
Vadodara	Rathwa, Bhil, Naikda	Agriculture and agricultural labour, unskilled wage labourers in mining operations.
Bharuch	Bhil, Dhanka Dublas, Gamit, Chodhara, Kotwalia	Agriculture and agricultural labour, labour in forest and firms, collection of forest minor produce, cutting of bamboos and labour work in mining.
(a) Surat-I	Choudhary, Gamit, Bhil Kotwalia, Dubla	Agriculture and agricultural labour and cutting of grass.
(b) Surat-II	Choudhary, Dhodia, Dubla (Halapati) Kotwalia	Agriculture and agricultural labour, basket making, labour work in forest coupes and diamond cutting.
Valsad	Dhodia, Kokna, Warli Dubla (Halpati) Kolcha	Agriculture and agricultural labour, Wage labourers for cutting grass, collection of minor forest produce, labour in gardens, and work on engine pumps.
Dangs	Bhils Kokna (Kunbi), Warli	Agriculture and agricultural labour, labour work in forest coupes, collection of minor forest produce and cutting of bamboos.

(1) In the Sabarkantha Tribal Sub-Plan Area Project, the tribals live mainly by agriculture. The main emphasis in the project should, therefore, be on development of agriculture and forest based industries. In short, the approach in preparing a blue-print for development will have to be flexible and tailored

to meet the needs of the tribals and local conditions.

Stated in brief, the strategy will vary from sub-area to sub-area depending upon the State of Socio-economic development in each sub-area.

(2) In Panchmahals Tribal Sub-Plan Area Project, the tribals live mostly upon agriculture. The area has the largest number of wage-labourers, who seek employment as unskilled workers in off-seasons outside the district. Unemployment problem is very acute, particularly because it is a drought prone area. The project, therefore, should provide for measures such as soil conservation, development of agriculture, dairying and forest based industries.

(3) In the Vadodara Tribal Sub-Plan Area Project, the tribals exist at a low level of development and agriculture is the main source of their livelihood. Special emphasis should, therefore, be on development of agriculture and small scale and forest-based industries.

(4) The areas covered by the Bharuch Tribal Sub-Plan Area Project are quite backward. There is great scope for developing the forest-based industries and cotton cultivation. The project should, therefore, provide for training the tribals for cooperative activities.

(5) In the Surat Tribal Sub-Plan Area Project-I, the tribal groups in the Talukas of Uchchal, Vyara, Valod, Songadh and Nizar are mainly farmers or agricultural labourers and therefore, greater emphasis will have to be placed there on development of both agriculture and industries.

The Surat Tribal Sub-Plan Area Project-II, covers talukas of Mahuva, Mandvi, Mangrol and Bardoli. The Tribal groups here depend on agriculture and allied occupations for maintenance. The emphasis, therefore, will have to be on development of agriculture and small scale industries. The tribals are subject to exploitation in a big way from non-tribals. Thus protective measures will have to be provided in this Sub-Plan Area Project.

(6) In the case of Valsad Tribal Sub-Plan Area, particular attention has to be paid to the economic and sociological problems of tribals. In the Umbergaon and Pardi talukas, the tribals are being inducted and absorbed into the industries developing there. Here development of technical skills through apprenticeship training needs emphasis.

(7) In the Dangs Tribal Sub-Plan Area Project, the economy of the tribals revolves round the forest. There is, therefore, considerable scope for the development of forest-based industries. Provision needs to be made for training the tribals for such industries. The economic level of the tribals is very low, which needs to be taken into account for quick pace of development.

NOTES

1. B.D. Sharma, formerly Jt. Secretary, Ministry of Home affairs, Govt, of India: "Administration for tribal Development", *Indian Journal of Public Administration-Special Number,* July-September, 1977, pp. 515-39.
2. *Tribal Area Sub-Plan* (Revised)-1974-79, Govt. of Gujarat, 1976, p. 17.
3. *Tribal Souvenir,* Adim Jati Sewak Sangh Delhi, 1979 p. 29.

3

HISTORY OF LAND SYSTEMS IN TRIBAL AREAS

Introduction

In the pre-British times, it was the lack of attempt on the part of Princely States, local governments and principalities, etc. with regard to framing comprehensive legislation on the system of land-holding and revenue. Consequently, issues of land reforms of the later period, called for the needs of land survey, settlement and regularisation of occupancy rights. Most of the problems of archaic land systems whether they related to British areas or areas governed by the then ruling dynasties, the land system was regulated by custom and usage. There were cases of special orders from the local governments regarding land occupation for military service, religious institutions, etc. In course of time these usages were hardened into customary laws. The Britishers more than the Mughals and others made fruitful efforts at systematising the principles and procedures of ownership and occupancy of land for the purpose of speedy and smooth collection of land revenue.

In Bombay Presidency, which included the region of Gujarat, various land regulations were made by the Britishers in the areas governed by them directly. The first ever regulation made by the British rulers regarding land revenue, based on the assessment of the quality of land, was made in 1827. After this Regulation, there were a number of modifications made in it in the form of enactments. Thus we have had (1) The Rent-free Estates Act (Act XI of 1852); (2) Summary Settlement Act of 1863; (3) Bombay Survey and Settlement Act 1965; (4) Act IV of 1868; (5) Bombay Revenue Jurisdiction Act of 1876 and (6) Bombay Land Revenue Code of 1879.

Some of the territories which are now covered by the Tribal Area Sub-Plan, were in the Princely States as well as under the control of the Britishers. There were also cases where a district in the historical past was being governed mostly by a number of petty landlords and princes. In view of this kind of situation, variations were to be found in the form of land management in various parts of the tribal areas. It is against this background of unsystematised land systems that a review of the land system situation in the eight tribal districts of Gujarat has to be made. An attempt is made here to indicate salient features of Tribal Land Systems that prevailed before reforms of various kind were introduced after Indian Independence. An account of the situation in eight districts is presented in the following pages under special headings and sub-headings in as much detail as possible.

Banaskantha District

The Banaskantha District has no full-fledged tribal taluka as such, excepting only two tribal pockets under the Tribal Area Sub-Plan. The following table presents the total number of villages forming the pockets in the talukas concerned.

Name of the Tribal Pocket	Name of the Taluka	Number of villages
Amirgadh	Palanpur	54
Danta	Danta	120

(a) *Amirgadh Tribal Pocket*

Amirgadh Tribal Pocket area formed part of the ex-Palanpur Princely State during the British period. After merger of the Princely State, this area formed part of Palanpur Taluka in Banaskantha District.

The land tract is almost hilly and rocky. The hills extend upto Arawalli Hills on the northern boundary of Gujarat. The whole area is inhabited by tribals who are known as Garasias and Bhils.

Three types of Land Systems prevailed in the ex-Princely Palanpur State as under:

(1) *Vighoti* (tax on size of land called Vigha) System prevailed in the Surveyed Khalsa Villages.
(2) *Kaltar* System (assessment by crop share system) prevailed in the village where *vighoti* was not introduced.

(3) *Halia* or plough tax system prevailed in most of the villages of the State. Under this system, a lump sum amount of grain per plough was charged from the cultivator. The rate of plough tax was fixed on the basis of the number of bullocks and the number of persons in the family of the occupant.

There were also *Jagirs* and other *non-ryotwari* and *inam* land tenures, related to regular or occasional services provided by landholder to the state. There was a village head-man called Patel and village revenue collector called Talati, to take care of revenue collection. They were responsible to the state for the regular recovery and payment of state dues by landholders in the villages. They were assisted by watchman called *Chokiat* who held cultivable land on service tenure in consideration of his services. The Patel also enjoyed a.certain amount of land free of Government dues called *Raj Hak*. The Chief of the State had sole powers of granting remission of revenue if a crop was destroyed by fire or if owing to scanty rainfall a crop was likely to be meagure.[1]

The cultivators in the state were almost tenants at will and had no power to make over their holdings to others by sale or gift. However, so far as a land-holder paid the rent, the prince or the Chief seldom disturbed him. If the Chief forced him to give up his land, the cultivator could not claim any money for labour spent by him in land improvement. Whenever a tenant built a water well for irrigation, he was paid Rs. 10 or Rs. 12 by the State who acquired thereby a proprietary right in the well and if the tenant gave up the land, he had no claim for compensation on his investment on the well.

(b) *Danta Tribal Pocket*

Danta Tribal Pocket area formed part of the ex-Princely State of Danta during the British period. After merger of the Princely State, this area formed part of Danta Taluka in Banaskantha District.

The land tract is hilly, wild and picturesque. In the past it was covered with thick forests which formed a natural habitat for wild animals. The land is generally fertile and capable of producing good crops. Major portion of land is covered by the mountainous ranges inhabited by tribals like Dungari Bhils, Dungari Garasias, etc. The villages were unsurveyed and unsettled. The Kalter (Crop-Share) system obtained in the Danta State. Area of landholding was shown in approximate acres. Normally one fourth of the crop share was recovered as revenue by the State. The State received revenues also from the collection of minor forest produce. But the largest revenue accrued to the state from pilgrims visiting the temple of highly venerated goddess *Ambaji Mata*.

In 24 villages round-about the temple of Ambaji Mata, there was a system to recovering government share called *Padri* or *Raj Bhag* on *Kharif* crops raised by a landholder at the rate of Rs. 2-00, Rs. 2-50 and Rs. 3-00 per households.

The system of land revenue in the co-shared villages was a levy of plough-tax at the rate of Re. 0-10 (Annas)[2] to Rs. 2-8 (Annas) per landholding. The *Vadas* (enclosed plot of land) of maize crops were in addition subjected to a plough tax of Re. 1-00 per plot of land.

There were five types of *Jagiri* villages in the State:

(i) *Swang* village (exclusively owned).
(ii) Bhagilu village (Co-shared).
(iii) *Patawat* village (Feudal service).
(iv) Jiwarat village (Cadet services).
(v) *Inam* village (Gift for security service).

The tenants were liable to be turned out at the pleasure of the Chief but in practice the tenant who paid his rent was seldom ousted. The proprietor of land had the right to raise the rates or crop-shares; but the amount of increase was limited by the capability of land and by public opinion sought by the traditional panchayat. In actual practice, however, changes were seldom made.[3]

Sabarkantha District

The Sabarkantha district has four tribal Talukas viz. Bhiloda, Khedbrahma, Méghraj and Vijayanagar covered under the Tribal Area Sub-Plan. There is no Tribal Pocket in this District. The first three of these talukas were earlier under the jurisdiction of the former Princely State of Idar, and their land systems are discussed in the following points (a) followed by point (b) concerning Vijayanagar taluka.

(a) *Bhiloda, Khedbrahma and Meghraj Talukas*

These three tribal talukas formed part of the former Princely State of Idar which was a First Class State in British India.

The Idar State was the largest State in the Sabarkantha district. According to the *Gazetteer of the Bombay Presidency* (Volume V), there were large areas of arable waste in the North and East of Idar states. These areas were offered to non-tribal cultivators on favourable terms but the settlers were scared by the wilderness of the countryside and of its fiercer Bhil inhabitants.

The land revenue was formerly extracted in the form of farm produce on the spot by the state. Later, it came to be collected directly from the cultivators after completion of harvesting the crops. The Bhil villages with no fixed village sites and widely scattered huts had no central place, temple or shop except a common headman called *Mukhi-Gameti,* village officers were not posted to collect land revenue. In non-Bhil villages, the headman was a hereditary go-between called *Matadar.* The village accountant called *Talati* collected the revenue from the cultivators and paid the same to sub-divisional officer called *Talukdar.* Later on, as per the advice of the British Political Agent, a Police Patel was added to the establishment of most of the villages. The village functionaries in Idar State were paid in cash and generally they held rent-free lands and enjoyed levying certain fees for personal benefits and perquisites.

In most of the *Khalsa* villages, the *Khatabandhi* or *Ryotwari* system of revenue in cash prevailed, while in a limited number of villages, the *Halwari* system was in force. In the former system the revenue was got by instalment, while in the latter, it was recovered for the land actually cultivated by landlord. In the Megharaj-Mewar frontier, inhabited mostly by Bhils, the lump sum amount of revenue was recovered collectively from the headman of the village.

The *Bhagbatai* system (crop-share system) obtained in just a few villages of the State. In the case when State share was recovered in cash, the amount of cash assessment varied from six annas to a rupee and half per acre for *Jirayat* land (dry land) and from three to eight rupees per acre of garden land. In the alienated villages, the revenue system was still the time honoured *Bhugbatai* (crop-share) type.

Some villages were leased out for fixed amounts or *Ankada,* and they were therefore known as *Ankada* Villages. These villages were leased to the local leaders by the state in the hilly and far-flung border areas of Bhiloda and Meghraj talukas. The leasers were called *Ankadedars* who on the other hand, were responsible for leasing out plots of land for cultivation to individual households who paid a fixed amount of *Ankada* to the State. This unique type of land system developed because of the distance of the villages and the difficulties involved in administering these areas. The Ankadedars were intermediaries or links between the state and landholders and had their own land for self-cultivation-*Gharkhed* gifted by the state.

Two-third of the area of Idar state was under the *Jagirdars* who were either *Bhumia* or grantees of former princely dynasty, or *Sardar Patawat,* the grantees of latter dynasty. The Sardar Patawats were originally granted *Patas* (fiefs) by the feudal Marwari Rulers for Military Services of allies and supporters. The majority of the *Jagirdars* were illiterate and they opposed any land reforms. The British administration Report of the year 1930-31, describes the rigidity of the *Jagirdars* and their extravagent nature, spending every thing on their personal luxuries and paying nothing to the state.

The *Ryots* of *khalsa* villages on the other hand enjoyed certain privileges not enjoyed by them under the yoke of *Jagirdars.* the people of the *khalsa* villages had to pay half of the cost on services for education, medicines, police, magistracy, roads and communications, etc. In contrast, the *Jagirdars* contributed next to nothing on the above items although their population comprised more than half of the state population.

The original survey and settlement in the state was carried out by the British Administrator Mr. Hall in 1868, and the Revision Settlement was carried out in the first decade of the present century, in respect to all the *khalsa* villages. Some *Jagir* villages were surveyed and settled under the Agency Administration, but in a few *Jagir* villages which remained unsurveyed, *Vaje* or *Kaltar* system of fixed revenue collection obtained. In some villages of Bhiloda Taluka, however, a plough tax at Rs. 8 was levied for the plot of land which would be cultivated by only one plough.

In some villages of Khedbrahma Taluka, *Uddhad Vero* (ad hock tax) for *kharif* crops was recovered at the lower rate of Rs. 4 or Rs. 5 per house from tribals. This pattern prevailed in 62 villages of Poshina princely *Jagir* and 9 villages of Kheroj *Jagir*, and also in some khalsa villages. For *Rabi* and Summer crops, a fixed crop share called *Kaltar* from the estimated produce, and a crop share equal to two, or two-and--half times (*Bijwa*) of the quantity of seeds sown in the field by the cultivator, was recovered.

One significant fact about the cultivators of the Idar State was that they were occupants of the land, whether they were put in the category of *Bhumia, Sardar Patawat, Bhayati, Inami, Seshani* or *khalsa* villages and paid *Vighoti* or *Vaje* to the state or to the *Jagirdars.* The land held by the cultivators was allowed to be sold, mortgaged, leased or alienated.

(b) *Vijayanagar Taluka*

The present tribal taluka of Vijayanagar formed part of the former Princely State of Vijayanagar. The Revenue system in the state was *Bhag-batai* in the dense forest villages in hilly and remote areas. Besides, levy system of lump sum payment to be paid to the village head-man on behalf of the state also obtained. It seems that the state had not introduced variations in fixing land revenue in hilly tribal areas under its jurisdiction.[4]

Panchmahals District

The district of Panchmahals has five tribal talukas viz., Santrampur, Devegadhbaria, Limkheda, Jhalod and Dahod all covered under the Tribal Area Sub-Plan. The district has also the following two tribal Pockets located in Halol and Godhra Talukas.

Name of Tribal Pocket	Name of Taluka	Number of villages
(1) Kathola	Halol	41
(2) Mora	Godhra	32

The historical situation of the land system in the areas is presented in four sub-sections after re-grouping the talukas and/or pockets as the case may be.

(a) *Santrampur Taluka*

Santrampur tribal taluka formed part of the former Sant Princely State. In those days, Ryotwari system of land-holding prevailed in this state. Land revenue settlement was introduced during the time of the Sant State. The rate of revenue called *Moksha-dar (Salvation tax)* varied from Rs. 2 to Rs. 4, on the plot of land for a plough. The revenue was being recovered in cash. Occupancy rights of the landholders had been recognised by the State. The sale and mortgage of the land to persons other than direct heirs, was made subject to the sanction by the Sant State.[5]

(b) *Devgadhbaria and Limkheda Talukas*

Devgadhbaria and Limkheda talukas formed part of the former Baria Princely State during the British period. The Circuit Survey in the State was commenced by Mr. Hall of the Gujarat Revenue Survey, in 1867 and completed in 1871. The survey and settlement of land revenue was made in the early part of the century and the revision settlement was made in 1920. The Ryotwari system of land-holding prevailed and the land revenue was assessed according to the fertility of land as in British-India. The average rate of assessment payable in cash came to be about Re. one per acre.* The occupancy rights were granted to cultivators who were registered land-holders on the data of conferment. A special State fee, called *Nazrana* was charged for grant of occupancy rights.

The Baria State land tenure had two special characteristics which could easily be rated as fairly progressive with regard to prevention of alienation of land.

(i) In the case of attachment and sale of land of occupant for redemption of debt or in execution of a decree of a Civil Court, immunity was granted to such portion of the holding as was adjudged by the Chief Revenue Authority for preservation of his status as an agriculturist and for maintenance of himself and his family, and

(ii) The prior approval of the Revenue Authority for sale or mortgage of land by a land-holder was imperative.[6]

(c) *Jhalod Taluka (Part of Sanjeli State)*

The present Jhalod taluka formed part of the British area and the Sanjeli Princely State. The Ryotwari system of land revenue prevailed in the former Sanjeli State and the occupancy rights were conferred on agriculturists. The lands were surveyed and classified and a uniform land system prevailed throughout the State.[7]

---

* *Land measures in metric equivalents*

1-Hectare	=	1000.00 square meter
1-Acre	=	100.00 square meter
1-Acre	=	50.00 square meter (appro.)
1-Bigha	=	23.00 square meter (appro.)
1-Guntha	=	1.00 square meter (appro.)

(d) *Jhalod (Outside Sanjeli State) and Dahod Talukas with Tribal Pockets of Kathola in Halol, and Mora in Godhra Taluka*

These areas formed part of British territory in the Panchmahals District. It is essential, therefore, to note that the Land Revenue Survey and Settlement was made in these areas under the Bombay Land Revenue Code, 1879, referred to in the first section of this chapter. However, the settlements of land-holding were revised between 1906-07 to 1926-27.

It may be noted that the Panchmahals district was handed over to British for management by the Marathan Rulers in 1853. The District was in the hands of the persons called *Revenue Farmers*. The *Farmers* realized land revenue dues from the headman of villages, Chiefs and large land-holders of several villages and from speculators who took on contract, the work of collection of revenue of group of villages.

The revenue in these areas was recovered under different systems. The large land-holders paid the amount of levy fixed by a rough estimate as revenue. The village head-men were made responsible for making rough calculation of what the village could pay and what it had paid before. Some villages were let out for revenue, in groups to the persons called *Revenue Farmer* on 5 years' lease with the condition of yearly increase in the rents.

In other cases, division of crops and a levy of plough cess varied according to the caste of the cultivator from Rs. 2 to Rs. 15 per plough or at the rate of seven acres (15 *Bighas*) per plough. A *Bigha* rate varied from 2 annas to Re. 1. An extra cess was levied for costly crops like spices, sugarcane, etc. In villages where a crop-share system prevailed, the government share varied from a third to a half of the produce.[8]

In Dahod taluka, an experimental settlement was introduced in 1878-79 because of the backward character of the tract inhabited by the tribals. It was sanctioned for 20 years in 1884-85, i.e., upto 1903-04. Practically the rate of revenue fixed in 1878-79 continued to remain in operation with slight modification. When land settlement was made, it resulted in immediate resignation, of 11,000 acres by occupants followed by decrease in population and cattle in the area. The predominant Bhils were backward and thriftless. However, in view of rise in prices comodities of domestic use and depreciation of land prices, a moderate increase of 10 per cent was proposed by the Settlement Officers. The Government sanctioned this proposal only for a period of 15 years.

The Dahod revision in land revenue set the pitch for Jhalod taluka. As in Dahod, introduction of survey rates resulted in resignation of over 5,000 acres of land. This was attributed by the District Collector to the rigid land system and the unfertile wild tract of this area. The Settlement Officer was guided by certain outdated considerations. On debit side was a loss of 28.5 per cent in population, increase in fallow and waste land, and a decrease in the occupied area. On credit side were introduction of a new railway line within 20 miles radius, a new metalled road to Limkheda and Dahod, a problematic rise in land prices etc. The old rates of land tenure were, however, continued for 5 years more.

The condition of the area deteriorated due to famine of 1899-1900, and Panchmahals was one of the districts which suffered heavily. Government had to consider the proposal for enhancement of revenue assessment in the light of local scarcity situation. On expiry of the five year's period, the Government ordered that an increase in revenue rates was not yet justifiable, and the original rates sanctioned in 1882-83 were further continued for a period of 10 years more.[9]

Vadodara District

The district has three tribal talukas viz. Chhotaudepur, Naswadi and Tilakwada under the Tribal Area Sub-Plan. The following tribal pockets are covered for development.

Name of Tribal Pocket	Name of Taluka	No. of villages
(1) Vadeli	Sankheda	53
(2) Bhatpur	Sankheda	51
(3) Karali	Pavi Jetpur (Jabugam)	52
(4) Bhikhapura	Pavi Jetpur (Jabugam)	46

It should be noted that Chhotaudepur Tribal Taluka was a part of ex-Princely State of Chhotaudepur. Also the present Naswadi tribal taluka has a number of villages of ex-Naswadi and ex-Ghadboriad Estates. Tilakwada tribal taluka and Sankheda Taluka which includes two tribal pockets, were the part of ex-Princely State of Baroda. The Pavi-Jetpur Taluka having two tribal pockets formed part of the ex-Princely State of Chhotaudepur. The following notes throw valuable light on the land systems prevalent in most of these areas.

(a) *Chhotaudepur State*

The ex-Princely State of Chhotaudepur was divided into four talukas for the purpose of Revenue Administration during the State regime. A section of Panvad division and Kawant Taluka were known as "*Rani*, i.e. Jungle land". All the villages with the exception of six villages in Kawant Taluka were surveyed, and revenue settlement rate was introduced therein. There were also 42 alienated villages were survey and settlement was introduced in the past.[10]

The Land Revenue Settlement in Chhotaudepur was based on the pattern of land system obtaining in the British Territory. The survey and settlement was introduced in the *Khalsa* villages between 1909 and 1919. The occupants had rights similar to those enjoyed by occupants under the Bombay Land Revenue Code of 1879. But there was no Record of Rights in the state, because amendment of 1913 made in the Code was not extended to this state. The people of backward classes were illiterate and improvident, and were prohibited from transferring their land to money-lenders without the sanction of the state, locally called *Darbar*. This was done to protect tribals and other weaker sections of land-holders from exploitation by money-lenders.[11]

(b) *Ghadboriad and Naswadi Estates*

These two Estates were included by the British in the Sankheda Mewas in the Rewakantha Agency. The Ghadboriad Estate was owned by the Chief of Rajput extraction of Chauhan clan, while Naswadi Estate was owned by the Chief of Rajput extraction of Solanki clan. In both these Estates, there was a custom of primogeniture with respect to inheritance of ancestral property.[12]

The various systems of revenue collection in the Estates of the Rewakantha Agency were as under:

(i) *Bighoti-tax*

Cash assessment per acre or *bigha* of land was fixed according to survey measurement and classification of soil.

(ii) *Khatabandi-tax*

The land-holdings were roughly measured into measure of *kumbha* and the assessment was fixed at certain cash rate on the *bigha* or *kumbha* according to the quality of land and its productivity. This rate was variable at the discretion of the princes.

(iii) *Halbandhi-Plough Tax*

In this category of taxation, a certain cash amount was levied on pairs of bullocks possessed by occupants of land irrespective of the extent of land cultivated. This kind of tax was levied on the people of most backward classes especially, the Bhils, Niakdas, and Kolis who generally lived among hills or forest tracts.

(iv) *Udhad, Ijara-Ankadia Tenure*

A certain number of villages were held by the headmen on what was called *Udhad, Ijara* or *Ankadia* tenure. The state received from them a lump sum amount only for the whole village, while the headman made individual collection of taxes in kind from the cultivators. The length and terms of tenure varied according to the circumstances in each case. Some occupants were hereditary, while others were kept for specified periods of time liable to revision or resumption of tenure.

(e) *Bhagbatai (Crop-share Tenure)*

Land tax was in the form of share of the grain or its equivalent in coin, as levied by the Princely Chief under this system. It look five forms. In the first four, cash recoveries of various amounts were made, while in the fifth, the state received actual share of the crop. When the crops were ready to cut, the state officials of the Thakor Chiefs themselves examined each field, and, with the help of appointed wise men and experts, made an estimate of the crop, locally called the *Kaltar.* In some cases, the estimate was made after the crop was reaped and harvested.

It may be noted that in Kathiawar, the state share was generally separated when the grain was ready and was afterwards sold by the State in the open market. But in the Revakantha area, the State received only the equivalent in cash according to the current price of the grain. The state share varied according to the reason, the kind of grain and the honesty of the assessors. This generally amounted to 1/3 or 1/4 of the produce, but in addition, certain cases the share under various names as *Havaldari, Sukhdi Kharjat*, etc. were sometimes levied. Under this system the cultivators, were left pretty much to the kind mercies and reasons of the State officials. However, where the amount of share was without any cesses, the inconveniences to cultivators were absent.[13]

Post-Independence Land Revenue Rules

There was a great need of rationalisation of the land revenue system specially in the merged areas of Princely States where survey and settlement was either introduced or not introduced at all. In some areas, no doubt, partial settlement was carried out. The main purpose of this rationalisation was to bring land revenue system of these ares on par with that of former Bombay State. The Bombay Land Revenue Rules of 1921 were strengthened by the insertion of Rules 19-N and 19-O for the fixation of the assessment of land revenue. The details of these insertions are presented below in suitable quotes as found in the latest Gazetteer of Panchmahals District.

"In the merged State areas, where the land revenue settlement was considered scientific, in order to bring the land revenue assessment on par with those obtaining in the premerger talukas of the state, Government framed the Land Revenue Rule 19-N. For fixing the land revenue assessment in areas which were not settled or not scientifically settled on lines similar to the Bombay Land Revenue Code, Land Revenue Rules 19-O was framed. Both these rules had been framed under Section 52 of the Bombay Land Revenue Code, 1879. These rules provides for fixing the assessment in all the unsettled areas on an *ad hoc* basis till the scientific survey and settlement are introduced under the provisions of Chapter VIII-A of the Land Revenue Code."[14]

"The land Revenue Rule 19-N applies to the merged territories only and provides for continuing the prevailing rates of assessment until the settlement of land revenue is fixed under Chapter VIII-A of the Land Revenue Code or the rates of assessment are fixed under Section 52 of the Code, whichever event occurs earlier. It also provides for reduction of the existing rates, if they are found to be higher than the Union areas rates after scaling them down by 25 per cent. Thus, the main objective of Rule 19-N is the continuance of the existing rates of assessment and necessary reduction therein by way of remission for removal of inequalities in the pitches of assessment."

"The Land Revenue Rule 19-O, however, applies to the whole pre-reorganised Bombay State comprising:

(1) the per-merger State areas.
(2) the merged territories.
(3) the merged area."

"It provides for fixing *ad hoc* assessment under Section 52 of the Code subject to the provisions of section 7 of the Bombay Merged Territories and Areas (*Jagirs* Abolition) Act, 1953. Detailed provisions are made for fixing the assessment by classifying the dry crop, rice and irrigated lands into good, medium and inferior, having regard to the sale value of agricultural lands, the yield of principal crops and the rental values of agricultural lands. After the classification of the lands as above, the average gross produce per acre of each sub-class of land for a period of 5 years is to be ascertained and the rates of assessment per acre for each sub-class of land calculated at 35 per cent of 1/6 of the prices of the average gross agricultural produce to be fixed in a group of homogenous villages as far as possible in respect of physical configuration, climate, rainfall, markets, communication and standard of animal husbandry. Such a detailed procedure is not to be undertaken in the case of unassessed lands in a settled village or an unsettled village surrounded by settled villages under the Land Revenue Code. In the case of such unsettled land and village, the assessment is to be fixed according to the standard rate obtaining in the same or neighbouring settled villages.

The rates of assessment fixed under the Rules are to remain in forces for 10 years or till the regular settlement is made under the LRC whichever is earlier."[15]

"Further, sub-rules (5) was added to the L.R. Code 19-O with effect from 18th May, 1956. It empowers Government to declare in the case of any merged territory that the provision of this L.R. Rule would not apply to the areas which were assessed immediately before the merger of such territory according to the survey and settlement law which generally corresponded to the provision of Chapter VIII and VIII-A of the L.R. Code. Accordingly Government has already declared the merged territories of the Gujarat States areas as falling in the above category. The effect of this sub-rule is that there will be no need to fix assessment in these areas according to the provisions of the L.R. Rules 19-O."

"It is clear that the Land Revenue Rule 19-O was framed in order to fix the rates of assessment in the surveyed and unsettled or unsurveyed and unsettled lands and villages on an *ad hoc* basis till scientific survey and settlement were introduced under the provision of Chapter VIII-A or the Land Revenue Code, 1879. This interim measure has been adopted by Government because it is not possible immediately to undertake the full dress survey and settlement for all such areas at a time."

"It may be noted that in merged areas, there were several villages held on Jagiri tenure. The Jagiri tenure was abolished under the Bombay Merged Territories and Areas (Jagirs Abolition) Act, 1953 and the assessment of each individual survey number or sub-division was fixed under Section 7 of the said Act by applying the rates of the adjoining homogeneous Khalsa village."[16]

Bharuch District

The Bharuch district has five tribal talukas, viz. Rajpipla (Nandod), Dediapada,, Jhagadia, Valia and Sagbara under the Tribal Area Sub-Plan. There is also one Tribal Pocket of Ankleshwar consisting of 38 villages in Ankleshwar taluka. The first four talukas originally comprised former Rajpipla Princely State. The Sagbara Estate was under the management of Rajpipala state. In the past, when the British Superintendence of the area was accepted by the Rajpipla state, the land of the districts (now turned talukas) were let out to persons of wealth and respectability, until 1823.[17]

The land revenue system in this area in general was based on the pattern of land system obtaining in British India. It was regulated by legislation more or less similar to the British enactments and land revenue codes. The *Ryotwari* System was first introduced in the year 1885 and perfected in subsequent years. The survey and settlement was completed in practically all villages in the year 1889-90 in both the *Rasti* (civilised) and *Rani* (jungle) areas, Revision Settlement was made in 1910.[18]

In 95 villages of Sagbara Estate, land was given out for cultivation on an extensive scale during the Rajpipla State regime, when they were not surveyed. The survey of these areas has been undertaken now by the Gujarat Government.[19]

Surat District

The district of Surat has 9 tribal talukas divided into two groups for the administration of schemes of Tribal Area Sub-Plan: (i) Surat-I comprises, Vyara, Valod, Songadh, Uchchhal and Nizar Talukas; and (ii) Surat-II comprises Mahuva, Mandvi, Mangrol and Bardoli Talukas.

The district has two tribal pockets taken under the Tribal Area Sub-Plan as under:

Name of the Tribal Pocket	Name of Taluka	No. of villages
Kamrej	Kamrej	43
Palsana	Palsana	35

The talukas of Vyara, Valod, Songadh, Mahuva, Mandvi and Mangrol including the two tribal pockets belonged to the former Vadodara State. The Bardoli taluka is a former British taluka, while the talukas of Uchchhal and Nizar formed part of the former West Khandesh district, a former British administered area. All these talukas of ex-British area were surveyed and settled according to the Bombay Land Revenue Code, 1879.

In the old Vadodara State the districts were formed out of the highest bidders and the cultivators enjoyed neither security of tenure nor of assessment. This kind of land management was called *Ijara Vahivat,* meaning monopoly management. Thereafter, where survey was conducted, the *Vighoti* system of land revenue was introduced. As a result, the pitch of assessment was raised to such an extent that the cultivators could not pay increased rate of land revenue, and so they fled to the adjacent British area. In order to remedy the situation, the term of original settlement was fixed for 15 years and the term of revision settlement was fixed for 30 years. This happened in the Talukas of Gandevi, Palsana, Kamrej and Mahuva. As Songadh Taluka was hilly and full of forests, and inhabited by hostile Bhils and Nayakdas, practically no land revenue was charged in the beginning of the Maratha Rule. Subsequently the Land of this taluka was given on *Ijara* (monopoly) pattern which was subsequently replaced by *Kaltar* and *Halbandhi* systems of land revenue.

The plough tax was recovered at their different rates, such as Rs. 10, Rs. 12 and Rs. 15. In the Vyara Taluka, original pattern was *Ijara* system of land revenue. It was followed by the *Kaltar* system, under which land revenue was recovered at the rate of six annas of the produce. In all Talukas of the ex-Vadodara state (now included the District of Surat) and those of Valsad district Navsari and Gandevi, the *Ryotwari* system was introduced during the state Regime. The most memorable land reform was the settlement of lands on just and equitable basis, according to the principle formulated in the *Joint Report of 1847 of the Bombay Presidency.* The principle was that "land should be assessed in accordance with its capabilities". The original settlements were made between 1880 and 1901 as per the principal laid down by the Bombay officers Mr. Illiot and Mr. Seddon. Later on Revision Settlements were also made according to the Bombay Presidency land revenue system.

Under these reforms the rights of occupants were considered permanent, heritable and transferable as defined in the Baroda Land Revenue Code. The *Barkhali* (alienated) land was settled accordingly in 1889 and made subject to payment of quit-rent. Although *Ryotwari* system was the common tenure in the state, there were two broad categories of *non-Ryotwari* tenures, viz. (i) *Narwadari — Bhagdari* types, and (ii) *Ankdabandhi* type.

In the Narwadari types of tenure the revenue was fixed for the whole village and collected from the *Narwadars* appointed for this purpose. The persons cultivating the lands of these villages were tenants not of the state but of the Narwadars. The tenants could not be ejected by Narwadars as long as they paid the customary rental. In the *Bhagdari* tenure, each field was separately assessed and the village as a whole paid the total sum of the land assessment as if in partnership. The State Government seldom interfered between the *Bhagdars,* and the tenants paid land revenue on the basis of customary joint responsibility. In the *Ankdabandhi* villages, a lump sum revenue was assessed from time to time for the whole village. The state did not interfere in the internal fiscal arrangement of the village controlled by traditional leaders.[20]

In certain backward areas of Vadodara State, laws had been passed in the interest of the backward classes (*Kaliparaj*) as well as tribals *Raniparaj*)[21] restricting the right of alienation of land (Literally *Kaliparaj* means dark people and *Raniparaj* forest people). In 1938, the State enacted the Backward Classes Land Protection Act. This was meant to protect the *Raniparaj* (Tribals) and other Backward classes who incurred debt and were steadily ousted from their lands by money-lenders. The *Kaliparaj* and *Raniparaj* people were illiterate, ignorant and poor and therefore, had to be protected from exploitation by money-lenders and other non-tribal communities. The money-lenders used to take possession of the land of these people but did not cultivate the lands themselves and leased out to tribals for cultivation on crop share bases. They used to give seed and maintenance or *Khavti* to the needy tribals at double the rates of recovery later on. As a result, the tribals could not extricate themselves from debt, and led a life of a serf for good. In order to protect tribals from this kind of exploitation, the law imposed restrictions on transfer, alienation or relinquishment of tribal lands. Under the law, transfer by sale, gift or alienation of land to non-tribals was prohibited though not between and among the tribals. This Act applied also to alienation of lands of backward classes without the permission of the State, except on base for one year only. The Deputy Collector called *Naib Suba* in charge of an administrative subdivision of a district was empowered to give permission of alienation provided the land was alienated to a person belonging to a person of backward community. The land which was alienated against the law was restored to the original owner by the Naib Suba, i.e. Deputy Collector.[21]

Valsad District

The district of Valsad has 5 tribal Talukas, viz. Dharampur, Vansda, Chikhli, Pardi and Umbergaon covered under the Tribal Area Sub-Plan. It has 4 tribal pockets located in 3 non-tribal talukas mentioned below:

Name of Tribal Pocket	Name of Taluka	No. of Villages
Rahej	Gandevi	31
Atgam	Valsad	20
Ronvel	Valsad	22
Sisodra-Ganesh	Navsari	37

The Chikhli, Pardi and Umbergaon talukas formed part of the former British area. The first two were the talukas in former Surat District, and the last one was in the Thana, now in Maharashtra District. These 3 talukas were surveyed and settled according to Bombay Land Revenue Code, 1879.

The Dharampur and Vansda talukas were formed of two ex-Princely State known by the same names, where tribals were the main inhabitants. Notes on land system in these two former tribal states are presented below.

(a) *Dharampur State*

In the former Dharampur State, the Ryotwari Settlement was in vogue. The bulk of population consisted of the *Raniparaj* (tribal) people. All the villages had been surveyed and settled after proper classification. The state paid Rs. 9,000 annually to British Government in lien of *Chauth Jakat* (one fourth of produce) tax formerly levied by Government in the state. It covered an areas of 704 square miles as shown by the survey. The revision survey commenced in 1919 and was completed in a few villages only. The maximum rates of assessment were:[22]

		Rs.	A.
(i)	Dry land per bigha	0-	14
(ii)	Rice land per bigha	8-	00
(iii)	Land fit for sugar plantation per bigha	2-	00

Out of total area of 369,192 acres: (i) 1,27,540 acres were under cultivation, (ii) 1,39,958 acres waste, (iii) 1,01,694 acres under Kharaba, (iv) 90,857 acres reserved forest, and (v) 60,355 acres protected forest.

(b) *Vansda State*

In the former Vansda State, the land revenue system was Ryotwari. The revision survey of land in the State commenced in 1914. The Survey operations were completed but the classification of land remained uncompleted in a few village. Old rates of assessment were in force. Total cultivable areas of the State was 69,296 acres of which 15,199 acres was waste land in 1920-21.

Maximum rates of assessment were:[23]

	Rs.	A.
Dry land per acre	3-	8
Rice land per acre	4-	0

An extra charge for water was levied by the state from the cultivators of rice land and *bagayat* land.

The last Revision Settlement was made in 1923-24 and assessment was fixed on acres according to the classification of lands. Land Revenue was recovered in cash into instalments. In order to safeguard the tribal interests against exploitation by unscrupulous purchasers or money-lenders, the Agriculturists' Relief Act and the Alienation of the *Raniparaj* Cultivators' Land Act were enacted. Under these Acts, any alienation of land by the *Raniparaj* cultivators were scrutinised by the Revenue officer and the *Dewan* (minister incharge) before the transaction was finalised.

Legislation was also enacted prohibiting usureous interest on loans to *Raniparaj* cultivators.

Dangs District

This district is both a district and a taluka, specially because of its size and character of population which was only 94,185 souls according to the 1971 Census. In Gujarat there are more than 18 talukas with larger population than Dangs. The whole Taluka has unique geophysical status and so treated as a tribal district for, administrative facility. It has a mark of distinction under Tribal Area Sub-Plan. The district is predominately hilly and forest and it lies on the spurs and slopes of undulating valleys. Its soils and land exhibit the characteristics of uneven and rough texture.

It is natural, therefore, that the basis of sub-area administration comprise of forests and not the agricultural land. The needs and interests of the Forest Department of the Government remain on the top. The ancestors of tribals of this area called Dangis were cultivating lands under the form of shifting cultivation. For this kind of cultivation, the revenue system of plough or *Halpati* tax was suitable and retained by the British. After Independence, the land has been surveyed and classified. But settlement of land revenue was not introduced until 1971. The survey has proved to be useful in locating the land in possession of cultivators, for which they now pay land revenue.

In the past, the cultivation of land in Dangs was allowed in patches in the protected forests only. This system of land use for cultivation came to be known as *Patedari* system. The lesses paid the plough-tax called *Halpati* of Rs. 6-50, of course, not on the basis of number of ploughs used for cultivation. The *Halpati* tax was actually levied on the cultivated area by one plough as well as a pair of bullocks. This tax rate was halved if cultivation was done by means of one plough drawn with one bullock or if no bullock was used and hand-plough was employed.

In the absence of classification and settlement of land revenue in the Dangs, the plough-system was found suitable. The Kunbi, Warli and other cultivators had to pay *Halpati* levy, but not the ruling Bhil Rajas, Naiks and their kins and affinal relations called *Bhaubandh*. The *Halpati* tax collected from cultivators used to be divided among several descendants of Rajas and Naiks according to the villages held by them. And, similarly their *Bhaubandhs* (kins and affines) also got their shares.

A bird eye view of past history will be useful to get on idea of old revenue administration in the Dangs. The chief rulers, the Bhil Rajas and Naiks, were powerful and supreme. They collected land revenue on the old pattern called *Autbandhi* system. This system provided for cultivation of land, not on the basis of a fixed survey number or a specified plot of land but on the basis of the area which could be cultivated by a farmer with one plough and a pair of bullocks. Under these circumstances, the revenues of the rulers were derived from fees charged on timber, and on all other forest produce carried away through the territory. Obviously therefore, the land revenue was meagure and was received in kind from the tribal population.[24]

Before the British acquired influence and jurisdiction over the Dangs, the Bhil Rajas and Naiks claimed to be owners of Dangs lands, as they were the original settlers and land-holders in the area. The forest lease system first introduced by the British did not give the British any right of ownership over the lands. The British were only given the right to exploit the forest in 1842. All lands held by the Rajas and Naiks continued to remain in their possession and they received land revenue from the lands cultivated by others in the forest area. However, these Chiefs remained ignorant for decades as to how the administration of forest area was carried out by the British. It was during this nascent period that the Divisional Forest Officer appointed by the British, saw to it that all lands in the Dangs came to be treated on record as vesting in Government and not in the Chiefs.

The Dangi tribals as said before, cultivated land anywhere in the Dangs on payment of *Halpati* tax of Rs. 6-50 even after the forest lease of 1842 with the British Government. The British had agreed to pay forest subsidy to the Chiefs. It was enjoyed in the lease that the "Government shall have the right to cut and remove timber in order to prepare land for cultivation and when the land is so prepared, to affix the assessment and make it payable to us", i.e. the Dangi Chiefs. But in the revised lease of 1862, two additional conditions were added, which placed restrictions on the Chief's right of cultivation and voluntary alienation of their lands. The Chiefs entered into an agreement with the British that:

(i) In the forest areas reserved by Government no one would be allowed to enter without the permission of the Forest Officer;
(ii) Sufficient land would be left outside the reserved forest for cultivation; and
(iii) The Chiefs would not alienate any *Vatan* or *Kunti* allowance or any other privilege to an outsider without the sanction of the British Government.

In 1879, the forests in Dangs were classified into two categories, (i) reserved and (ii) protected. This resulted in the abridgement of rights of the Chiefs, i.e., Bhil Rajas and Naiks with regard to cultivation and alienation of land. Their right to cultivate land was confined to protected forest areas. Dangi tribals however, indulged in wonton destruction of the forest and commenced cultivation of virgin lands by lopping off trees. To pacify the disobedient tribals and Chiefs, the British had to increase the amount of forest subsidy to the rulers called Rajas. The Chief, however, remained unreconciled with the interference of British Government.

To meet the resistance of the Dangi tribals, the British immediately appointed a Divisional Forest Officer and a Dangs Diwan. Before the appointment of these officers, the land revenue was collected directly by the Chiefs. But after appointment of these officers the revenue was collected by them and made payable to the Chiefs, on the alleged ground that the Chief oppressed the cultivators. Thus the direct link of the Dangi Chiefs with the actual tribal cultivators was broken.

In 1903, the Divisional Forest Officer was upgraded as the Assistant Political Agent for Dangs with First Class Magisterial powers. He was assisted by the Dangs Diwan who was also invested with Second Class Magisterial powers. From 1903 onwards upto 1943, these officers tried to maintain a *status quo* so far as land administration was concerned. As stated in the Annual Administration Report for Dangs 1944-46, the basis of land administration in this area was the forest and not the field. The needs and interests of the Forest Department were recognised as paramount and had to be primarily attended to since the revenue was mainly derived from the forests and not from the cultivable land.

In the year 1969-70, the Gujarat Government issued orders to give suspension and remission of *Halpati* tax to the Dangis having regard to the scarcity conditions in that year. In Dangs, unlike other districts, Local Fund cess and Education cess are not levied on the leviable land revenue. The land in the Dangs district was thus historically vested in the Government. It was entirely a forest area. No private ownership of land was granted. The Dangis were allowed to cultivate land in the protected forest areas on an *Eksali* (yearly) basis.

The Government of Gujarat took a historic decision to grant occupancy rights to the Dangis, with effect from 1st January, 1970, in respect of the land under their cultivation in the protected forests. The rights over non-reserved trees situated on the land have not been conferred. The occupants, however, shall be entitled to lop the trees standing on their lands for the purpose of agricultural operations. If any tree or trees obstruct the operation of cultivation, such tree or trees shall be cut down by the Forest Department at the request of the Dangi occupant. Their rights over the surved lands are recorded in the record of the rights and they are provided with *Khatavahies*-registration indicating individual title to the land.

Government of Gujarat also granted lands to the former Bhil Rajas and Naiks on new and impartible tenure, but free of occupancy price. Lands were granted for their maintenance to these traditional Dangi Chiefs as they had no moveable or immoveable property, and none of them was educated or well settled in life. Taking into consideration the extent of land in their possession, practice of keeping rotational fallow lands, future increase in number of family members and rise in living standard, sufficient land was allotted to them. They were allowed to select fallow lands in their own forest villages. Before 1953, they did not pay any *Halpati* levy, but for the lands under their cultivation. But after the formal grant of occupancy rights they have been subjected to payment of *Halpati* tax on the land under their cultivation.

It may be noted that these changes did not appear to have made may material improvement in the conditions of Dangi Rajas and Naiks. They did not take sufficient interest in the management of their lands. They were by and large illiterate, ignorant, extravagant, and addicted to drinking and living under debts. They did not take interest in the management of their own affairs, nor were they keen to educate their children. Their estate managers called *Karbharis* were ignorant Adivasis. Presently they depend mainly on political pension granted for their livelihood.[25]

NOTES

1. *Gazetteer of the Bombay Presidency,* Vol. V, 1880, See also, F.S. Master, *Palanpur Agency Directory,* Vol., I, 1908, pp. 34-35.
   Gazetteer of the Bombay Presidency, Vol. V, *Kutch, Palanpur and Mahikantha,* 1880, pp. 304-305.
2. In British currency 16 Annas were equal to one Rupee.
3. (i) *Gazetteer of the Bombay Presidency, Op. cit,* pp. 386-87.
   (ii) G.D. Patel, *Land Alienation Report of Danta State,* (Unpublished) 1951.
4. It may be noted that foregoing material has been summarised from the sources listed below:
   (i) Campbell, J.M., *Gazetteer of the Bombay Presidency, Op. cit.,* p-386.
   (ii) Master F.S., *The Mahikantha Directory,* Vol. 1, Rajkot, 1922, pp-122-123.
   (iii) G.D. Patel, *The Report of the Alienation Enquiry Officer, on Idar State,* 1951.
   (iv) *Annual Administration Report of the Idar State,* 1930-31. p. 85 and 1933-34 p. 14.
   (v) *Gujarat State Gazetteers: Sabarkantha Dist.,* Revenue Administration, Chapter XI, 1974.
5. *Ibid.,* pp. 565 and 573. See also. *Report on the Administration of the Sant State for the year 1940-41,* p. 6.
6. *Report on the Administration of the Baria State,* 1942-43, p. 10.
7. (i) *Administration Report of the Sanjeli State,* 1936-37, p. 4.
   (ii) *District Gazetteer Panchmahals,* 1972, p. 565.
8. Campbell, J.M., *The Gazetteer of Bombay Presidency,* Vol. III, Karia and Panchmahals, 1879, pp. 261-262.
9. *District Gazetteer; Panchmahals,* 1972, Revenue Administration, Chapter XI.
10. Rewa Kantha, *Gazetteer of the Bombay Presidency,* Vol. VI-B, Cambay and Surat Agency, 1927, p.1.
11. *Administration Report of the Chhotaudepur State,* 1945-46, pp. 6-8.
12. L.H. Parmar, *The Revakantha Directory,* Vol. 1, 1903, pp. 74-76.
13. *Ibid.,* 1903, pp 104(c) to 104 (c)
14. G.D. Patel, *Panchmahal District, Gujarat State Gazetteers,* 1972, pp. 574-76.
15. *Ibid.*
16. *Ibid.*
17. *Bombay Government Records,* No. XXIII, 1856, pp. 587-590.
18. *Rajpipla State Administration Report*-1942-43 Chapter II
19. *Gujarat State Gazetteers, Bharuch District,* 1961, p. 629.
20. *Baroda Administration Report,* 1944-45, pp. 37-46.
21. *Ibid,* p. 200.
22. *Administration Report of the Dharampur State,* 1940-41 Chapter II, and *Gazetteer of Bombay Presidency,* Vol VI B, *Revakantha* Cambay and Surat Agency, 1927, pp. 69-70.
23. *Administration Report of the Vansda State,* 1944-45 Chapter II; and *Gazetteer of Bombay Presidency, Op. Cit* pp. 81-82.
24. *Records of Bombay Government,* No. XXVI, New Series, 1856, p. 166.
25. G.D.Patel, *Dangs District Gazetteer,* Revenue Administration, Chapter XI, 1971.

4

LAND REFORM MEASURES, ALIENATION AND RECORD OF RIGHTS

Introduction

In the foregoing pages, details have been given about the past history of land systems prevailing in Tribal areas in the eight Districts of Gujarat, which originally formed part either of ex-Princely States and/or of ex-British Territories. Now, we shall firstly review the position of land systems under the pressures of change through post-independence land reforms in general. Secondly and importantly, discussion on implications of the same on the conditions of scheduled tribes in the eight districts will follow. Lastly, alienation of tribal land, record of rights and results of implementation of land reforms in tribal areas will be presented on empirical basis.

After the independence and merger of the former Princely States, it was earnest and immediate necessity for State Governments to resolve the land problems inherited from the past. The future of land management and optimum agricultural productivity constituted the most fundamental issue of national development. The reason is not far to seek. The pattern of economic and social organisation in the country will greatly depend upon the manner in which the land problems faced by tillers of the soil are resolved to meet social justice. As revealed from the foregoing account, there were various land tenures upon which land was held by agriculturists and others. These tenures were a product of long evolution determined by the geographical, economic, social and political conditions prevailing in an area at different point of time in history. The past land systems originated in the exigencies of administration and the overriding considerations of political expediency.

It was not out of any generosity that the previous rulers whether Hindus, Muslims, Marathas, or the British had allowed alienation of villages and lands to reliable and faithful land-holders or occupants. All grants and rights of land ownership were dictated by the political necessity that worked to strengthen and support the existing rule of law and secured land revenues to the state. In order to achieve these objectives, the leading and powerful persons living under the jurisdiction of the areas under ruling princes, were appointed variously as *Watandars, Inamdars, Jagirdars,* etc. and granted land rights. They were given gifts or *Inams* of land in the form of entire villages, plots of lands, etc. and made to work as collectors of land revenues from the tillers of the soil.

During uncertain political conditions in the past, when the means of physical communication and administration had not developed on rational and scientific basis, the rulers had to fully depend upon the support of their kinsmen, devoted friends, faithful allies etc. Most of the holders of *Inam* lands were the trusted men of the rulers and princes. When different parts of India came under the British Empire, the quasi-political and feudal linkages of the past were weakened. And, with advent of the Indian Independence, the hold of rulers, princes, *Inamdars, Watandars, Jagirdars*, etc. as intermediaries between Government and tillers of the soil became out-dated and redundant. Such intermediaries outlives their utility in the new democratic set-up as embodied in the Constitution of the Indian Union. As a result Government of India laid down a policy for removal of all such intermediaries from the ownership and administration of agricultural land by enacting special acts and legislations.

The new Land Reform Programmes in Gujarat are the direct outcome of these epoch-making changes initiated in the whole country.

In brief these programmes of land reforms have two specific objects. The first is to remove such impediments between the land and its tiller, as they are harmful to agricultural production. Various kinds of lacuna and drawback in agricultural production arise from the lopsided agrarian relations detrimental to the tillers of the soil. The paramount national goal has been to put an end to this paralytic situation. In order to pursue this goal, it was essential to create conditions for evolving, as speedily as possible, such agrarian relationships which can enhance agricultural economy with higher standards of management efficiency and productivity.

The second object which is closely related to the first, was to remove all forms and elements of exploitation and social injustice built-in within the pre-independent agrarian relationships. This was because it is most essential to provide security to tillers of soil and to assure their socio-economic status. This is the only way to create equality of opportunity and freedom from want specially among the small and marginal farmers, and also landless labourers.

Abolition of Intermediaries

The principal measures taken by the Government for securing these objectives were abolition of the intermediary in the management of land. The old tenures had to be replaced by security of tenure of Government land to farmers. The reform of tenancy relations with land-holders including reduction of rent and regulation of agricultural wages called for urgent attention. Wherever applicable, the government had taken steps in implementing tenancy reforms which led to conferment of occupancy rights of the tenants who were the tillers of the soil.

It is important to note at this juncture that prior to 1st May, 1960, the eight Districts covering the tribal areas of Gujarat were falling under the jurisdiction of the former Bilingual Bombay State. After 1-5-1960, the Gujarat and Maharashtra States were carved out of the Bilingual Bombay State. Thereafter, the enactments for the abolition of intermediaries and special land tenures of the past remained in force in Gujarat, along with other Acts enacted subsequently by the latter. A general list of these Acts, applicable also to tribal areas of Gujarat is presented below for ready reference.

1. The Bombay Talukdari Tenure Abolition Act, 1949.
2. The Bombay Paragana and Kulkarni Watans Abolition Act, 1950.
3. The Bombay Personal Inams Abolition Act, 1952.
4. The Bombay Merged Territories (Baroda *Watans*) Abolition Act, 1953.
5. The Bombay Merged Territories and Areas (*Jagirs* Abolition) Act, 1953.
6. The Bombay Merged Territories *Ankadia* Tenure Abolition Act, 1953.
7. The Bombay Merged Territories Miscellaneous Alienation Abolition Act, 1955.

8. The Bombay Inferior Village Watans Abolition Act, 1958.
9. The Gujarat Patel Watans Abolition Act, 1961.
10. The Gujarat Devasthan Inams Abolition Act, 1961.
11. Gujarat Surviving Alienations Abolition Act, 1963.

The enactments stated above for abolition of intermediaries, and the use of special land tenures in general hold good in respect of tribal areas also. The special features of various enactments passed by the Gujarat Government provide a dynamic view of the historic changes brought about to justify abolition of the rights all category of intermediaries in the state. An assessment of the great task performed by the State Government, is presented in the following points throwing valuable light on implementation of these Acts.

1. *The Bombay Talukdari Tenure Abolition Act, 1949*

The petty feudal chiefs (or intermediaries) called *Talukdars* holding the *talukdari* lands and the young cadets holding similar lands under hereditary rights were recognised as occupants of land in their possession. However, they were liable to the payment of full assessment of Land Revenues to Gujarat State. The permanent tenants and inferior land-holders who paid land revenue at the prescribed rate of assessment to the Talukdars have now become eligible to the rights of occupancy since 1st March, 1955. For this, they had to make payment of 6 or 3 times the assessment respectively to the Talukdars. These multiple *ad hoc* payments convey the occupancy price and the compensation for the right of reversion to intermediaries. The occupants were then onwards made liable to pay full assessment of revenues to government.

2. *The Bombay Paragana and Kulkarni Watans Abolition Act, 1950*

It may be noted that in Gujarat area, only *Paragana Watans* tenure were applicable. Those who held the position of *Paragana Watandars* were variously called Amin, Desai and Majumdar. They were the chief agents and instruments assisting government in collection of the land revenues right from the times of Muslim Rulers.

These *Watandars* paid *Judi* a kind of composite tax, varying from 3 to 8 annas in a Rupee assessment of total revenue of the area under their jurisdiction (one rupee was equal to eight annas). They were given necessary *Sanads*, i.e., or written documents sanctioning undisputed rights as Revenue Collecting agencies.

This Act was made to abolish these titles with all their incidents. When the ownership of these *Watan* lands was resumed from time to time in the past, the ex-*Watandars* were not dispossessed of their lands, but made eligible for regrant of the same. This required them to pay for regrant of land to new tenure by way of occupancy price equal to six times the assessment of revenue. Such an assessment was fixed on the land within a period of five years from 1st May, 1951. In case a person desired that the *Watan* land granted to him earlier is made transferable or partible, he had to pay a *Nazarana* (gift to an overlord) equal to twenty times the assessment of land revenue. And, such a payment had to be made to government in six instalments within a period of one year.

The *Watans* in Panchmahals were however alienable, and therefore, they were not done away with under Section 4(3) of Revenue Code. Here, the resumption of *Watan* lands was effected only by levy of full assessment of revenue once and for all. These *Watandars* were neither asked to pay occupancy price nor *Nazarana* to the government.

3. *The Bombay Personal Inams Abolition Act, 1952*

The personal gifts of land called *Inams* were the private properties in the form of villages or plots of land. The *Inamdars* held this kind of property by way of written contractor promise from the government concerned, subject to payment of a tax called *Judi* mentioned before. The rights to trees, forests, mines and minerals, wherever not specially reserved by the government, were conceeded to the holders of *Inams*. The *Inam* grants were multipurpose in their character. In the Panchmahals, personal *Inam* was granted by the British Government for defending the fort of Dahod to the defenders during the Mutiny of 1857.

All categories of *Inams* were abolished from 1st August, 1953. The *Inam* Abolition Act put an end to all the incidents of the *Inams* and resumed cash allowances and *Amals* i.e., assessment fee of land revenue. All lands which were partially or wholly exempt from assessment were made liable to payment of full assessment of revenue. Under the Act, the Inamdars and the inferior land-holders paying assessment to the former, were conferred with occupancy rights.

4. *The Bombay Merged Territories (Baroda Watans) Abolition Act, 1953*

The ex-Baroda State had granted *Watans* to certain leading men of villages whose designation and titles are mentioned in point two before. *Watandars* were the chief agents through whom the state collected village revenue. In earlier times of the state regime, the *Watandars* were the pivots of village administration. The essence of the *Watan* grant comprised of a kind of service to the state, the remuneration of which was made to *Watandars* either in land or cash. Thus the origin of the *Watans* lay in revenue management of the villages or groups of villages. The Baroda Watan Rules never recognised any proprietory interest of a *Watandar* in the *Watan* villages and land.

It should be noted that *Watan* grant was inalienable even for the life-time of a *Watandar*. In the case of unauthorised alienations, the *Watan* lands were made *Khalsa* by the state. Such lands were then entered as waste land and put to auction, indicating that the State treated the *Watans* purely as service grants. The defaulters were thus declared as Service *Kapat*, that is, cut in the service on failure to performance of personal duties. Rules relating to succession of *Watan* grant were very strict in the sense that even a person sharing the benefit in the *Watan* was not allowed to inherit another *Watan* or share in another *Watan* without the permission of the State. Women were of course permitted to inherit *Watan* grants, but were entitled to maintenance allowance only. At every succession, the *Watan* grants were subject to *Pedhi Kapat* succession, that is, cut due to transfer of rights to next generation.

The service and succession cut *Kapat* were quite common, and they made the *Watan* grants a gradually vanishing phenomenon in the course of a few generations. This unique feature distinguished the Baroda *Watans* from those in other parts of Gujarat which were permanent in character.

The Act abolished services after its enactment and resumed all the *Watan* lands for which the *Watandars* were made eligible to regrant of resumed lands on payment of occupancy price equal to six multiples of assessment of land revenue fixed on the land. The regrant of the old *Watans* was on the new tenure only. For making the occupancy transferable or partible, for non-tribals who alone were the *Watandars* in Baroda State, the concerned occupants had to pay to Government, a *Nazarana* equal to 20 times the assessment.

Thus, for regrant of the resumed land on old tenure, the amount aggregating to 26 times the assessment of the land revenue was to be paid to Government.

5. *The Bombay Merged Territories and Areas (Jagirs Abolition) Act, 1953*

As mentioned earlier, the term *Jagir* broadly refers to land grants for maintenance, appreciation of services or remuneration for services rendered to the state. The land revenue to be collected from *Jagirdars* was in the form of *Bhaghatia* or *Vaje* and the state's share in the collection was fixed on an *ad hoc* basis.

The *Jagirs* are broadly divided into two functional categories, viz; (1) land granted for maintenance to kinsman and members of the royal family, and (2) land granted to individuals for loyal services rendered to the State in times of peace or war. The *Jagir* grants were variously called as *Jiwarak, Jiwai* or *Ayada* and were held generally by the younger brothers of the Rulers and cadets or serviceman in armed force. In some of the former Princely States, *Jagirs* were given to the Sardars and heads of army division for military service as gifts called *Pattas* in the form of documents to hold plots and stripes of land. These *Jagirs*, were, therefore called *Patavati Jagirs*.

In the furtherance of the Government policy or abolishing various kinds of intermediaries in the agrarian sector, all these *Jagirs* were abolished under the Bombay Merged Territories and Areas (Jagirs Abolition) Act, 1953 with effect from the 1st August, 1954. The Act classified *Jagirs* into main two types, (i) proprietary and (ii) non-proprietary, but it also recognised a third type called (iii) *Jiwai Jagirs*, a life-long grant.

Occupancy rights were recognised in respect of self-cultivation *Gharkhed* lands held by princely *Jagirdars* and cadets. The tenants in proprietary and non-proprietary villages were made eligible to the rights of occupancy on payment of the occupancy price equal to six multiples of assessment both to the *Jagirdars* and the State. A kind of protection to the *Jagirdar's* rights to mines and minerals and forests in the area had remained untouched in this Act.

6. *The Bombay Merged Territories (Ankadia Tenure Abolition) Act. 1953*

The *Ankadia* system of land revenue grant by a state originated in the case of those areas which were not easily accessible. The difficulties inherent in administering the far-flung and hilly regions of the border lands, and areas of uncertain political stability and situation of weak administration of 18th Century, were common in Gujarat. The then ruling powers badly needed strong and confident allies who could control the village land-holders, collect revenue on their behalf and pay in return a fixed sum called *Ankada* without fail.

In villages outside Baroda state the amount of *Ankada* paid by an *Ankadedar* was fixed under lease contract for a number of years. But in Baroda State itself, the amount of *Ankada* was either fixed for 30 years or 10 years according to two kinds of villages, e.g. stationary *Ek-Ankadia* villages or *Farta-Ankadia* mobile lot villages. The payment of dues were regulated by leases and *pattas* renewed at the discretion of the Ruler. The *Pattas* also refer to land grants prescribed for the performance of police duties. The *Ankadia* villages in ex-Baroda State were held by persons of different castes and ethnic groups such as Rajput, Koli, Thakarda, Barot, Brahmin, Charan, etc; while in other states they were held by the Thakarda and Koli groups only.

The Government of Bombay, in furtherance of its policy of abolishing intermediaries from the agricultural sector, framed a special legislation for abolishing the *Ankadia* tenure under the Act which came into force from 15-8-1953. The new Act abolished the *Ankadia* tenure with all its incidents. All the leases and agreements relating to the *Ankadia* villages were made null and void. All the *Ankadia* villages were consequently resumed, and all lands in those Villages were made liable to payment of land revenue under the provisions of the Bombay Land Revenue Code, 1879. A former *Ankadedar* was recognised as an occupant in respect of the land which was meant only for *Gharkhed* and self-cultivation.

A person whose name was entered in the record as an occupant *(Katjedar)* and was liable to pay land revenue to the *Ankadedar* was also recognised as an occupant in his own right. The *Ankadedars* in respect of *Gherkhed* lands and cultivators paying land revenue have both been recognised as occupants. Except such persons, other cultivators who continued to remain as tenants under the provisions of the Bombay Tenancy and Agricultural Lands Act 1948 got occupancy rights only on the payment of purchase price. Thus Ankadia Tenure Abolition Act has made the *Gharkhed* and *Jiwai* lands, (which were wholly exempt from payment of land revenue), liable to full assessment of land revenue under the Bombay Land Revenue Code, 1879.

7. *The Bombay Merged Territories (Miscellaneous Alienations Abolition) Act, 1955*

The above Act covered the alienations consisting of scattered lands, fixation and assignment of land revenue and cash allowances only made by the ruling authority before merger. These grants included *Wanta* and *Giras* lands given to princes' sons and other members of the royal family and revered holy persons, as remuneration of services connected with the administration of the state. The Act applied to the merged territories only and therefore the alienations in the merged areas were not affected.

8. *The Bombay Inferior Village Watans Abolition Act, 1958*

The status of inferior village servants had been quite the same in Gujarat as in other parts of India. They were hereditary village officers of lower degree than revenue officer, Police Patel and Village Accountant many of whom were *Watandars*. The inferior service village *Watans* land granted to them were held hereditarily under the then *Watan* law. These were granted for the performance of duties connected with the administration, collection of revenue of a village, village police duties, the settlement of boundaries, and other matters of civil affairs in a village. Such inferior service village *Watans* land continued to remain hereditary occupancies even where the services had ceased to be in need.

In the light of changing agrarian policy of the Bombay Government, the Inferior Watans Abolition Act, 1958 was brought into force. The Act Abolished all the inferior village *Watans* with their incidents. The Watandars were liable to regrant of the resumed land on payment of occupancy price equal to 3 times the amount of the full assessment of revenue of the land. These inferior village servants were thus made occupants of their land within the purview of the Bombay Land Revenue Code, 1879. Occupancy of the land re-granted is not transferable or partible without the previous sanction of the Collector and except on payment of the occupancy price determined by government for this purpose. The occupancy price was fixed at equal to 3 times the amount of full assessment of such lands. The Act provides for application of tenancy law to any *Watan* land lawfully leased by the inferior Watandar.

9. *The Gujarat Patel Watans Abolition Act, 1961*

Reference has been made in the previous point to the grant of Patel Watans for a superior village officer. The Patels were mostly hereditary village headman in Gujarat. Hereditary Patelship was created also for different kinds of of village officers including a Revenue Patel and Police Patel. Under the *Watan* Law, the *Watans* land was granted for the performance of duties connected with the administration, collection of revenue, village police, settlement of boundaries, and other duties of civil administration of a village. The *Watans* Law permitted the continuation of such offices even where the services originally associated with it had ceased to be demanded. Under this system there were Revenue and Police Patels, either separate or combined in one person. Along with the revenue account (talati), a Patel was the village executive to whom government looked for assistance in village affairs in general and revenue administration in particular.

10. *The Gujarat Devasthan Inams Abolition Act, 1969*

From times immemorial, the rulers of Gujarat,like those in other parts of India used to make grants of land, right of collecting land revenue, cash allowances, etc. for maintenance of religious and charitable institutions. Such grants were called *Devasthan Inams*. They consisted of grant of entire villages and portions of villages, exemption from land revenue, assignment of collecting land revenue of a village or a portion thereof, and allowances in cash or in kind.

The Act was enacted and brought into force with effect from 15th November, 1969. It is extended only to the former Bombay area included in the State of Gujarat, and excludes all Saurashtra and Kutch districts from its purview. This abolition Act applies to *Devasthan Inams* consisting of land only and not cash allowances or allowances in kind to religions institutions.

The Act has made the *Devasthan Inams* liable to the payment of land revenue while retaining occupancy right. These rights are granted to following three categories of land-holders: (i) *The Inamdar*, where such land was in his possession and had been cultivated on behalf of the *Inamdar*; (ii) authorised land-holder or inferior land-holder, where such land was in possession of such a person; and (iii) the *Inamdar* where such land was in possession of a person other than the *Inamdar*, whether authorised holder, unauthorised holder or inferior holder.

Where any Devasthan land was in possession of an unauthorised holder, it shall be resumed and an unauthorised holder shall be summarily evicted. If in the opinion of the State Government such eviction was likely to cause hardship in view of investment made by him in the development of land or in non-agricultural use, the State Government may direct the Collector to regrant the land to such holder on payment of such amount and subject to such terms and conditions as the State Government may determine. If such land was not so regranted, it shall be liable to be disposed of under the provisions of the Bombay Land Revenue Code, 1879.

It should be further noted that this Act provides for abolition of, (a) exemption enjoyed by institutions for public religious worship under Section 88B of the Bombay Tenancy and Agricultural Lands Act, 1948, (b) exemption which was available to the *Devesthan Inams* in regard to the provisions available to the landlord in respect of termination of tenancy, and (c) exemption which was provided for *Devasthan Inam* land in the Ceiling Act.

11. *The Gujarat Surviving Alienations Abolition Act, 1963*

This Act was brought into force with effect from 1st October, 1963. The Act abolished all surviving *Inams* (gifts) which were not abolished by any of the tenure abolition laws. The Act extended to the whole of Gujarat State, abolished alienations altogether with incidents thereof and alienated lands have been made liable to the payment of land revenue. These alienations include *Jiwai* (livelihood) lands held by the Bhayats (agnates) of ex-rulers and other service *Inamdars*.

Prevention of Fragmentation and Consolidation of Holdings

The excessive sub-division of agricultural land is the main impediment to agricultural production. The consolidation of small and scattered holdings is accepted therefore as a preliminary step towards the formation of co-operative farming. The consolidation programme is therefore thought of in the context of entire land policy of the state.

Bombay was the pioneer State in preventing fragmentation of land-holdings. Provisions for prevention of fragmentation were made in the Bombay Prevention of Fragmentation and Consolidation of Holdings Act, 1947. It was also applied to the merged areas and territories from neighbouring regions.

Under the Act, standard areas and unit of holdings were laid down for all districts. All holdings below standard *areas* were entered in a register with the ultimate object of their being consolidated into economic holdings of standard size. The Act provides for prevention of fragmentation in agricultural holdings and also provides for consolidation of the scattered parcels of lands into compact holdings.

For the purpose of implementation of the Act, standard areas have been fixed for all Talukas in the State and any area below the standard area is deemed to be a fragment, and noted as such in the village records.

A transfer (other than lease) of a fragment cannot be made except to the owner of a contiguous Survey number and recognised sub-division of a Survey number. Loans can, however, be advanced to a land-holder by government Land Development Banks or Cooperative Societies by taking the fragments and Survey numbers on lease.

In proceedings for partition of land among the heirs of a joint family or co-sharers, the following procedure is adopted. If a co-sharer cannot be given his due share without creating a fragment, he was to be compensated in money for his share. The amount of compensation was to be determined according to the provisions of the Land Acquisition Act. In determining which of the co-sharers shall get the land, the matter is to be decided by agreement or by drawing lots. If none of the co-sharers to whom land is allotted pays compensation, the share shall be sold in auction and the purchase money paid to the co-sharers not getting land in proportion to their respective shares.

Penalty for transfer or partition contrary to the provisions of the Act is provided. Such transfer shall be void and the owner shall be liable to a fine up to Rs. 250. Any person who takes possession of the land which has been transferred or partitioned in contravention of the law, shall be liable to ejectment.

Where an owner is unable to transfer his land under the

conditions imposed by the law, a provision is made which entitles him to transfer the land to the Government on payment of compensation at market value.

The Rules provide for the following order of priority according to which the land shall be offered for transfer.

(1) To the tenant of the holding or his heirs;
(2) To the owner of the adjoining holding provided he cultivates it personally or to the tenants of the adjoining holding; and
(3) To such *bona fide* cultivators in the village as have insufficient land of their own for maintenance. No sub-division of a land-holding shall be made except with the permission of the State Government.

The advantages of Consolidation are that it saves time and labour of a farmer, facilitates improvement of land through irrigation as well as dry farming practices, provides an opportunity for replanning development of holdings and providing other amenities. Consolidation programme is no doubt in progress in the State.

The study of land records, in villages in the tribal areas, has, however, revealed that there are several bottlenecks in the implementation of the Act at the ground level. Firstly, on the partition of family land on the death of a tribal *Khatedar*, his heirs sub-divide land in as many parts as necessary, each parcel of ancestral land of the family, wherever situated, so that each heir can get the benefit or otherwise of quality of soil of each plot equitably. Contrary to this kind of ground position, the Record of Rights shows occupancy in joint names of the heirs on record. But each parcel of land in practice is sub-divided into fragments and cultivated separately on spot by the heirs. A number of small fragments thus exist on each parcel of land. But their names appear as joint land-holders, indicate falsely that individual parcels of land are kept intact and that the law of prevention of fragmentation is respected in full.

This naturally makes the task of consolidation of land-holdings very difficult and complicated. The Record of Rights would not show the correct position obtaining in the fields of plots, whether they call for consolidation. If a fragmented parcel of ancestral land is passed on to our heir or co-sharer, he has difficulty in making payment to heirs of each fragment. This is because, he may not have money to give compensation to other heirs or co-sharers on account of his impoverished condition.

It is also revealed that the plots of tribal land including fragments arc of various types i.e., rocky, stony, sloping in various degrees and also plain. The tribals may have also. *Kayari* lands for growing paddy, where water from the neighbouring areas flow down to low lying plots. Such uneven positions of plots of land have also induced the tribals to share such fragments or survey numbers with the co-sharers so that the benefit of good crops can be available to each heir from possibly the fertile and rich land.

This tradition of fragmenting each parcel of uneven character the of land in hills and hillocks is responsible for not evoking whole hearted response from the tribals in the implementation of the Act of consolidation of land-holdings. The present study has also revealed that in tribal villages, where consolidation of land in tribal areas is completed and new record of rights is rewritten, the actual possession of the newly formed land Blocks has not been taken over by the parties concerned.* Possession of land as per the old Record has not changed, but the new Blockwise record is written and the crops are also noted in the new Blocks which are formed of old Survey numbers. This all is contrary to ground position, and has resulted in grave anomaly, because the Record of Rights prepared after the consolidation scheme does not show the correct position of lands on the spot. In sum, it means that the tribal agriculturists have neither abandoned their possession, of old parcels of land nor have taken over the possession of new parcels of land as per consolidation Blocks on paper. The implementation of the law thus seems to be virtually falsified in almost all cases in Tribal areas concerned.

The Government of Gujarat instituted a special committee on the problems encountered in implementation of the Bombay Prevention of Fragmentation and Consolidation of Holdings Act, 1947 under the Chairmanship of Shri H.K.L. Kapoor in 1964. The committee had in all 35 sittings during which a large number of problems were discussed. The most significant findings of the committee were pertaining to the problems of consolidation of holdings in socially

---

* The formation of this kind of land block has been devised specially for consolidation of land-holdings in order to ensure economic viability of land in cultivable size.

backward arêas such as those inhabited by the Scheduled tribes. The committee indicated in brief whether the ground position is (a) suitable, (b) unsuitable or has (c) intermediate categories of areas with regard to consolidation of land-holdings. Most of the tribal areas are obviously unsuitable for this purpose. However, the programme of consolidation had already taken place in certain tribal areas where it has met with resistance on account of more than one difficulties. The main characteristics leading to these difficulties have been identified by the Kapoor Committee as follows: (p. 40).

(i) Tribal areas have undulating and hilly terrain;
(ii) Tribal areas have disproportionately large varieties of soil;
(iii) Tribal areas have an insignificant problem of scatterdness; and
(iv) Tribal areas have large percentage of Adivasi population or of those who are socially backward.

Whatever is reported earlier as the reasons of ineffectiveness of implementation of the consolidation scheme is clearly brought to light in this commendable report. It seems, therefore, reasonable that in future this programme be reviewed from place to place, but definite measures be taken for its implementation as and when appropriate.

Tenancy Legislation and Occupancy Rights

Before the advent of British rule in India, the relations between the landlord and the tenants were mostly governed by mutual contracts, local usage and customs. In course of time, the Government of Bombay devised Section 83 of the Bombay Land Revenue Code, 1879. This Section provided that a person placed as a tenant on the land shall be regarded as holding the land at the rent and for the services agreed upon between him and the landlord. If the duration of tenancy was not known by reason of antiquity, such tenancy was to be presumed to be co-extensive with the tenure of the landlord. Such a tenant was considered a permanent tenant. In the absence of any satisfactory evidence of the capacity in which a person held the land for which he rendered service or paid rent, he was presumed to be in possession of land as a tenant.

In Section 86-87 of the above code, provision was also made for recovery of rent from the tenants. There was neither the security of tenure nor security of rent. With a view, therefore, to safeguard the rights of tenants in the former Bombay State, the first tenancy legislation, called the Bombay Tenancy Act, 1939 was enacted. This Act introduced a concept of "Protected Tenants" covering those tenants who held land continuously for a period of not less than six years. For the first time, it gave to the tenants fixity of tenure, ceiling on rentals, rights in house-sites and trees, and protection from eviction under certain circumstances.

After Independence, this Act was replaced by a comprehensive legislation in 1948. This Act was amended extensively in 1956. The amendment provided that on the 1st April, 1957, described as the "Tillers' Day", every tenant whether permanent, protected or ordinary was seemed to have purchased from the landlord, the land leased to him. This was subject to the condition that the tenant cultivated the land personally and his total holdings did not exceed the ceiling area, and the purchase price did not exceed 200 times the assessment. In the backward areas, the maximum assessment was fixed at 80 times the assessment by government notification. If an issue arose whether a person was a tenant or not, Section 70(b) provided that the issue may be decided by the Mamlatdar. Provision was also made that the purchase price may be determined by Agricultural Lands Tribunal under the provision of the Act by taking various factors under consideration.

The act was also further amended from time to time after 1956 amendment. The original Act as amended in 1956 made comprehensive provision for regulation of rent, security of tenure and transfer of ownership to tenants, the ceiling on existing holdings as well as future acquisition, restriction on transfers of agriculture land, management of uncultivated lands etc. were also regulated. Under this many sided law, the maximum rent was not to exceed five times the assessment or Rs. 20 per acre and not to be less than twice such assessment. Where the amount equal to twice the assessment exceeded, the sum of Rs. 20 per acre, the rent was fixed at twice the assessment of land revenue.

It should be noted that the permanent tenants had been given complete security of tenure. Other tenants were given security subject to landlord's right to resume lands not exceeding 3 economic holdings or 16 to 48 acres of land on the condition that every tenant was able to retain half the area leased. A small land-holder was defined as a person who had leased land not exceeding one economic holding, i.e. 16 acres and whose total income did not exceed Rs. 1500. A holder of this category could resume half the area leased from a tenant in all cases.

Certain constraints on resumption were also provided. The main constraints were that the income by the cultivation of land of which a person was entitled to take possession, was the principal source of income for his maintenance and that the land leased stood in his name or in the name of his ancestors on 1st January, 1952. If a landlord after terminating the tenancy did not cultivate the land personally within one year of resumption or after having commenced cultivation or discontinued the same within 10 years, the tenant would be entitled to restoration of the land cultivated by him.

Transfer of ownership to permanent tenants was provided with effect from Tillers' Day i.e. 1st April, 1957. He was required to pay six times the assessment to the landlord, as he was required to pay under the various Tenure Abolition Acts enacted previously. Other tenants except those of the small land-holders were also deemed to have acquired ownership from that day. As regards tenants of small land-holders, the law was subsequently amended to provide transfer of ownership to tenants in respect of non-resumable lands with effect from 1st April, 1962.

During the course of implementing tenancy legislation, it came to the notice of the Government that in several cases, there was a possibility of purchases by tenants becoming ineffective because they did not present themselves before the tenancy courts and were unwilling to purchase these lands. In many cases, their purchases were likely to become ineffective due to non-payment of due instalments of the purchase price to the landlord. In order to remedy the situation, the Government of Gujarat tried to prevent such ineffective purchases by two important amendments. (A) Under one amendment, the tenants who remained absent before the tenancy courts and who expressed their unwillingness to purchase the land, were given an opportunity to apply for purchase of land, if the same were not still disposed of by submitting an application within one year from 29th December, 1965. (B) By another amendment, the State Government extended the period of paying arrears of instalments by three years more. The Government also framed Rules under the Agriculturists Loans Act for advancing *tagavi* loan to assist them in paying the arrear amount of instalment within the extended period of three years.

The Amended Act of 1973 was brought into effect from March 9, 1973 for plugging the existing loopholes. Some of the important features for amending the Act are as follows:

(i) Surrender of tenancy rights in favour of landlords have been barred. All surrenders can be made only in favour of the State Government and such land will vest with the State Government free from all encumbrances for disposal according to provisions of the Act in accordance with priority list;

(ii) The date for all the postponed cases for acquiring occupancy rights was extended;

(iii) Tenants who were dispossessed of land without due process of law between June 15, 1955 and March 3, 1973 can be restored possession of such land provided that the land in question is not sold away by the landlords or put to non-agricultural use on or before March 3, 1973, and the tenant agrees to cultivate it personally. The *suo moto* action can be taken by the Mamlatdar if the initiative for such restoration is not taken by the tenant;

(iv) No tenancy of a tenant belonging to Scheduled Castes or Scheduled Tribes can be terminated by the landlord on the ground of personal cultivation or for non-agricultural use;

(v) If even after normal surrender of the tenancy between June 15, 1955 and March 3, 1973, tenant has continued to remain in actual possession of land with or without the consent of the landlord, he is made eligible for acquisition of occupancy rights;

(vi) Tenants, who in the past either did not appear before the Agricultural Land Tribunal or refused to accept the tenancy rights, thereby rendering their purchases ineffective, are given opportunity to acquire occupancy rights. If such lands are not disposed off, the time limit for making applications by such tenants to the Tribunal for a declaration that the purchase of the land has not become ineffective has been extended upto December 31, 1974 by Act. No. 7 of 1974;[1]

(vii) The defaulting tenants, who could not pay the purchase price by falling in arrears of four instalments are given a further opportunity to pay purchase price before December 31, 1974 by the Act No. 7 of 1974, thus making their purchase effective;

(viii) With effect from May 2, 1973 the agricultural labourers and artisans are deemed to have purchased the homestead lands belonging to the landlords if the dwelling houses are built by them on such sites, and occupancy rights conferred on them on payment of occupancy price, to be fixed by the tribunals, which is to be within 20 times the annual rent of the site;

(ix) The definition of the expression "to cultivate personally" has been made more restrictive in as much as the land is required to be cultivated by the person concerned or by a member of his family i.e. his wife or his male descendants. The land cannot be considered as personally cultivated by an individual if he does not reside in the village in which the land is situated or in a village not farther than 15 km. away;

(x) Where the purchase of land by a tenant becomes ineffective, the land vests in the State, thus eliminating the possibility of collusion between the landlords and the tenants;

(xi) An absolute ban has been imposed on purchase of land for agricultural purposes by a person who is a non-agriculturist and whose income from other sources exceeds Rs. 5000 per annum; and

(xii) The Agricultural Land Tribunals set-up under the Act have been empowered to issue temporary injunction restraining the landlords from dispossessing the tenants from the land.[2]

Ceiling on Land-holding

The Gujarat Agricultural Land Ceiling Act, 1960 was enacted and enforced with effect from 1st September, 1961. It provides for ceiling on existing holdings as well as on future acquisition. The ceiling is fixed on a person that includes the joint family under the headship of the person concerned. No limit is fixed for the size of joint family for this purpose.

The ceiling area is not rigidly prescribed. It varies according to the class of land as it should be. In the case of dry crop land, ceiling varies from 54 acres to 132 acres, in the case of rice land, from 38 acres to 88 acres, in the case of seasonally irrigated land, from 38 to 88 acres, and in the case of perennially irrigated land from 19 acres to 44 acres. Thus the areas of ceiling varies from 19 acres to 132 acres according to local conditions and classes of land. The level of ceiling on a person desiring to have future acquisition is the same as that on existing holdings mentioned above.

The State identified nine different classes (A to I) of local areas along with different ceilings within the limits prescribed above for each class of local area for (i) Dry crop land, (ii) Rice land, (iii) Seasonally irrigated land, and (iv) Perennially irrigated land. See Table 4.1:

TABLE 4.1: Category of land and size of Ceiling Area

Class of local area	Ceiling area in acres			
	Dry crop land	Rice land	Seasonally irrigated land	Perennially irrigated land
1. Class A	56	38	38	19
2. " B	60	40	40	20
3. " C	72	48	48	24
4. " D	80	54	54	27
5. " E	84	56	56	23
6. " F	96	64	64	32
7. " G	108	72	72	36
8. " H	120	80	80	40
9. " I	132	88	88	44

About the transfer of land, very stringent provisions have been made. No transfer or partition can be made by a person holding agricultural land in excess of the prescribed ceiling area after the commencement of the Act. If a person committed transfer or partition of any land between 15th January, 1959 and 1st September, 1961, he shall be deemed to have made it with a view to defeating the object of the Act unless the transaction is declared otherwise by the Collector. Such transfers or partitions shall be ignored in computing the surplus land held by the person in his name. In the first instance, a surplus land shall be determined from the extent of land available with him. The balance, if any, shall be taken from the transferee to whom the transfer was made after 1st September, 1961. Thereafter, the balance, if any shall be taken from the transferee to whom the transfer was made after 15th January, 1959 and before 1st September, 1961.

Under the Ceiling Act, the land-holders are enjoined to declare the surplus agricultural land in their possession within the prescribed time limit. The law provides elaborate procedures for computing and determining surplus lands. Broadly, the land ceiling was determined as the land-holding size that could provide a family an income of Rs. 1,200 at the 1960 price level annually.

The law provides exemptions also. The following categories of lands are exempted from the ceiling limits:

(i) lands held in compact blocks of efficiently managed farms on which heavy investments or permanent structural improvements have been made and breaking of which will lead to a fall in production;
(ii) lands leased to or held by bodies or persons for growing fruit trees and used for that purpose for not less than 3 years before the implementation of the law;
(iii) lands held or leased by approved Land Development Banks;
(iv) lands held or leased by approved Co-operative Societies for improvement of economic and social conditions of peasant, or for ensuring the full and efficient use of land;
(v) lands leased or held by approved industrial undertaking whose *bona fide* carries on any industrial operations; and
(vi) lands being the property of a public trust for an educational purpose, hospital, *Panjrapole, Gausala* or an institution for public religious worship, the entire income from which is for the purpose of the trust.

The Ceiling does not apply to above lands. They will not be taken into account in computing the ceiling areas of a person, institution, etc. but if the extent of the land held under such categories exceeds the ceiling area, the person will not be permitted to retain other lands.[3]

It is significant to note that the land which vests in the Government under the Ceiling Act is allotted to persons or institutions by preference. The first preference goes to Co-operative farming societies having Scheduled tribe members alone. The second preference is given to a co-operative society, the membership of which is held party by persons belonging to Scheduled Tribes and partly by persons belonging to Scheduled Castes. Thereafter, the preference is given to a Co-operative Society the members of which belongs to Scheduled Castes.

The third preference for allotment of land vested in the government under the Ceiling Act, is a Co-operative Society, the membership of which is not solely held by persons belonging to Scheduled Tribes or Scheduled Castes. When this kind of preference has to be considered for individual persons, the persons belonging to a Scheduled Tribe get precedence over other persons, and the persons belonging to Scheduled Castes get precedence over persons other than those belonging to a Scheduled Tribe.

The government could grant 2.47 lakh acres of land of all categories as surplus. The actual possession was taken for 1.49 lakh acres which amounted to be just 60 per cent of the total, and of this 80 per cent was given to the Co-operative Societies of economically backward people, scheduled castes and scheduled tribes.

Amendment to the Ceiling Act

As indicated before, radical changes were incorporated in the Gujarat Ceiling Act 2 of 1974. Land standing in the names of major sons of a persons was excluded from computation of his holding. Also, provision was made to enable a family or joint family consisting of more than five members including minor son, widow of a pre-deceased son or unmarried daughter of a pre-deceased son, where his or her mother is dead, to hold (on the specified date when the Amendment Act of 1972 come into force) land in excess of ceiling area to the extent of 1/5th of the ceiling area for each member in excess of five, so however, that the total holding of the family does not exceed twice the ceiling area. If any of the member of such family holds separately land, such lands shall be grouped together.

The Amendment provided that any person who, after 24th January, 1971, but before the specified date, has transferred whether by sale, lease, mortgage, with possession or exchange, lease surrender or otherwise partitioned any land held by him, he shall be deemed to have done so in order to defeat the object of the Act and the Court will have to satisfy on the merits of the case that the document which is not registered is a *bona fide* document executed within the said period and is not ante-dated as a result of collusion between the parties. Transfer or partition to a major son will not however be affected.

The person affected by the transfer or partition during the said period will have to make an application to the Collector for a declaration that the transfer or partition was not made in anticipation to defeat the object of the Act. The Collector after giving due notice to the parties for hearing and after considering evidence shall decide the matter.

The Amendment also provided that exempted land shall not be transferred or partitioned without the permission of the Collector. In case, the exempted land was utilised for maintenance of *Panjrapole* or *Gaushala*, a separate trust was required to the created. A committee consisting of the Collector, officer of Animal Husbandry Department nominated by the Director, Animal Husbandry having regard to the number of cattle normally maintained or cared for in the institution, provided the lands are used solely and directly for the purpose for which such lands are held and not for the purpose of deriving income for the institution, will specify the extent of land exempted from time to time, from the Ceiling Act, for the purpose of grazing of cattle or storage of grass for cattle.

Land Alienation

In the ex-Bombay State, the land tenures could be divided into (i) Survey tenure, (ii) the *Inam* tenure, and (iii) the *non-Ryotwari* tenures. The problem of tribal land alienation is related more intimately with survey tenures and, therefore, it will be the focus of attention in this section. The problem also has different implications in pre- and post-independence times as indicated in the following two points.

(a) *Pre-Independence Period*

The Survey tenure is one which consists in the occupancy of ordinary (*Khalsa*) Government land. It has two forms, viz, the old or unrestricted and the new or restricted tenure. The difference between them in the conditions upon which the land is held by a person. In the case of the old tenure, the right to alienate land by sale, mortgage or any other form of transfer is unrestricted; whereas in the case of the new tenure land, such right is restricted.

Under section 73 of the Bombay Land Revenue Code 1879, land is deemed to the heritable and transferable subject to the change of land revenue and conditions lawfully annexed to the tenure. Under the Bombay Land Revenue (Amendment) Act, 1901, Section 73-A was inserted. Under this section, the State Government is empowered to declare that in any tract or village to which government may by notification published in the official gazetteer before the introduction thereon of any original survey settlement, occupancies shall not after the date of such notification be transferable without the previous sanction of the Collector. The Government may, by notification in the official gazette, from time to time, exempt any part of such tract or village or any person or class or persons from the operation of this Section.

This restricted tenure came to be adopted in order to safeguard the tenants against themselves and their improvident readiness to alienate their lands to non-tribal agriculturists. In the times of the famines and plague in the two decades of the nineteenth century and as a result of arrears of land revenue in Gujarat, averaging about 50 per cent of the total demand, unfair transfers of land had become quite patent. The new tenure has been therefore best suited to the socially and economically backward tribals of the areas such as Panchmahals and those in the Surat and West Khandesh districts. New occupancies are ever since granted land generally on new tenure only.[4]

It should be noted that the Section 73-A did not apply to areas where Survey and Settlement was introduced, and such areas were therefore not covered under the Section. This was because under Section 68 of the Bombay Land Revenue Code 1879, an occupant was entitled to use and enjoy occupation of his land for the period, if any, to which his tenure was limited or if the period was unlimited or a survey settlement was extended to the land, in perpetuity, conditionally or by payment of land revenue for the sale and on the fulfilment of any other terms or conditions lawfully annexed to his tenure.

Had there not been any restriction on transfer of land of the persons in backward areas, it would have created a huge problem of their being rendered landless and without any means of sustenance. Government therefore, inserted a proviso to Section 68 of the Land Revenue Code making it lawful for the Collector to grant permission to any person to occupy any unalienated unoccupied land, whether Survey-Settlement has been extended to the land or not, on such conditions as may be prescribed by Government. The special terms may include a restriction on transferability. Alienation by transfer can be restricted. So also, by insertion of the new Section 73-A, in areas notified, where Survey-Settlement is not introduced,

Government can declare that occupancies shall not after the date such notification is issued be transferable without the permission of the Collector. Under the same Amendment Act, Government inserted a new Section 79-A enabling eviction of a person unauthorisedly occupying or wrongfully in possession of any land which is not transferable without the previous sanction under Section 73-A, by the Collector.

Thus the tribal land-holders could be protected from alienation of their lands to money-lenders etc. only if the lands held by them, (i) were in areas where survey and settlement was not introduced and notification was issued under new Section 73-A and (ii) were originally Government wastelands (i.e. unalienated unoccupied land) were granted after the Proviso to Section 68 was inserted in the year 1901. The result was that the tribal land-holders in areas which were already surveyed and settled prior to 1901, could not get any protection from alienation of their lands to money-lender etc. as the survey tenure of most of the lands was old tenure.

(b) *Post Independence Period*

The Government of Gujarat issued a notification on 4th April, 1961 in exercise of powers conferred by Section 73-A. The essence of the notification presented in Appendix-I is summed up in two points, and the implications elaborated in the pages that follow. Firstly, it declared that the provisions of Section 73-A shall be applicable to all those villages in the Scheduled Areas in the State of Gujarat in which the survey and settlement under the said Code was not introduced and to which the provisions of the said Section have not been made applicable before the issue of this notification. Secondly, it exempted from the operation of the said Section 73-A all persons not being members of scheduled tribe, holding lands in the villages to which the said Section 73-A was to be applicable by this notification.

The list of Scheduled Areas included the whole area of Dangs Taluka, select villages of Uchhal Taluka, Nizar Taluka, Vansda Taluka, ex-Rajpipla State area, Chhotaudepur Taluka, Ghadboried estate villages included in Naswadi Taluks, villages of Devgadhbaria and Limkheda Talukas, villages included in Santrampur and Jhalod Talukas and villages of Vijayanagar, Khedbrahma, Bhiloda and Meghraj Talukas. The survey-settlement introduced if any, during the ex-States' regime under the ex-States' orders was not deemed to have been done under Chapter VIII-A of the Bombay Land Revenue Code 1879, and so such areas come under the scope of Section 73-A.

In the Scheduled Areas where originally survey-settlement was not introduced, the Section 73-A put restriction of transferring the occupancy of tribal land. The object underlying was to project the weaker and unwary section of the tribal society against exploitation by crazy and greedy money-lenders who, in defiance of the law, thrived upon ignorance, penury and misery of this section of the society. In order to protect against deprivation of their land, the state could restrict the unfettered right of transferability of occupancy by issuing notification under Section 73-A. This was a measure of social reform. Section 79-A for summary eviction of persons unauthorisedly occupying land was inserted by Section 12 of the Bombay Land Revenue Code (Amendment) Act, 1901. It provides a remedy and forum for summary eviction of persons in unauthorised occupation or unlawful possession of land. This is the legislative provision of summary eviction of the unauthorised persons on tribal lands in scheduled areas where Section 73-A is made applicable.

The reasons for tribals alienating their lands are not far to seek. They are impoverished in general, have scanty means to depend upon agriculture, have to undertake extra labour wherever they can find either in the village or in the neighbourhood or outside the sub-region, have to respond to social obligation, have to provide for foodgrains to the family to last for the whole year. If the produce of the crops do not bring necessary income, they have to borrow money for clothes etc. and meet with expenses for daily necessities of family members. Sometimes they have to send their grown up married sons with some members of family for labour outside, and they also to move with the whole family in search of work. Their only source of livelihood to fall back upon in the hour of immediate and dire need is land. To satisfy their creditors, they have to offer agricultural land for sale or mortgage with or without agreement. When the tribal was able to repay, he redeemed the mortgage, if such was the condition agreed upon. The transactions were either oral or by registered or unregistered deeds. Knowing that there is a ban on transfer of their land, the Tribals prefer to make oral transactions.

With a view to implement the provisions of Section 73-A of the Bombay Land Revenue Code 1879, in the ex-merged areas for which notification was issued by the Government of Gujarat on 4th April, 1961, special officers of Deputy Collector's cadre were appointed in the year 1976 for tracing out and deciding cases of unauthorized alienations of tribal lands. If was noticed during the inquiries of these officers that the alienations had taken place in the following types of cases:

(i) Transfers of tribal lands between tribals.
(ii) Transfers of tribal lands between tribals and non-tribals.

The main object of application of Section 73-A of the land Revenue Code was to prevent exploitation of the tribals by non-tribals and to ensure that the tribal lands are not snatched away from them at low prices.

The Government of Gujarat, therefore, issued instructions for the guidance of the Collectors to grant permission for alienation of tribal lands, only between the tribals, in the following types of cases:

(i) The purchaser tribal must be purchasing at the market price.
(ii) The sale should be *bona fide*;
(iii) The execution of sale should not be on account of indebtedness or helplessness due to other causes;
(iv) The tribal selling the land should not be rendered landless or he must have other sufficient source for maintenance;
(v) The tribal must be leaving the village for permanent residence elsewhere for better living;
(vi) The tribal occupant being old or infirm is unable to cultivate land personally;
(vii) The land with the purchaser should not exceed one economic holding (i.e. 16 acres *Jirayat* land)
(viii) The purchaser must cultivate land personally;
(ix) Exchange of lands between tribals must be for *bona fide* purpose of residence;
(x) Exchange of tribal lands for agriculture is possible provided they are valued at the same price and the lands are of the same type;
(xi) Cases in which it is customary to give lands to daughters for maintenance; and
(xii) Partition cases in which land is held in the name of the elderly person of the family. (Family partition is excluded from the scope of Section 73-A of the Code).

Finally, it should be noted that in cases in which the above conditions are not fulfilled, and still if the Collector is of the opinion that sanction should be given, he may refer the case to the Government with full details.

The Government of Gujarat also issued two main instructions for the guidance of the Collectors for dealing with cases on alienations of tribal lands between tribals and non-tribals.

(i) Cases of alienation of tribal lands to public institutions which merit sanction by the Government should be referred to the Government by the Collectors if they think proper; and

(ii) If the sale is in favour of non-tribal for use of land for non-agricultural purpose and for public purpose and if the Collector is of the opinion that sanction deserves to be given, he may refer such cases to government with full details.

After the issue of the Government Notification dated 4th april, 1961, if the tribal lands in the notified areas are leased to tenants, provisions of Section 73-A will apply.

In cases of alienations of tribal lands, where permission is not given, recourse is to be taken under Section 79-A of the Land Revenue Code for eviction of the unauthorised person and then putting the tribal into the occupation of land.

It is significant to note that Clause (1) of Section 73-A was made applicable to some areas of West Khandesh District of ex-Bombay State by Government Notifications issued during the period from 1902 to 1932. No tribal area in the present Gujarat State forming part of ex-British area was covered then by Section 73-A. This was probably because survey and settlement was already introduced in the tribal areas of Gujarat which then formed part of the ex-British area of the Bombay State. Thus, it is not possible to apply Section 73-A to these tribal areas even at present as the old tenure is guaranteed under Section 68 of the Code. This means that the Jhalod, Dahod and Umbergaon Talukas are not covered by the operation of 73-A of the Code and so it is not legally possible to prevent alienation of tribal lands from going into the hands of money-lenders, exploiters, etc. at present.

The ex-Princely States in the country were merged with the Indian Union area after independent i.e. in the year 1948. The ex-Princely States of Gujarat comprising parts of tribal areas of

Gujarat (after merger) formed a part of ex-Bombay State. However, the latter did not take timely action to issue notification to apply Section 73-A to the merged areas of ex-Princely States of Gujarat. It was after twelve years that the Government of Gujarat issued a notification on 4th April, 1961 for the application of Section 73-A to the tribal areas of ex-princely States. Thus the transactions of alienations of tribal lands which had taken place in this intervening period after the merger remained uncovered by Section 73-A allowing no legal remedy to deal with such alienations.

From the above account, it will be seen that in Gujarat State there are still two types of alienations of tribal lands held under the occupation of the money-lenders, exploiters, etc. for which there is no legal remedy. These two types are:

(i) alienation of tribal lands in the surveyed and settled areas;
(ii) alienations of tribal lands in the ex-Princely States which occurred during the period after merger in 1948 until 4th April, 1961 in respect of areas notified therein.

In order to bring the above two types of cases of alienations of tribal lands within the purview of the legal bounds, it is recommended that Sections 68 and 73-A of the Land Revenue Code may be suitably amended to cover all tribal areas and all transfers to tribals as well as non-tribals alike. This is because, a new upper class in tribal society is rising and becoming exploitative to poorer tribals on account of their favourable power position and substantial land-holdings. They have already cornered privileges and resources in the areas of agriculture, irrigation, education, employment and placement on key-posts reserved for all categories of scheduled tribes.

It should be noted that the Maharashtra Government has given retrospective effect from 1st April, 1957 to deal with all cases of alienations of tribal lands to non-tribals and for restoration of such lands to original tribal occupants, in the light of the Maharashtra Restoration of Lands to Scheduled Tribes Act, 1974 by suitable amendments in the Maharashtra Land Revenue Code.

Record of Rights

The maintenance of correct and up-to-date land records is a

pre-requisite for the implementation of land reforms. Following the abolition of intermediaries, introduction of tenancy reforms, ceilings on land, prevention of fragments and consolidation of holdings, etc. the land records, had to be re-written and brought up-to-date. The work of preparing the Record of Rights, so far as the tribals are concerned requires utmost care and vigilence because most of the tribals are illiterate and ignorant of the implications of various enactments. The approach to this work should be a human one rather than legalistic and should take full cognisance of tribal customs and traditions.

The Committee on Special Multipurpose Tribal Development Blocks rightly observed in its report that, "The tribal people are bound to their land by many and intimate ties. Their feeling for it is something more than mere possessiveness. It is connected with their sense of history, for their legends tell of the great journeys they made over the wild and lonely hills and of the heroic pioneers who made the first clearings in the forest. It is part of their reverence for the dead, whose spirits still haunt the countrysides. The land is the mother who provides for them in response to the labourers of their hands and who, when supplies run short, feeds them with a hundred natural gifts. It is the setting of adventure, in love, in hunting and in war, which can never be forgotten. The land is the foundation of a sense of security and freedom from fear; its assured possession is a lasting road to peace".[5]

There is thus the prime necessity that the Land Records in tribal belt showing the rights of tribals should not only be maintained up-to-date but should also reflect real position on the ground.

The Record of Rights prevalent in the former Bombay State, in respect of agricultural lands became applicable in the state of Gujarat after the reorganisation of Indian States, because it formed part of the then Bombay State. The Record of Rights is being maintained in the combined Village Form (VF) which is commonly known as V.F. VII-XII[6] This combined Village Form consists of two parts, viz. Village Form VII and Village Form VII-A and XII, printed on the single page and maintained for each survey number or part of a survey number by allotting separate page for each parcel of land. Village Form VII is printed on the upper part of the page and gives details about the area of the field with *Pot Kharab* or uncultivable portions if any, its assessment, name of the field, name of the occupant, nature of tenure of the land (i.e. new tenure, restricted tenure) etc.

It also contains column of "other rights", wherein other rights subsisting on a particular parcel of land are shown. Besides, on the lower part of the page are printed V.F. VII-A and V.F. XII. The V.F. VII-A gives the name/names of tenants, area cultivated by them etc. The V.F. XII gives details about crops, area under each crop, irrigated or unirrigated and sources of irrigation details about trees etc. The lower part V.F. VII-A & XII-A contains columns for yearwise entries and can be used for 10 years.

The entries in the upper part i.e. V.F. VII are of a permanent nature and no yearwise entries are made but any change in information in respect of any column is made by effecting a mutation entry in Mutation Register which is called Village Form VI.[7] In Village Form VII, the change is made in any information in respect of any column by quoting only entry number of V.F.-VI, whereas by seeing the mutation number, one can see the details of the mutation in the Mutation Register V.F. VI. The V.F. VI and the combined V.F. VII-XII constitute together the Record of Rights.

V.F. VI is maintained in a bound Register while V.F. VII-XII contains loose pages kept in sizable bunches or blocks and tied together. Each block book contains pages about the serial Number of land or their sub-divisions situated in a particular portion of the village. Thus there may be one or more block books for the village.

The Village Form VII-XII is not carried as a bulky Register in order that the Village Officers (*Talatis*) can easily move with it in the fields during field inspection and for – making entries of various kinds, including crops grown, etc.

As stated in the earlier chapter, most of the tribal areas in Gujarat State formed part of ex-Princely States. There was no regular and uniform system of maintaining up-to-date land records in most of the ex-Princely States. The Rulers maintained the land records according to their own requirements without bothering for the rights of the tribals. It was only after the merger of the ex-Princely States, with the former Bilingual Bombay State in the year 1948, that the Record of Rights in the village Forms VI & VII-XII was introduced in the villages of the ex-Princely States. In unsurveyed villages also, survey operations were carried out. Steps were taken to bring the Records of Rights up-to-date because of implementation of various land reforms, etc.

In spite of efforts made by the State Government to keep land records up-to-date, it has been observed during field inspections that Land Records in tribal areas are not so up-to-date as expected so as to reflect the real position of land-holdings on the ground. Various factors are responsible for this state of affairs and these factors can be attributed to defaults not only of administrative machinery but also of tribals and non-tribals alike. The various factors related to the situation are mentioned below:

(i) During the olden times, it was the general practice in most of the ex-Princely States to demand forced labour commonly known as *Veth* from villagers. Every land-holder called as *Khatedar* had to supply one person, one bullock cart, etc. to do free labour for any job decided by the Ruler. In order that the *Khatedars* may not have to supply more persons for free labour, they tried to restrict the division of land-holdings i.e. *Khatas*. It was ,therefore, the established practice among the tribals to enter the name of the eldest male heir of the family while carrying out the heirship of the deceased *Khatedars*, though there may be other male heirs of the deceased who might have distributed lands on the spot for self-cultivation according to their shares. This practice of entering the name of the eldest male member in the record of rights was being continued for several generations.

After merger of the ex-Princely States, of course the practice of demanding forced labour does not exist at all. However, the old custom and practices of carrying out heirship of land-holdings among the tribals has not completely vanished with the result that instances of this type are to be seen. In recent years it has been the practice to enter names of all heirs jointly in the land records in respect of the land-holdings of the deceased, but divisions of lands for self-cultivation are made according to the shares of the heirs on the ground.

(ii) The different parcels of lands held by a tribal land-holder, are situated at different places, some on rocky and hilly areas, while a few in some-what plane area. The tribals land-holder generally constructs his residential houses/huts in the land which is in somewhat plain area. The fertility of each parcel of land is different. The ultimate result is that each and every heir of the deceased land-holders sub-divides each parcel of ancestral land and gets his own share in every parcel instead of getting shares in the form of intact parcels of land. This results in small and uneconomic fragments and at times these fragments are of the size below the standard area prescribed by the Bombay Prevention of Fragmentation and Consolidation of Holdings Act. However, so far as land records are concerned, joint names of all the heirs of the deceased family-head are shown against each parcel of land though the position on the ground is different. The village officers *(Talatis)* who are maintaining land records are also helpless to effect showing heirship position on the ground as there are breaches of the provisions of the Bombay Prevention of Fragmentation Act and so they safely enter the joint names in respect of each parcel of land.

(iii) The provision contained in Section 73-A of the Bombay Land Revenue Code does not permit alienation of tribal lands to non-tribals and even to tribals without the Collector's permission. However, the tribals are in the habit of incurring debts for social ceremonies, family maintenance in times of scarcity, and other requirements. For this purpose they have to give as security their lands to their creditors. These are secret transactions and both parties being interested, they are not brought to the notice of officials and are never reflected in the Records of Rights.

(iv) The programmes of re-survey and revision survey have been undertaken in tribal areas. However, the surveyors do not, and cannot take responsibility to show all fragments of every parcel of land existing on the ground because of the provisions of the Bombay Prevention of Fragmentation and Consolidation of Holdings Act. Appendix-II gives present position of land record programmes in Gujarat.

(v) The scheme of consolidation of holdings has also been introduced in some tribal villages. However, it is observed in the field that the tribals do not exchange their lands and do not occupy the lands allotted to them while forming blocks. There are various reasons for this. There is great emotional attachment among tribals to their ancestral lands. Again as the fertility of various pieces of land is not uniform, the tribals do not exchange ancestral lands with lands of others allotted to them according to consolidation scheme. Thus the consolidation scheme remains on paper only, without any changes in occupation of land on the ground. The village officers *(Talatis)* therefore find it very difficult to do crop inspection etc. as their records are re-written according to blocks formed under the consolidation scheme while the position on the ground is as it was before the introduction of the scheme. The consolidation staff generally obtain a written declaration from the cultivators in regard to exchange of consolidated holdings. However, the cultivators either do not act as per declaration and exchange the possession as per scheme or even if exchange of possession is carried out, they tend to revert to the original position thus rendering the scheme ineffective.

Implementation of Land Reforms and the Empirical Situation

This concluding section throws light on the actual implementation of (a) Tenancy Law, (b) Ceiling Act and (c) Provisions of Section 73-A of Land Revenue Code. The data presented in the three tables and described under relevant titles were collected during 1977-79 through correspondence from the officers in the districts concerned.

(a) *Tenancy Law*

The results of implementation of Tenancy Law was available in respect of 14 tribal talukas and one tribal pocket and are given in the Table 4.2. It may be added that this data come from 14 tribal talukas and one tribal pocket. Information on remaining tribal areas was not available. The figures in hectares and rupees are round figures. This table shows that the maximum number of tribal tenants who got occupancy rights as deemed purchaser under Tenancy Law were 32285 in Vyara Taluka of Surat districts, and they got occupancy rights of 69292 hectares of land. The minimum number of tribal tenants who got occupancy rights was 274 in Santrampur Taluka of Panchmahals district. The extent of occupancy rights received by them was of 193 hectares only.

Similarly, the maximum number of tribals who paid their landlords instalments of Purchase Price was 27,363 in Vyara Taluka and the minimum number was 203 in Santrampur Taluka.

The maximum number of tribals who paid purchase price to their landlords by taking loans from Land Development Bank was 1215 in Jhagadia Taluka with the loan amount of Rs. 4,23,900. It was interesting to note that in Jhalod, Santrampur, Limkheda, Devgadhbaria Tribal Talukas and Sisodra Ganesh Tribal Pocket of Navsari Taluka, not a single tribal received such a loan for payment of purchase price from the Land Development Bank.

TABLE 4.2: The Results of implementation of Tenancy Law in Tribal Areas

Name of Taluka or Pocket*	No. of Tribals who were conferred occupancy rights as deemed purchasers and area involved		No. of Tribals who paid instalments of purchase price themselves		No. of tribals who paid instalments of purchase price by taking Tagavi loans from			
					Land Development Bank		Govt. by Tagavi loan	
1	2		3		4			
	No. of Tribals	Area hect.	No. of Tribals	Amount Rs.	No. of Tribals	Amount Rs.	No. of Tribals	Amount Rs.
Panchmahal								
Jhalod	5046	2042	498	44166	—	—	4245	517838
Dahod	12917	13251	11349	1468559	20	15590	955	644019
Santrampur	274	193	203	67368	—	—	71	26481
Limkheda	1641	998	1611	4088	—	—	19	12252
Devgadhbaria	3640	3280	3019	948953	—	—	381	64427
Vadodara								
Chhotaudepur	10406	9109	8982	1574030	77	74500	751	312470
Tilkawada	3278	3278	2639	632486	34	55629	334	185191
Bharuch								
Jhagadia	8933	20429	5698	3050740	1215	423900	820	688940
Surat								
Vyara	32285	69292	27363	7575539	929	472206	2415	463725
Mahuva	12935	9241	10753	3355943	452	156927	1132	433424
Songadh	20675	11584	18300	205971	17	18714	1688	360637
Valod	8555	10934	6697	2046942	507	459719	883	437086
Bardoli	830	626	440	333147	11	29180	180	78884
Valsad								
Pardi	18315	7825	110496	2914268	215	108973	389	152960
Navsari								
Sisodra-Ganesh (P)	3477	2578	3227	1148376	—	—	191	72192

Contd.

TABLE 4.2: *(Contd.)*

Name of Taluka or Pocket*	No. of tribals who were not able to pay instalments of purchase price		Tribal tenants who voluntarily surrendered lands in favour of landlords		Tribal Tenants who lost lands for personal cultivation by landlords	
1	5		6		7	
	No. of Tribals	Amount Rs.	No. of Tribals	Area Hect.	No. of Tribals	Area Hect.
Panchmahal						
Jhalod	303	64183	3	1	23	44
Dahod	593	159769	4	4	13	16
Santrampur	—	—	—	—	—	—
Limkheda	11	3280	—	—	—	—
Devgadhbaria	240	38986	—	—	—	—
Vadodara						
Chhotaudepur	596	151037	1315	1137	177	358
Tilkawada	271	61827	—	—	52	103
Bharuch						
Jhagadia	1200	1455240	502	1234	39	80
Surat						
Vyara	1578	113266	118	49	—	—
Mahuva	1298	184805	15	18	118	86
Songadh	670	75000	—	—	89	418
Valod	468	195107	89	68	142	121
Bardoli	199	82323	39	61	22	13
Valsad						
Pardi	1215	53797	1227	628	775	856
Navsari						
Sisodra-Ganesh (P)	59	26763	5	3	—	—
Total			3317	3203	1450	2095

* The above information is in respect of 14 Tribal Talukas and one Tribal Pocket(P). The information in respect of the remaining 18 Tribal Talukas and 14 Tribal Pockets is not available. Figures in Hectares and in Rupees are round Figures.

The maximum number of tribals who paid the purchase price to their landlords by taking Tagavi loans from the Government was 4245 in Jhalod Taluka in Panchmahals district with the loan of Rs. 518738. The minimum number of cases in this regard was 19 in Limkheda Taluka with the total loan of Rs. 12,252. The Table 4.2 shows that the State Government advanced Tagavi loans in this regard to every Taluka while the Land Development Bank did not cover each and every Taluka.

The maximum number of tribals who were not been able to pay the amount of purchase price to their landlords was 1578 in Vyara Taluka with the outstanding amount of Rs. 1,13,266. The minimum number of tribals in this regard was 11 in Limkheda Taluka with the outstanding amount of Rs. 3280. All tribal tenants in Santrampur Taluka had paid the amount of purchase price to their landlords and none is remaining to be paid now.

Column 6 of the Table 4.2 shows that no tribal tenant surrendered any land to his landlord in 5 tribal talukas, viz., Limkheda, Devgadhbaria, Tilkawada and Songadh. The maximum number of such tenants was 1315 in Chhotaudepur Taluka where 1137 hectare of land were surrendered. The minimum number was 3 in Jhalod Taluka and the land area surrendered was one hectare only. Further more, column 7 of the table 4.2 shows that no tribal tenant lost his tenanted land on account of personal cultivation by landlords in 4 tribal talukas and one tribal Pocket, viz., Santrampur, Limkheda, Devgadhbaria, Vyara and tribal pocket Sisodra-Ganesh (P) in Navsari Taluka. The maximum number of such tenants was 755 in Pardi Taluka of Valsad, where 856 hectares were involved. The minimum number was 13 in Dohad Taluka with the area of 16 hectares of land.

It is seen from columns 6 and 7 of Table 4.2 that in respect of Tribal Talukas and one Tribal Pocket, 3317 and 1415 tribal tenants respectively had to give up their lands admeasuring 3203 hectares and 2095 hectares by voluntary surrender to their landlords and for personal cultivation by landlords.

It must be remarked that 4767 tribal tenants would have been benefited to retain 5,298 hectares of land, and they would have become deemed purchasers, if the amendments to tenancy legislation banning voluntary surrender by tribal tenants, and getting land back for personal cultivation by landlords from tribal tenants, was made by the State legislature much earlier, say at the very outset of enacting the tenancy law.

(b) *Ceiling Act (Table 4.3)*

The information regarding results of implementation of the Ceiling Act and relinquishment of lands (under Section 74 of the Land Revenue Code, 1879) by non-tribal for allotment to tribals in respect of 14 tribal talukas and one tribal pocket is in Table 4.3.

It is seen from the column 2 of the Table 4.3 that no land was declared surplus in 4 tribal talukas and one tribal pocket viz, Santrampur, Chhotaudepur, Tilakwada, Vyara and Sisodra Ganesh (P) of Navsari Taluka. The maximum number of occupants whose lands were declared surplus under the Ceiling Law was 72 in Jhagadia Taluka in Bharuch district with an area of 112 hectares. There was only one person in Devgadhbaria Taluka whose 61 hectares of land was declared surplus.

Column 3 of the Table 4.3 shows the number of tribals who were allotted surplus lands under Ceiling Act, and the size of area involved. The maximum number of tribals who were allotted surplus land under the Act was 769 in Pardi Taluka of Valsad district and the area allotted was 316 hectares. On the other hand, the minimum number of tribals who were allotted surplus lands was 13 in Valod Taluka in Surat district and the area allotted was 29 hectares.

Further more, the column 5 of the Table 4.3 shows the area of lands relinquished in favour of tribals by non-tribal occupants and the ex-gratia amounts paid to these occupants, while column 6 shows the number of tribals who were allotted relinquished lands, and the amount of price charged for allotment. The actual relinquishment of lands has taken place in Pardi Taluka and Sisodra-Ganesh Pocket of Navsari Taluka. These lands were presumably grass lands known as *Ghasia* lands. By this relinquishment, 2394 tribals were benefited and become occupants of 1116 hectares of land by paying Rs. 3,90,970 as against the ex-gratia amount of Rs. 9,83,865 paid to non-tribal occupants.

This experiment to solve the problem of Grass lands (*Ghasia* lands) in Pardi Taluka of Valsad district by way of relinquishment of lands by non-tribals and allotment of the said lands to the Tribals has been very successful. It may be possible to recommended some such measures for other tribal areas for allotment of land to the tribals wherever feasible.

TABLE 4.3: Implementation of Ceiling Act in Tribal Areas and relinquishment of land in favour of Tribals

Name of the Taluka or Pocket*	Lands declared surplus under Ceiling Law		Number of Tribals allotted surplus lands and area		Area of surplus lands remaining to be allotted and reasons		Area relinquished under Section 74 of Bombay Land Revenue Code and ex-gratia amount paid to occupants			Number of Tribals allotted relinquished lands and amount of concessional occupancy price charged		
	No. of occupants	Area declared surplus hect.	No. of Tribals	Area allotted hect.	Area hect.	Reasons	Number of occupants	Area relinquished hect.	Ex-gratia amount paid	No. of tribals	Area allotted hect.	Amount of price charged
1	2	3	4	5	6	7	8	9	10	11	12	13
Panchmahals												
Jhalod	3	285	68	112	173	Uncultivable and assigned for gauchar etc.	—	—	—	—	—	—
Dahod	3	56	34	51	—		—	—	—	—	—	—
Santrampur	Nil											
Limkheda	2	49	77	49	—	—	—	—	—	—	—	—
Devgadhbaria	1	61	96	61	—	—	—	—	—	—	—	—
Vadodara												
Chhotaudepur	Nil											
Tilakwada	Nil											
Bharuch												
Jhagadia	72	112	69	106	6	—	—	—	—	—	—	—
Surat												
Vyara	Nil											

Contd.

TABLE 4.3 *(Contd.)*

1	2	3	4	5	6	7	8	9	10	11	12	13
Mahuva	10	137	102	137	—	—	—	—	—	—	—	—
Songadh	6	202	201	202	—	—	—	—	—	—	—	—
Valod	2	33	13	29	4	—	—	—	—	—	—	—
Bardoli	11	33	—	—	33	Stay order	—	—	—	—	—	—
Valsad												
Pardi	53	334	769	316	18	Hilly land	700	1066	924972	2339	1066	332077
Sisodra Ganesh (p)	—	—		—	—	—	10	50	58893	55	50	58893
Navsari												
Total	163	1302	1429	1063	234		710	1116	983865	2394	1116	390970

(c) *Cases of Land Alienation (Table 4.4)*

The position of the cases for restoration of alienated land under Section 73-A of the Bombay Land Revenue Code, instituted and dealt with at the end of August 1979, is given in Table 4.4.

The total number of cases instituted in all the 8 tribal districts was 16815 out of which 3800 cases were found to be non-conductable and 2625 cases were considered to be dropped. Out of the remaining 10390 cases for restoration of tribal land, 8188 cases were disposed off until August 1979. Out of 8188 cases decided by the court, 7980 cases turned out to be in favour of tribals and 208 cases against. Out of the 2202 cases which were pending, 276 were pending below 6 months, 902 below one year and 1024 for more than one year.

The highest number of cases to be conducted amounted to 5223 in Bharuch district, next in order were 2910 cases from Panchmahals district, and the lowest number of cases was 52 from Surat district. As a result of the court proceedings, the number of cases decided in favour of tribals was 3396 in Bharuch, 2871 in Panchmahals and 42 in Surat district.

Of all the decided cases in favour of the tribals, possession of land was restored to 6349 tribals admeasuring 19536 acres of land.

However, there were 1631 cases in which possession was not restored for the land admeasuring 4489 areas. In the district of Bharuch, the largest area of land restored to tribals was 7810 areas. Next in order comes Panchmahal where the figure of the land restored was 5868 acres.

The Special programmes of the State Government for strengthening the administrative machinery to detect cases of unauthorised alienation of tribal lands, made it possible to decide 7980 cases for restoring tribal lands admeasuring a total of 19536+4489, i.e. 24025 acres of land.

(d) *Consolidation of Land-holdings*

The situation regarding fragmentation and consolidation of land-holdings in tribal areas is interesting. Out of 39 sample villages of Tribal Talukas, there were only 4 villages with more than 300 fragments in each village. In the 15 sample village of Tribal Pockets, the maximum of 200 to 300 fragments were to be found only in one village.

TABLE 4.4: Cases of tribal land alienation instituted and dealt with until August 1979

District	Total No. of cases instituted	Out of Col. 3 No. of cases			No. of cases disposed off at the end of August 1979		
		Conductable	Non-conductable	To be dropped	In favour of tribals	Against tribals	Total
1	2	3a	3b	3c	4a	4b	4c
Banaskantha			Nil				
Sabarkantha	1669	896	155	618	376	25	401
Panchmahals	3218	2910	230	78	2871	11	2882
Vadodara	4475	905	3256	314	905	—	905
Bharuch	5701	5223	159	319	3396	161	3557
Surat	244	52	—	192	40	11	51
Valsad	1088	69	—	1019	60	—	69
Dangs	420	335	—	85	323	—	323
Total	16815	10390	3800	2625	7980	208	8188

TABLE 4.4 *(Contd.)*

District	No of cases pending				No of cases in which possession was handed over to tribals		Cases in which possession remained to be restored to tribals	
	Below 6 months	6 months to 1 year	Above 1 year	Total	No. of cases	Area in Acres	No. of cases	Area in Acres
	5a	5b	5c	5d	6a	6b	6c	6d
Banaskantha	Nil							
Sabarkantha	214	245	36	495	296	474	80	92
Panchmahals	28	—	—	28	2810	5868	61	162
Vadodara	—	—	—	—	785	3232	120	366
Bharuch	21	657	988	1666	2158	7810	1238	3131
Surat	1	—	—	1	13	38	27	24
Valsad	—	—	—	—	47	115	22	39
Dangs	12	—	—	12	240	1999	83	705
Total	276	902	1024	2202	6349	19536	1631	4489

On completion of the consolidation scheme, possession of land was to be inter-changed, so that the land-holders take possession of their newly formed Blocks in place of their old Sr. Nos. and/or Sub-divisions.

During the course of field survey in the sample villages of Tribal Talukas and Pockets, it was revealed that the work of consolidation was completed in 6 sample villages of Tribal Talukas and 7 sample villages of Tribal Pockets, i.e. in 13 sample villages only.

(i) In the following 7 villages the fragments were not exchanged.

Name of villages	Taluka	District
1. Kanjod	Valod	Surat
2. Titwa	"	"
3. Virpore	"	"
4. Chakhalia	Jhalod	Panchmahals
5. Vanjolia (Pocket)	Pansana	Surat
6. Navapara (Pocket)	Navsari	Valsad
7. Loti (Pocket)	Sankheda	Vadodara

(ii) In the following 3 villages, possession was reported to be partially exchanged.

Name of village	Taluka	District
1. Barasadi (Pocket)	Palsana	Surat
2. Butlav (Pocket)	Navsari	Valsad
3. Aritha (Pocket)	Sankheda	Vadodara

(iii) In the following villages, possession was reported to be fully exchanged.

Name of village	Taluka	District
1. Sarsad	Jhagdia	Bharuch
2. Kanti	Mahuva	Surat
3. Karala (Pocket)	Palsana	Surat

Out of the total of 13 villages, distributed in three categories the consolidation scheme was not successful in 10(7+3) villages as shown in categories (i) and (ii) above.

In cases of (ii) and (iii) categories of villages where there was partial and full implementation of the consolidation scheme, it was found that most of the lands belonged to non-tribals. Out of total of these 6 villages, 4 villages come from tribal pocket areas and 2 from tribal talukas.

In the "Report on Consolidation of Land-holding Gujarat State" by H.K.L. Kapoor Committee, it was pointed out that the areas having one or more of the following characterisations were obviously unsuitable for implementation of the consolidation scheme:

(1) Areas having undulating and hilly terrain;
(2) Areas having disproportionately large varieties of soil;
(3) Areas where there was an insignificant problem of scatterdness; and
(4) Areas having a large percentage of Adivasi population or that of other inhabitants who were socially backward.

Firstly, it seems that the above 10 villages where the consolidation scheme has not been successful were taken up before the preparation of the Kapoor Committee's Report, and one or more of the above characterisations seem to have affected the results. The above characterisations may be kept in view when the question of taking up tribal villages for introduction of the consolidation scheme arises in future. The feasibility of the scheme, the willingness of the land-holders for implementation etc. must be thoroughly examined while taking up a tribal village for implementation of this scheme.

Secondly, it seems that the Record of Rights (in these 10 villages) was rewritten according to the Consolidation Scheme as if the possessions were exchanged according to the formation of Blocks, and as such Block numbers were shown in place of survey numbers along with Sub-divisions of Survey numbers. However, the position on the ground was different in cases in which the land-holders had not exchanged their possession.

This resulted in a lot of difficulties for the village officers (*Talatis*) concerned in doing crop inspection and keeping notes of the crops in the Block numbers in village records. Since possession was not according to consolidation Blocks in such cases, serious administrative difficulties were faced in day to day working of the village officers.

In principle, the Record of Rights is the Record of Possession of land by an occupant. This is not observed under these conditions. The vital statistics of crops collected at various levels are also affected.

In the end, it seems appropriate to suggest that the Record of Rights in villages in which Consolidation Scheme is not successfully implemented, it should be brought in conformity with the possession of holdings on the ground.

NOTES

1. This date is changed from time to time and has been recently extended upto 31-12-1980.
2. *Report of the National Commission on Agriculture 1976*, Part XV, Agrarian Reforms, pp. 117-118.
3. Section 6(3) of the Gujarat Agricultural Lands Ceiling Act, 1960.
4. G.D. Patel, *The Land Problem of Reorganised Bombay State*, 1957, p. 99.
5. *Report of the Scheduled Areas and Scheduled Tribes Commission*, Government of India, Vol. I, 1960-61, p. 121.
6. V.F. VII-XII is treated an one combined Village Form commonly known as "Index of Lands" which includes information on various aspects of land ownership, crops, mode of cultivation, etc.
7. V.F. VI is commonly known as "Mutation Register" and it traces the history of changing pattern of ownership and other rights over a parcel of land.

5

DYNAMICS OF LAND REFORMS

Introduction

The problems of land in general and land reforms in particular is a dynamic issue. Ever since the remote ages, man depended heavily on the resources available from land for maintenance and development of human culture. In the middle ages, there were a number of changes and challenges in the political power structure of India. These changes occurred on account of invasion from the outside world and also due to internal feuds and expansionist policy of one neighbour at the cost of the other. The feudal-lords and the princes alike changed hands in the control of one territory or the other as a result of victory or defeat. The inhabitants of these territories had to undergo a lot of suffering on account of a number of changes in the supremacy and ownership of lands by one power or the other. Not all the rulers, princes, feudal-lords and petty chiefs were able to maintain satisfactory relationship with the tillers of the soil from whom they exacted remuneration or rental in kind or cash for the maintenance of themselves, their armies and their supporters. Right from the most powerful ruler to the lowest category of a feudatory, there has been a continuous tendency to delegate power and responsibilities to their own kinds, affairs, office functionaries and trusted milita man who looked after the affaines of lands and other resources.

We have seen in the previous Chapter, existence of a variety of land systems with specific reference to the collection of land revenue from farmers living in different kinds of Princely States. This was common in the districts under study before and after the establishment of British control of different areas in the country. From this historical background of land systems of the past, one can easily see that most of the princes and the feudal-lords collected land revenue through one or more intermediaries. For this, they evolved either crude customary taxation usage or somewhat refined method of assessment of revenue from various categories of land-holders either directly or indirectly. The collection of revenue was made possible with the help of requisite orders, enactments, regulations, laws, etc. In the early days of occupying new territories or in extending their suzerainty over local rulers, the Britishers had to rest content initially by entering into temporary agreements with the rulers and chiefs in order to receive share in the produce of land.

The present study of land reforms in tribal Gujarat is, therefore, concerned broadly with the emergence of concealed tenancy, improvement in conditions of land tenure, right of tenants vis-a-vis feudal masters of the land, and prevention of fragmentation and consolidation of land-holdings. Over and above these specific aspects of land reforms, there is another and more significant problem tackles by the Government of free India established on the principles of democratic decentralization of power concerned with social, economical and cultural well-being of the people. This was the crucial problem of policy, imposing a ceiling on the ownership of agricultural lands. The available agricultural lands can thus be distributed to a larger number of common farmers who can derive benefits by improving the methods of agriculture through application of new techniques, methods and technology for higher production.

In view of the general consideration of the study of tribal land systems outlined above, it is essential to lay emphasis on the following specific items for presenting findings of the study. These items are: (i) Abolition of Intermediaries, (ii) Tenancy Reforms, (iii) Prevention of fragmentation and consolidation of holdings, and (iv) Ceiling on Agricultural land. The fifth item that is of paramount importance so far as the Tribal Land System for predominantly hilly areas is concerned, is (v) Proper use of Forest Lands. In this Chapter, we shall discuss the first four items which are directly concerned with the dynamic aspects of land reforms. The problems of Forest Land are many but as they are confined to limited areas of tribal land in general, the problems of its cultivation for agricultural purpose is to be looked into. We shall deal with the problems of Forest Land in the next Chapter.

It will be useful to mention at the outset that the data collected and used in preparing this whole report comes from various resources. An open end questionnaire was used as a guide for indepth interviews of cooperative respondents. It was also mailed to select persons to get data through mail. A copy of the questionnaire is given in Appendix-III for reference. The important sources from which most information has been presented in this Chapter, and some of the subsequent ones, comes from field interviews and discussions with different types of people. Broadly speaking, these people belong to *official* and *non-official* categories. Firstly, officials comprise District Collectors , Dy. Collectors, etc. and various heads of development departments at district as well as taluka levels. Secondly, among the *non-officials* were the political leaders, elected representatives, heads of voluntary organisations and different types of social workers. We have also collected information with the help of formal interviews through semi-structured schedules from heads of tribal house-holds and village leaders, on the basis of selective sample design. The opinions, attitudes and behaviours of all these people are reflected in the responses we tried to elicit on the prevailing hard realities connected with land-holdings and land reforms in order to safeguard the interests of marginal and small farmers. Suggestions to eliminate exploitation and to put tribal land to optimum utilisation for the benefit of the people at large have also been advanced. Behavioural dimensions of the land reforms are difficult to fathom but are easy to comprehend from what is actually happening at the ground level. These are also referred to in the narrations of some of the persons interviewed in the course of field investigations.

We shall now present some aspects of districtwise accounts providing dynamics of land reforms. The tribals of every district face different kinds of problems in relation to Panchayati Raj, Community Development, alienation of land, conferment of occupancy rights of land in his possession or of land received on account of tenancy legislation, and the moratorium on old debts. There are also back and forth references to the past and present-day agrarian relationships of the tribals with the defunct administrative authorities and the feudal lords concerned. The Bombay Land Revenue Code Section 73-A and its impact on the problems of land alienation are discussed in relation to specific conditions and situations obtained in every district.

The points of view of and assessments of problems by the *officials* and the *non-officials* reported from the field sometimes widely differ due to varying perceptions and divergent micro situations in the field. Respondents of both these categories are tribals as well as non-tribals. The problems of land is obviously related to money-lending, indebtedness and forestry including collection of minor forest produce, etc., by the tribals. The issues and problems which have not been dealt with in adequate details in this Chapter, are taken care of in subsequent Chapters.

The districtwise accounts presented here are divided into the reactions of official and non-official categories of respondents, some of whom were more reserved than others.

Banaskantha District

(a) *Assessment by Officials*

In all there were ten officials contacted for collecting data on this subject, but hardly any one of them was to the point. The assessment of the situation and information given by nine non-officials only is therefore presented below.

(b) *Assessment of Non-Officials*

In the former Danta State of this district the condition of the tribals was reported to be quite satisfactory. They used to get from their habitat almost all their small domestic requirements free of cost in the times of crisis. For instance, if they wanted fire wood, it was possible for them to get it free of cost from the State forest. There was no need of a special permit to be obtained for this purpose. In the times of scarcity of rain or heavy and damaging rainfall, the Maharaja of Danta State used to give to the tribals special permits for cutting *pucca* wood to earn their living. So far as the problem of land revenue was concerned, there was a custom of *Kaltar* type of revenue system. According to this, the state collected the share in the total produce of the farm. But in the case of lean or difficult years when agricultural produce was not sufficient, the state used to supply food-grains free of cost, viz., maize, *Jowar* or *Bajra*. Also, when tribals dug wells for irrigation and used stones for this purpose, the state gave them freedom from the payment of revenue for a specified period of time.

The non-officials said that unsurveyed and unsettled land in the state was surveyed and settled in 1956-57. At this time all the tribals who were cultivating land in their possession got occupancy rights.

Although the up keep of Record of Rights was fully implemented in favour of most of the tribals, their lands were actually mortgaged in concealed way with the businessmen or money-lenders from whom they had to borrow money. In course of time some of the tribals began to do unauthorised cultivation into the forest areas, either to supplement their income or to pay exhorbitant interest on the money borrowed from the businessman. Although a large number of tribals of this area is not landless, they are by no means well-to-do. This is because of the poor quality of the land as well as smaller holdings. The most exploitative trick of the money-lenders was that they would not take away the possession of land from the tribals, but exact interest in the form of entire agricultural produce every year, leaving them poor and dependent year after year.

Most non-officials believed that the role and impact of land reforms in this district was minimised because the tribals are permanent tenants of the land under their occupation. There is not much of a radical change in actual occupancy in spite of land reforms. The problem of ceiling on land does not arise because there is not much of surplus land, except in a few villages where it was distributed among the members of schedules castes. The prevention of the fragmentation of land-holdings was however badly needed. The Act on Prevention of Fragmentation is actually on paper without being properly implemented.

The fragments of tribal land were actually many more than recorded in the Village Forms by the revenue officer (*Talati*) working at village level. The reason was that the number of fragments that members of a tribal family occupied were not recorded separately in the name of each cultivator but in the name of one person who was the head of the joint house-hold. The land which remain entered in the name of the eldest member was actually divided into several fragments to suit the claims of a number of heirs.[1] All the younger sons were in usage, deprived of legal rights over the land of the father because of the custom of ultimogenature. However, in practice, the eldest brother allows younger brothers to cultivate parcels of land of different categories for their maintenance. A complicated informal land distribution system of this kind made it most difficult for consolidation of land-holdings of small plots of land under the ownership of several different parties at the ground level.

The non-tribals admitted that the post-independence governmental declaration of "Land to the Tillers" made many a landless tribals, the land owners in principle, on account of tenancy legislation. This, however, did not happen in practice in spite of fixation of Ceiling on land.

As a general rule, the tribal cultivator had not to pay land revenue so far as the land under his occupation did not exceed 7½ acres. However, he had to pay local cesses, i.e., educational cess and Panchayat cess. These cesses were beyond the capability of some of the tribals to pay on account of poverty. There were a few cases however, of the well-to-do tribals not paying these cesses for want of personal honesty. In such cases the development officers had to file suits against the parties concerned and get cesses recovered in the presence of 12 persons of public standing as witness. Sometimes, even police party had to be called for recovery of dues. However, in general, a strict action of this type was not taken by the authorities unless government Takavi loan, etc. were to be recovered. Hardly any action by the authorities was taken specially if it was a matter of recovery of land revenue. However, if an action to auction land was taken at all, the problem faced by the Government was that nobody was prepared to buy the land of a tribal defaulter.

Under the Devasthan Inam Abolition Act, about 31 tribals got occupancy right in Banaskantha District. It amounted to a total size of 49 hect., 51 are and 4 sq. meters of land. Those who got benefit under tenancy act were many. In one part of the district, there were cases of 40 fragments of the total size of 23 hect., 68 are and 43 sq. meters, while in another area, there were 10 fragments measuring 5 hect., 64 are and 53 sq. meters of land. In the third case of fragments of land-holdings, the total number of 47 fragments were recorded, amounting to 17 hect., 79 are and 40 sq. meters. These were distributed among deserving persons.

Under the Patel Watan Abolition Act, two tribals received occupancy rights of land amounting to 3 hect., 64 are and 26 sq. meter. There were four persons who received this benefit under the tenancy legislation and become occupants of the land which they were cultivating before.

Sabarkantha District

(a) *Assessment by Officials*

The number of *officials* interviewed in this district was 14 and *non-officials* 5. The discussion-cum-interviews were held both at the district headquarters and at Khedbrahma Taluka.

The officials said that no difficulty was reported in the recovery of land revenue in the district since the rate of land revenue was considerably low. However, the politically motivated social workers sometimes tried to instigate the tribals under their influence not to pay land revenue to the government. This seems to be one of the reasons why payment of land revenue fluctuated between 60 per cent to 80 per cent in normal years. Also it was reported that the village headman (*Sarpanch*) and the *Talati* did not like to displease a few powerful farmers in the village who continued to evade payment of land revenue. Most of the officials however felt that recovery can easily be made if the revenue was collected promptly during harvesting period. In some areas, difficulty continued to be there in this matter because the *Talaties* were loyal to local social workers who, due to political reasons, were not interested in allowing the government to take coersive measures.

The problems of restoration of lands mortgaged to money-lenders by the tribals was serious in this district. Even after the orders issued by the Government for the restoration of lands to tribal land-holders, there were practical difficulties preventing physical possession of the land by the tribals. It was also reported that some of the tribals even refused to take possession of their own land because of long standing loyalty and economic dependence they had established with the non-tribals concerned.

According to the officials, the problems of abolition of intermediaries was not easy to be solved particularly for the tribal area on account of underhand practices and concealed tenancy existing in spite of legal provisions against it.

On 1st April, 1957, the Tiller's Day, the tenants cultivating the lands were made deemed purchasers' of such lands in their occupation. However, most of the tribals had lost possession of lands prior to that date due to following devious and deciteful methods and arguments used by non-tribals under the provisions of the Act then in force.

(1) Voluntary surrenders of tribal tenants in favour of landlords.
(2) Relinquishment or disuse of lands by tribals.
(3) Declaration that the tribal was not a tenant under Section 70(b) of the Bombay Tenancy and Agricultural Lands Act.

To set right all these unfair means resulting in loss of possession of tenanted lands by tribals, the Government amended the Act in 1973, by inserting Section 32(1)(B) of the said Act to give real benefit to ousted tribal tenants. Such surrenders or relinquishments or declarations of this nature were made against their own interests by the tribals because of illiteracy, or ignorance, or pressure of indebtedness, or obligation of usurious money-lenders and landlords. In contrast, non-tribal tenants did not surrender their lands to their landlords as the tribals did.

An officer reported that when the government made an attempt to restore the lands to the tenants in general, a hue and cry was raised by the parties concerned and so the implementation of Section 32(1)(B) of the Tenancy Act was held in abeyance. He also said that the cases of the tribals with respect to alienation are covered by Section 73-A L.R.Code, the problem of the stay of Section 32(1)(B) does not affect the ownership rights of the tribal on land.

Out of 1504 cases of land alienation in Khedbrahma, Meghraj, Bhiloda and Vijaynagar Talukas under the Tribal Area Sub-Plan Projects, 57 cases of alienation of land by the tribals to the non-tribals had taken place. The remaining were cases of mutual transfer by tribals to tribals. This fact was revealed from Village Forms VII and XII and it included the cases of sale as well as mortgage. These were all illegal transfers of land because in no case of this kind of alienation, sanction is given to any body by the Government.

Section 73-A L.R. Code imposes restriction on sale of tribal land without the permission of the District Collector. In the case of a tribal who wanted to sell his land on account of personal reasons was faced with constraint. This referred to the fact that the tribal in the non-British areas was not permitted to sell his land either to a tribal or to a non-tribal. Since tribal land was alienated on account of indebtedness, wherever there was a case of a "tribal money-lender", the restriction on his being able to buy the land of the tribal borrower could not be made compulsory. The officials believed that this kind of restriction should be only on "non-tribal money-lenders" alone.

One of the greatest setback of alienation of tribal land of whatsoever kind is that it creates uncertainty in the progress of agricultural development. Stability of land tenure is very essential for genuine interest of tribals in land and its progressive development. However, on account of radical measures taken by the government, there have been changes in agrarian relationship which initially created unstable situation in agriculture. The notification of 1961 related to Section 73-A L.R.C., in the former non-British areas preventing transfer of tribal land without the permission of the Collector. In the district of Sabarkantha there were 1600 cases of alienation of tribal land in spite of legal measures of the government against it. Out of these total number of cases, 247 cases were reported to be of alienation of land from tribals to non-tribals, while there were 1353 cases of alienation between tribals and tribals. Out of the cases of internal transfer, 75 per cent of the total of 1600 alienations were among the relations and about 10 per cent were said to be alienations due to intra-group indebtedness or exchange of land. The latter kind of alienations were supported by the tribal people in general and so it was suggested that there should not be any restriction on alienation of land among tribals themselves.

In some parts of the district, it was believed that the grant of occupancy rights to tribal tenants were not realised due to lack of resources and assets for the purpose of good cultivation. The land reforms leading to occupation of the land in the hands of the tribals remained ineffective for practical purpose. Unless a tribal was able to pay occupancy price of land allotted to him, and was also able to make the best use, merely legal measures can not be of any help.

The law regarding the prevention of fragmentation of land-holdings was no doubt applicable to all areas in the state. However, this law is not effective in the tribal areas because of the customary rights of equal inheritance applicable to all the sons in the property of the father. This is because minute partitions are made by the heirs on account of a great variety of differences in the quality of land in different plots of ancestral land in the village. The law of consolidation of land-holdings was not fully implemented in this district because of the complication it involved due to land inherited in the form of fragments as mentioned above.

The question of imposing ceiling on land does not hold good for most of the tribal areas in the district because there are few land-holders with surplus land under their occupation. It is reported that a large number of tribals are actually in possession of small fragments of the size of less than two acres of *Jarayat* land or 20 *gunthas* of *Kyari* land. This is one of the reasons why some people suggested construction of check-dams for the purpose of irrigation facilities in this area.

In the opinion of some of the non-official informants, *Jagiri* abolition in this district has considerably affected mainly the tribals. In general, concessions are given for the payment of occupancy price to a tribal of *jagiri* land. In the case of a non-tribal becoming land-holder after implementation of *Jagirdari* Abolition Act, he had to pay 24 times, but a tribal occupant had to pay only 6 times the price of land assessed.

(b) *Assessment by Non-Officials*

Whatever was said earlier by the officials of Sabarkantha District regarding benefits received by the tribals on account of land reforms, was not corroborated by the non-officials. Some of them reported that the administrative machinery in the field sometimes take decisions against the tribal tenants vis-a-vis non-tribal exploiters in the case of disputes.

On account of lack of surplus land in the area, there were very few cases of tribals getting land under the land ceiling law. No tribal in this district was benefited under the regulation of "Land to the tiller", and none had employed anybody as a tenant. Only in the village of Dehgamada some surplus land was given to the tribals.

The non-officials further said that a number of transactions of land alienation between the tribals and non-tribals were concealed, as were generally oral. The money-lenders entering into this type of transactions with the tribals, did not charge interest in the form of cash money. Even the possession of land was not taken on mortgage basis. The physical occupation of land remained with the tribal land-holders, but the money-lenders took share in the produce of crops in the place of interest on the money given on loan.

Panchmahals District

(a) *Assessment by Officials*

The actual tribal cultivators are the marginal and small farmers facing the difficulty of getting government subsidy for various purposes. This difficulty arose as their economic status was treated low on account of smaller holdings. The programmes of helping the tribal land-holders by the Land Development Bank was also reported to suffer on account of heavy arrears pending payments by the tribal borrowers from various sources. It seems that there was greater incidence of the tribal lands passing on from one person to other, either within their own group or to the non-tribals. This, however, was unrecorded, leading to a number of complications for establishing eligibility of a person for getting subsidy and loan from governmental as well as from other institutional resources.

It was reported by some officials that quite a few tribal land-holders wanting to sell their land undervalued the land in order to avoid spending money of court stamp, and also to avoid being caught in the net of prohibitory provisions of alienation under Section 73-A. There was another difficulty also. Since smaller divisions of ancestral land cultivated by a number of brothers was not recorded in the Village Forms, a tribal family was put to a great disadvantage at the time of selling the land because it was already undervalued for avoiding stamp duty.

Out of 6000 cases of alienation of lands under various underhand-dealings, about 1400 cases were reported to be of those where the tribals refused to take the possession of their own land under protection of the law. There were clear evidences of at least 900 persons cultivating their own land as servants or farm labourers of money-lenders to whom they had alienated land on account of heavy debts.

In a number of tribal villages in the district, the village records were incomplete and entries were not certified because mutations cannot be done on account of the following reasons.

(1) The law of fragmentation of holdings was violated;
(2) A number of the transfers were illegal;
(3) The social custom of retaining the land in the name of head of the family recently deceased, came in the way of registering mutations in practice; and
(4) There were cases of underhand dealings to avoid illegal transfers coming to light.

It was generally observed by officials that about 30 per cent of the tribals migrated to other places for earning livelihood after Diwali, and they come back home at the time of Holi festival every year. There were adverse effects of this kind of long term migration of the tribals. These included: (a) neglect of agriculture at home and (b) temporary lease of land to other persons, resulting into disputes arising at the time of return to the village.

The prevention of fragmentation and consolidation of land-holding Act covers Section 9 and 7 for imposing penalty upon a person for violation of the provision of the Act. However it was recommended that in certain cases, there should be exemption from the application of the law in the cases of fragmentation on account of following three reasons.

(i) Heirship of land (ii) Co-ownership of land, and (iii) Partition of land during the life time or after the death of the head of the family. The officials believed that exemption of the same kind should also be provided for in the application of Section 73-A with regard to fragmentation of land-holdings during the life time or after the death of the head of the household.

Officials believed that if the Record of Rights had been prepared properly and kept up-to-date, there would not have been any need of putting limit on the use of the Village Form VII and XII.

The fragments were generally not recorded specially in the case where family partition had taken place. Provision should specially be made in the law for getting this type of fragmentation recorded by the village accountant. The Government Regulation R.D. No. ADM/1075/11085-2 dated 3-7-1976 regarding the violation of Section 73-A and restoration of the possession of land to the tribals was applied in 3046 cases of breach of this law. In all 2523 cases were disposed off, while 757 cases, where transfer of land had been oldered, were yet to be restored to the persons concerned. In the cases of 348 persons, land was actually handed over. In the case 409, the process of handing over the land to the owner was postponed on account of the crops standing for harvesting. The transfer was, therefore, pending after the month of April. There were 1764 cases in which there was no violation of Section 73-A. There the mutation had taken place on account of the partitions of the ancestral land cultivated by the heirs during the life time of the head of the household.

According to the officials, the belief that the RTS (Review of land transfers) teams of revenue officers to up-date records of rights sent by the government for the investigation of cases of mutation would be able to find out a large number of cases, was not borne out by facts. Out of 3000 cases only 25 cases were reported to have been of non-tribals who were either,

(1) Merchants having shops in villages,
(2) Koli-Barias,
(3) Chamars, and
(4) Ashram shalas.

Had the Records of Rights been prepared and kept up-to-date, there would not have been any need for creating the RTS team for investigation of the case of violation. The team was no doubt doing useful work in up-dating the Village Forms VII & XII on the basis of papers prepared by them.

As indicated earlier by the officials, the fragments of land-holdings at the family level were not recorded in the Records of Rights maintained by village accountant. It was essential that the fragments of land-holdings cultivated by individual family members were properly recorded and that it should not be treated as a violation of the Rule if such fragments were made at the ground level and practically cultivated by different heirs of the same family.

The Section 73-A for prevention of alienation of land-holdings of the tribals was generally applicable in four talukas of Panchmahals district. These talukas are Jhalod, Santrampur, Limkheda and Devgadh Baria. It was however not applicable in certain areas of ex-Princely States of Devgadh Baria, Sanjeli and certain villages of Santrampur and Limkheda talukas. In all, there were 882 villages where Section 73-A was not applicable because these villages remained unsurveyed and unsettled when this Section was made applicable. These 882 villages made a total of 53 villages from Jhalod, 244 from Limkheda, 399 from Santrampur and 186 from Devgadh Baria. If it was required to apply Section 73-A in certain cases for prevention of alienation of land, it can be done by the government notification No. LND-7961-41509/G.D., dated 4-4-1961.

According to the officials, the action was taken on 3-7-79 by the Government regarding the violation of Section 73-A for the restoration of land alienated earlier, back to the tribals (Revenue Department Ref. No. ADM-1075/113085-2). The findings recorded after the action taken by the RTS team in this matter are as given below.

The investigations by the team revealed that there were 3046 cases of breach of the Section 73-A in this district. Out of these, 2523 cases were disposed off, and there were 757 cases in which the land transferred from the tribals to the non-tribals were ordered to be restored to the original land-holders. Of these cases of restoration, 348 were actually handed over possession of land, while 409 cases were pending actual handing over of the possession on account of standing crops. It was decided that the possession of land in these cases be given to the persons concerned after the completion of harvesting in the month of April.

It was reported also that there was no case of violation of Section 73-A with regard to 1746 cases. The reasons were different in several cases such as:

(a) There were partitions of ancestral property, (b) Lands were cultivated by heirs during the life time of the land-holders, and the partitions approved by him. These were the facts discovered and reported by the RTS teams appointed for the investigation of violation of Section 73-A. From what is reported above, it was clear that the application of the Section 73-A was quite effective and that the changes and alterations in the possession of the lands were fairly restricted.

The officials reported that even after four generations in the life of tribals, one may find cases where division of land had not been made. This was one of the reasons why it was not possible for actual land-holders, namely, the descendants of the head of the household to be able to get Government loan against land in his possession for various purposes. It is, therefore, suggested that the Government take into consideration actual ground position regarding land-holdings rights so that they can give loans and other benefits of schemes to individual land-holders. There were also unauthorised mortgages of land as well as transfers which ultimately deprived the actual land-holder from taking benefit of loans and Government subsidies.

In some cases, the tribal cultivating land of a non-tribal having surplus land (under the Land Ceiling Act) was shown by the tribal concerned in the name of his son. This amounted to violating tenancy legislation. Moreover, ceiling law was ignored by connivance of the tribal himself who was not benefited in any way. In such cases of concealed alienation of land from the tribal to the non-tribal, the former was not only deprived of land under Ceiling Act but also of compensation that is due to him.

In the case of river projects for building dams, canals, etc. constructed in the tribal areas, there were cases of not only deprivation of tribal land but also of non-payment of compensation by the Government. Many problems were faced by the displaced tribals from the construction site of Kadana and Ukai river projects. Those people whose lands were recorded in the name of the grandfather or great-grandfather were entitled to get compensation either in land or in cash fixed as the price of land. But that was not done in certain cases.

The officials generally observed that the recovery of normal land revenue among the tribals did not pose any difficulty. This was because of the fact that terms of land revenue were very nominal. However, difficulties were said to have been experienced by irrigation department for recovery of dues for the use of canal water in tribal areas.

(b) *Assessment by Non-Officials*

The non-officials generally did not have much to say on technical aspects of land reforms. However, some of those who were politically conscious said that the advanced tribals (the *Patelia*) should not be allowed to have more land from other poor tribals who were far behind in progress. They learnt that 172 acres of forest land had been given by the Government to the tribals in recent times. In such cases of recent allotment of land to the tribals, as well as in cases of inherited land, it was recommend that the names of actual cultivators among the tribals be recorded in the Village Forms maintained by the Revenue Department.

Some of the non-officials in Panchmahals were aware that after the merger of the Princely States with the Indian Union, the areas under British occupation were surveyed and settled. In the case of the States of Baroda, survey and settlement of land had already taken place on the British pattern. There was, however, no forest policy, or policy regarding use of land in the forest areas. Most of the Princely States generally prohibited cutting of trees from the forest within the area of their jurisdiction. It was suggested that at least survey of forest land should be made in some of the Princely States and the land revenue settlement be finalised on scientific principles.

In the case of remote tribal areas in general, land revenue was to be recovered in kind since the people were cut off and were backward. They were not able to pay revenue in cash on account of lack of adequate monetisation of their economy. Some of the non-officials expressed satisfaction that the small land-holders were exempted from the payment of land revenue in the times of draught and scarcity. This was really a very enlightened measure which worked as a protection to the tribals from being exploited by money-lender, whose help they had to take in the times of adverse circumstances. In any case, the Government did not take coercive measures for recovery as the normal land revenue itself was very meagre. The question of auctioning land of a tribal by the government for recovery of unpaid revenue, *tagavi* loans, etc. was out of question as great emphasis was given on helping the tribals rather than putting them to any kind of troublesome situation. In some extreme cases and circumstances, however, when the tribal land was put to auction by Land Development Bank on account of loan arrears, it was just not possible to find any other tribal to come forward for buying the land.

Section 73-A of Land Revenue Code has no doubt been useful in preventing alienation of tribal land in this district. There were, however, cases where land transfers took place in concealed manner. The land recorded in the Village Forms did not reflect actual transfers on the spot. The land records at village level were in many ways far from the truth and reality. Obviously this created adverse impact on the morale of the tribals specially in the talukas of Dahod, Jhalod and Chhotaudepur. A survey conducted on land alienation in about six villages of this area showed that the tribals had not benefited much from the implementation of Section 73-A. Some of the non-officials felt that in the last 30 years, quite a large proportion of tribals lost their land in spite of preventive measures of the government. It will be useful, therefore, to make a legal provision on the lines of the Government of Maharashtra to take care of such an unhappy situation. The original provision of the law in Section 73-A did not provide for the restoration of transfer or mortgage of land even among tribals. This need to be remedied as soon as possible. The tribals benefited under the abolition of *Talukdari* and *Inam* lands in this area. Earlier, they were paying the annual rent to these land-holders under the revenue assessment called *Sant* (plough tax). This had greatly changed under the post-independence tenancy legislations as tribals become the owners of occupied land on permanent basis. Wherever, documentary evidences were not available on the previous conditions of rent paid by the tenant, the possession of land was given with the condition of paying occupancy price to the tune of 20-25 times the actual assessment.

Vadodara District

(a) *Assessment by Officials*

The application of Section 73-A was implemented in almost all tribal areas of Vadodara district. The idea was that the alienation of land of the tribals should not be permitted, even if the exchange takes place between two tribals. This is because according to officials, there was a great danger of the elitist or rich tribals exploiting the poor tribals.

The Section 73-A was applied to a total of 409 villages of two tribal talukas. The taluka of Chhotaudepur had 280 villages and Naswadi had 129 villages. There were unauthorised transactions of tribal land to the tune of 7204 cases in this area. On the other hand, the partitions among the heirs during the life time of a tribal land-holder (*Khatedar*) were 4200. The cases of sale of land to the tribals were 2200 and the cases of sale of land to non-tribals were 800. The Deputy Collector of the District took legal steps against 800 cases of land transfers to non-tribals. As a result, 700 non-tribals were compelled to dispose off their land in favour of the tribals. The remaining 100 cases were about sales to public institutions such as Vadodara District Backward Classes Services Society, District and Taluka Panchayat, Cooperative Society and Anand Niketan Ashram and also sales for house sites and shops to non-tribals. The latter were cases of non-agricultural use of land and could not be persuaded in the court of law because of stay orders from the Government.

The results of 700 disposed off cases in favour of tribals can be assessed from the following points.

(i) In 200 cases, the possession of land with the original tribal holder remained intact, but in the village records the land stood in the name of the non-tribals money-lender. In such cases, only possession of land had to be changed in village records in favour of tribals;

(ii) In other 200 cases, orders were issued to restore land to the tribals concerned;

(iii) In 100 cases, the process of handing over possession of land to the tribals concerned was in progress at the time of the study.

The Deputy Collectors' orders regarding these cases had to be executed by the *Mamaldar* (Sub-divisional officer) with his normal departmental staff. In normal situation like this, the Mamaldar's staff was not expected to attend this type of work promptly;

(iv) In the remaining 30 cases, the Collector issued stay orders against the Deputy Collector's orders which amounted to interim stay order preventing tribals concerned in taking possession of the land; and

(v) In the remaining five cases, the High Court issued stay orders, not disposing money-lenders holding tribal land.

The officials remarked that the results of implementation of Section 73-A was that the registration of documents regarding transfer of tribal land had disappeared. But it was replaced by concealed oral transactions leaving little room for taking any case to the court of law. There was also another problem that arose in this connection. As there was no provision for grant of compensation in restoration of alienated land, money-lenders preferred to sell land to another non-occupant tribal in order to recover the amount loaned to the original occupant. There were 10 such cases reported to the Government, the decision on which was pending according to the Government Regulation of 21.1.78. This was because such transactions were falsely reported to be the transactions of land between two tribals.

An interesting case of identifying a particular category of non-tribal as of the scheduled tribe was reported in connection with the problem of the land alienation. The problem of identification referred to the distinction between the people called *Koli* and Rathwa Koli and between Rathwa Koli and Rathwa. According to the Scheduled tribes list of the Constitution of India, only the Rathwas are considered Scheduled tribes and not the people called simply Koli or Rathwa Koli who claim to be tribals. The money-lenders who dealt with land of these people took the stand that they loaned money to the non-tribal Koli or Rathwa Koli of this area and not to Rathwa tribals. There were 40 such cases of dispute between money-lenders and the Koli and Rathwa Koli tribals pending in the Court of Deputy Collector.

The experience of the officials of land alienation in the Songadh taluka was that Section 73-A was not very effective. Parsis and Bhaniya money-lenders advanced loan to the tribals on usurious rates and got the land of the poor tribals alienated in a concealed manner.

The Deputy Collector incharge of LND-5 Units was there to detect cases of unauthorised land alienation and take necessary actions.[2] It was an observation of a Deputy Collector that local social workers supposed to work for the benefit of the tribals had taken up the position of money-lenders by taking tribals into confidence. They were said to be exploiting the tribals rather than helping them. Not only this, some of them did not allow younger selfless social workers to come forward to work among the tribals. Similar was the case of non-tribal office bearers working in the cooperative societies of the tribals. Some of the office bearers dominated the working of cooperative societies and exploited the tribals.

Raising significant issues, the officials said that the land reforms for the benefit of the tribals were no doubt put into operation. However, most of the land reforms remained good in theory. They had not done as much good to the tribals as it was envisaged by the policy-makers in the Government. This was not to say that all land reforms were a waste. Many of them became cumbersome on account of lengthy and complicated administrative procedures and resulted into ineffective implementation, in spite of frantic appeals of the aggrieved parties.

Quite a number of cases regarding land in general never got settled in spite of legal provisions. Procedures to settle cases in dispute, need to be streamlined so that one or two appeals by the *bona fide* party concerned would help in bringing a case to a final decision. It seems necessary that social institutions with technical knowhow and legal knowledge come forward to give guidance to tribals in this matter and help establish their rights over land and secure final possession. There was also another side of protecting the tribals from getting into the clutches of money-lenders who tempted the tribals to borrow money during Holi festival and ceremonial functions.

The money-lenders were not the only people who exploited the tribals. The village *Talatis* who were maintaining Village Form and other land records were also partly responsible for creating problems for the tribals. Some officials themselves felt it would be useful to appoint an educated tribal as a village *Talati*. Moreover, the practice of appointing *Talati*-cum-Secretary for statutory village Panchayat in tribal areas need not be continued. It was said that *Talatis* were found engaged in political activities of the President of Village Panchayat. It was felt essential that they work only for the revenue department as in olden times. In many cases, the complaints were made that the transfer of a "non-cooperative" *Talati* was done at the instance of the President of the Panchayat, although formal orders were to be issued by the District Development Officer. The records of *Talati* were kept physically in the official centre called *Seza* village which is his headquarters from where he operates in the neighbouring villages, the limits of which are decided by the Government.

Some times, in spite of Section 73-A, the restoration of alienated land remains on paper. In one case, even after the restoration order, the possession remained with the non-tribal purchaser of the land. The restoration orders were executed by *Mamlatdar,* but it would be appropriate if this was done by the Deputy Collector looking after LND-5 operations.

There were cases of legal benefits received by the tribals on account of tenancy legislation and other land reforms. In one village, four tribals were able to get some land under the tenancy law, and 22 under *Jagirdari* abolition law. In another village 42 persons received land under tenancy law. In still another illustration reported by the officials, the actual area of land received by the tribals was significant. Here, 19 tribals got about 45 hectares of land under Jagir Abolition Act, and 4 tribals got 6 hectares, 19 are under the Tenancy Act. Still in another village, 27 tribals got occupancy right over 105 hectares, 38 are and 92 sq.m. due to Jagirdari Abolition Act. And, other 13 tribals got 10 hectares, 72 are and 45 sq.m. under Tenancy Act.

(b) *Assessment by Non-Officials*

Some of the non-officials from Vadodara, who provided information were highly educated persons engaged in legal and other upper class occupations. One of the non-officials mentioned that Section 73-A was treated in some Talukas of the district as restricted tenure, viz. in the Talukas of Chhotaudepur, Naswadi, and Tilakwada part areas. These areas form part of partially excluded areas under the Act of 1935. Under the constitutional provisions, they became scheduled areas in 1950 and the Section 73-A became applicable to them in 1961 by government regulation. The actual implementation of the Section 73-A became operative after 1965.

Somewhere before the above period of time, about 200 to 300 cases of unauthorised transactions violating the provisions of the Act had already taken place. Of these, about 50 to 60 cases of alienation were declared null and void by the Government. About 50 per cent of these transactions were considered *bona fide* as between the members of Scheduled Tribes and Scheduled Castes or between Scheduled Tribes themselves. The political and social workers moved the Government for regularising all such transactions. These efforts were not helpful in improving socio-economic conditions of the tribals concerned. For instance: (i) socially, they created constant illfeeling among the parties involved in the transactions; (ii) economically, expenditure on litigations increased and become prohibitive; (iii) agriculture production from disputed land decreased; and above all these, (iv) violence and physical attacks between contending parties increased.

The prevention of fragmentation and consolidation Act of 1947 also led to similar untoward and undesirable conflicts between parties concerned. Eventhough, entries of transfers in land records were certified by revenue officers, the *Talati* and the *Mamlatdar* concerned took certain measures which created tension among the people.

Referring to the Bombay Tenancy Act of 1948 with special reference to Section 32-M, 32-PP, 32-PPP, 43 and 70(b), read with Sections 4, one of the knowledgeable non-officials reported following limitations and serious defects involved in its implementation:

(i) In the beginning, tenants were not conscious of rights bestowed upon them by the Act;
(ii) Social pressure for illegal surrender of land for unauthorised transfer with the help of Talatis and Revenue Officers became common;
(iii) Mamlatdar, Deputy Mamlatdar and Deputy Collector functioning as Tenancy Courts trying tenancy cases were under great influence of cliques of the landlords; and
(iv) In the Village Form VI showing actual possession of the tenant, the land was surrendered by a tribal to the landlord.

The impact of these hard realities is presented in the following points:

(a) Unauthorised changes in mutations in VF VI and VII–XII took place between 1950 and 1956;

(b) There were a number of fictitious surrenders of land by the ignorant tribals who were tenants before;

(c) There were cases of wrong or incorrect decisions given by the tenancy courts either deliberately or by connivance of facts;

(d) A number of gullible tenants made fake surrenders of surplus land in favour of their landlords; and

(e) In spite of lawful purchase under Section 32-G, certain land-holdings were sold to others leading to violations of restrictions of Section 43.

Under these circumstances, the Nationalised Banks, Co-operative Banks or cooperative societies were reluctant to advance money to the tribals. These financial institutions were dominated and managed by the local influential persons. The poor tribal tenants were therefore not able to get timely financial assistance from these agencies. It created adverse impact on the development of agriculture by those tribals who become land-holders under tenancy legislation. They had little means to use improved methods and inputs for increasing their agricultural income. The land-holding granted to the tenants were not economically viable. The schemes of Small Farmers' Development Agency (SFDA) organised by the State Government for benefiting marginal and small land-holders could not help as these schemes were left in the hands of a few dominant persons, the age old exploiters of these people. Even the Government staff entrusted with the work of implementing the well-thought out programme were not free from negative attitude and bias against the capability of the tribals to take advantage of this programme.

In the opinion of the non-officials tenancy legislation had no doubt benefited a number of tribals. However, most of these lands were mortgaged to other parties, and they thus become landless again. In the Naswadi taluka for instance, 75 per cent of the tribal tenants were supposed to have lost their land in this manner. The worst episode had been that they had to mortgage land for paltry amount of money borrowed from prospective money-lenders. Moreover, the programme of restoration of agricultural land to the tribals should have been taken up starting from cases of alienation which had taken place 15 years ago. All such transactions should be declared unauthorised with the introduction of a collective appeal to put an end to this shady deal of land alienation.

It was a general practice that the caste disputes of tribals were settled in the open court under the leadership of traditional leaders. It helped a great deal in avoiding expenditure in taking cases to the Statutory Courts. In the village of Zaria in this district, young social workers helped the tribals in settling the land disputes with non-tribal money-lenders through informal negotiations and compromise. Most of the tribals would certainly prefer such methods so that they may not have to incur debt for expenditure in taking the cases to the court of law.

The actual alienation of tribal land took place in various ways and under different circumstances. One of the major reasons of land alienation was connected with the debts that a tribal had to incur for meeting minimum requirement of his food and other daily necessities during lean months of the year. This is the most dangerous time when he falls in to the hands of the money-lenders who prefer to charge a special type of interest called *Hatiu Vyaj*. The term *Hatiu Vyaj* means that a borrower has to pay the interest every week when he returns after selling minor forest produce in the weekly market called *Hat*. Under normal circumstances, if the burden of his family responsibilities was not very high, a person was able to pay a part of this type of interest every week to the money-lender. More often than not, there was accumulation of this kind of interest alongwith the original amount that a person borrowed from a money-lender. The result obviously was that he remained perpetually in debt and was compelled to mortagage his land to a money-lender.

One of the leading social workers reported that ignorance of the local tribals was so great in some parts of Vadodara district, that they came to know about the advantages of Section 73-A of 1961, after six years in 1967. When people came to know about the provisions of this Section, applications in thousands were made in 1969 for restoration of their land alienated to non-tribals. This led to a kind of mass agitation by the tribals to capture their rights to become land holders. In 1970 the cases were taken up in judiciary courts, and lands were ordered to be restored to them but the aggrieved persons brought stay orders and prevented restoration of land. The problem of restoring land to a number of tribals in these areas could have been solved if the jurisdiction of the Civil Courts was barred in respect of cases under Section 73-A. It was estimated that 12 lakhs acres of land could have easily gone to the sons of the soil had such a change taken place in time.

There was the practice of forced labour in vogue in olden times in the Princely States of Gujarat. According to this custom, every land-holder had to send one person from the family to provide free labour to the state as and when required. This was one of the reasons, why land-holders, whether tribals or non-tribals preferred to keep the land of the family in the name of one person. In practice, the land was divided between several brothers or male members of the family. This meant that a family had to spare only one person and not all male members who established their families and cultivated separate plots of land of their ancestors. Generally, such plots of land cultivated by the members of a joint family were more or less fragments not bigger than two acres. The non-officials felt that if the government desired to achieve the goal of consolidation of land-holdings under conditions of this kind, they should be encouraged voluntarily, rather than be implemented through legislative measures.

Bharuch District

(a) *Assessment by Officials*

The problem of land alienation in Bharuch District was related to social and economical conditions of the tribals in the area. Section 73-A of Bombay Land Revenue Code was applicable in 5 *Talukas* in this district.

Under tenancy legislation, the tribal tenants were made deemed purchasers on payment of purchase price which was fixed upto 80 multiples of assessment. This, however, was actually not thought of a very heavy purchase price. However, a poorer tribal was not in a position to pay such a purchase price as a result of which he had to borrow money from the landlord whose very land he cultivated for a number of years as a tenant. He, therefore, mortgaged his original acquired land to this money-lender without any documentary records so that he was able to pay the occupancy price. Thus the tenancy legislation lended many of the poorer and ignorant tribals into vicious circle of this type. Not only the tribal of this kind lost the actual possession of the land, but was forced again to work as a tenant in disguised form for the original landlord from whom he wanted to be free. Instead, he continued to borrow money for purchase of the very land given to him as tenant or for other social purposes as before.

There were also several cases where the tribal preferred to mortgage land to his relatives without written documents. In such cases, if the land was virtually cultivated by the relatives concerned as tenants, the purchase price to be paid to the original land-holder was not at hand. So, it became necessary for the person concerned to approach other relatives and money-lenders for borrowing money. In any case, the result was that land received by a tribal on account of tenancy legislation did not remain with him although on record he remains a tenant purchaser.

The officials informed that as per rules, the Deputy Collector passes order to restore possession to a tribal in case of unauthorised alienation to a non-tribal under Section 73-A of Bombay Land Revenue Code. Thereafter he issues notice under Section 202 of Land Revenue Code to the alience to vacate the land within a period of one month. During this period the alience gets a stay order from the court. It is during this period that the non-tribal money-lender who holds the land, goes to the court and gets stay order. Lawyers help these influential people in this matter. A situation such as this leads to serious doubts in the mind of a tribal concerned about any possibility what-so-ever of becoming the tenant-purchaser of the land under this cultivation.

It is quite natural that in such cases, delayed processing of transfer of ownership from the non-tribal to the tribal causes a lot of frustration among the poor tribals. Such a delay can be overcome by handing over the possession of the land to a tribal in person under the supervision of a Revenue Officer concerned so that it may not leave any room for stay received by the alience.

It is, therefore, proposed to insert a new Section 73-AA[3] barring Jurisdiction of the Civil Court in this matter so that tribals can get immediate possession of previously alienated land. This measure can inspire confidence in the minds of the tribals in amelioratory schemes of the Government. Restoration of alienated land to original tribal cultivator without interference of the civil courts shall be of great help in allowing immediate possession of land to be given. If necessary, special legal provision should be made in this regard. The Government measures to help the tribals in various ways to become land owners will work, if it is possible to take concrete steps to remove difficulties coming in the way of getting the land transferred legally to the tribals.

Notwithstanding solutions to the above problems, it must be

admitted that the tenancy legislation has made a considerable impact on the social and economical life of the tribals towards their betterment. Of.course the application of ceiling law has not helped much because the land in general is scarce. It may bc useful to suggest that the orders under tenancy or any other law, giving occupancy rights to tribal tenants, should be sent immediately to the Village Officer called *Talati*. The *Talati* should make necessary arrangements for entry of transfer of land in the name of the tribals in the Village Forms and return the same to the concerned parties for confirmation. The certificate copies of VF-VII and XII should be specially printed for indicating: (i) date of application, (ii) fees charged, and (iii) date of delivery. Since there is a continuous demand of copies of VF VII and XII by the tribals ever since 1955, arrangements should be made to give concessions to the tribals for purchasing these documents.

In principle, the Section 73-A gives protection to a tribal land-holder from transferring his land under hard circumstances to non-tribals greedy of more lands. Unfortunately it led to internal transfer of about 95 per cent of land from one tribal to another tribal, who may work as a go-between, between the tribal and money-lender who makes money available under concealed alienation. The ambiguous order of no transfer of tribal land to others provided in Section 73-A can be a source of indirect exploitation of poor tribals because there is no provision for post-facto regularisation of land transferred between tribals themselves.

In this district of Bharuch as in others, Section 73-A has come in the way of genuine tribal tenants cultivating lands of big tribal land-holders. Introduction of notification applying Section 73-A to tribal areas of ex-Princely States, has come in the way of the right of small tribal tenants against large tribal land-holders who leased their lands to the former. The tenancy of small tribal tenants became null and void under Section 73-A and the land in their possession were to be restored to original large tribal holders. Thus large tribal holders were benefited.

In the case of the problem of consolidation of land-holdings, the officers implementing the scheme had not to work under the supervision of the Collector. Many transactions, in some villages, of illegal nature were reportedly found in contravention of the prevention of fragmentation and consolidation Act. In the new VF VII–XII prepared after the so called consolidation, illegal occupants of land were shown in the village records. Another draw-back in the implementation of the Consolidation Act was that a number of smaller fragments of land had taken place as a result of which the very purpose of this programme was defeated.

Detections of breaches of new tenure land of Section 73-A, Tenure Abolition Acts, Prevention of Fragmentation and Consolidation Act, were being made by the Officer of the rank of a Deputy Collectors. In special cases they work under the name of LND-5 programme. The operations of this programme were conducted in five talukas of Bharuch district. This programme was implemented initially in only two talukas, viz. Sagbara and Dediapada. Similar cases of detection of breach of Section 73-A in remaining talukas viz. Nandod, Jhagadia and Valia were conducted by the Assistant Collector of Rajpipla.[4]

The results of detection of land alienation among the tribals under LND-5 operations in three talukas viz. Sagbara, Dediapada and Valia may be presented below: This refers to the cases of violation of Section 73-A as reported during 1977-78.

Violation of 73-A	Non-transfer & intervention	Breach of land-holdings
1677 cases	224 cases	57 cases

There were also cases of breaches regarding conditions under which land was purchased. They were as follows:

Mortgaged or leased/ purchased land to others	Concealed transaction by violation of 73-A
311 cases	5 cases

The number of cases leading to various complications on account of violation of Section 73-A are presented below indicating the number of cases and the total size of the land involved in each category.

(1) Cases of breaches detected so far	4050
(2) Cases disposed off	1863

(3) Orders issued for restoration of land 1111
(4) Actual possession given to tribals 967

Actual coverage of land was 2933 acres and 38 gunthas. The remaining cases which had to be settled under Government orders were as follows:

(1) Stay order cases referred to Supreme Court 114
(2) The cases under process of giving possession of land by Standing Orders 119

It will be useful here to refer to the work of detection of illegal alienation by the LND team. The team was reported to have examined 9553 Village Forms VII and XII in order to scrutinise validity of entries of land-holders and to detect breaches committed, if any.

In the Sagbara taluka, 27 villages were submerged in the construction of Ukai reservoir. The displaced villagers purchased land in other villages of the same taluka, with the help of money received as compensation. All these displaced persons were the tribals and therefore the breach of 73-A, if any, involved in the transfer of land for the rehabilitation of these people was to be condoned. Section 73-A was misused in the Sagbara taluka, especially in Selamba village which was a local marketing centre of the taluka. The Marwadi and Khandeshi traders and the Patidars from Nandod in this district as well as some parts of Surat went to this village and purchased the land of the tribals on cheaper rate. When tenancy legislation was made applicable, the landlords brought a stay order from the Supreme Court in 1972 in order to protect their rights over the land. Under these circumstances, the tribal tenants were not able to get the possession of land in spite of favourable tenancy legislation on their side.

The Sagbara-Mehwasi Estate Abolition Act of 1962 was earlier under operation. The notification regarding prevention of alienation of land under Section 73-A was dated 4-4-1961. This raised a question as to whether the transaction of land between different parties could be considered valid, if they were implemented between these two points of time. In any case, the problem of tribal land-holders became complex after they became the occupants of the land. They immediately faced the problem of how to cultivate land with meagre resources at their disposal. The needs of agricultural implements, inputs, etc. can be not through money-lenders to whom land had to be mortgaged on short or long term basis. The final solution was to succumb to concealed alienation.

(b) *Assessment by Non-Officials*

The point of view of the non-officials regarding the alienation of tribal land vary from person to person. According to one opinion, a large amount of tribal land in Bharuch district continued to remain with non-tribals who belong to higher castes and economic class status in society. However, when the tribals were asked about the ownership of land, they said that "it was in their occupation". No amount of land legislation in favour of the tribals can be of much use under these doubtful circumstances. It was reported that in some talukas of this district 50 to 60 per cent of tribal land was mortgaged to non-tribals. The tribals preferred to continue to remain under this type of relationship with the landlords in order to see that their day to day economic needs were met. Another opinion was that the tribal land had been acquired illegally by the non-tribals on account of ignorance of the tribals. It was also believed that the tribal feel absolutely incapable of going through legal formalities either for establishing their right over land or for getting legal possession of the same by going from court to court. As reported by some of the officials, the landlords got stay orders on transfer of land to the tribals and thus prevented implementation of Section 73-A.

According to non-officials, there was a considerable amount of corruption practiced by village level Government servants who are appointed to deal with such cases in favour of tribals. The tribals felt that the Government should make on the spot, the studies of cases of violation of Section 73-A and give instant decision in order to protect their rights. It is useless to involve poorer tribals in the long process of legal correspondence and other measures in order to remove their grievances.

It was also believed that in spite of Section 73-A, the Courts were made to favour interested parties, doing more injustice to poorer tribals. In more than 70 per cent of the cases of land alienation, the transactions had taken place either between tribals and tribals or between tribals and non-tribals. The Section 73-A was virtually not operative in the district, specially when both the parties become willing partners in illegal transfers leading to land alienation.

The Government had made a provision of enabling the alienation of land of a tribal to another tribal by payment of Rs. 75 per acre and with the permission of the Deputy Collector. Even this accommodative measure suited to the tribals was misused and quite a number of cases of impersonation of non-tribals passing as tribals were reported in the transfer of tribal land. This facility of the Government misused by unscrupulous persons was withdrawn from the powers of the Deputy Collector in 1977. The Government, took over these powers for effecting transfer of land in special cases and under special circumstances.

Whenever the Deputy Collector took measures to make Section 73-A applicable in some cases of land alienation, the aggrieved party concerned approach District Collector for revision of the order and got a stay order. For instance, a case was duly heard by the Collector, and he passed the necessary orders based on his own judgement. When the orders of the Collector went against the aggrieved non-tribal landlord, the case was sent for revision to the Special Secretary in-charge of the land disputes. The orders passed by this high official were also subject to appeal by the aggrieved party, who went to the Civil Court. The Civil Court granted injection against the orders of the Special Secretary and prohibited any party to enter the land under dispute. Since the possession of the land was with the transferee, the injection order of the Court became absolute until the final hearing was given by the Court. In the written statement the transferee made the plea that he was the tenant of the land and so the matter was referred to the Tenancy Court under Section 85-A of Tenancy Act.

At the end of all these legal wranglings and procedures of the Court, the order was passed in favour of the tribal land-holder. Then again the matter went to the Court of the Mamlatdar for actual handing over of the possession of the land under dispute. This led to another interesting complication as the transferee with his economic and political powers put an obstacle in effecting the actual handing over of the possession of the land to the tribal concerned. Moreover, unfortunately for the tribal, the Government passed orders not to hand over the possession of land to the legally established owner when the crops were standing in the field. Thus from the very beginning of putting up the claim over the land under tenancy legislation, until he was able to get the possession of the land, in practice, a tribal had to wait and wait, for years in order to possess the land of which he was ones the owner tenant.

A few suggestions made both by the officials and the non-officials are presented in the following points in a generalised form.

(i) Government orders no doubt said that the possession of land should not be given to a tribal tenant with standing crops in the field cultivated by the landlord. But this order was misused by the landlord who continued to raise new crops immediately after harvesting the previous one. Naturally this came in the way of handling over the possession of the land, almost indefinitely, to the rightful tribal tenant. It calls for corrective measures by the government;

(ii) Like the cases regarding tenancy, those falling under the per-view of Section 73-A should be also excluded from the jurisdiction of the Civil Court so that the government order or restoring the land to the tribal concerned can be executed without delay;

(iii) It is necessary to provide free legal aid to a tribal fighting in the court for restoration of the alienated land to him because many a times such cases continue to extend over a long period of time, and eventually become costly; and

(iv) Government should provide alternative arrangements for credit and loan to a needy tribal so that there is no room for him to approach a money-lender who may otherwise contrive to get his land mortgaged and alienated in a concealed manner.

Surat District

(a) *Assessment by Officials*

The tribals in some villages of tribal talukas in Surat District became deemed purchasers of lands cultivated by them as tenants. The lands stood in the names of Parsi and Bhaiya landlords. The officials reported that in one village, there were 386 tribal and 21 non-tribal occupants. About 91 tribals purchased the land under tenancy law a total of 111 hect., 26 are and 88 sq. meters of land. Under the Ceiling law, 25 tribals were allotted 23 hect., 23 are and 92 sq. meters of land. Two tribals got 0 hect., 89 are and 6 sq. meters of land under Inferior

Village Servants Act (Watan Abolition Act). Another two tribals got 0 hect., 87 are and 1 sq. meter of land under Bombay Merged Territories Act 1955.

Regarding the effect of Section 73-A there have not been substantial cases of violations in this district. Actually, wherever these cases were traced, they were of the period prior to 1961. The alienation of land with regard to such cases had taken place during the period of the ex-Princely State of Baroda.

According to the tribal custom, the land was registered in the name of the eldest male member of the family and, therefore, the names of other male heirs were not entered in the record of rights even though all the adult members were in actual possession of their share used for maintenance of their family. This meant that the record of rights as maintained by the village *Talati* did not reflect the ground position of actual possession of land. It was not even possible to make this type of precise records possible on account of the prevailing traditions and custom among the tribals to keep the ancestral land under the name of an elder person. The RTS teams who visited tribal areas to check up records of rights, took the heirs of the same family cultivating plots of land as tenants. The cases of this type had to be dropped by the Tenancy Courts.

The work of the RTS team meant to detect violation of tenancy law in the talukas of Vyara and Songadh remained in arrears. This was because on conferment of the occupancy rights to tenants, the entries in VF VI were not done as it should have been made. This was not done in many cases. But where entries in the village record VF VI were made, they were not incorporated in VF VII and XII. It may also be noted that there were no heirship cases unrecorded as was found in other districts. In general, an individual tribal was not conscious of his right over land and, therefore, he did not approach the village *Talati* for recording his name in village form.

The Government problem of recovery of land revenue from the tribals was not so serious as the problem of recovery of other dues, specially the instalments of occupancy price of the land sold to the tribal under the tenancy and ceiling laws.

(b) *Assessment by Non-Officials*

According to non-officials in Surat district, the concealed land alienation was reported to have taken place in certain tribal areas.

There were at least 5 per cent of such cases of tribal lands found in some villages. Generally, the poor tribal who received marginal land-holdings preferred to mortgage his land to a non-tribal. But he did not get agreement signed. A well-to-do tribal allowed the mortgage to be put on the paper, but kept it secret. In some cases, debts were written off if large part of it was paid by the end of a five year period. In other cases, the debts persisted and the stamp paper agreement kept secret was renewed every five year. The land, however, remained with the original tribal land-holder and was allowed by the money-lender to cultivate on his behalf. Sometimes the land was given for cultivation to another landless tribal labourer. In general, the tribal land situation in the district was probably as bad as elsewhere, because here also the mortgage or transfer of land to non-tribals did not appear in the record of rights.

The non-officials reported that the programme of consolidation of land-holdings in the tribal areas of Surat District had not taken place although the law existed. There was an urgent need of putting together scattered pieces of land owned by a person for better cultivation. Consolidation would also help in putting together the plots of land received under tenancy legislation. This is not to say that the consolidation of land-holdings had not been put on paper in all the villages of the district. It is however, regrettable to note that in practice, the owners of plots of land scattered in a village continued to cultivate them separately, and thus made a mockery of the consolidation law in practice.

Valsad District

(a) *Assessment by Officials*

Wherever survey and settlement of land was not made in this district, the Section 73-A was applied for restricting sale of land to non-tribals. It required advance sanction of the Collector of the District. Section 79-A made it possible to effect summary eviction of unauthorised non-tribal occupants of tribal lands. A special bill for restoration of tribal land transferred to money-lenders for loans advanced by them to tribals was under the consideration of the Government. So far as the problem of termination of tenancy of a tribal occupant by the landlords for personal cultivation was concerned, it is strictly prohibited under the tenancy legislation.

There are some talukas in this district where the Section 73-A was not applicable. Lands obtained by tribal tenants as deemed purchasers under the Tenancy Act were alienated to non-tribals or to tribals simply because of emergent necessity of money required by the tribals. Thus the situation gave ample scope for violation of the conditions of restricted land tenure under tenancy legislation. There were cases of land granted under the Patel Watan Abolition Act and Inam Service Abolition Act. Such lands were also alienated because the tribals were not able to pay instalments of fixed occupancy price. This also led to violation of tenancy legislation.

The tribal land-holdings in Valsad district generally vary from the minimum of 20 guanths to 3 to 4 acres. However, the standard area of economic land-holding is considered to be 20 guanths *kyari* land and 2 acres of irrigated land. Any piece of land less than this standard land area was considered a fragment for the purpose of agriculture. Most of these fragments were notified by the Government and recorded as such under the law.

Whenever alienation of land took place, it was this kind of fragment which was mortgaged, sold or given on lease to non-tribal by the tribal. It was obvious that the cases of this kind led to violation of Prevention of Fragmentation and Consolidation of Land-holdings Act. The land granted under the Section 32-G (sale) were also subject to alienation. The restoration of this kind of alienated land was possible under Section 84-C failing which the lands were forfeited by the Government.

Taking an over-view of the situation, it was reported that the tribals with less than 2 acres of land-holdings were not materially benefited by tenancy legislation. The reasons of this are as follows: (a) all lands obtained under the Tenancy Act were not cultivated; (b) those lands which were not cultivated were leased to grass merchants and dealers from whom the tribal got lump-sum amount of money every year in advance. This led to exploitation of tribals as the amount given to him as advance was meagre; (c) on account of very small holdings, the tribals were not able to undertake agricultural improvements by using better seeds, pesticides, etc. They were also handicapped because many of them did not possess bullocks to plough the land; (d) they found it difficult to pay the purchase price of land even by instalments on account of poverty; (e) they were unable to repay instalments of loan obtained through Land Development Bank, Government Tagavi, etc. This led to their disqualification to get further credit from other sources also.

The officials informed that under the Ceiling Act, 14,000 acres of surplus lands were available mostly in three talukas, viz. Pardi, Umbergaon and Dharampur. This lands were allotted to tribals only for occupancy. Out of these lands, the tribals came to be in possession of nearly 70 per cent of the land. This means that about 30 per cent of land were alienated to non-tribals. Those tribals who alienated the land were not able to pay instalments of purchase price on the basis of which they could become occupants. They were also not able to pay loans and Tagavi taken from the Government. The situations like this would not have taken place if these tribals were in occupation of the land allotted to them by the Government.

Regarding the status and position of details in the record of rights, the lands in Dharampur taluka were reported to be in the name of the ancestors of tribals who died 30 to 40 years ago. This made the record of rights outdated. Secondly the land-holdings remained in the joint name of successors of a person after his death. In practice, the land was already partitioned among the adult male members or the heirs for self-cultivation. The cultivation of land was done by the different descendants on parcels of land of the ancestors concerned. This practice continued to be the same as was found during the time of the Dharampur princely state. It was during this period that a *Khatedar* (land-holder) was called upon by the State or Darbar to render free labour as and when required. In order to lessen the burden of free labour on the members of the family of the *Khatedar*, the old practice of keeping land in the name of the ancestors became helpful. This was fine as far as it went in the olden times, but after Independence, the heirs of deceased *Khatedar* found it difficult to get their names recorded in the record of rights. The local *Talati* who maintain this record did not take sufficient interest in removing the hardships experienced by the tribals in getting possession of the land inherited by them. Some of the reasons of this kind of negligence on the part of *Talati* were: (i) most of the *Talatis* lived at the taluka headquarters in the town of Dharampur; (ii) the villages were isolated in the interior hill areas and so there was no easy access to them; (iii) most of the tribal families lived in dispersed hutments making it difficult for a person to contact every household; and (iv) there was reported corruption and lethergy among local officers, which contributed to the difficulties of tribals.

The tribals found it difficult to stick to their land that was sloppy, stony and poor. This kind of unfertile land required to be properly levelled and enriched without which it was difficult to convert it in to *kyari* land. The programme of soil conservation was therefore a very important activity which the Government encouraged with the help of the enlightened tribals. There was already a programme of *kyari* bunding under the block development activities and funds were easily available for this purpose. However, the general carelessness of the tribals was said to be responsible for lack of constant efforts to improve land and try agricultural inputs.

Valsad taluka had 95 villages suffering from a large number of cases of violation of Section 73-A against alienation of tribal land. There were a total of 1129 cases of such violations in this taluka. One of the Deputy Collectors, therefore suggested that: (i) Section 73-A should be made applicable to the land held by the tribal irrespective of whether the land was surveyed or not, and (ii) land should be forfeited to the Government, if and when alienation took place on account of the personal problems and ignorance of a tribal. It was felt necessary, therefore, to make a special provision in the Act for this purpose.

In one of the talukas of Valsad district, quite a number of cases of breaches of Section 43 of Tenancy Act and 50 cases of breaches of new tenure lands (wastelands granted on new tenure) were reported. The violation of 73-A was also reported in 975 cases among the tribals of which 23 cases pertained to non-tribals. In all 41 cases of lands alienated to non-tribals were dealt with under Sections 73-A and 202. In all, 38 cases were actually heard under the above two sections; and out of them 18 persons refused to take back the land even when offered free of cost. The refusal was reported to be on account of honesty of the poor tribals who respected above all, the obligations of non-tribal land-holders. There was no provision to help the tenants of this kind in the practice of law. In the remaining 20 cases, orders were issued for restoration of land to original tribal occupants or to their heirs. In these cases, further action was stayed on account of decisions pending in the High Court.

In last three cases out of the 41 cases, stay order was granted in one case by the High Court, while in other two cases, the Collector had regularised sales in favour of the non-tribal occupants.

In the Umbergaon taluka of Valsad district, the lands available to the landless tribal labourers were of two kinds: (a) surplus lands available under the ceiling Act; (b) lands relinquished under Section

74 LRC by landlords on payment of ex-gratia amount of Rs. 500 per acre and charging occupancy price equal to 200 times the assessment of land revenue from the tribals. This amounted to Rs. 80 to 100 per acre by incurring loss of Rs. 400 per acre. In the first category, the surplus land from the ceiling law, available to tribals amounted to 7103 acres, and in the second category 2141 acres of land was relinquished by landlords which benefited 1380 tribal and scheduled caste households.

Most of the tribals, who became occupants of the land held by their landlords, benefited on account of tenancy legislation. Among these landlords who surrendered land were Parsis, Jambu Brahmins, Jain Baniyas and Anavil Desais.

The law of prevention of fragmentation of land-holdings does not apply to the fragments held by tenants on 1.4.57. But the cultivation of fragments is uneconomical and not protective. Therefore, those tribals who became occupants of such fragments had to leave their plots unattended, in order to cultivate the lands of the landlords from whom they can earn livelihood. On the other hand, it was convenient for them to give their fragments for cultivation to adjacent tribal land-holders. About 50 to 60 per cent of lands of the tribals were cultivated by those who were not the land-holders. In reality, the produce of such fragments were enjoyed by the persons who were in possession of these fragments. The original land-holders remained without substantive advantage of the fragments. The tribals who had more than 2 acres of land were really the beneficiaries of produce of their land.

In Umbergaon taluka, the number of tenants on whom occupancy rights were conferred were 19423, holding an area of 46426 acres of land.

The Dubla tribals named *Halpatis* by Mahatma Gandhi, live in Umbergaon Taluka alongwith Warli and Dhodia tribes. Elsewhere, the Dublas were the least benefited of the tribals from various advantageous of land reforms and development schemes after independence. However, in this taluka, they have become land-holders because of tenancy legislation and land ceiling law. In other talukas of this district, and parts of Surat District, they are landless labourers. One of the drawbacks coming in the way of development of Dublas was said to be their lethargic habits. In comparison to them, the Dhodia and Warli, have done better in the field of education and development. Dhodia and Warli tribals were found to be industrious and therefore, able to retain their precious land-holdings.

As reported by the officials, until 1978, the Land Development Bank was advancing loans to these tribals for the payment of occupancy price of land allotted to them. But because of the mounting arrears of repayment of installments, the bank stopped this facilities to the tribals. In the place of the Land Development Bank, the Government have now come into the picture and are giving Tagavi loans in order to help the tribals for payment of occupancy price of the land given to them.

When the money was advanced to the tribals for payment of occupancy price by the Land Development Bank, the rate of interest was 11 per cent, of which 5 per cent was paid by the Government under the Tribal Area Sub-Plan. This was, of course a facility given to those persons who could pay instalments of the loans regularly. Those who were the defaulters were not advanced loans by Government financial institutions. The conditions laid by the L.D.B. for advancing loans in order to pay occupancy price by the tribals were that the land cannot be transferred, leased, gifted or subject to agreement for transfer. The above conditions were, however, relaxed in favour of cooperative societies from which a person may like to take more loans against land in his occupation. In spite of a number of ameliorative measures taken by the Government, there were many cases of concealed alienations as well as concealed tenancies in which a large number of poorer tribals were involved.

(b) *Assessment by Non-Officials*

There were a few non-officials who came forward to give information on the subject of land in relation to tribals of Valsad district. They said that tenancy legislation had not helped tribals in a material sense. Tribals did not take trouble to use better management methods and inputs for the purpose of improved agriculture. They were happy and contended by earning their livelihood from the grass grown in the fields. Even for this purpose, they became dependent on grass merchants who took away grass from them at a very cheap rate. It was said to be merely a waste on the part of the Government to have given the land to tribals under the Tenancy Legislation and Ceiling Act.

In general, the money-lenders gave loans to these people and took away the benefit of whatever crops and grass that the tribals grew on their land. The village level workers were aware of such cases. However, they did not take any action to help the poor tribals. In brief, the name of the tribal was on the record of rights, but the full advantage of the produce of the land was reaped by non-tribals. Thus the Section 73-A was not of much avail even though it was implemented on paper. The money-lenders recently began to advance loans to the tribals not on land, but on the crops cultivated by them. This kind of shift of money-lending from land to the crops made most land reforms redundant. In reality, Section 73-A did not serve any purpose in giving protection to the tribals against concealed land alienation.

In the Dharampur taluka referred to earlier, Kukna tribals were the main land-holders. But that was not the case in Umbergaon taluka where most of the tribals got occupancy rights on land under the tenancy legislation. Considerable small holdings were over a period of time reduced to small fragments which were by no means economical.

With a little bit of awakening, land hunger in this taluka has increased. The well-to-do Dhodias and Dubla Halpatis have began to go in for agriculture. This tendency of earning livelihood from agriculture was found to be the least among the Warli tribals. The Warli's were habituated to heavy drinking which did not allow savings and capital formation at house-hold level. Similarly there were backward Halpatis who alongwith Warlis were landless labourers, and were subject to exploitations by the money-lenders.

The administrative procedures of implementing land reforms and management of the land system in this area was found to be difficult for tribal to understand. Management of land was highly cumbersome and had to be replaced by simple and flexible administrative procedures for dealing with illiterate tribals. Whenever an illiterate tribal asks for help from the office of the Mamlatdar, he requires to be assisted by knowledgeable person of his own group. Otherwise he is likely to be misled and ultimately exploited by those who pretend to help him.

We may conclude by giving an over all view of the land problem in Dharampur taluka. There were 77 villages under the preview of this taluka, out of which 27 went to the State of Maharashtra, after the bifurcation of the Bilingual Bombay State. This 27 villages were mainly forest areas formerly dominated by Parsi land-lords. One of the reported reasons why these 27 forest rich villages were allowed to go to the State of Maharashtra was that they were dominated by the Communist workers and the State of Gujarat did not show much interest in retaining them. The present group of 50 villages of this taluka had very poor soil and nothing grew except gram and rice. This was one of the reasons why a number of tribals lived in the village of Umbergaon and daily commuted to rich villages located in the State of Maharashtra for work and livelihood.

Dangs District

(a) *Assessment by Officials*

In the district of Dangs, the problem of application of Land Reforms such as, tenancy legislation, abolition of land-holdings, ceiling on land-holdings etc. is not relevant. The first survey of land under cultivation was taken up by the Government of Gujarat in the Dangs forests only between 1957-64. The settlement had not been undertaken. The occupancy rights of most of the Dangis were confirmed in all except four villages. The land revenue collected at present is called *Autbandhi*, which is a continuation of the old practice of plough tax amounting to Rs. 6.50 per plough. It is important to note that Section 73-A is applicable with regard to land alienation in the district. The Tenancy legislation is applied in the two villages belonging to ex-Vadodara State and the tenants there were declared as deemed purchasers of the land which they were cultivating before. The land revenue called *Autbandhi* in Dangs area is generally collected from the farmers before the Holi festival in the month of March every year. Those who had one plough and two bullocks, had to pay Rs. 6.50 as land tax. Those who cultivated land by manual labour on the other hand, has to pay Rs. 3.25. The village Patel and Karbhari have not to pay the land revenue for the land that they may be cultivating. In general, whether a person owns ten acres of less than one-and-a-half acre of land, he has to pay revenue of Rs. 6.50 per plough. There is no practice of reduction in the rate of land revenue on the basis of quality of land, because as reported earlier, the settlement of land revenue has not taken place in the Dangs so far.

There had been inequality in the old pattern of distribution of the land among the Dangis. In general there were on one side a few big land-holders while on the other, there were many tribals who were landless and owners of the marginal and small land-holdings. This kind of situation could have reminded intact if after independence, the Government has fixed some reasonable limit on maximum and minimum size of holding for a household before conferring occupancy rights. The Dangi farmers held lands on lease, which were in actual possession of Dangi Rajas. So far as the usual pattern of cultivation in the forest areas of Dangs is concerned, the customary *Eksali* leases of land is common as was the practice in the past. This practice continues to be still in vogue. The terms and conditions of the *Eksali* leases to cultivate land in Dangs were as under:

(i) A Dangi tribal remains in the actual possession of the land, if he was found to be so on January 1, 1970;
(ii) The above privilege is given only to the Dangis;
(iii) The land is not liable to transfer being on new and impartable tenure;
(iv) If a person in possession of such land desires to get loan or subsidy from other sources, he can get it hypothecated to cooperatives or nationalised banks; and
(v) The trees in such land remains vested in the Government and the grantee of the same is not entitled to cut these trees. However, under special circumstances trees can be cut by the person holding the land with the permission of the forest department. In any case, lopping of branches of trees can be done by the land-holder as and when required by him.

It may be noted that in a village named Maligam, 84 persons were given land on occupancy rights which amounted to 314 hectars and 82 Are. Formerly, these people practiced shifting cultivation, but after becoming occupants of the land allotted to them, they are as good as any other settled farmers. Whether a person holds 10.05 hectars or 0.09 hectars of land, the land revenue that he pays is Rs. 6.50 only.

(b) *Assessment by Non-Officials*

Before independence, the land in the forest in Dangs remained under the control of the local Dangi Rajas and the British Government. Under this circumstances, there was little scope for land reforms which can be of benefit to the tribals. The people of Dangs were under the clutches of the local Rajas and the Britishers, who maintained control through the forest department. Under historical reasons, there were hardly any cases of forest land put under cultivation in a big way. There were also no cases where the land was recorded in the name of a person who was in actual possession of large section of forest land.

As reported by non-officials, when the land was distributed to the Dangis in 1970, it created some basic problems of maintenance of forests. From the point of view of development of the forest in Dangs, this measure of allowing land for cultivation in the district was not considered proper. In the recent past, however, schemes were implemented to do soil conservation in this area by earth work and bunding, so that the people may be able to cultivate the land on long term basis. This programme was implemented by the Dang's Development Council. Under this programme, it was decided to help a farmer to develop only one acre of land under his possession. The idea was to see that one acre of such land becomes so fertile that it can be comparable to the income from forests land of about 10 acres where only Nagli, a coarse millet can be grown. It should be noted that this programme was not successfully carried out. The reason for the failure of this programme was that altogether wrong type of land was considered for this purpose, and therefore 4 to 5 times more money had to be spent for development of a piece of land. In spite of this, the land remained so barren that the purpose of soil conservation become redundant. Such lands turned out to be useless even for growing Nagli. It may also be noted that the limit of one acre of land fixed for this programme was also not adhered to.

It was more or less during this period that the land was recorded in the name of those who were said to be in possession the land, specially without putting a reasonable ceiling on land. This was one of the reasons why 75 per cent of the people of Dangs had to put up with limited plots of land which could not sustain them. Had this been done after determining the ceiling of 5 to 15 acres of land per tribal household, it would have been possible to have a plenty of surplus land distributed between a large number of landless Dangi tribals. Actually what happened was that a person who was holding 90 acres of land without full use was able to sit over it, while a hard working cultivator with only 3/4 acre had to remain satisfied with such an uneconomical holding. The surplus land which could have been used for distribution among needy farmers by a proper programme of ceiling on the land of large-holders, could have benefited a number of landless or small farmers.

It will be useful here to understand some of the historical reasons behind the present land situation in this district. Formerly, it was under the control of five local Rajas and nine Naiks. The land under their control was subject to land revenue decided at their sweet will. The land, however, was not under the ownership of the cultivators. When the Britishers came, they first established administrative rights over the forests of Dangs and through this they also controlled the local Chiefs and the Rajas. After independence, the Government took over the administrative control of the whole district. This included the control of the administration of the forest which was the exclusive right of the former forest department instituted by the British Government.

Under these circumstances, the local tribals called Dangis had no right what-so-ever over the ownership of the land. They were merely the serfs of the local Chiefs. The Dangi farmers were compelled to do free labour called *Veth* on behalf of the forest department. This is one of the reasons why agricultural land of this district did not at all improve and most of the tribals remained backward. Whatever land was given to the tribals, it was not fully under their control. The Forest Department divided forests into two types, i.e. Reserved Forests and Protected Forests and as a result, at the time of survey, the land of many a tribals covered by the reserved forests was lost. Thus many tribals who were earning livelihood by cultivating these lands by relatively primitive method of cultivation were deprived of the land.

When the land was transferred in the name of some of the Dangis in 1970, it was generally recorded in the name of the head of the household. The land is recorded in the name of only one person in the Village Form of the revenue department. This was a cultural tradition of associating land with the eldest member of Kinship or ethnic group among the tribal. Rest of the common tribals have been left with small pieces of land which cannot sustain a large number of persons of their households. In general, there is a great dearth of land for cultivation among a number of able bodied male members belonging to almost landless groups. This works as a deterrent to a person who is enthusiastic to earn his livelihood through agriculture.

The non-officials deplored that right from the olden times, the Dangi Chiefs did not introduce systematic land reforms for the benefit of local tribals. These people,. therefore, remained deprived of all advantage of cultivating lands and even improving upon it for betterment of livelihood. All throughout the past history they worked almost as slaves and aliens under the Rajas and the forest department of the British Government. No one had until Independence, come forward to encourage the local Dangi tribals to improve age-old agricultural practices. Moreover, any one who had taken a land on lease in the olden days was not in a position to get it registered under his occupation in a rightful manner. Moreover, the land reform under Section 73-A has not been applicable to the tribals of this area.

Those who have been conferred upon rights over the land after 1970 are not able to mortgage the same to a businessmen or to anybody else when they need hard cash in emergency. When a Dangi farmer dies, it is not easy for the heirs to acquire right over the land without the permission of the Collector. It is important to note that until today, not a single person in Dangs has sold his land to a money-lender or a businessmen.

The basic characteristic of the land of this hilly district is that, it is dotted with forest, rocky and stony areas. The soil is very shallow and of inferior quality from the point of view of agriculture. It is difficult to expect high-yields of agriculture under these circumstances. Besides, there are no tanks or catchment areas where water can be stored and used for irrigation. The chances of raising crops is, therefore, dependent on monsoon rains. The crops, however, are of inferior variety and they abound in coarse grains, such as, Nagli, peddy, banti, etc.

In the opinion of the non-officials, the highlights of the problem of the Dangis today is that the former chiefs and administrators such as, Police, Patel, Karbhari, etc. have cornered cultivable land to the extent of 75 acres each. The Dangis Bhils who were the original settlers and owners of the area are left almost without any cultivable land in their possession. They work as labourers for the village Patel, Karbhari, etc. who exercise complete hold in the area. The Bhils are almost like dumb animals and are not able to express their points of view and press their legitimate demand to the required extent. If the Government is able to control the power of Kunbis, the recent settlers of this area, it may be possible to do something for ameiiorating the economic conditions of the Bhils. There is a big timber depot in the place called Vaghai which has led to scarcity of land for the people of that area. If it is possible for the Government to give some land for cultivation from the contiguous Protected Forest area for cultivation, the local people can take advantage of the same.

NOTES

1. This practice was in vogue in olden times. At present, the names of all heirs are entered jointly in the village records although the heirs generally sub-divide each parcel of land on the spot for self-cultivation.
2. The Revenue Department instituted LND-5 Units for detecting unauthorised land alienation of tribals, and to take steps to restore the same. Each Unit was headed by 1 Deputy Collector and assisted by 2 Deputy Mamlatdars, 4 Circle Inspectors and 1 Assistant. Earlier these Units operated as planned scheme, but at present they fall under non-planned schemes and are called LND-8.
3. This proposal of inserting Land Revenue Code Section 73-AA, referred to in this report, was confirmed by government order on 1-2-1981, almost one year after the submission of the present report.
4. It is important to note that two instances of the work of LND-5 operations are presented in Appendix-IV indicating the complexity involved in detection of tribal land alienation and breaches in implementing land reform measures. The initial government orders of LND-5 Unit have undergone three revisions with the result that at present there are five headquarters in tribal areas where LND-8 Units, with more effective operations are reported to be in action.

6

DYNAMICS OF FOREST LAND AND FORESTS

Introduction

For most of the tribals, forest is a real habitat. Their ancestors earned livelihood, and their very existence depended upon whatever the forest could offer to them. They were the original inhabitants of the hills and forests and the term "aboriginal" is probably derived from the secured abode or habitat that the tribals found in forest. Over many generations, the tribals settled in the form of dispersed or clustered village habitations and cleared parts of the forests and brought land under cultivation. From this time onwards they maintained themselves by hunting, fishing and gathering minor forest produce as well as by cultivating patches of land in the forest by burn and slash method called *Jhum* cultivation in Gujarat as in many parts of India.

The government administration looks after maintenance of forest for the benefit of public as well as the State. This involves a planned programmes of conservation of forests from being destroyed out of ignorance of the tribals as well as the tendency of exploitation of wealth of the forest by non-tribals. This is why restrictions have to be imposed by the government for preservation of forest and at the same time allowing certain privileges to tribal users who are original inhabitants of the forests. The tribals are the main groups of the population in a country who face various kinds of restrictions of the forest department. In Gujarat, as else where, the forest department identified two different categories of forest viz. (1) Reserve forests and (2) Protected forests. In this chapter we shall deal with forest problems connected with the use of forest wealth and various types of forest lands by the tribals.

The problems dealt with in the following pages cover: (i) what are the customary rights enjoyed by the tribals and are they recognised by the government; (ii) has the forest department conceded occupancy rights to the tribals in respect of forest and land; (iii) what is the preference of the government, conservation of forests or cultivation of land by the tribals; (iv) if rights of cultivation of forest land by tribals are conceded what are the safeguards for maintenance of ecological balance; (v) what is the impact of forest laws on the livelihood and living conditions of the tribals; (vi) what is the role of forest labour cooperative societies in helping the tribals to earn their livelihood, and (vii) what is the role of Forest Department Corporation in protecting the forest wealth as well in helping tribals develop an integrated approach towards forests in order to promote social forestry and other innovative approaches to forest life and environment.

The problems of forest and forest land in relation to the tribals is presented here keeping all the above seven points in focus. Micro level classification or distinctions of the information have been avoided. The presentation gives a composite picture of the situation. However, the outstanding cases of distinction with regard to the available interesting information is highlighted as and when required.

Customary Rights on Forest

The only right admitted to the tribals in reserved forest at the time of forest land settlement in most of the districts, is the right of way and access to water courses. However, in some areas special privileges and concessions are enjoyed by tribals living in villages. These are: (i) villagers having right of way and use of water are entitled to a path way of 50 ft. wide with fence of thorn, free of charges from the forest; (ii) free grazing of cattle by forest and non-forest villagers. The cattle of neighbouring states are not entitled to this concession, and in case they want the facility, they will have to pay the fees prescribed by the forest department; (iii) no forest will be closed to grazing within a quarter of a mile of a village site; (iv) access to grazing areas in interior areas of forests will be granted by allotment of a sufficiently wider shortcut approach road; (v) access to remove stone and earth from places approved for *bona fide* agricultural and domestic use; (vi) access to remove fallen leaves and grasses for *bona fide* agricultural and domestic use; (vii) access to remove coupes of felled timber not useful to contractors, and branch-wood of trees of stipulated size, for domestic or agricultural use; (viii) access to remove timber of inferior species of trees required for temporary huts to replace houses destroyed by accident or fire, (ix) access to remove timber in some quantities from coupes of the Forest Labour Cooperatives for construction and repairs of new houses and agricultural implements; (x) access to remove fallen and dead material of non-reserved species on head-load basis without passes and permission. The government approvals of forest uses listed above comprise age old customary rights of tribals.

Occupancy of Forest Land

Some tribals were cultivating forest land since ages, so to say, unauthorisedly. Although this act of the tribals has been against the rule and interest of the government and the practice of forest conservancy, it was always considered sympathetically in favour of tribals. The government had passed resolutions on this issue and as per the latest resolution on the subject, of 1972, all tribals cultivating land for three years before 31-12-67 were given right on land under their cultivation subject to ceiling of 8 acres of land. This also included unauthorised land in possession of a tribal. It may be noted that in the Dangs district, extensive lands from the protected forest were granted to tribals.

In the opinion of a non-official, the ceiling of 8 acres of land to be allowed to tribals for self-cultivation was not implemented properly in some areas. Those who were eligible as occupants of such lands did not receive occupancy rights for the purpose of agriculture. However, on account of great hunger for more land for cultivation, the functionaries of forest department, as well as leaders of political parties, were alleged to have worked-up tribals to cultivate forest land by stealthy means.

The land cultivation under forest areas can be divided into two categories, viz. (i) land in forests village settlements, and (ii) unauthorised forest land. The occupancy right of tribals is accepted for generations in the first category of land. But no occupancy right is recognised in unauthorised cultivation of forest land. The reasons for not recognizing occupancy right in the second category is that it would increase incidence of illegal encroachment upon forest land by the tribals.

In some areas conflict of interests developed between the forest department and the tribal settlers in the forest. If the land was under forest, it was government property and the tribal was merely a labourer. If the same land was under cultivation, the tribal became an owner and was able to reap full benefits of his efforts. This situation led naturally to increasing deforestation. If it has to be stopped, the status of the tribal even in the forest land has to be raised from a labourer to that of an owner. Then he can be persuaded to raise trees in the same land instead of crops. This requires a fundamental change in the forest policy.

One of the officials from the Panchmahals felt that it was no good giving occupancy rights to the tribals to cultivate forest land. In Dangs, it was reported that the tribal cultivators who cultivated forest land in earlier days were given occupancy rights in the protected forest areas. In the district of Bharuch, the lands cultivated by the tribals in the forest without authority were subject to litigation by the forest department. Such cases were withdrawn on account of the work of social workers. The government issued orders in 1967 that those who had cultivated land before 1964-65 should be given occupancy rights, but many of the tribals were not benefited done to previous government regulations. It was suggested that if this regulation was applied after 1974-75 a large number of tribal cultivators in forest would be benefited. The tribals had given up the cultivation of unauthorised land and so the question of making alternative arrangements may go against the regulations of the government. From the taluka of Rajpipla, a non-officials suggested a critical appraisal of a number of points connected with occupancy rights of land to the tribals in forest areas. The suggestions are as follows:

(i) Tribals were cultivating forest land for many years without authorisation and are, therefore, entitled to get occupancy rights in the forest land;

(ii) Tribals are required to produce a token payment of fine for which receipts were issued by the forest beat guards. These receipts can stand as testimony that they were cultivating forest land in the past. The forest beat guards were alleged to take advantage of the situation. After getting the fine or penalty money from a person with a large area under his cultivation, receipt of only a small amount of fine was issued. The rest of the money was said to be pocketed by the guards.

Generally, the tribals did not object to this practice, but it went against their basic interest, because the receipt of a fine of smaller amount meant that he was holding a smaller plot of land than that he actually did;

(iii) In some cases, the forest guards did not at all give receipts of penalty paid by a person, particularly when he was cultivating unauthorised forest areas. In such instances, a poor tribal was completely deprived of concrete evidence of the rights over land occupied by him in the forest. A tribal occupant subject to this kind of malpractice loses land-holding rights for good;

(iv) A tribal cultivating unauthorised forest land even for a number of years in the past, but unable to produce fine receipts was not able to get the benefit of government land reforms and supportive measures to own the land occupied by him in the past;

(v) In many cases, the local forest officers were supplied fine receipts as evidence by the tribals at the Rajpipla headquarters. But the authorities neither acknowledged the submission of the receipts, nor took necessary action to clear the case of occupancy of the tribal concerned. This kind of carelessness on the part of the forest authorities concerned resulted into total loss of occupancy rights to the tribals;

(vi) When the forest officers pay visits to tribal villages for checking the case of actual cultivation, they are asked for receipts of fines as a proof. A tribal who has already sent the receipts to the Rajpipla headquarters, is not able to provide them as evidence on the spot. The plea that he is the real occupant is not accepted by the inspecting forest officers. Thus he loses his occupancy rights due to negative report of verification of the inspector;

(vii) Glaring pitfalls like this were demanded to be looked into by the tribals cultivating forest land, for an impartial inquiry with the help of non-officials deputed by the government, so that the cases of injustice can be looked into;

(viii) The officers of the forest department on the other hand point out that many clandestine tribal claimants have sprung up after the government regulations to help give occupancy rights to tribals in the forest land. This tendency of cheating the government should be curbed. Such allegations are however, refuted by the tribals who say that all of them were definitely cultivating forest land in one way or the other in the past. Shifting cultivation was a common practice among the tribals;

(ix) The attitude of the forest department towards giving occupancy rights to the tribals was to oppose the rights of the tribals, and sit tight on the applications of the claimants; and

(x) There are, however, forest villages in which the forest department have regularised the occupancy rights of tribals. These villages were not governed by the Statutory Village Panchayat Act and so the people residing there were not entitled to get benefits of development programmes. Tribals of such villages were not eligible for government subsidies for wells, pump-sets, fertilizers, bullocks, etc.

Conservation of Forests and Customary Rights

Forest has been the basic source of livelihood of most of the tribals. They get from it timber, firewood, grazing areas for cattle, minor forest produce such as *Mahuda* fruit, *timru* leaves, edible oil seeds, etc. Forests also bring indirect benefits such as (i) ameliorating climatic conditions, (ii) checking soil and water erosion, and (iii) keeping up waterlevel in wells and reserves. This is the reason why conservation of forests should be given highest importance as compared to the cultivation in forest areas. However, increasing burden of the population living in forest can be removed only by giving education to tribals and getting them encouraged for other occupations in firms and factories in urban areas.

The Gujarat State is having only 10 per cent of land under forest as against 33 per cent standard land area prescribed as per national forest policy. This means that it is extremely necessary not only to make concerted efforts for conservation of existing forests in Gujarat, but to increase land coverage of forests. There is a need of overhauling the whole policy of the forest department. Whenever, there is a scope for raising forest, water facilities should be supplied on a large scale. After this the forest should be systematically protected by the department. This includes the possibilities of encouraging and raising of private jungles also.

There should be strict prohibition on the cutting down of trees, and wherever cutting of trees takes place, forest officials should be held responsible. The intermediaries, agents contractors, etc. have no doubt been eliminated from operating in the forest areas after the establishment of forest labour cooperatives. But even these cooperative societies have developed vested interest. The by-laws of these cooperative societies should be improved upon so that responsibility of raising new forest areas is taken up by them. To avoid destruction of forests for fuel, the use of *gobar gas* plants should be widely propagated. This can save timber from being burnt for domestic purposes. The government should provide as much as 85 per cent of subsidy to a group of village of farmers for constructing *gobar gas* plants for fuel and lighting.

According to one opinion, the tribals should be given rights to make forest plantations so that they can take the profits therefrom. The special cases of individual tribals cultivating the land in forest should be considered favourably for occupancy if it is good for cultivation. Occupancy rights on such land should be confirmed and made permanent, but no land should be given in the midst of the forest. The land being cultivated by the tribals until 1972 should be given to them and the limit of the forest should be fixed thereafter. In many cases, the forest land is unfertile and not suitable for cultivation. According to one official, barren land will not produce anything worthwhile. It would be better to retain such land under the forest department. The forest department can also develop certain areas into pasture land from which fodder requirements of villagers can be met and the surplus fodder sold to other villages in the district. A programme of this type was already started in the district of Banaskantha specially in Deodar taluka. The Government of India was advancing 100 per cent grants for the benefit of drought-prone areas. This scheme can be introduced in any taluka of the tribal districts.

In the district of Dangs, a programme of raising private forest was started by the government. If this continues to be accepted, it will be helpful to the people of Dangs in the long run. Until recently the theft of trees (illicit cutting) was reported to be negligible. However, since last four years or so, the incidence of unauthorised destruction of trees has increased. The peripheral forest areas of Maharashtra on South-east boarders are under the occupation of private parties and therefore the tribals of that areas encroach upon Dangs forest and take away the trees. In order to put an end to this kind of illegal thefts from across the boarder, it is necessary that strong protective measures be taken for the forests of the villages of Bardipada, Bheramari, Chanchli, Pipaldahad, Galkund, Saputara, Manhudi, etc.

Under no circumstances, the tribals should be given occupancy rights in reserved or protected forests because there are all chances of theft of wood taking place in such areas. The forests of Rajpipla, Panchmahals, Dharampur and Vansada areas have already been destroyed because of the lenient attitude and policies of the forest department. In the olden times, the government was taking special care to see that lopping of trees for cultivation was done under strict supervision. But now, because of lack of precautions by forest department, not only lopping of trees takes place, but also the whole trees are cut down. The danger of destruction of forest in the area of Hadkaichod had increased to such extent that unless there was a strong patrolling, it was likely that the whole forest of the Dangs would fall to destruction in twenty years' time.

Earlier, there was the customs of marking forest areas in a systematic manner. This method was replaced by clear felling of trees on the fringe . Under this new system of felling of trees, the hills were washed away and the soil erosion increased from year to year. A very serious problem was reported from the Dharampur forest. Here the main crop was of *Nagli* millet. In order to raise the seedlings of Nagli, there was an old custom among the tribals to use *ash* or *rab* which requires lopping of trees and burning the wood. These tribals were told many a times that it was not necessary to use *rab* in order to raise *Nagli* seedlings. However, out of ignorance and habit of *rab* cultivation the people did not accept the advice given to them by government functionaries. The lopping, therefore, continued unabated at the cost of the forest wealth.

In the Surat district, the programmes of afforestation had been taken up in recent past and it had helped the tribals in many ways. However, it was reported that the tribals remained idle and did not come forward for labour to help the programme of afforestation.

Measures to Safeguard Forests

One of the non-officials from Surat district suggested that the best way to safeguard the forest was to develop small forest villages in such a way that instead of keeping them separate, they could be inter-connected by communication links and a large reserved forest area could be developed. However, in the opinion of one of the officers, it was difficult to keep and safeguard the maintenance of the forest if the land was given to tribals for cultivation. Therefore, it was suggested that no agriculture should be allowed in the forest area. It was also believed that if the right of the tribal in cultivation of forest land was protected then conservation of forest will be difficult. In case, it was not possible to restrict tribals from cultivating forest land, they will have to be involved in forest activities of various types such as protection, afforestation and development of the forests.

The safeguards of forest was indeed necessary, because it is this that will ensure economic benefit to the tribals without reducing the forest cover on the land. The question of the tribal rights in the forest by way of preference did not arise. The department of the forest would certainly desire that only the forest land given to the tribals for cultivation be brought back for afforestation in the interest of the tribals as well as the forests. According to this opinion, forest should be reserved for plantation and the cultivators allowed to cultivate with the condition that they take active participation in afforestation programme. There should be a close watch against cutting of trees in surroundings areas. The cultivation should go along with protection of forest trees specially, in the areas cultivated by tribals. There should be a programme of plantation and rearing of trees every year for safety and growth of the trees with the involvement of the tribals themselves.

According to another non-official, there should not be any scope of giving land to the tribals for cultivation in the forest under any circumstances. If the forests have to be protected, it should be ensured that the forest was not washed away by indiscriminate cutting of trees. The forests are to be seriously taken as potent treasurers for protection of land from floods and other forces of destruction.

Over a period of time, vested interests of various types grow in forest lands. The plots of land were reserved for grazing village cattle, but in many cases, they were cultivated for personal benefit by the strong man in the area. If such lands were given to the families of poorer tribals for agriculture in a multi-caste village, after keeping grass land for the cattle, they can be put to proper use. There was another category of vested interests in land by the timber contractors. They involved the tribals in felling trees indiscriminately and force them to get the land developed and cultivated. When the tribals fully develop these areas and raise crops for a few years, the money-lenders and contractors tempt them to take money on loan for religious or social purpose and get the land mortgaged. Lands of this type lead to illegal and unauthorised alienation of land in forest areas. Most of the tribals became the owners of this land which fell in the category of concealed alienation. The ultimate result was that the forests were gradually destroyed. It is, therefore, useful to inculcate a new concept and idea of social forestry among the tribals. This seems to be the best way to meet the need of future development of forests.

In the district of Banaskantha, a large parts of the forest were cut unauthorisedly by the tribals to meet bare minimum requirements of living in times of draught and natural calamities.

During drought and scarcity conditions, tribal men and women would go to forests at night, cut the wood stealthily and sell in the local markets. This needs to be looked into for safeguarding forests in this area. It may also be noted that in many parts of this district, agriculture was not taken up as a main occupation by the tribals. They somehow supplemented their income from non-agricultural activities, and illicit cutting of trees was one of such activities. The valuable species of trees such as Dhawda, Khair, Bamboo, etc. have already become victims of illicit cutting. It may be noted that 9.00 per cent of the forest measuring 1359 sq. kilometers of areas covers the whole of geographical areas of the Banaskantha District.

There were estimated 14 lakhs cattle from Kutch-Rajasthan and other parts of Gujarat that were said to be grazing in the forest of Banaskantha district. The normal prescribed area for grazing in non-forests villages was 40 acres for 100 heads of cattle, and 20 acres for forest villages for the same number of cattle. If this standard is taken seriously in the interest of protection and preservation of forests, there would not be enough grazing area either in the forest or in government wasteland in the district. According to one opinion, the number of non-milch cattle in the district was very high. This uneconomic burden of the cattle can be taken care of if unwanted cattle are destroyed. The remaining cattle could be divided into two main categories, as milch and those useful for other purposes. The former should be provided with better care and feeding while the others may be given inferior variety of food. This kind of discriminatory treatment can ultimately help in reducing the pressure on grazing area in plains and forests.

In some parts of South Gujarat, special rights were granted to the tribals on concessional rates for cutting wood from the forest for domestic and agricultural use. The people there cut wood for building new houses and for repairing agricultural implements. The forest department marks trees so that the tribals know the exact types of trees which were permitted for cutting without being punished. The marks on the trunk of the trees indicated clearly whether he will be extended the right to free cutting of certain types of trees for the next 25 to 34 years. When the illicit cutting of trees was done for trade by timber contractors and merchants, a serious notice was taken by the forest department. The immediate remedy to control this type of activities was to have strict control imposed through forest laws most difficult for easy violation. If the forest laws were not fool-proof, it was likely that in the court of law, the evidences cannot be produced in punishing the guilty parties iudulging in illicit plundering of forest wood. One of the strong recommendations for preventing illicit cutting and misuse of forest wealth was to develop intensive monitoring and management of the forest officers. Moreover, if diversification of occupation was introduced among the tribals, it would be possible for them to find alternative sources of income, and the extent of damage done to forests can be reduced.

The complaints against the tribals' misuse of forest are generally filed under Section 26 of Forest Act, 1926. The Act mainly prohibits cultivation of land in reserved forests. In the Panchmahals, the main problems of safeguarding forest wealth arose on account of unauthorised cultivation, illicit cutting and grazing the cattle. Here the cost of timber was very high and the tribals, therefore, stole the wood which they cannot afford to purchase from the market. If they used the stolen wood for their own purpose, it may not have done much damage to the forest, but when they began to sell the wood to the contractors, they not only damaged the forest by illicit cutting of trees, but also got themselves badly cheated by the contractors in terms of pitiful payment in return.

In the case of cattle let loose in the forest for grazing, a lot of damage was done. However, in order to prevent tribals from grazing cattle in the forest, they were said to have been assaulted by the forest beat guards. Wherever, there were plantations, the forest area was closed for grazing for five years. The rest of the area was kept open for free grazing. But some tribals over-stepped the limit determined for free grazing, and took their cattle into the prohibited areas, and committed violation of forest regulation. This kind of violations can easily be avoided if tribals use the grass from non-prohibited areas.

It is also reported from the Panchmahals that the illicit cutting of trees was done by the tribals in gangs for the sake of earning their daily bread. When they were persuaded to participate in the programme of afforestation, they were reluctant to cooperate. This was because they were said to be fond of migrating to other areas in off season times. In the scheme for prevention of illicit cutting of fodder, the forest department encouraged plantations of *Koobaval* trees which provided green fodder. This scheme was undertaken also be voluntary agencies to help the tribals. However, it was noted that illicit cutting went on and a lot of damage was done on account of political cover and pressure not to take actions against the guilty parties.

Although the village Panchayats in certain forest areas were supposed to encourage tribals for raising trees, sometimes they issued permits for cutting the trees. This kind of action defeated the very purpose for which the Panchayats had undertaken developmental programmes in tribal areas.

It may also be noted that the Gujarat Electricity Board undertakes huge programmes of laying down grid lines through tribal areas. This leads to cutting down of trees. In some areas the tribals were made to take disadvantage of the situation and do further damage by unauthorised cutting of trees in the neighbouring areas. There are traditional customs of celebrating arrival of a son in the family at the Holi festival by bathing the hill (Dungro Navdave). In reality it was a practice of putting trees symbolically on ritual fire. Besides setting fire to forest trees, shrubs and grass under oath, the usual activities of collecting Mahuda fruits and flowers, and damaging trees in the state of drunken conditions were reported. One of the non-officials suggested that the functionaries of the forest department should be given special training in understanding tribal society and culture.

All the village Panchayats should have a special committee for protection and development of forests. The activities of this special committee can be of great help to the functionaries of the forest department in taking advice and guidance from time to time. The 3rd and 4th category of functionaries of forest department should be given suitable educational programme so that they can understand how to work with local Panchayats. The tribal leaders at the district, taluka and the State level should be invited specially on such occasions when the training is given to the functionaries.

At the time of the study, there were critical remarks heard about the forest beat guards who were called Ravan guards. Such negative values and feelings can be done away with if coordination and cooperation exist between the tribal leaders and the forest functionaries. It was said that at times the forest functionaries have committed so much crime in the past that it defies description in words. Whatever may be case, the climate of hostility and mistrust needs to be cleared in the interest of forest development.

Impact of Forest Laws on Tribals

The forests, are not only the gift of nature to the tribals, but also to all other people in the country and if the wealth of the forest is judiciously utilised, it will not only provide livelihood to the tribals, but many valuable gifts of nature to future generations. The present picture of the forest laws vis-a-vis tribals or non-tribals is that they are not afraid of the laws. The attitude of apathy and negligence towards protection of the forest by the tribals particularly, results in rapid deterioration of valuable forest resources. We hear a great deal about the love of the tribals for the forest, but it is unfortunate that they themselves become responsible for destroying the forest. Their careless attitude towards the forest law, on the whole proved damaging to their future condition of willing. It is high time the tribals themselves feel concerned about safeguarding the forests.

There are certain areas such as the reserved forests where the forest laws are somewhat lenient allowing the tribals certain privileges in order to facilitate their age-old mode of life dependent on natural resources. The management of the forest, if taken care of by the government as well as by the local Panchayat bodies, it will be a great boon to the growth and development of forests.

The government regulations requiring tribals to sell minor forest produces to the contractors, appointed for this purpose, leads to a kind of exploitation of the tribals. The items such as gum, honey, musli, etc, instead of being sold to the contractors, if sold to a regular cooperative society and in the open market, it would prevent exploitation of the tribals.

The forest laws are generally meant to prohibit unscrupulous elements indulging in illicit cutting of trees, grazing of cattle and unauthorised cultivation. They are immensely helpful in the preservation of the forest providing livelihood to the tribals. The forest laws are also helpful in preserving the natural habitat and environment of the forest which promote and strengthen the culture of the tribals.

Notwithstanding these advantages, the economic trends of constant rise in prices of forest produce are so great, that tribals are tempted to indulge in unauthorised operations detrimental to forest development and conservation. When forest laws are enforced strictly, they are strongly resented by the tribals for obvious reasons. One of the officials was of the opinion that the tribals in some areas should be gradually weaned away from cultivating forest land. This becomes necessary if they are not good cultivators and are not committed and painstaking in improving agrarian skills.

In the forest of Dangs, most of the land belonged to the forest department. The government was, however, allowing the cultivation by the tribals in the protected forest areas for the sake of convenience. In this area, most of the tribals used to raise food-grain crop called *Nagli* in the wet season only. The yield of *Nagli* per acre fetched the income of Rs. 35 to Rs. 50 only. If more advantage has to be taken from the cultivable land of the forest in Dangs, it is advisable to raise plantations of bamboo and *sag* trees and teak wood. If the tribals can be persuaded to do this, they may be able to get a return of Rs. 250 to Rs. 500 per acre. It is heartening to note that ever since 1977, i.e. after twenty years of planning in India, this programme has been accepted by the people. This is an illustration showing how we can mend forest laws to introduce innovations in management of forest for the benefit of tribals.

In other areas of Gujarat, many tribals were unsettled from the forest on account of notifications issued by the forest department under Sections 6 and 20 of forest law. The old inhabitants of this area were forced to leave their land which they used to cultivate for a number of years without payment of any dues to the government. The occupancies of these areas were also not given to tribals in reserved forest. Most of these cases were reported from Sabarkantha where the forest was under the *Jagirdari* system of land tenure. The abolition of *Jagirdari* system of revenue collection was responsible for eviction of many tribals by the forest department. The ultimate result of this kind of sudden change in the abolition of old tenurial system and its strict implementation was that the tribals were forced to become thieves of forest wood. Sometimes the raids by the forest department resulted in imposition of a fine of about Rs. 1000 compelling a tribal towards incurring heavy debt.

One of the adverse impact of the forest laws reported to be an increasing trend of corruption among the beat-guards of the department. These guards allow the tribals to cultivate land and cut trees illegally on payment of bribe. This meant that the aggression on the forest land increased instead of decreasing, in spite of forest laws. The ultimate result is that the forests are likely to be destroyed in the next ten years where ever such contrabad and liberties are extended to tribals by the forest guards. In some tribal belts the situation was so deplorable that not only the trees were cut, but even the roots are dug out by the poor tribals, and used as fuel.

Role of Forest Labour Cooperative Societies (FLCS) and Forest Development Corporation

According to a non-official, the Forest Labour Cooperative Society in Banaskantha district was formed in 1970 for the benefit of the tribals. However, for want of work and lack of cooperation from the forest department, the society had to be closed down. The Forest Development Corporation, however, came to the help of tribals in selling honey, wax, gum and *timru* leaves collected by the tribals in this areas. The government also started establishment of fire wood depots in order to see that the dead and fallen wood collected by tribals from the forest, fetch reasonable price in the market. The wood depots of this type were established at seven places such as Palanpur, Danta, Ambaji, Amirgadh, Ikbalgadh, Malan and Virpur. The purchase price of 20 kilograms of fire-wood by the depots was fixed at Rs. 2 and it was sold at the rate of Rs. 3.50 in the market. This amounted to sale by depots on the basis of no loss no profit. That was basically helpful in preventing exploitation of the tribals by the outsiders. This scheme of fire wood depots was so popular that there was a great demand from other tribals to have the depots started in their villages.

In the district of Sabarkantha, the Forest Development Corporation had setup centres for purchase of *Mahuda* flowers at the rate of Rs. 8 per maund which was being sold at the higher rate of Rs. 40-42 by the Forest Development Corporation. It was suggested therefore that the sale should not be restricted to the corporation only. If the tribals were willing, they can go to the open market where they may be able to get a better price. It was suggested by one of the officers that the programme of soil and moisture conservation, afforestation, social forestry and employment oriented labour, at the minimum wage of Rs. 5.50 be ensured to the tribals.

In the district of Panchmahals, it was reported by an official that the forest labour cooperative societies did not have wide-spread interests. Their activities were limited only to certain areas. This was the reason why the real impact of FLCSs had not been perceptible. The over-all situation as reported was that the forest areas were in a poor condition and it was therefore worth-while to stop further exploitation of the forests in the district, at least for a period of 10 years. The time had come to concentrate on plantation activity on one hand and protection of the forests on other.

In the district of Dangs, 29 Forest Labour Cooperative Societies (FLCS) were functioning according to the information supplied by a non-official. Twelve of these societies were originally started by the Vedchhi Ashram, and were run under the direct guidance of the cooperative societies of the Government. Other societies were run by the voluntary agencies called Serva Seva Sangh of Bilimora. Several other societies newly started were seven in all and were helped by the Government in various ways. It was reported that the FLCSs in this district were managed generally by the outside elements as a result of which it was difficult to expect them to be of real benefit to the people for whom they were meant. In other areas, a prescribed standard of 80 per cent and 20 per cent profit of the FLCSs were distributed between the Government department and the members of the Societies. This formula was also applied to the FLCSs operating in this district also. For instance, if a Society earned the profit of two crores rupees, tribals were given a share of Rs. 40 lakhs according to this formula. This of course was a very encouraging method of helping tribals through voluntary agencies running these societies. However, it was necessary to actually evaluate the manner in which these societies were spending money on the welfare of the tribals.

The managers of the societies, such as, Chairman, Secretary, Managing Directors, Accountants, Clerks, etc. were generally the tribals themselves. They had thus certainly replaced the contractors and the non-tribals who were formerly exploiting tribal labourers. It was, however, an open question whether this, 'new contractors' became also the exploiters of the labourers, and could be easily replaced by active members of the poor labour community among the tribals. According to another non-official, the Secretaries and other functionaries of the FLCSs in the Dangs were non-tribals who came from contiguous talukas of Vansada, Anaval, Mahuva, Vyara, etc. He strongly felt that these non-tribal functionaries be replaced by the tribal youths who were equipped to undertake this kind of responsibilities in Dangs.

In some societies the members were given bonus in the form of utensils and such other gifts. The method of purchase of gifts of this kind was objectionable and defective. The purchase of bonus gifts in bulk should in principle be made directly from the manufacturers rather than from the middleman and shop-keepers. If this was done, the commission taken by the shop-keepers could have been saved. Some Societies purchased bonus gifts in the form of utensils worth lakhs of rupees and it was necessary, therefore, that some control on the method of purchase was imposed.

A non-official in the district of Bharuch was of the strong opinion that there should not be even a single non-tribal number or officer in the Forest Labour Cooperative Societies. In his opinion, even an officer is likely to take the disadvantage of this kind of situation. Even though most of the forest contractors were eliminated in this district and 100 per cent work of coupes was entrusted to the FLCSs, the tribal labourers were not able to get the full payment of their labour. The FLCSs were managed also by the non-tribals and the stocks of timber and coal were sold at higher price, these necessary. Although apparently, the labourers were given gifts of brass or copper utensils and blankets by way of bonus, the amount spent for other social benefits was so meagre that the real profits were eaten away by bad elements in the management. Most of the FLCSs practically did nothing to help the tribal labourers to build their own huts, provide school facilities medical aid, water supply, etc. Unless the FLCSs came forward to use their profits for all round socio-economic developments of the tribals, the age-old problems of exploitation would continue.

An illustration of a good FLCSs was not doubt reported, where all managers were the tribals themselves. This society was reported to have given labour to the tribals worth Rs. 2 lakhs in a year. The society also spent Rs. 10,000 for the *Balwadi* and school for education of the children. In the field of health facilities, the society spent Rs. 700, and for digging *kucha* wells it spent about Rs. 800. Moreover, at the end of the year Rs. 20,000 were spent in giving gifts as bonus in the form of woolen blankets etc. Above all, it was indicated that the daily wages given by the society to the labourers were according to the standard fixed by the wage board.

There were twelve forest labour cooperative societies in this district managed by the District Adivasi Seva Sangh. Not only was there a lack of concern in helping the tribals through these societies as mentioned earlier, but they were not able to provide full employment to all the tribals working in the areas. The cutting of bamboo trees for the Songadh Pulp Mills was not being done through the forest department and so the tribal labourers were not able to get better wages. If this was done through forest department, they would have at least got wages according to the standards prescribed by the government.

This certainly would have gone a long way in helping a larger number of tribals who were said to number about four thousand. It was mentioned that there were five coupes in this district from which 700 tribals were able to get employment. Moreover, excepting a non-tribal accountant of the coupes, all activities were taken care of by the tribals. One of the officers felt that the FLCSs should be able to provide labour to the tribals in a big way if they started forest based industries such as bee-keeping, *kattha* manufacturing, basket making, etc.

The general impression of the role of Forest Labour Cooperative Societies from the district of Surat, Vadodara and Valsad was more or less the same as reported from the districts referred to earlier. The FLCSs were said to have been a good boon to the labourers who were able to get fixed wages at prescribed rates. However, the real problem was that the profits were misappropriated in one way or the other on account for malpractices and bad management. Together with internal politics, this had led to the weakening of these societies. During the times of Bombay State, it was late Mr. B.G. Kheri and Mr. Morarji Desai who introduced the FLCSs in Vadodara district, but as usual these societies continued to be dominated by non-tribals for many years. One of the non-official from Valsad indicated that when some of the FLCSs were started by the government, even non-tribal office bearers such as Secretaries, Chairmen and other officers were truly service minded. However, after more than 15 years of running of these societies, it was found that most of these office bearers were rolling in luxury. From where did they get so much money was a matter to be investigated by the government. Not only this, an independent inquiry committee, without any political party workers, should be instituted to go into this and other issues of exploitation of the tribals through these societies.

One of the officers from this district however indicated that in the Dharampur area, the FLCS was purchasing the minor forest produce collected by the tribals and distributing regular payment in return. The money on hand helped the tribals in purchasing goods for the daily necessities. This was definitely a great boon to the tribals who were otherwise badly exploited by the traders who used to sell them goods in exchange of the forest produce, employing the age old system of barter.

An additional note on the Forest Labour Cooperative Societies is presented later in Table 6.1. The data have been collected through correspondence from various districts and roughly covers one year period of 1977-78.

It is interesting to note from the Table 6.1 that most of the FLCSs had negligible number of non-tribals as its members. For instance, in the Dharampur taluka of Valsad District, there were 11 societies having 19080 tribal members and 22 non-tribal members. It is from this taluka also that payment of tribal wages was turned to be considerably high as compared to those in most of other talukas. The exception however was in Songadh taluks of Surat District where the total amount of wages earned by tribals in a year was R. 29,81,226. This is the taluka in which there were 10 FLCSs having 3940 tribal members and 29 non-tribal members. In the District-cum-Taluka of Dangs, the number of societies were 27 having 10056 tribal members.

It can be said in general that the FLCSs had begun to play a satisfactory role in providing employment to a considerable number of tribals, making it possible for them to earn wages between the range of Rs. 60 to Rs. 700 per head per annum in various talukas of the Tribal Area Sub-Plan.

Forest Officials and Tribals

A great deal of information on complaints of the tribals vis-a-vis the forest officers was referred to in earlier sections.

Some of the forest officers were asked to react and present their own points of view on the subject. One of the officers said that the tribals complained and expressed grievances against the forest officers in spite of allowing special privileges granted to them by the

TABLE 6.1: Forest Labour Co-operative Societies in Tribal Areas: 1977-78

Name of District and Taluka	No.of FLCS	Coupes allotted	Number of Members		No. of Tribals Employed	Total amount of wages earned (Rs.)	Average income per head in taluka (Rs.)	Average income per head in district (Rs.)
			Tribals	Non-Tribals				
1	2	3	4	5	6	7	8	9
Sabarkantha								
Vijaynagar	1	Nil	197	30	Nil	Nil	Nil	Nil
Khedbrahma	1	Nil	80	5	Nil	Nil	Nil	
Total	2		277	35				
Vadodara								
Chhotaudepur	8	23	3288	33	1265	149000	117.78	113.87
Pavi Jetpur	2	5	1024	16	140	11000	78.57	
Total	10	28	4312	49	1405	160000		
Bharuch								
Nandod, Dediapada, total								
Sagbara	13	41	3299	–	4182	1468487	351.14	351.14

Contd.

TABLE 6.1 *Contd.*

1	2	3	4	5	6	7	8	9
Surat								
Uchchhal	10	26	2145	12	1550	558364	360.23	
Songadh	10	33	3940	29	3808	2981226	782.88	
Vyara	10	—	6547	12	5224	1587293	303.84	
Valod	2	—	—	—	—	--	—	
Mandvi	6	—	2214	1	2957	626688	211.93	347.66
Mangrol	5	—	2393	3	3913	536887	137.20	
Mahuva	1	—	780	—	780	48090	61.65	
total	44	59	18019	57	18232	6338548		
Valsad								
Dharampur	11	40	19080	22	16958	1985382	117.07	
Vansda	4	10	3969	4	2881	241488	83.82	111.52
Chikhali	1	2	426	4	343	20204	58.90	
Pardi	1	2	489	3	275	34425	125.18	
Total	17	54	23964	33	20452	2281499		
Dangs								
Dangs	27	33	10056	—	43071	7583299	176.28	176.28

* Information of remaining areas were not available.

government. The tribals were allowed to enjoy living facilities in the forest and in nearby areas. Many of them had no lands or small plots of land for farming, and so depended upon the minor forest produce for earning livelihood. The illiterate tribals did not have the foresight of long term benefits which accrue to them from the forest, which they should use with utmost care and caution. They were generally concerned about their immediate needs and in order to meet them, they committed offences by way of illicit cutting of trees and other unauthorised activities damaging forests and forest land.

While making the Indian Forest Act of 1926, the interests of tribals were given utmost importance. There is the need to educate the tribals about the forest development policies of the government. This can be done through visits and holding workshops and discussions with the people. If the intentions of the forest department to preserve the forest is properly understood by the tribals, they would not keep any grievances against the forest officers.

One of the officers strongly felt that the forest department never interfered with implementation of area development and welfare scheme for the tribals in any way. On the contrary, thousands of acres of land for major and minor irrigation dams, schemes of rehabilitation, road building, etc. have been given away by the forest department. The forest department thus stood for the welfare of the whole community and particularly the tribals living in forest area.

DYNAMICS OF INDEBTEDNESS AND EXPLOITATION

Introduction

One of the most important economic burden of the tribals is indebtedness, the main cause of land alienation. A number of social and religious obligations lead them to incur debt received from mostly the non-tribals.

The tribal debt no doubt form a part of the general rural indebtedness the liquidation of which is complicated and difficult to achieve. The practice of indebtedness among the tribals is associated with age-old custom of bonded labour, which in the recent past was eliminated in its archaic and mundane form from various parts of the country. The bonded labour connected with indebtedness had assumed a number of forms of inter-personal relationship between the creditor and debtor. Bonded labour has been legally abolished in India, but it continues to persist in disguised form on account of continuous economic helplessness of the poor tribals. One of the important reasons leading to tribal indebtedness and bondage has been the custom of barter system of exchange of services and commodities between the tribals and the non-tribals. Most of the transactions between these two categories of communities, one advanced and the other backward, were based on inequality of payment in the exchange of the loans advanced and recovered under doubtful conditions.

The repayment of loans taken by the tribals from non-tribals include both the amounts of capital and the interest thereon. The unknown system of monetisation for tribals involved in the exchange of goods and services becames a great barrier to establish equitable relationship between the non-tribal giver and the tribal borrower. Since most of the tribals live in subsistence economy, the whole situation leads to indebtedness not only for purchase of agricultural implements, seeds etc. but also for fulfilment of socio-economic and ritual obligations in society. On account of onslaught of draught and scarcity combined by deprivation of their produce from forest at cheaper rate of exchange, they suffered great losses year after year. The chain of misfortunes of this kind haunted many of the tribals and they were forced to go to money-lenders under extreme circumstances to buy daily necessities of foodgrains, oil salt, kerosene, etc.

It is clearly found from the revised document of the Tribal Area Sub-Plan of the Government of Gujarat — 1976, that no reliable statistics regarding tribal indebtedness was available. In the present study, a general effort was made to collect data through correspondence with the concerned departments of State the Government, to find out the number of applications made for debt redemption by tribals as well as amount of debt within the perview of Gujarat Rural Debtors' Relief Act of 1976. The data on incidence of indebtedness and court cases of money-lending in tribal areas for the year 1976-77 were also collected. We shall present the important findings of these studies at the end of this chapter. What we have attempted in a big way, in the following pages is however an exploration of various aspects of the problem and behavioural dimensions of indebtedness and exploitation of the tribals.

The information that goes into the following points was derived from the field interviews conducted with the help of an inventory of facts administered to officials and non-officials. The responses to a special questionnaire addressed to the subject matter departments have also been incorporated in the report. The various answers and responses have been classified broadly under five points as follows:

(i) Causes of debts and prevention, and impact of Money-Lending Act of 1946 on extent of indebtedness,

(ii) Steps taken by the government to restore tribal land and other valuable articles from the creditors,

(iii) Extent of freedom achieved from indebtedness by tribals and extra-ordinary circumstances such as social pressures and malpractices of petty officers, contractors, etc. leading to exploitation of tribals,

(iv) Ameliorative and relief measures against indebtedness through institutional finance, cooperative marketing, social workers, missionaries, etc, and

(v) Traces of bonded labour.

It may be pointed out that the problem of indebtedness and money-lending is a technical issue as it involves the rate of interest, mortgage of land or other valuable articles such as ornaments etc., so far as legal-rational aspect of exchange is concerned. However, it is largely a human problem of inter-personal relationships and it goes beyond the purview of duties and responsibilities prescribed by the government for the cooperative societies and the officers looking after eliminating private money-lending in general. It should also be noted that the concepts of indebtedness and exploitation are relatively new to tribals and therefore, it is necessary to deal with them in a general sociological frame of reference than only from the point of view of legal rational relationships.

Prevention of Debts and Money-lending

According to a senior officer in the office of the Registrar General of Co-operative Societies of the Government, the main reason of indebtedness of tribals was their extremely poor economic conditions. Tribals incur debts sometimes on account of getting daily necessities of life such as cloth, foodgrains, etc. But they incur heavy debts for expenditure specially at the time of marriage and mortuary rights. Those people who have land, tend to incur debts in order to supply inputs and other necessities for raising better crops.

The real problem, the tribals face if that they are utterly ignorant about what is good for them in changing times. They stick to their old customs and practices even though they get into pitiable condition and endanger their economic stability and well-being. There is dearth of new leadership to educate them and bring them out of ignorance inherited from the past. There are also wested interests developed among tribal leaders who exploit the common persons of their own group.

The above elaborate and frank reasons provided by an official regarding the causes of indebtedness among the tribals were generally shared not only by other officials, but also by non-officials from various tribal areas in the State. We shall point out any special and outstanding information on the subject as and when required, but before doing this, we may also record the opinion of some senior officials on the measures that may be taken for removing indebtedness among the tribals.

The officials believed that there was no special provision in the Money-lenders Act of 1946 which can be helpful in preventing, reducing or eliminating the debts among the tribals. The U.N. Dhebar Commission, however, gave a serious thought to this problem and recommended appointment of fifteen cooperative officers for field visits and detect money-lending in each tribal area. No doubt, the Gujarat Rural Debtors' Relief Act initiated on 15th August 1976 has been implemented, but nothing much seems to have been achieved by this Act in general. However, so far as the tribals were concerned, small and marginal farmers have specially benefited from implementation of this Act.[1]

One of the reasons of tribal indebtedness lie with the shop-keepers living in the vicinity of the tribal villages. These shop-keepers not only indulge in exploitative trade practices with the tribals, but also lend money without obtaining a money-lending licence from the Government for this purpose. If on the other hand, the tribals are asked to report about unlawful practices of the shop-keepers, they decline to admit that they have taken money from anybody on interest. However, when the crops are reaped, they are taken straightway to the shop-keepers who while paying purchase price exploits the tribals. They also charge exhorbitant rate of interest for the money borrowed by them. This kind of dual exploitation can be prevented if the economic condition of the tribals can be improved with the money advanced from the cooperative societies, for investment in agriculture, irrigation, animal husbandry and such other productive purpose.

One of the social workers of Sabarkantha district reported that ignorance was the main cause of indebtedness among the tribals. They do not know how to handle money and keep accounts. Moreover, they were addicted to vices such as drinking, smoking, etc. and spent beyond their means. However, it was notable that a large number of district level cooperative societies were active and come to the help of the tribals in getting easy loans. The activities of the Land Development Bank also came to their rescue. The Government provided Tagavi loans as a result of which very few tribals were in debt in this district. The Money-Lenders Act was also implemented alongwith the Debtors' Relief Act, and curbed the unlawful activities of money-lenders.

According to another non-official (MLA), the various Acts meant for protecting the tribals from exploitation through unauthorised money-lenders did not work satisfactorily. The cooperative officer and the money-lenders worked in collusion with one another and encourage the tribals to incur debt without putting anything in writing. This was the main reason why non-officials in general felt that no practical solution was in sight for saving the tribals from the clutches of money-lenders.

One of the officials from the Dangs was forth-right in giving a picture of indebtedness of the tribals in the area. He said that in earlier times when tribals were engaged for labour in forest, they were advanced loans and exploited by the contractors. The method of exploitation was that they were given less wages against more work leading to non-clearance of loans. The rights for agriculture in the Dangs district was extended from year to year by forest department and therefore, the tribals did not put their heart and soul into the land. Many a times, the poor tribals had to loose the seeds invested in sowing on account of excessive rains as well as lack of proper development of land. All these disabilities of the tribals in the Dangs compelled them to take the help of money-lenders. The ignorance and helplessness of the tribals were fully exploited by the money-lenders who reduced them to the condition of more and more indebtedness.

It was reported that nearly 70 per cent of the tribals in the Dangs were reduced gradually to utter poverty in the past. It was suggested that the situation can be remedied if a special fund called Dangs Loan Fun was raised by the government. It is from this fund that the tribals can be given economic assistance at the time of religious, development or social events. They can also be helped by providing assistance for education of children, medical aid and loans for starting new vocations. The present practice of making loan available to tribals from a variety of different sources should be replaced by a single agency such as one suggested above. There are a number of schemes of agriculture and cooperative assistance through which arrangements were made to give loans to tribals. However, the experience had shown that the possibilities of getting loans from a cooperative society remain meagre because of their weak economic status. The principle of credit worthyness becomes an obstacle. The rate of interest taken by these agricultural cooperative societies is also very high. On the other hand, the forest labour cooperative societies were more helpful and worked effectively for the benefit of the tribals.

In some parts of Surat district, the private money-lending was considerably reduced and the tribals were liberated from the clutches of the money-lenders. In one taluka, tribals were able to get back their land to the tune of about 50 acres.

One of the non-officials from the Vadodara district pointed out that small land-holdings, lack of better manure, seeds etc. lead to poor crops in the tribal land. The facilities for irrigation were also not provided in the tribal areas and specially at the time of draught there was no hope for rescue. Tribals, therefore, suffered a great deal. They also were the victims of wasteful social customs which compelled them to take money on loan from money-lenders. The rate of interest sometimes taken by the money-lenders ranged between 50 to 300 per cent, which seems to be unbelievable. As if this was not enough, some money-lenders charged at the rate of 600 per cent of interest which is known as *Zadap* (hurried) interest.

The occasions of the tribals getting into this type of indebtedness was common before the starting of monsoon season when food-grains with the family got nearly exhausted. The money-lenders for instance would gives him one maund of *Jowar* grains against three times the cotton pods to be returned to him. This meant that a person was to pay about Rs. 100 to the money-lender for taking one maund of *Jowar* worth Rs. 20 only. It was regrettable to note that there was no satisfactory alternative to lending money to the tribals, in time of unforeseen calamity, than the usurious money-lender. Some people were thinking of solving these problems through rural credit banks, but it was difficult to envisage as to when this type of programmes would be implemented.

The general picture of the relationship between the tribal debtor and the money-lender was under strain on account of The Gujarat Rural Debtors' Relief Act. Those tribals who filled up forms prescribed by the Government for abolition of the debts were point blank refused money on loan from the private money-lenders. This lend many of them into great hardships during urgent need of money for social purpose. In view of the unpredictable need of the money, many of the tribals made a point to pay up the borrowed money from the private money-lenders, so that they can again be trusted for loan during emergency. The situation become so serious at times that the money-lenders who used to advance money purely on personal bond was reluctant to do so. It was not possible to get private loan without invariably mortgaging ornaments or other valuables. In Dangs, the tribal debts for unproductive purposes amounted to about 28.41 per cent for domestic consumption, 9.12 per cent for repairs in the house, 5.75 per cent for marriages and other ceremonies and 2.27 per cent for the purpose of medical aid.

Since there was a time limit prescribed for the implementation of the Rural Debtors' Relief Act, only those who applied for this in time were likely to be benefited. In fact, a large number of debtors did not do so on account of intimate relationship with private creditors. The dependable image of government willingness to help tribals calls for greater improvement. The huge sums of money spent by the government for the development of tribals was reported to be wasted in the absence of missionary zeal among government officials. Despite the Rural Debtors' Relief Act, exploitation of tribals went on at the hands of money-lenders. The gravity of the situation did not subside as a new class of well-to-do tribals fashioning as money-lenders were also active. This made it easy for them to orally mortgage land to tribal creditors who were not subject to prevention of land alienation despite Section 73-A.

An official from Surat district, however, was of the opinion that the tribals benefited generally on account of debts being mostly wiped off or scaled down due to Debtors' Relief Act. The other opinion, however, was that the Debtors' Relief Act created difficulty for an ignorant tribal to take advantage of it. According to the Act, applications have to be given to Panchayat or Municipality for abolition of debt by a tribal. These authorities have to issue notifications inviting objections to the applications within a period of 30 days. All the applications with objections received against money-lenders have to be further forwarded to the Debt Settlement Officers (Non-Gazetted-III). Some of the administrative problems involved in this procedure were difficult for the ordinary tribals to take care of and it led to adverse side effects on the credibility of a tribal. These were some of the reasons why the Debtors' Relief Act reportedly failed to achieve results in practice in favour of ignorant tribals.

Steps to Restore Land and Valuables

There was no appreciable impact of Debtors' Relief Act on the restoration of mortgaged land and other valuable property of the tribals. It was, therefore, out of question as to how much land was restored under the preview of the Act and also whether sizable number of tribals received any benefit on account of the same. One of senior officers of the Registrar General of Cooperative Societies in the State government clearly indicated that they did not have figures to supply on the extent of restoration of the land to the tribals on account of Debtors' Relief Act.

It was reported by an official from the district of Panchmahals that in 359 cases out of 764, the possession of land was restored under the Debtors' Relief Act. The impact of these actions in favour of the tribals by the government was difficult to measure until figures on extent of other sources advancing credit were available.

It was revealed by an official from Rajpipla taluka of Bharuch district that actions were taken for restoration of land to the tribals under Section 73-A. It led to restoration of tribal land to the tune of 876 acres. From the Palsana taluka of the Surat District, an officer said that private money-lending was removed and about 50 acres of the land of the tribals was restored. In the Chhotaudepur taluka of Vadodara district, it was reported that actions for restoration of land under Section 73-A was in progress, and it was quite evident that land of the tribals would not be taken away by money-lenders. Tribals had started taking great interest in agriculture, education and other development activities. In many ways, this liberated them from the debt of money-lenders.

A team of Deputy Collector, LND-5 operating in Chhotaudepur taluka for detection of alienated land had made it possible to restore 766.35 acres of land to as many as 230 tribals. However, a non-official said that in some cases, a lot of side money had to be spent for restoration of the land, and no substantive advantage occurred to the tribals. The reason was that the results of Debtors' Relief Act were not fully realised. So far as the problems of land alienation is linked with unemployment among the tribals, such issues cannot be solved satisfactorily. Many tribal labourers had remained under conditions of concealed bondage as they follow their own codes of customs and stick to their traditional debtors.

It is not possible to achieve full results of Debtors' Relief Act unless the tribals' unemployment problems are solved. There are no doubt cases where Debtors' Relief Act had helped in liberation of bonded labour. Some of these people were able to get land on account of tenancy legislation and under Ceiling Act. Banks and Cooperative Societies came forward to give them money on loan and quite a few of them had really begun to enjoy peaceful and happy life.

Writing on the causes of land alienation in Gujarat, S.N. Dubey and Murdia writes, "In view of ignorance of the tribals of the existing laws, their inherent sense of honesty, integrity and loyalty, the number of cases identified as illegal represents only a fraction or the actual cases of land alienation in the State. Further, a recent study on the subject in the State of Gujarat by the Tribal Research and Training Institute, Gujarat Vidyapith, Ahmedabad, points out that the land is mortgaged with the money-lender and is not immediately sold for the loan. The land is recovered after payment of the debt. The tribal prefers a person of his own community, to whom he mortgages his land."[2]

Freedom from Indebtedness and Exploitation

As revealed from earlier accounts many a legislations and acts have been promulgated to relieve the tribals condition of want and poverty. However as will be revealed from the following pages, tribals have faced many a problems of raising their standard of living by circumventing exploitation of various types. In the district of Banaskantha, the money-lenders were Bohra, Memon, and Baniyas in general who maintain shops in the tribal areas. These people, purchased agricultural products of the tribals as against the money or goods borrowed after the end of a year.

According to one non-official, the Bohra shop-keepers took away crops of a tribal and promised to pay back on their behalf, Tagavi loans etc. to the government. But in fact, they did not really help the tribals in relieving of his burden of this kind. The tribal take goods from the shops of these people without asking the price. The borrowings of goods may be in the form of grains, pulses, clothes, shoes etc. In this kind of relationship with the shop-keeper, he has not to go far away into a village or town to buy these commodities.

For this, he has to pay exorbitant price in the form of new crops taken away by the shop-keeper. One of the mechanisms of the Bohra shop-keepers was said to be to keep the Sarpanch of the village Panchayat on their side and do whatever they liked with other tribals. It was reported that there were quite a few shops and processing units of the Bohras operating in this area almost for the last 200 years.

In certain cases, the interest taken on loan was at the rate of Rs. 7 for Rs. 10 after one year. Some of the tribals mortgaged their ornaments with the Bohra shop-keeper against loans which ultimately resulted in the liquidation of valuables mortgaged. Sometimes, when mortgaged ornaments were returned to a tribal, they managed to get them converted into light weight than the original deposited with them. Not only this, in many cases, the original piece of ornament was not at all returned under the pretext that the ornament was taken away by another debtor after payment of his debt, out of mistake. This kind of unfair methods, cheating and rampant exploitation by the money-lenders, led to perpetual penury of ignorant tribals.

Added to the misfortune of wanton exploitation by others, a tribal was highly addicted to drinking which not only damaged his health, but also washed away his meagre earnings. Some of these habits are connected with the social customs. A person is compelled to commit expensive ceremonies and rituals by the caste panchayat which also became responsible for his indirect exploitation.

The Police Department was also blamed for eating away substantial amount of earnings of a tribal in bribe, on account of his tendency to commit social crimes of light or serious nature. In a village called *Dhagadhia*, it was reported by a non-official that one tribal with two wives got into trouble when one of his wives died after taking some poisonous medicine. The in-laws of the diseased wife went against him to take revenge for death of the woman. The kins-men not only took money for the purpose of mortuary cremation of the woman but also compelled him to pay a customary amount of money to mitigate the social offence he was supposed to have committed in the incident. This is one of the dimensions of exploitation of a person permitted within the tribal social systems itself.

The village functionaries, such as a village level worker, etc. who are supposed to make the subsidy available to a tribal for buying cattle or sinking a water-well were reported to help the tribal only after some gratification. He will raise technical problems of credit-worthiness, etc. against a particular person. This would prompt a person to come forward with commitment for some bribe. In some cases half of the amount of subsidy advanced had to be given to the village functionary for supporting his case, and getting the money released.

The tribals were able to get loans from the cooperative societies at a lower rate in interest. This money, sometimes found its way in the hands of non-tribal money-lenders. Thus the purpose for which the cooperative societies came to the help of the tribals to keep them away from the clutches of the money-lenders was practically lost. The thumb impressions of illiterate tribals taken by the creditors on paper keep them under their obligations for a long time. There were said to be thousands of cases of this type leading to no solution of the exploitation of the tribals through private money-lenders. Their debts kept on increasing in spite of various schemes of the government of relieving them of debt bondage. The non-officials who gave this information were of the opinion that the village shops of the Bohra money-lenders from the tribal areas should be completely removed. This was the only way to put an end to the exploitation of the tribals. In the place of these shops, it was suggested that Danta Krushi Mandal should be made to open branches in the form of ration shops in tribal areas. Such shopping centres be used as centres of exchange of goods and daily necessities between and among the tribals.

Some of the tribals were fairly health conscious and they took advantage of health services of the primary health centres in their areas. Here also they were sometimes exploited by unscrupulous health staff. This kind of exploitation took place in different forms, such as: (i) he had to pay a special charge for admission in indoor department, (ii) he was charged for injection administered to him, (iii) he had to pay for getting even prescription, and lastly (iv) he had to pay for ambulance service through his nose. It was indicated by an official that a private medical practitioner in the Danta taluka was very generous to the tribals and stopped exploitation of the tribals in need of health services, by himself providing cheap treatment to patients.

Another category of tribal exploitation was out right cheating by the traders who bought minor forest produces from them. Sometimes a person was not even able to earn the rightful wage for his labour because the traders purchase their goods at a much lower rate. On the contrary they buy their daily necessities from the traders at a very high rate of payment amounting to double edged exploitation.

The staff members of various government departments touring tribal areas were looked after by the tribals as hosts. The hospitality required a great deal of time and expenses to a tribal in general.

Arrangements for this type of free services by a tribal to a visiting official are also forms of indirect exploitation.

In the process of money-lending, there was a finer element of exploitation when a person first made token payment of Rs. 10 to Rs. 15 for making a money-lender open his money bag. This meant that a tribal was given only Rs. 85 to 90 in cash for borrowing Rs. 100. Further more, an amount Rs. 24 to 36 was cut by way of interest of a whole year in advance. If a person was not agreeable to make the payment of interest in advance, he had to make one person available to money-lender by way of bonded labour for one year. As if this was not enough, immediately after the harvest season, the person had to return loan in the term of grain. At this time also, the money-lender fixed the price of the grain at a much lower rate than what was prevalent in the market. In some cases, the value of the grains was not counted on the spot, and in its place an ad hoc quota of grains was credited in the name of the tribal. After five or six months again, the accounts were made and the tribal was not given any interest of the grains credited in his name with the business man. Connected with this type of exploitation was also another mechanism in which a trader sold domestic goods to a tribal much below the weightage for which he was charged.

In the districts of Banaskantha, Sabarkantha, Panchmahals and to some extent Vadodara, the money-lending was done by Bohra and Bania traders in general. Moreover, there was a tendency among money-lenders to withdraw and wind-up money-lending business with the tribals and occupy themselves in some other occupations. We shall later see that in the remaining districts, the money-lending was done by many other social groups of traders. In any case, what we have recorded in various forms of exploitation of the tribals by money-lenders remain common to all districts. There were still other methods and bases of indirect exploitation which may be briefly noted here.

The weekly markets called *hats* are held regularly in tribal areas. They are the most common centres of exchange of goods of domestic use and minor forest produce between tribals and the non-tribals. It is at the weekly *hats* that the members of trading community worked to find ways and means of cheating the tribals in weightage and payment of lower prices for the things sold by the tribals. Most of the tribals had to sell their goods at a lower rate and buy their necessities at a higher rate. There was also another category of exploitation of the tribals through market mechanism. The public sector cooperative societies also build up their resources by taking unfair benefits in the management of giving loans and receiving re-payment either in cash or in kind. This kind of exploitation was reported in the study of various labour cooperatives. We have provided quite a few instances of this in the previous chapter. In some areas such as Panchmahals district, the fair price shops were opened by cooperative societies but they were later on indirectly run by the Bania or Bohra traders.

The tribal educational institutions such as Ashram Shalas are run by voluntary organisations who sometimes appointed unqualified staff for responsible educational positions and received grants from the government. Many of such schools however utilise government grants for the benefit of managers in the name of building institutional resources. What the tribal children get by way of education is extremely a poor return of the money invested by the government. Tribals who migrate seasonally to other areas for labour between Diwali and the onset of monsoon can not send children to schools regularly. They are cheated in payment of lower wages by their employers who neither made arrangements for children's education nor for suitable huts to live in. Where mango trees were found in the land of tribals within the boundary of a village, they had to take permission of Panchayat Sarpanch and Mamlatdar for cutting the trees. The tribal was paid at the rate of Rs. 50 to 100 per tree by the Panchayat while actually it was worth Rs. 500 or so. This kind of exploitation of tribals was done by interested parties.

In the district of Dangs there were hardly any licence-holding money-lender. In recent times however, six applications were received by the government from small traders, many of whom struck advantageous dealings with the backward Kotwalia tribals in this area. Kotwalias were made to cut bamboo on behalf of these traders in the place of advances received from time to time. Quite a number of Kotwalias were reported to be under the debts of these traders almost permanently. In the survey of a village, it was found that 75 per cent of the house-holds were indebted to the tune of Rs. 110-71 per household.

In the districts of Bharuch, Surat, Vadodara and Valsad, the money-lenders came from many social groups. They included varieties of Maharastrians from the border areas, Marwadi, Sindhi Muslims, Parsis, Makrani, Ghanchi, Bhaiya, Pathana and Lohana. Added to this, some of the rich tribals themselves became money lenders. It was alleged that tribal money-lender were more ruthless exploiters of poorer tribals than the non-tribal money-lenders.

It may also be noted that a kind of cultural exploitation of tribals was also done by the non-tribals. It was reported from the district of Bharuch that a lot of moral degradation had set in among the tribals. The music, dance and other artifacts such as dress, ornaments, etc. of the tribals were used for commercial purpose. The educated non-tribals sometimes sold rare pieces of folk art at higher prices to outsiders. The innocent tribals sold at throw away prices their old folk art treasures in order to buy cheap variety of plastic and other goods manufactured in factories. Sometimes they would sell their pieces of tribal art simply in exchange of worthless goods towards which they are attracted on account of false sense of prestige.

One of the important domestic animals required by the tribals for agricultural assistance is the bullock. The itinerant Sindhi Muslims who trade in bullocks pay a visit to the tribal areas and sells bullocks at exhorbitantly high rates to the tribals. Generally, it is not possible for a tribal to pay the price in cash, and so he had to make urgent arrangements for the payment of at least the 1/3rd of the fixed price. In case a tribal was not able to pay the remaining amount on a prescribed date, (usually second day of the bright half of the month of *Falgun*), the bullocks were just taken back by the Sindhi trader, and the tribal had to forefeit the 1/3rd of the price already paid in cash or kind.

It is interesting to note that in some areas, the tribal Sarpanch himself was made to lift the bundle of records of village Talati-cum-Secretary for transporting the same to the taluka headquarters. For this, the tribal Sarpanch was paid Rs. 2 to 3 by the Talati who pocketed rest of the money. Such stories reported from some areas may be over-blown, but the fact remains that even the elected tribal leaders sometimes suffered at the hands of unscrupulous village functionaries, who infact, are supposed to assist Village Sarpanch.

In some parts of the Valsad and Surat districts, vast grass-lands provide a lot of labour to the tribals for cutting the grass. As elsewhere, here also, they were exploitated because of low wages under which they worked. The Warli tribals in general worked in various occupations such as cutting of trees in forest, tapping juice of toddy, making salt-pans and collecting fish from the sea. In all these activities, they were exploitated by the intermediaries and various types of contractors. These contractors had easy access to tribal workers because not only they posed themselves as political workers, but also as social workers.

Ameliorative Measures by Financial Institutions and Voluntary Agencies

There is substantive programme of institutional finances through Tribal Area Sub-Plan schemes. We shall not go much in detail in this chapter about the work done by the tribal area project administrators. However, it is pertinent to refer to the institutional finances provided for debt redemption to tribals through Land Development Bank (LDB). The activities of LDB has no doubt been of great help to many a tribals. However, there were certain practical difficulties and problems which went beyond the influence of LDB in helping the tribals. The private money-lenders as reported earlier advanced loans on the crops of a person. As soon as the harvesting time was near and crop was ripe the money-lenders recovered their dues in grains at cheaper rate. The LDB was not able to keep a watch over this kind of situation to save new crops from being taken away by usurious money-lenders.

Many a times, a person took loans from the LDB in cash by mortgaging his land and made payment against his debt to old-time money-lender. This indirectly helped a tribal in taking courage to go in for loans beyond his means from private money-lenders. It is also true that subsidy was available from various government agencies for agriculture and other developmental programmes. However, as indicated earlier, they were not able to get subsidy in time. Before more damage was done to a particular person by his actually going to a private money-lender, it was necessary that payment of subsidy was promptly made.

In any case, it was reported by one of the non-officials from Khedbrahma taluka of Sabarkantha district that the loans advanced to a tribal through government schemes and institutions such as LDB etc. were not enough for his requirements. The development programmes undertaken by a person therefore suffered a great deal. This refers to sinking of a well, buying a motor and pumping machine for irrigation etc. If the LDB and the government could give enough money required to an individual tribal, he will not have to go to a money-lender and become a debtor. Whatever limited money was received through these sources by a tribal, it helped him complete only a part of the developmental work. The total task on hand remained incomplete. For instance, when LDB advanced money for well and irrigation pump-sets on the basis of the bill produced, there was still need for more money to take care of other accessories. The money required for buying corrugated tin sheets, cement, etc. for building houses etc. including the labour costs was not being given by these sources. Obviously tribals had to go to a private money-lender to meet extra costs. One of the officials reported that under the present circumstances, voluntary agencies were lagging behind in helping the tribals to overcome various problems. The vacuum created by their inaction was filled by the Christian missionaries in due course of time.

Most of the financing institutions come forward to advance loans to the tribals for productive purposes only. They therefore, find it very difficult to meet their expenditure of non-productive nature related to social events, ceremonies and festivals. They have, therefore to go to Bohra Bania, Parsi and other money-lenders as discussed earlier.

In the case of taking loans for seeds, tools, etc. for productive purposes, there is a great need of saving tribals from being exploited by businessman. This can be done if more and more of Large Agricultural Multi-purpose Cooperative Societies (LAMPS) are established at taluka level in tribal areas. It should be possible for LAMPS to meet the requirements of the tribals in lieu of the entire produce of their land. These societies should be managed completely by the tribals themselves with the technical advice and guidance of government officers. There should not be any social worker or a private person to become a member of LAMPS. The most important thing to be kept in mind in this context is that there should be only one institutional agency that should advance loans to the tribals for all their requirements. A programme of this type will help a great deal in controlling the Christian missionaries pressing in the loans for various purposes advanced to a tribal. Moreover, if these institutions are managed by the tribals as members, there is likelihood of less corruption in the process of buying and distribution of basic necessities in tribal areas. Some new cooperative agencies can also be started to take up the responsibility of opening fair price shops with a large number of tribal membership so that profits go to the tribals themselves.

The Christian missionaries were actively working to help the tribals in some parts of tribal areas. In the monsoon they come forward to provide grains, buffaloes etc. The Dangi Bhils take special advantage of this facility. One of the adverse impact of this help seemed to be that some tribals lost initiative for hard work and were getting dependent on almost free help. For instance, the missionaries advanced a loan of Rs. 2200 to tribals for buying buffaloes. Against each such loan, he would get the loan of Rs. 1,100 from the Bank of Baroda. The remaining half of the amount was recovered from the income of the milk supply of an individual. One of the non-officials suggested that the Tribal Development Block should be used for providing such help to the tribals. It was reported that the missionaries were operating actively in Dediapada, Sagbara, Netrang, Jhagadia, etc. The Collector of Dangs provided land to the missionaries for work facility in the areas of Ahwa and Pimpri. According to one source, it was the land of the tribals given to missionaries that led some of the local social workers file objections with the Gujarat Government. Some non-officials said that the missionaries take trouble to carry the buffaloes right at the door steps of the tribals. Not only this, one of their persons toured every village and monitored the manner in which the buffaloes were taken care of. They also provided veterinary services and made necessary arrangements for sale of milk in the morning and in the evening. The fodder was regularly provided and charges were recovered from the income of the milk. The money saved after deductions of the various charges was recovered against instalments of loans. The remaining savings were handed over to the tribal concerned.

In the district of Bharuch, similar programmes were organised by the missionaries. The needs of immediate importance for the welfare of the tribals were also looked after by the missionaries. For instance, they helped the sick persons for medical aid, hospitalisation, etc., as well as free legal aid for redressal of their grievances against money-lenders. For the latter, they employ requisite experts to carry out legal proceedings until the settlement of the case in the court of law.

In Rajpipla, the government had opened a Centre called Free Legal Aid Project (FLAP) in 1975. The FLAP heard the grievances of tribals and offered legal aid if required. This kind of centres were started in five talukas of this district. Every centre had one field worker who was to find out from the people as to the manner in which FLAP cases are handled. It was on the recommendations of the field workers that the advocates connected with the centre scrutinised the applications and discussed merits of the case with parties concerned. The legal aid programme covered a wide range of problems such as: (i) implementation of Section 73-A, (ii) Tenancy Act, (iii) Debt Relief Act, (iv) Minimum Wages Act, and (v) Miscellaneous Acts including Alienations Abolition Act of 1955.

Before the introduction of free legal aid project, it was reported that the tribals did not get copies of record of rights from local *Talatis*. In case copies were provided, they were on payment of bribe in the form of cash, foodgrains or even ornaments. This referred mainly to the availability of copies of Village Forms VII and XII from the *Talati*. The interested and influential parties who were affected by the legal actions saw that the tribals did not get the copies of Village Forms. They, therefore, exercised all kinds of pressures on the *Talati* at the village level.

One of the officials from Bharuch district was of the opinion that missionaries took roots into some parts of tribal areas on account of failure of local leadership. Not only this, voluntary agencies became politicised to such an extent that they lost the vigour of helping the really poor tribals. The great advantage that the missionaries have is that they do not suffer from disunity among themselves. The tribal leaders were not only sometimes fighting among themselves, but also become puppets in the hands of powerful non-tribal leaders in the area. The foreign missionaries on the other hand remained politically neutral. They not only provided economic help but also run educational and health care institutions. The managers of the scheduled banks are also happy in advancing loans to tribals through them. They are sure about the recovery on the basis of deposits in the accounts of missionaries.

The impact of missionaries in the districts of Surat, Vadodara and Valsad was limited. This may be on account of relative advancement of most of the tribal talukas in these districts. Though there are a few talukas in the district of Valsad where some of the most backward tribes are helped by missionaries.

Presented below are two Tables 7.1 and 7.2 providing information on a number of applications for debt redemption and amount of tribal debts recorded in several talukas in the year 1976. The second table gives information on incidence of court cases of money-lending for the years 1976 and 1977. The information in both these tables are separated in terms of tribal talukas and tribal pockets. It is revealed from Table 7.1 that the largest number of applications numbering 1688 involving the amount of Rs. 3,95,513 came from the Vyara taluka of Surat district. This shows that the average amount of debt per case was not so large as revealed from the figures of Sagbara taluka in Bharuch district reporting 833 applications involving Rs. 16,14,114. Similarly from Naswadi taluka, 805 applications involving Rs. 15,56,000 were reported. The cases from Devgadh Baria in Panchmahals and Bardoli in Surat tend to show that the applications for debt abolition were much less as compared to the amount involved. In the district of Valsad, there seems to be more or less a uniform pattern of number of applications. The money involved was more or less comparable.

TABLE 7.1: Number of applications received and amount of debt recorded under Gujarat Rural Debtors Relief Act of 1976

Name of District	Name of Taluka	No. of applications received	Amount of debt involved
1	2	3	4
	I. *Tribal Talukas*		
Sabarkantha	Vijaynagar	19	20,400
"	Khedbrahma	109	72,798
"	Bhiloda	5	19,299
"	Meghraj	165	1,59,808
Vadodara	Chhotaudepur	554	5,06,239
"	Naswadi	805	15,56,000
"	Tilakwada	209	6,58,449
Panchmahal	Jhalod	121	15,01,650
"	Dahod	64	76,070
"	Santrampur	335	4,09,221
"	Limkheda	10	5,375
"	Devgadh Baria	237	4,37,175
Bharuch	Sagbara	833	16,14,114
"	Dediapada	169	1,39,410
"	Valia	152	1,27,107
"	Jhagadia	504	4,82,700
"	Nandod	439	6,27,238
Surat-I	Uchchhal	—	—
"	Vyara	1,658	3,99,513
"	Valod	332	95,601

Contd.

TABLE 7.1 *Contd.*

1	2		3	4
Surat-I	Songadh		89	50,112
"	Nizar		–	–
Surat-II	Mahuva		10	15,820
"	Mandvi		67	17,636
"	Mangrol		115	1,06,451
"	Bardoli		96	1,50,026
Valsad	Dharampur		31	34,677
"	Vansda		146	28,470
"	Chikhali		35	52,975
"	Pardi		32	32,079
"	Umbergaon		117	81,090
Dangs	Ahwa		–	–
Total for I			7,458	94,77,503
	II. *Tribal Pockets*			
Banaskantha	Palanpur	Amirgadh	6	29,105
"	Danta	Danta	64	90,324
Panchmahals	Halol	Kathola	32	85,666
"	Godhra	Mora	161	93,928
Vadodara	Sankheda	Vadeli		
		Bhatpur	–	–
"	Jabugam	Karali		
	(Pavi-Jetpur)	Bhikhapura	1,801	26,63,225
Broach	Ankleshwar	Ankleshwar	296	2,14,913
Surat	Kamrej	Kamrej	6	1,475
"	Palsana	Palsana	1	100
Valsad	Gandevi	Rahej	–	–
"	Valsad	Atgam	–	–
"	Valsad	Ronwel	–	–
"	Navsari	Sisodra-Ganesh	–	–
Total for II			2,367	31,78,736
Total for (I) & (II)			9,825	1,26,56,239

TABLE 7.2: Incidence of Court Cases of Money-lending in Tribal Areas: 1976 and 1977

Name of District	Name of Taluka/ Pocket (P)	Year	Total Licensed Money-lenders	Cases of breach of ML Act	Cases Committed to Courts	Cases of Departmental Action	Cases pending Action	Cases Filed
1	2	3	4	5	6	7	8	9
Banaskantha	Amirgadh (p)	1976	99	1	1	–	–	One case filed in Court decided in 1978
		1977	9	–	–	–	–	
"	Danta (p)	1976	10	–	–	–	–	
		1977	7	–	–	–	–	
Sabarkantha	Vijaynagar	1976	11	6	–	–	6	
		1977	5	8	–	–	8	
"	Khedbrahma	1976	36	4	4	–	–	–
		1977	35	1	1	–	–	
"	Bhiloda	1976	62	56	56	–	–	Court decided 56 cases
		1977	49	16	–	–	16	Court decided in a case filed in 1975
"	Meghraj	..... Not received						
Panch-Mahals	Jhalod	1976	54	318	315	3	–	103
		1977	37	156	155	1	–	18
"	Dahod	1976	52	3	3	–	–	3
		1977	37	2	2	–	–	2
"	Santrampur	1976	62	34	3	16	15	–
		1977	31	45	2	30	13	–
"	Limkheda	1976	6	640	347	293	–	10
		1977	5	17	17	–	–	3
"	Devgadhbaria	1976	61	1	1	1	–	–
		1977	57	5	5	5	–	–
"	Mora (p) of Godhra Taluka	1976	4	2	–	2	–	2
		1977	4	1	1	–	–	Case decided by Court in 1978
"	Kathola (p) of Halol Taluka	1976 1977	..... Not received					
Vadodara	Chhotaudepur	1976	58	33	–	33	–	33
		1977	54	16	–	16	–	16
"	Naswadi	1976	22	21	–	11 (decided)	10	–
		1977	17	1	1	–	1	Pending with ADR (ML) Surat
"	Tilakwada	1976	20	1	1	1	–	–
		1977	20	6	–	6	–	–

Contd.

TABLE 7.2 *Contd.*

1	2	3	4	5	6	7	8	9
Vadodara	Bhikhapura (p) of Ravi Jatpur	1976 1977	.... Nil					
"	Karali (p) of Pavi Jetpur	1976 1977	.... Nil					
"	Bhatpur (p) of Sankheda	1976 1977	.... Nil					
"	Vadeli (p) of Sankheda	1976 1977	.... Nil					
Bharuch	Sagbara	1976-77	14	11	—	11	—	—
		1977-78	10	2	—	2	—	—
"	Dediapada	1976-77	1	1	—	2	—	—
		1977-78	1	1	—	1	—	—
"	Valia	1976-77	4	1	—	1	—	—
		1977-78	4	2	—	2	—	—
"	Jhagadia	1976-77	6	2	—	2	—	—
		1977-78	4	1	—	1	—	—
"	Nandod	1976	20	8	—	8	—	—
		1977	15	7	—	7	—	—
"	Ankleshwar (p)	1976 1977	.... Not received					
Surat	Uchchhal	1976	10	2	—	2	—	—
		1977	—	1	—	1	—	—
"	Vyara	1976	24	12	1	12	—	—
		1977	6	4	1	4	—	—
"	Valod	1976	22	—	—	—	—	—
		1977	20	3	—	3	—	—
"	Songadh	1976	21	7	—	7	—	—
		1977	24	5	1	5	—	—
"	Nizar	1976	1	2	—	2	—	—
		1977	1	1	—	1	—	—
"	Mahuva	1976	6	—	—	—	—	—
		1977	6	2	—	2	—	—
"	Mandvi	1976	8	—	—	—	—	—
		1977	4	—	—	—	—	—
"	Mangrol	1976	8	—	—	—	—	—
		1977	8	3	—	3	—	—
"	Bardoli	1976	15	—	—	—	—	—
		1977	14	9	2	8	—	—
"	Palsana (p)	1976 1977	.... Nil					
"	Kamrej (p)	1976 1977	.... Nil					
Valsad	Dharampur	1976	1	—	—	—	—	—
		1977	—	—	—	—	—	—
"	Vansda	1976 1977	.... Not received					
"	Chikhali	1976	7	3	—	3	—	—
		1977	5	—	—	—	—	—

Contd.

TABLE 7.2 *Contd.*

1	2	3	4	5	6	7	8	9
Valsad	Pardi	1976	1	–	–	–	–	–
		1977	1	2	–	2	–	–
"	Umbergaon	1976 1977		.... Not received	....			
"	Atgam, Ronwel (p)	1976	14	6	–	6	–	–
	Valsad taluka	1977	12	4	–	4	–	–
"	Sisodra Ganesh (p)	1976	14	3	–	3	–	–
	Navsari Taluka	1977	22	8	–	8	–	–
"	Rahej (p)	1976	14	14	–	14	–	–
	Gandevi Taluka	1977	14	–	–	–	–	–
Dangs	Dangs	1976	5	–	–	–	–	–
		1977	1	–	–	–	–	–

The position in the tribal pockets was clearly different and more moderate in terms of limited debt of the tribals, except perhaps in Karali pocket of Vadodara district wherein the number of applications were 1801 involving Rs. 26,63,225. In the pocket of Ankleshwar in Bharuch district there were 296 applications involving debt of Rs. 2,14,913. On the other hand, in Kathola pocket of Panchmahals and Danta pocket of Banaskantha, the applications received were 32 involving Rs. 85,666 and 64 involving Rs. 90,324 respectively. The case of Mora pocket of Panchmahals where applications received for debt abolition were 161, involving Rs. 93,928. This seems to be an exceptional case.

The incidence of court cases of money-lending presented in Table 6.2 were specially considered from the point of view of cases worthy of departmental action. Secondly, emphasis was also laid on the number of licenced money-lenders reported from various tribal talukas and pockets. From the Limkheda taluka of Panchmahal district, it was revealed that the total number of licenced money-lenders in 1976 were six, though there were 640 cases of breach of Money-Landing Act. Of these 347 cases were committed to the court, and 293 admitted for departmental action. From the Chhotaudepur, it was revealed that the total number of licensed money-lenders were 58, as against 33 cases of breach of ML Act. All the 33 cases were taken up for departmental action. In the Sagbara taluka of Bharuch, 14 cases of licensed moneylenders as against 11 of breach of ML Act were taken up for departmental action. The other outstanding case was found from Vyara in Surat district where in 976,24 licensed money-lenders against 12 cases of breach of ML Act were to be found. Here again all the 12 cases were taken up for departmental action. Now looking at the relative figures of total licensed money-lenders as such, we find that Sabarkantha, Panchmahals, Vadodara and some parts of Surat and Valsad districts were most enlightened in this matter. One may therefore, conclude that private money-lending was relatively controlled in parts of these districts as compared to other districts.

Traces of Bonded Labour

The Indian Parliament passed the Bonded Labour Systems (Abolition) Act, 1975 which came into force on 25th September, 1975 and provided for abolition of bonded labour system throughout India. However, in Gujarat as perhaps in other states of India, the evil of bonded labour has not been fully abolished. It seems to persist in some form or the other and landlords. They allowed bonded labourers to build their living quarters on plots of land and provided meagre means of livelihood and social expenditure.

The traces of bonded labour were however found in areas where the tribals had to incur debts from private money-lenders. In the opinion of the officials as well as non-officials in general, the bondage of a poor person selling his labour cannot be got rid off until he has to depend on the private individual for meeting expenditure on the emergency situations and unforseen social events. This implies that the better off tribals were rarely the victims of bonded labour because of their ability to get credit from various sources without much difficulty. The statement of a non-official from Vadodara district revealed that bonded labour in some parts of the district continued to exist in some form or the other. The farm servants and labourers in some parts of Surat and other districts were also reported to be working as bonded labourers.

NOTES

1. It may be noted that the general expression "Money-Lending Act", "Debt Abolition Act" etc. appearing in the text refers to (i) Bombay Money-lenders Act, 1946 and (ii) The Gujarat Rural Debt Relief Act, 1976 respectively.
2. S.N. Dubey and R. Murdia, Eds., *Land Alienation and Restoration in Tribal Communities in India*, Himalaya, Bombay, 19 pp. 79-80.

8

DYNAMICS OF DEVELOPMENT AND PANCHAYATI RAJ

Introduction

One of the aims of the present study was to make an assessment of the impact of the Five Year Plans and their implementation leading to improvement of general socio-economic conditions of the tribals. Various kinds of developmental programmes and schemes generated in the process of planning for the tribals was bound to have created impact on the manner in which land reforms, forest policies, agricultural development, tribal debts and other programmes became successful. In this chapter, we shall deal with some aspects of execution of community development among the tribals through planning in general and Tribal Area-Sub-Plans in particular.

As in the case of earlier chapters, presenting dynamic aspects and other dimensions of tribal land problems, the data presented here were derived from indepth interviews and responses collected with the help of a set of guide lines in the form of a questionnaire. The two major types of respondents providing various kinds of information were the officials and non-officials. The efforts connected with the programmes of planned change have been geared to achieve development and growth of tribal society with social justice and economic equality. The central focus of planning however was on strengthening tribal economy, removal of geographical isolation of tribals and increase in levels of education and literacy. The problem of providing gainful employment to surplus tribal population, so far dependent only on resources of the land, was to be solved forthwith.

The information covers a wide range of subjects calling for action from Panchayati Raj institutions. They are soil conservation, consolidation of holdings, provision of irrigation facilities, agricultural inputs, etc. which directly help increase agricultural output leading to strengthening tribal economy. The Five Year Plans provided a number of avenues for social development through various kinds of funds sanctioned by the government for tribal development. The funds are related to various schemes of not only agricultural development, but to other walks of life also and it is necessary therefore to take a stock of difficulties encountered in implementing tribal development schemes. As it is well known, the introduction of Panchayati Raj institutions has been the prime instruments of not only planning, but also of implementing developmental programmes. The community development programmes have been formulated and implemented at various levels of Panchayati Raj institutions. So far as tribal development programmes are concerned, special programmes were evolved in various parts of the country for intensive development of specific areas.

The latest programmes of Tribal Area Sub-Plan in the country and in Gujarat is operated through special Sub-plan administrators at Block or Taluka levels with the help of village panchayats duly elected by the tribals themselves. The Panchayati Raj Act of 1961 empowered Panchayati Raj bodies to make District level plans, and delegated responsibilities of various activities to implement development schemes. These and various other issues connected with tribal development shall be discussed within the framework of the following broad points:

(a) *Planned Development*

(i) Development schemes pertaining to agriculture, irrigation, etc., (ii) improved agricultural practices and methods including animal husbandry, poultry farming, etc. (iii) allocation of funds for development and problems of implementation.

(b) *Panchayati Raj Organisations*

(i) Powers of panchayat in management of land resources, (ii) allocation of special funds for Scheduled Tribes, (iii) special schemes for improvement of live-stock, poultry farming, fishing, dairy, etc., (iv) village development schemes including housing, etc., (v) educational incentives and rural works programmes, (vi) schemes of

Tribal Sub-Plan and problems of coordination.

(c) *Departmental Assessment of Various Schemes and Programmes*

(i) Benefits of agricultural schemes, etc. (ii) veterinary services and milk societies,, (iii) Ashram Shalas, primary schools and secondary schools, (iv) employment and industrial training.

Issues of Planned Change

The tribal area Sub-Plan schemes were started in 53 T.D. Blocks in 1957 as an important asset to the Five Year Plan programmes for the tribals. The tribal area Sub-Plan Projects were started in those talukas of Gujarat where more than 50 per cent of the population come from Scheduled Tribes. For instance, in the district of Valsad, there are eight talukas of which the Sub-Plan Projects were instituted in the Vansda, Dharampur, Chikhli, Pardi and Umbergaon talukas only. Under the Sub-Plans, the tribals were given government help in agricultural improvement by supply of improved seeds, fertilizers, insecticides, agricultural implements and other crop protection assets. A tribal farmer was given 50 per cent assistance on behalf of the government by the Sub-Plan Project administrators.

With regard to irrigation, there are programmes of building check-dams, lift irrigation, irrigation through minor canals, etc. The tribal farmers are also provided help for putting up pumping sets on wells for lift irrigation. The tribals in many parts are also benefited specially by subsidies for buying bullocks, buffaloes, bullock carts, etc. These assets are a great help to some of the tribals interest areas. The complimentary and supplementary vocations of cattle breeding, poultry farming, etc. associated with the economic life of a farmer are also assisted from the Tribal Sub-Plan Project funds.

Some officials reported that although there were village level workers appointed in the rural areas, to help the tribals in getting better knowledge on problems of agriculture, it was necessary that these people remained constantly in touch with advanced tribal farmers so that they are able to give demonstration effects to others. This could be done by the village level workers who with other qualifications, are the holders of diploma in agriculture. In certain tribal districts, the efforts for improvement in agriculture in general were very successful and helpful in improving economic conditions of the tribals. The individual tribals were certainly benefited from the economic assistance received for special schemes through Sub-Plan Projects.

However, certain types of common works such as approach roads, housing for village schools, etc. which required collection of contributory funds from the village people were not executed properly. One of the bottleneck in the development of tribal areas was the absence of good communication facilities. It was not possible for the village functionaries to easily keep in touch with the tribal population or to make suitable living accommodation for himself in tribal villages. Unless a village worker is able to establish quick personal contracts with the farmers at the right point of time, their services are not likely to be fully utilised. The policy of collecting matching funds from the poor tribal community for certain developmental programmes remained unfulfilled and therefore it should not be pursued rigidly.

One of the non-officials from Sabarkantha district reported that voluntary agencies such as Adivasi Seva Samiti and Seva Kendra of Shamalaji, Sisodra and Vijayanagar were actively working to help the tribals in getting the best advantages of development programmes under Sub-Plan Projects. A large number of tribals took the advantage of the services of these voluntary agencies and improved their socio-economic conditions.

One of the officials from a taluka in Panchmahals district reported that the development programmes such as lift irrigation, tanks, irrigation canals, wells, etc. were no doubt helpful in improving water supply for agriculture. However, it was not possible for all the tribal farmers to adopt such facilities and methods of agriculture because of extremely poor economic condition. The rate of water supply for irrigation should be fixed at a low level so that more tribals can take its advantage and increase agricultural output. The rates for supply of water for irrigation were more like a punishment and a deterrent to a poor tribal. Sometimes, a tribal farmer had to pay water charges much beyond agricultural income he was able to get. This led him to incur debts which ultimately resulted in concealed alienation or mortgage of the land. It is, therefore, most urgent to see that the rates of water supply for irrigation are nominal or very low.

Another officials from the Panchmahals reported that the soil conservation was required to be done on a massive scale as this had a high priority in ensuring better agricultural produce in the tribal area.

As this programme was taken up under watershed programme which covers the needy area quite slowly, it piles up payment liability of a farmer. Moreover, supply of water was increased, but integration of other necessary requirements of soil conservation, inputs etc. was not simultaneously ensured. The funds sanctioned and allotted for tribal development in general were not full utilised because implementation was done departmentally without any scope for monitoring and scrutiny of the same at the district level. The development machinery was not effective in the tribal area which did not have good communication facilities. Such areas in particular required special programmes directly relevant in overcoming difficulties of communication. The standard pattern of development schemes for such areas just did not find favourable responses.

As reported by an official about 25 different schemes were implemented in a tribal area for two years under different sectors of activities such as agricultural production, soil conservation, minor irrigation, etc. The response of the tribals was quite encouraging specially in the use of input kits, irrigation and soil conservation. This helped them increase their agricultural production by adopting improved methods of agriculture. These achievements in general, could be attributed to liberal financial credit policy of the government and subsidies provided for various activities. Besides the extension services such as organising training camps for the tribals, conducting demonstrations in various improved methods of agriculture also yielded satisfactory results. There was however, comparatively lesser utilisation of government funds due to late arrival of piece-meal sanction of certain schemes. The other implements were illiteracy of the tribals, lack of special staff for agricultural activities and availability of matching grants through cooperative societies and other financial institutions.

An official of the State Government looking after the programmes of animal husbandry, said that the main thrust under the programme was on cross-breeding of local cattle with high yielding exotic breeds of foreign cattle. The special breeds selected for this purposes were Jersey and Holstein Friesain cows known for enhancement of the production of milk. There were 29 cross-bred bulls located in different areas for providing natural services for genetic improvement of cattles in tribal areas. Almost every district has a live-stock Inspector incharge of an animal husbandry centre. In the district of Dangs, there were four live-stock production centres.

More than 400 milch animals were distributed at 50 per cent subsidised rates for the tribal families. This scheme was very well accepted by the tribals and they were accepting more such help which led to enhancement of financial outlay for this purpose. With regard to poultry development, Intensive Poultry Development Blocks (IPDB) for the augmentation of supply of eggs and poultry were started in various Tribal Sub-Plan areas. The special Blocks of this kind were provided with supply of a day-old chicks, feed, and feed additives, medicines, credit facilities, adequate health cover, marketing facilities, etc. It was through the Fifth Five Year Plan that six IPDBs were started at Valsad, Dohad, Valia, Vadodara, Vyara and Himmatnagar. There were other programmes with regard to veterinary services and maintenance of health etc.

The animal husbandry programmes outlined before have been implemented in order to develop dairy activities among the tribals. This has brought tangible financial help to the needy tribals for the development of schemes under dairying and milk supply. In the concluding year of the Fifth Five Year Plan, viz. during 1977-78, budget provision of Rs. 24 lakhs with or without one milk chilling centres was made available at select district centres.

There were mixed reactions to the efficacy of provisions of funds and implementation of agricultural and animal husbandry programmes under Sub-Plan Project. A number of points of criticism have been recorded. Here we shall try to lay emphasis on some of the structural aspects of implementing Tribal Area Sub-Plan.

Most of the criticism of the Sub-plan came no doubt from non-officials. There were also officials who were critical of various aspects of Sub-Plan Project. One of the officials was reported to have said that it was an unproductive experiment. Its working should actively be put under the control of the Collector if speedy implementation was to be guaranteed. Generally, the government officers of various departments were not fully concerned with the results and there was no feed-back of information in the process of implementing schemes. Instead of a Project administrator in-charge of Sub-Plan programmes, a Reviewing Officer for measuring results of implementation should have been appointed.

One district level officer left that the sub-plan did not cater to the genuine needs of the needy tribals. It made rich richer and poor poorer, specially among the tribals themselves. Moreover, there should not be sectoral planning for development of the tribal economy. A special functional classification of tribal economy varying from area to area should be done before planning and implementing the programmes. It was why the sub-plans schemes remained silent on employment generation resources for the tribals.

It was also mentioned that Tribal Sub-Plan was a misnomer since the actual implementation of schemes was done by various subject matter departments. The old concept of Intensive Tribal Development Blocks continued to prevail. The only difference was that a nucleus budget was available under Sub-Plan, but no planning scheme was based on monitoring local needs and specific problems of urgent attention. It was also alleged that there was no independent evaluation of the impact of sub-plan, and no new directions from the Government. The official concerned was critical of an experiment by Indian Institute of Management, Ahmedabad, for intensive development of economic resources of a specific tribal area in the taluka of Dharampur in Valsad district. It was looked upon by the observers as an *ad hoc* programme catering only to the strata of poor and unemployed tribals only. It did not have the character of an over-all project for integrated economic planning of tribal community in a specific area.

Some of the non-officials also came out with the criticism of the machinery of Tribal Area Sub-Plan. In one opinion, the work of Tribal Sub-Plan would bring better results if it was implemented directly by the Panchayats. The District Development Officer would have taken the responsibility to see that the Sub-Plan Projects were properly implemented. If this was done, the Talati-cum-Secretary of Village Panchayat and the V.L.W. would have taken the responsibility of distribution of subsidy and providing various other assistance to the tribals. Another non-official felt that it was strange that the President of District Panchayat was kept out of the sub-committee of the Tribal Area Sub-Plan. Moreover, the District Development Officer was not given the status of Chairman of the sub-committee. One of the non-officials remarked that the government had spent crores of rupees for tribal development, but 76 per cent of the tribals were still living below subsistence level. He was critical of the scheme of building huts worth Rs. 800 each for a tribal household. He opined that this was not practical since a hut would cost at least Rs. 1800 and not less. Keeping in mind the nucleus budget of a sub-plan at Rs. 13.50 lakhs, he felt that the money thus allotted was almost spent at random.

A critical appraisal of administrative and policy dimensions of the Tribal Area Sub-Plan may be added at this juncture. Most of these programmes are worked out in the Project Implementation Committees. This committee consist of (i) Project Administrator, (ii) Project Officers, (iii) Mamlatdars, (iv) Taluka Development Officers, (v) Deputy Engineers, (vi) Medical Officers of Primary Health Centres and other Officers connected with special schemes. This committee is supervised by the Committee of Direction under the Chairmanship of District Collector who is the coordinating and advisory link between various departments for implementing sectoral programmes. In this capacity, the collector is appointed as the Chairman of the sub-committee.

The total amount of funds to be spent for various sub-plans schemes were not directly handled by the Project Administrators. One of the officials felt that both the staff of various development departments and the funds should be put under the Project Administrator. Another official was of the opinion that various departments implementing Sub-Plan Projects were overburdened, and so they required to be strengthened by additional manpower. Moreover, the development departments which were generally functioning under the Panchayati Raj institutions did not sometimes work in harmony with other departments of District Administration. Under these circumstances, the Project Adminis- trator found it very difficult to see that the programmes were implemented in harmony and without conflicts.

It was further felt that if the status of Project Administrator was raised to that of an additional Collector in a District, it would become easy from him to sort out administrative bottle-necks. This kind of change in the status of the Project Administrators would save time and energy of the staff members and making his role viable and useful in developmental programmes.

The execution of most of the programmes of Small Farmers Developmental Agencies was done through the Taluka Development Officers who were implementing Tribal Sub-Plan schemes. This overburdened the T.D.O's working in sub-plan areas. The programmes of SFDA are also extended to non-tribal areas, and it was possible under these programmes to provide loans against the finances given to a tribal who was advanced previously, the loan by the banks. This would come to the rescue of many tribals who were declared defaulters by the banks from whom they had taken loans before.

We may here throw light on some of the crucial burning problems of tribal development. One of the non-officials was of the view that the Sub-Plan Project was generally aimed at development of the whole area inhabited by the tribals. But the programme of area development when implemented in practice happened to benefit the limited number of more articulate and influential population in the area. For instance, the construction of roads, minor and major irrigation projects, etc. ultimately benefit the better off people much more than the poor tribals. It was, therefore, suggested that in certain backward areas, schemes should be prepared specifically to help individual tribal households which can become economically self-sufficient and independent in course of time.

The problems of river dam projects were also discussed by tribal leaders. When the Meshvo Dam was built in the Khedbrahma taluka of Sabarkantha district, 12 villages were sunk under water. The land of these villages of Bhiloda area were the best in the taluka and most of it belonged to tribals. The compensation received by tribal land-holders was so meagre that it was not possible for an individual to buy even quarter of the original land-holding from the money received by him. Moreover, the forest land in which they were rehabilitated was so barren and difficult to develop that their economic status would not come up for years.

The money advanced by the Government for a displaced person to buy land turned out to be a burden to him because he was not capable of not only paying instalments fixed, but it was not possible for him to pay even the interest of the money advanced to him. This kind of over-all developmental programmes had accumulated thousands of rupees of debt in the name of the displaced tribals. As if this was not enough, the outsee tribals were neither able to get the benefit of the water for irrigation nor other advantages connected with the project of the dam. The Meshvo Dam in fact benefited the well to do farmers in parts of Kheda and Ahmedabad districts. The betterment levy imposed by the government on Dash Koshi area should have been given to outsee tribals. Instead, it was given to the Panchayats of Dash Koshi villages. This again was very unfair because the collection of betterment levy was possible at the cost of enormous sacrifices given by the people of the villages from Bhiloda area.

Issues of Panchayati Raj

In the Gujarat Panchayat Act, 1961, there is no special provision regarding management and use of land occupied by tribals. However, there are general provisions for viable management of fixed categories of the landuse pattern, such as grazing areas or Gauchar lands, etc. Village Panchayats imposed certain restrictions and conditions on the use of other plots near house-sites. These provisions were common both for non-tribal villages as well as tribal villages. It many villages, Gauchar lands were occupied unauthorisedly by influential and powerful land-lord families.

Earlier, the power to collect land revenue vested with the government. After the establishment of Panchayati Raj, the land revenue collection is done by the Gram Panchayats with the help of Talati-cum-Secretary. The Taluka Panchayats are given power to grant permission to make non-agricultural use of agricultural lands in class-2 villages while District Panchayats are given similar powers in Class-1 villages. However, powers to fix tax on non-agricultural assessment of land remained with the Collectors. Of course, the collection of non-agricultural assessment of tax is done by Gram Panchayats.

Panchayats are also given powers to dispose of open village site-plots with the previous sanction of the competent authority. Such open village site-plots are also managed by the Panchayats and put to use for implementing common schemes and construction of buildings for the common use of villages.

A variety of funds coming under the Tribal Area Sub-Plan are earmarked for Scheduled Tribes. The budget estimates are fixed under various heads and the money is spent according to the rules and regulations of the government for tribal development schemes. In every agricultural development schemes, the tribals are given special treatment for getting subsidy for various purposes. In order to enable a person to get it, 50 per cent subsidy is admissible for implements, soil conservation, bullocks, machinery, lift irrigation, etc. The sub-plan also provides facilities for subsidy to tribal farmers for undertaking travels to demonstration centres with a view to learn and improve agricultural practices. In certain areas, where scarcity, draught, or heavy rains come in the way of better yields in agriculture, the poor tribals should be given more than 50 per cent subsidy to meet expenditure of various agricultural activities. The government should make special arrangements for loans under such unforeseen calamities through Tribal Development Corporations or scheduled banks. In certain cases, if and when necessary, even 75 per cent of subsidy should be provided to deserving tribal farmers.

During normal programmes of Tribal Area Sub-Plan, the schemes for agriculture were implemented through district Panchayat and officers were specially appointed to supervise the work. For all schemes, the grants were given to the district Panchayats, directly by the department concerned. This was passed on to the taluka Panchayat that were directly responsible for implementing agricultural schemes under Sub-Plan Projects. The work no doubt showed signs of improvement, but if it was to be more fruitful, it was absolutely necessary that special staff was appointed at taluka level for looking into proper implementation of Sub-Plan Projects.

In many areas, the usual staff of various departments were not able to give full justice to the special programmes of tribal development. The over-all situation was that the poorer tribals were unable to take advantage of a number of schemes for agricultural development, specially because of the condition of a fixed percentage of contribution to be matched with the amount of subsidy to be sanctioned. As a result, only richer sections of tribal farmers were able to take benefit of these schemes. One of the officials felt that it should be the endeavour of the government to see that full benefits of Sub-Plan Projects go to the last tribals in the last village. This cannot be done if unrealistic conditions are linked with subsidy. He recommended 100 per cent subsidy for the poorest of the poor tribals.

The programmes of animal husbandry etc. was formulated for the Tribal Sub-Plan under various schemes. The schemes of poultry farming, rearing ducks, dairy farming, etc. were acceptable to the tribals. Panchayats took considerable interest in augmenting these schemes and helping tribals in raising their income. The pisciculture programmes was however, not taken up by the village Panchayat in certain areas of the Tribal Sub-Plan. The lack of pond water in tribal areas may be one reason of lack of interest in this occupation.

In the implementation of phased programmes, village community development schemes were undertaken. In many parts of the country and even in Gujarat, these schemes were implemented without difficulties in non-tribal areas. So far as the tribal areas were concerned, there were difficulties in implementing village development schemes in Gujarat. This was because the tribals were not found to be building their residential huts at one site in a village. They mostly built their huts in the midst or border of the land they were cultivating. Specially in the hilly regions these types of villages are called dispersed villages by the sociologists. Generally, many tribal villages, were spatially spread over in the area ranging from 2 to 3, 4 or even 6 miles in length, if not in breadth. This made it necessary to demarcate groups of house sites into spatial divisions and sub-divisions, sometimes called Failas in tribal villages. Panning for such villages required further provision of physical amenities and facilities such as water wells, schools, Panchayat houses, etc., accessible to most of the inhabitants of such villages. So far as their problem of water for cattle in the village was concerned, some of the tribals dug water wells in their own lands. Suitably located tribals took advantage of common reservoirs like rivers, tanks or streamlets.

In the opinion of an enlightened non-official, the problem of house tax to be paid by the tribals in dispersed villages, was difficult to solve. For, most tribal land-holder paid revenue for the land including house sites. There was a lot of opposition from individual tribals who refused to pay separate house tax to the village panchayats. As a result of this, village Panchayats were not able to have sufficient funds which they can utilise in minor developmental programmes. Whatever the income that the village Panchayats was able to get from other sources was spent in the maintenance of registers and records of Panchayat office, including salary paid to a peon, and thus it was not possible to bring efficiency in the working of village Panchayats in tribal areas predominated by dispersed village settlements.

There were also group Panchayats consisting of more than one dispersed as well as nucleated villages with independent village sites. In the nucleated villages, facilities of school, road, light, sweeping, radio, waterworks, police *choki*, etc. were feasible. The cost of these facilities were provided from the common government funds of the group of Panchayats. These nucleated villages enjoy at the cost of the dispersed villages, where no such facilities could be provided as the tribals there lived scattered in individual fields, as no village site existed for building houses at one place only. As the people of dispersed villages could not avail of developmental facilities, they felt disheartened and so, the composition and working of group

Panchayats requires to be reconsidered. Dispersed villages may be given independent village Panchayats or group Panchayats keeping in mind how their resources can be utilised and amenities can be made available to the people of dispersed villages having no village sites.

In fact, the pattern of the village housing in the tribal areas was more suitable when tribal farmers lived in the huts built in their fields. This helped them in paying more attention to various agricultural activities. They were also to look after protection of their crops. Moreover, all domestic waste and refuge was immediately used as manure in the fields. On the other hand, wherever the villages were built within an enclosed fencing, the roads were dirty with refuge heaps, etc. which made the environment of the village unhygienic. There were many other factors of nuisance in nucleated tribals villages which were not to be found in dispersed villages.

Keeping in mind all these various aspects of village development and panchayats in the tribal areas, the non-officials suggested that the entire structure of village Panchayats for tribal areas should be reformulated. Both the problems of village development on one side and Panchayati Raj structure on the other in tribal areas should be such that they can easily create integrated developments of the tribals without becoming counter productive, specially in remote and hilly areas.

One of the important mechanisms to attract tribal children to attend schools was to provide mid-day meals to them during school hours. Eventhough this is a programme for the improvement of nutrition in general, it serves to boost up the attendance of children and indirectly helps literacy drive considerably. The situation regarding the mid-day meals programme varies a great deal from taluka to taluka and from district to district. Both the officials and the non-officials reported that only some village schools in the areas of their purview were provided with mid-day meals, while in others that was not done on account of various reasons. There were also cases of mid-day meal programme for the tribal children becoming useful to schools in the peripheral area where non-tribal children were also admitted.

The programme of construction of rural-works undertaken with a sense of priority to help developmental programmes in backward areas are taken up on the basis of high priority for all round developments of tribal areas. For instance, in the district of Dangs, most of the people were tribals and therefore, the question of deciding priorities of rural works programmes remained out of question. Wherever, the problem of getting employment was acute for the tribals, the Collectors of the districts, concerned are empowered to prepare special schemes to help the needy people. This means that the programme of Right to Work was to be introduced in all villages of the tribals so that poorer tribals do not suffer from want. According to a non-official, 25 to 30 per cent population increased every ten years in the tribal areas. Though this seems a great exaggeration, there was some element of truth and urgency in the statement. Increasing number of tribals do not have land enough for their maintenance and besides, they have no other alternative occupations to fall back-upon. This calls for serious thinking on how to introduce Right to Work programme for the tribals.

It was after 1974 only that most of the Panchayats in the tribal areas were represented by the elected tribals themselves. This was in sequal to the amendment in 1973 in the earlier Panchayat Act of 1961 for tribal areas, based on the report of Zinabhai Dharji Committee. It helped backward classes to occupy and enjoy greater representation in village level democratic bodies. The tribals are not able to occupy the seats of powers in Panchayats and other bodies and it is after this stage that more and more of developmental resources are geared to help tribals to take advantage of various schemes.

With regard to the attitude of non-tribals towards developmental programmes for tribals, a lot has been said before. Here we may note that under normal conditions, non-tribals play an important role in the programmes of tribal welfare. However, when their business interests were affected adversely, they showed resentment towards the Government programmes for the tribals.

Some non-tribals were against giving more powers to the Sarpanch or Panchayat Committee in tribal areas because they cannot take full advantage of the system on account of illiteracy. There are political dimensions to the problem of decentralisation of power for Panchayats in tribal areas. These Institutions are sometimes highly politicised, and the decisions are not taken in time and with a sense of direction. In the first place, therefore, tribal leaders should be educated. Secondly, the village panchayats as such cannot become operative unless communications are established between a village and taluka headquarters. This means that roads must be built on high priority basis in tribal areas. It will also help literacy over a period of time if children are sent to schools located in other villages or towns in developed regions.

Assessment of Development Schemes and Programmes

In the preceding two sections we have presented qualitative assessment of a variety of issues related to development of tribals. It raises problems of value judgements and attitudes of officials and non-official respondents. In order, therefore, to put the record straight, the data received from various levels of administration of Tribal Area Sub-Plans have been analysed for an *ad hoc* assessment of the achievements of tribal development. The analysis is presented in the following pages.

The data were received from the various subject matter departments through correspondence during 1976-77 and 1977-78. The information covers four subjects such as (i) agriculture, (ii) animal husbandry, (iii) education, and (iv) employment in general.

1. *Benefits of Agricultural Schemes*

In the following points we throw light on four important agricultural activities such as, (i) subsidised distribution of input kits, (ii) promotion of vegetable cultivation, (iii) distribution of improved agricultural implements and (iv) Benefits accrued.

(i) *Input Kits for Crop Improvement*

In the year 1976-77, the total units of input kits supplied in various districts were as under: (a) in Valsad district 1,072 units benefited the same number of tribal households, for which Rs. 87,765 were advanced as subsidy, (b) in Vadodara district 453 units benefited 433 households, for which Rs. 27,847 were advanced as subsidy, (c) in Sabarkantha 543 units benefited the same number of households, for which Rs. 27,172 were advanced as subsidy.

Again in 1977-78 the position of subsidised distribution units of input kits were: (a) in Valsad district 4796 units benefited 4259 tribal households, for which Rs. 3,61,114 were advanced as subsidy, (b) In Vadodara district 8681 units benefited 6188 tribal households, for which Rs. 7,52,805 were advanced as subsidy, and (c) in Sabarkantha district 7353 units benefited the same number of tribal households, for which Rs. 5,98,844 were advanced as subsidy.

(ii) *Input Kits for Vegetable Cultivation*

In the year 1976-77 the total number of vegetable units of input kits supplied were: (a) in Valsad district 284 units benefited the same number of households, for which Rs. 3,469 were advanced as subsidy. Again in 1977-78, in the same district, 919 units benefited 619 households, for which Rs. 10,593 were advanced as subsidy, (b) in Vadodara district, in the year 1977-78 the total number of vegetable units supplied were 1691 which benefited 1165 tribal households, for which Rs. 17,300 were advanced as subsidy.

(iii) *Distribution of Agricultural Implements*

In 1976-77, the distribution of improved agricultural implements were as under: (a) in Vadodara district 14 items were given to the same number of tribal households, for which Rs. 605 were advanced as subsidy. In the same district in 1977-78 the number of distribution of implements was 397 which benefited 94 tribals households, for which Rs. 6,972 were advanced as subsidy, (b) In the year 1977-78, in Valsad district 283 improved implements were distributed to the same number of households, for which Rs. 25,308 were advanced as subsidy, (c) In the year 1977-78 in Sabarkantha district, 241 improved implements were distributed to the same number of households, for which Rs. 7286 were advanced as subsidy.

(iv) *An Analysis of Benefits Accrued*

The above information of development clearly indicate the fact that more and more of tribal households were deriving benefits from various agrarian schemes. The data on impact of adaption of various agricultural practices for improved agriculture in specific areas were available from a few districts and a few tribals pockets. An *ad hoc* account of the same is presented in following points:

(a) In the Valsad district; (i) cropping pattern changed to some extent as a result of which paddy cultivation increased due to input kits, (ii) areas under improved high yielding varieties increased, (iii) tribals understood technical know-how of proper dose of fertilizer, insecticides, etc; (iv) vegetable cultivation improved and surplus yield was marketed to nearest towns. All these change occurred because of adoption of quality seeds of vegetable; (v) tribals sow vegetable on irrigated patch of land even by hand watering; (vi) Winnowing fans became popular in case of paddy; and (vii) use of improved implements steadily increased.

(b) In the Vadodara district: (i) the tribals adapted improved methods of agriculture; (ii) specially they began to utilise fertiliser, improved seeds and insecticides; (iii) crop pattern under went considerable change; and (iv) the subsidy benefits were derived only by tribals with at least 5 acres of land.

(c) In the Sabarkantha district: (i) tribals benefited by improved methods of agriculture, such as seeds, use of fertilizers and insecticides; (ii) they took advantage of supply of bullocks and milch cattles with the help of subsidy; and (iii) they constructed irrigation wells for augmenting crop production and income.

(d) The tribal pocket of Kareli in Pavi-Jetpur taluka of Vadodara district derived benefits of improved implements, purchase of storage bins, plant protection appliances and subsidy for fruit plants.

(e) The Danta pocket of Sabarkantha district derived the benefits of supply of fruit plants, wheat kits, hybrid maize kits, construction of wells and subsidy for study tours.

Almost all the items indicated above had better acceptance and the number of tribals benefited were 486, to whom a total of Rs. 61,697 were advanced as subsidy. It may, however, be noted that the scheme of supply of fruit plants was greatly popular. The total work done amounted to 240 plantations that benefited the same number of tribal households, for which Rs. 8,105 were advanced as subsidy.

2. *Animal Husbandry and Milk Societies*

The data on centres for veterinary services, treatment of cattle diseases, milk societies etc. were available from five districts through correspondence. The data collection coverd a period of two years i.e. 1976-77 and 1977-78. It was not possible to have similar reliable data from other districts.

(a) In the district of Valsad, there were five veterinary dispensaries, 16 veterinary aid centres which helped in treating 130130 cattle. The number of milk societies in all the five talukas of the district were 76 and they were associated with the Sumul Dairy Cooperative Society of Surat;
(b) In the district of Dangs, there was only one veterinary dispensary, eight veterinary aid centres which treated only 53 cattle suffering from a disease called the fever of Bovine Surra. There were seven milk societies in Dangs;
(c) In the two pockets of district of Banaskantha, there was only one veterinary dispensary, four veterinary aid centres, which helped in treating 12153 cattle. There was no milk society;
(d) In the three talukas of district of Vadodara, there were three dispensaries, seven aid centres which treated 21020 cattle. There were in all 21 milk societies associated with Baroda Cooperative Dairy;
(e) In the six talukas of Surat district, there were six dispensaries, 18 veterinary aid centres, 29 artificial insemination centres which treated 25895 cattle. The six talukas of the district were associated with Sumul Cooperative Society of Surat.

We may add a brief note on the problems of running milk societies in the tribal areas of the five districts. Some of these are listed below:

(a) In Valsad district the road conditions in tribal areas were very bad. This made the transport of milk costlier and resulted in more cost in storage of milk. Secondly, there was a great dearth of qualified staff to manage milk societies. Thirdly, the lack of knowledge regarding modern techniques of animal husbandry and related practices continued to persist among the tribals. Fourthly, there was a lack of adequate training facilities for cattle owners and the staff of milk societies;
(b) In the district of Dangs, facilities for roads and necessary infrastructures were not easily available. This was the greatest difficulty of introducing developmental programmes in general and dairying in particular. Moreover, there continued to be a lot of ignorance on account of illiteracy, lack of awareness and

carelessness among the tribals which come in the way of their taking advantage of veterinary services available in the area;

(c) In the district of Banaskantha, the villages were dispersed and scattered. This was one of the great difficulties in spreading timely veterinary services in a satisfactory manner to all the tribals;

(d) In Vadodara district, there was a need for suitable roads for villages distantly situated, specially in Chhotaudepur and Naswadi talukas. This made it most urgent to establish quick and safe transport facilities for centres where chilling plants could be located. In the taluka of Naswadi, the buffaloes required green fodder which can be made good adequately by providing irrigation facilities;

(e) In the district of Surat, there was a lack of qualified staff and management skills among the tribals for taking advantage of animal husbandry and related improved practices. Similar difficulty in the way of improving dairying was to be found in the talukas of Uchchal and Songadh. In the taluka of Mahuva, there was a need of one full-time animal husbandry officer for taking care of cattle for providing milk to various milk societies. There was also the problem of storage of medicine for veterinary services and transportation facilities for exporting milk cooperative dairy in Surat.

3. *Primary-Secondary Education and Ashram Shalas*

The most important thing about the Ashram Shalas in tribal areas was that they were managed by about 25 different voluntary agencies. Most of these voluntary agencies looked after the management of Ashram Shalas in quite a number of villages. The earliest Ashram Shala aided by the government was started in 8-2-1954 in Dharampur taluka of Valsad district. A number of other Ashram Shalas were established in 1977 in several villages distributed in Vyara and Mandvi talukas of Surat, Umbergaon taluka of Valsad, Dediapada taluka of Bharuch and Chhotaudepur and Sankheda talukas of Vadodara districts. Most of the Ashram Shalas imparted education ranging from 2 to 7 standards while only a few had facilities for giving education between 8 to 10 standards. There were only nine such Ashram Shalas where the standard of education was raised to 8 to 10 standards. It may be noted that most of the students attending

Ashram Shalas came from neighbouring villages and the norms of selection were determined by the voluntary agencies running the Shalas.

The data on the Primary Schools and Ashram Shalas in the districts of Bharuch, Valsad and Dangs for the year 1977-78 were available. They throw some light on the number of Ashram Shalas and Strength of students for groups of villages in several talukas concerned.

The information received through correspondence indicated that relatively the Ashram Shalas were more popular than the Primary Schools in remote tribal areas. This was done to adequate facilities and provision of food, clothing and residential facilities in Ashram Shalas. In Dediapada taluka of Bharuch district, there were 142 villages with Primary Schools attended by 8651 students. It was further reported that 71 per cent of the students in the usual kind of Primary Schools turned out to be drop-outs. In the whole of Dediapada taluka, there were six Ashram Shalas and the number of students on roll amounted to 559. On the other hand, there were 129 Primary Schools with 8651 students. The percentage of students in Ashram Shalas was 93 per cent, while that in Primary Schools was 67 per cent. In the remaining tribal talukas of Bharuch, viz., Rajpipla, Sagbara, Jhagadia, Valia and Ankleshwar talukas, the attendance of tribal students was more in Ashram Shalas. The reason of poor attendance in the Primary Schools in Bharuch district was reported to be ignorance, illiteracy and poverty among the tribals.

In the Dharampur taluka of Valsad district there were 238 Primary Schools attended by 23,700 students with a drop out rate of 12.5 per cent. In contrast, there were 2 Ashram Shalas attended by 240 students with a drop out rate of only two per cent. The Ronwel tribal pocket in Valsad taluka had 42 primary schools attended by 5209 students, and in Sisodara Ganesh in Navsari taluka, the total number of Primary Schools were 37, attended by 3495 tribal students. In both these schools, the drop out rate was about 7.5 per cent. The data on Ashram Shalas were not available for these pockets. Some of the reasons of drop-outs of tribal students in Primary Schools in Valsad district were reported to be on account of illiteracy, ignorance and poverty of tribal households who were compelled to send their children to work for supplementing family income. The cases of drop-outs appeared to be most prevalent among the age group of 9 to 14 years.

In the district of Dangs, which is also a taluka, there were 343 Primary Schools attended by 20,622 students. In contrast, were also 10 Ashram Shalas attended by 1200 students. The percentage of drop outs in the Primary Schools in Dangs was reported to be 73.3 per cent, and in that Ashram Shalas 5 per cent only.

(b) *Secondary Schools*

In the district of Panchmahals, there were 1107 villages. The secondary school education facilities existed in five tribal talukas. In 1977-78, they were 81 in the category of Normal Schools and five Uttar Buniadi schools. The total number of students in Normal Schools was 20080 and in the Uttar Buniadi schools, it was 700. The Uttar Buniadi schools were available only at Dahod Taluka (4) and Jhalod Taluka (1). The Santrampur taluka had 24 Normal Schools serving 399 villages and having a total number of 4884 students. In the district of Bharuch, the total number of villages served by secondary education facilities was 815, having 32 Normal Schools and one Uttar Buniadi schools. The number of students in Normal Schools was 8697 and in Uttar Buniadi schools it was 205.

The question of suitability or otherwise of common general syllabus of Uttar Buniadi schools in the district of Panchmahals was reported to be satisfactory for tribal students. However, it was felt that special coaching and hostel facilities were essential for helping the students. The subjects taught in these schools were agriculture, cattle breeding, etc. In practice, the programme of teaching encountered certain difficulties because of lack of cultivable land for making demonstrations and experiments as teaching methods. This was the reason why drop out rate of the tribal students in Uttar Buniadi schools in Panchmahals ranged between 20 to 25 per cent. In fact, there were other reasons reported for this high rate of drop out. They were, (i) brilliant students went away to join medical, engineering and science education; (ii) school hostels had limited seats; and (iii) a compulsion of devoting one hour more for craft work was disliked by students.

In the district of Bharuch, the reasons of lack of interest in secondary education in general were quite different. It was felt that science, mathematics, agriculture and environmental problems be added to the list of subjects.

The Uttar Buniadi syllabus geared to educating tribal students did not become popular due to the following reasons: (i) tribals experienced difficulty in subjects of mathematics and languages; (ii) students found it difficult to concentrate on studies as they had to help parents in earning livelihood; and (iii) students found it difficult to make progress because of lack of suitable social environment. The drop out rate in Uttar Buniadi schools in the district were reported to be 15 per cent and the main reason was said to be the economic and social backwardness of the tribals.

We present here some basic information on Ashram Shalas to begin with followed by additional data from some specific areas. The total number of Ashram Shalas in respect of which the information has been collected is 105.

4. *Registration for Employment and Training*

The data on registration of Scheduled Tribe (post-graduates) candidates through University Employment Information and Guidance Bureaux and their employment in different kinds of services in 1976-77 were received from five universities in the State. This includes data from the Gujarat Agricultural University also. The total number of registered and employed candidates in general as per educational qualifications was as follows. The registered candidates (i) with post-graduate qualifications were 40 of which 5 were employed, (ii) among degree holders with technical qualifications, 12 were registered and 2 employed, (iii) among the medical graduates, 15 were registered and 2 were employed, (iv) among law graduates, there were no candidates, and (v) among others, there were 11 registered candidates of whom two were employed.

In all there were 78 candidates registered for employment of whom only 11 were employed, amounting to 14.10 per cent of those successful in getting employment through University Employment Information and Guidance Bureaux. It should be noted that the South Gujarat University in Surat was a better venue through which many applications of various categories of qualified tribal candidates were received. It is likely that the registration in the rest of the four Universities was poor either because the tribal students did not know of this facility or did not get themselves registered due to distant locations of the universities.

The following information throws some light on employment of educated scheduled tribe candidates registered through Government

Employment Exchange Bureaux in 1976-77. The information on the subject for eight tribal districts indicate that there were 13553 candidates below S.S.C. examination of whom 2162 were employed. Of the 8113 S.S.C. pass candidates whose names were registered, 835 were employed. The total undergraduate candidates were 379, of whom only 9 were employed. Among the graduate tribal candidates numbering 1115 who got registered in the Government Employment Exchange Bureaux, 85 were employed.

The overall picture shows that there were 23160 Scheduled Tribe candidates registered for employment of whom 3091 were employed. The percentage of employment to registration on the whole was 13.35 per cent only. For the year 1976, the total number of registered educated candidates were 12912 of whom 1396 were employed, amounting to 9.25 per cent employment rate. In 1977, the total number of candidates registered was 10248 of whom 1695 were employed, amounting to 6.04 per cent rate of employment.

It is significant to note that the percentage of employment to registration of candidates comes to be lower in 1977 as compared to that in 1976, the previous year. The candidates who were employed in different types of services through Government Employment Exchange Bureaux got jobs either in government offices, Panchayati Raj institutions, Municipal offices, etc. The total number of candidates employed in the government in 1976-77 was 3091, amounting to 13.35 per cent of total number of 23,160 educated Scheduled Tribe candidates registered for services through Government Employment Exchange Bureaux. Employment of tribals in other institutions like Panchayat and Municipal offices, Corporations, textile mills and factories and other firms was comparatively poor.

The data on admission of Scheduled Tribe candidates to Industrial Training Institutes for one year course in nine centres, viz., Palanpur, Modasa, Godhra, Dohad, Baroda, Ankleshwar, Surat, Billimora and Ahwa throw valuable light on the extent of change and development in tribal areas. Though there were reserved seats for the Scheduled Tribe candidates in the total number of sanctioned seats in these institutions, tribal students had sought admissions in two specialities. These two specialities were the courses for the skills of welder and carpenter. There were no tribal candidates for the speciality of moulder, mechanics, plumber, stenographer, etc. These IIT centres also offered two year courses but the problem of choice of tribal students to go in for them did not improve.

In contrast to this, there were I.T.I. courses under Tribal Area Sub-Plan located in Dohad and Ankleshwar where Scheduled Tribe students were admitted for technical education.The results here were quite encouraging. Of the total number of 32 seats sanctioned for armature winding, 29 candidates were on roll; of 32 for wireman, 31 were on roll and of 24 for welder, all the 24 were on roll. It seems reasonable to think that the I.T.I programmes implemented through Tribal Areas Sub-Plan are likely to get better results, as these courses were liked by tribal candidates.

9

SOCIO-ECONOMIC DEVELOPMENT AND EDUCATIONAL SITUATION

Introduction

We have made cursory references to social and cultural changes taking place in tribal society. Passing information has already been presented on tribal groups, communication, education, training, occupation, etc. in some of the earlier chapters. These topics are discussed here in greater detail. The change in the values, attitude and behaviour of the people towards various problems connected with land tenure, agriculture, indebtedness, bonded labour, etc. have also been reflected in the earlier pages. The research workers of the Tribal Research and Training centre and students of M.D. Maha Vidyalaya of Gujarat Vidyapith, Ahmedabad have tried to do justice to special studies on various subjects of tribal life and culture. They have been reproduced in printed or cyclostyled form and are available in the form of booklets, books and dissertations. Most of their studies have been conducted mainly at micro levels with focus on specific problems. On the other hand, the data presented here have largely meso and macro focus helpful in creating a composite perspective of the tribal situation in Gujarat before 1980. It should be added that the information presented is in no way exhaustive due to the limitations of time and resources imposed by the terms and conditions under which the present project was completed. In brief, this is an attempt at providing a profile of socio-economic and cultural development of the tribals, nearly a decade ago.

Salient Features of Tribal Population

The data on tribal populations from the districts concerned were not exhaustive. This was partly because of the fact that only a few talukas and a few villages in each taluka were visited during the course of interviews with officials and non-officials at district levels. In the district of Banaskantha, the main population of the tribals resided in Amirgadh and Virampur areas of the Palanpur taluka. The important tribes are Dungari Bhils and Dungari Garasia. The former are reported to be very cooperative in nature while the latter group of tribals were not so easy to approach. They also did not observe national festivals possibly because they refused to be mixed with the mainstream of national life. The Dungari Garasias consider themselves to be of high racial origin. Legends say that their forefathers came from the ruling dynasty of the State of Udaipur in Rajasthan. This is the basis on which they look upon themselves as Rajputs.

In the district of Sabarkantha also, the main tribal groups are Dungari Bhils and Dungari Garasias. The dress and ornaments among their sub-groups resemble those of Rajputs in Rajasthan. The gradual spread of literacy and education have brought some changes among most of these sub-groups. Although agriculture is the main stay of life, in recent times the jobs of teaching and clerical work are being adopted by the youths. Out of the six sub-groups of Dungari Garasias one had undergone great transformation in education, occupation and dress so much so that they can be clearly distinguished by most of their tribal groups. The tribe of Naikdas is also found here, but the most backward are the Kathodis living in the areas of former Idar State. The Kathodis are highly skilled in making a spice from bark of trees, called Katha from which their name is derived. They are landless and many of them live in poor conditions of life. A few of them may be found in other districts also.

In the district of Panchmahals, the most backward tribes are reported to be Naikdas and Rathawas. These two groups were almost landless labourers. The Bhils of this area are not so poor. Among the Bhils, the group called Patelias are rich and affluent and they look almost like non-tribals. The Naikdas were so poor that they were reported to be able to eat food once in 2 to 3 days only. They rarely wore clothes, although women were slightly better clad. It was reported that they were not classified as Scheduled Tribes and therefore were not able to get the benefits of the tribal areas sub-plan. Similarly, the group of tribals called Kathala are deprived of developmental benefits. The Patelias are refined Bhils, influential and well-off economically, and they took full advantage of most of the benefit of development programmes and schemes.

In the district of Vadodara, the most distinguished group of tribals has been Koli as well as Rathawa-Koli. The other two groups of importance are Dungari Bhils and Tadavi. There are also Nayakas who are physically strong and sturdy, but economically extremely poor. This is because they have no land of their own and earn their livelihood working as herdsmen and chowkidar. The Tadavi on the other hand are relatively advanced and follow the occupation of carpentry, black-smithy, agriculture, etc. Quite a few Tadavis are in administrative and teaching services. It may be noted that the Bhils of this area are also divided among two groups, viz. Dungari Bhils and Medani Bhils, the latter are said to be economically more advanced and intelligent than the former.

In the district of Bharuch, the main tribal population is of Bhil Vasava who measure about 45 per cent of the total tribal population in the area. The next group of the tribals are the Tadavi who were also called Dhanka. They were about 10 per cent of the tribal population, while Kotwalia and a special group of Cowherd Bhils were about five per cent only. The rest of the population in the district was of the non-tribals. The Vasava Bhils are specially numerically dominant in Jhagadia and Nandod talukas. The other groups of tribals more or less distributed in the district are Chaudhri, Gamit, Vitolia, etc. In the taluka of Nandod, there were Tadavi and Vasava Bhils in the north east and south west areas respectively. In Dediapada taluka, Vasava and Kotwalia were to be found in large number. In Sagbara taluka, Vasava, Tadavi and Chaudhari and Kotwalias are to be found. In the taluka of Valia, Kotwalia and Chaudhari are to be found in large number. In the taluka of Jhagadia, main population of the tribals were Vasava with a sprinkling of Tadavi.

In the district of Surat, the Dubla tribals, who are also known as Halpati, are distributed in almost all talukas. The next important tribal groups in the district are Dhodia who are advanced and progressive agriculturists. In recent times, they are reported to be taking more and more to industrial labour. Some the Dhodias are also taking to advanced occupations of school teachers, clerks, etc., specially because they have been in closer contact with non-tribals as compared with other tribals. The Chaudhari are also industrious and politically conscious about their rights and privileges.[1] They have taken up various kinds of occupations which could put them into the class of wage-earners, of relatively advanced category.

The other important groups of the tribals are Dhankas whose main source of livelihood is agriculture. They are, also engaged in labour of various kinds, as well as collection of minor forest produce.

The fifth group of tribals in Surat district are the Gamit concentrated in the taluka of Vyara, Songadh, Uchchal and Nizar. They are land-holders and mainly occupied in agriculture. They are economically better off not only because they are only good agriculturists, but are also hard working people. Gamits benefited from skilled and semi-skilled labour works in Ukai Dam Project in recent times.

The sixth group of people are Kotwalia concentrated in Vyara and Songadh talukas. They are also found in Mandvi taluka. They were the most backward and poor group of tribals without land in the district. Their main occupation is Bamboo-craft including preparation of fishing traps, winnowing fans, brooms, etc. The seventh group of the tribals are Kathodi who are less in number as compared to others. They were greatly attached to forest life and their main source of livelihood was manufacturing charcoal and other kind of forest labour. On account of their backwardness and poverty they were suffering from stigma of untouchability, besides many other social disadvantages. There are also groups of tribals called Kolcha and Kolgha who are to be found in a few talukas and were also looked upon as untouchables because of their socio-economic backwardness.

In the district of Valsad, the tribal population is concentrated around the area called Bhilad. The main tribals are Warli, Dubla, Dhodia, Chaudhari, Naikda, Konkan, Kolgha and Kolcha.

The Warli and Dhodia tribals are in majority in the whole of Valsad district. The Dhodia and Choudhari are relatively lesser in number but are educated and some of them are affluent. This is one of the reasons why the leaderships of the tribals in the district is vested with Dhodias.

The Dublas are also in sizable number in this district. They are mainly concentrated in the district of Surat, but are also to be found in the two contiguous districts of Bharuch and Valsad. Most of the Dublas are landless agricultural labourers and since ages, so to say, they have been exploited by their masters. They have had a long standing association with high caste Hindu landlords, working as agricultural labourers. Therefore, their way of life, customs, norms and values have been influenced by the Hindus. All of them speak Gujarati language and have around 30 per cent of literacy among them. The level of political consciousness is fairly high although economically extremely weak. After independence, some of them got agricultural land which they cultivated as landless tenants. Excepting a few, many of the Dublas have not benefitted by land reforms and the development programmes of the government. As a special case, in Umbergaon taluka, they are landholders because of benefits received due to Tenancy Act and Ceiling Law. In most of the other talukas they are landless.

The other economically poor tribals are the Warli who are mainly agricultural labourers. Some of them hold marginal land, and are not advanced farmers. They grow inferior variety of coarse foodgrain such as *Nagli*. They are said to be inclined towards nomadic life, largely engaged in fishing and hunting. They do not care for the second day, if they get food on the previous day. Although Warlis as a group are to be found in large number in Valsad, a sprinkling of them are found in Dangs and Surat districts also. Some of them migrate to towns and go as far as Bombay in search of labour. They also work as domestic servants but are not inclined to take up independent occupations.

The Dhodias as indicated earlier are fairly educated and advanced group of the tribals. Some of them work as teachers and clerks in schools and offices. Others either engage themselves in agriculture or take to trade. Most of their habits, food, clothings, etc. resemble those of high caste people in the area. Some of the Dhodias are landholders and devote their time to agriculture. There are also some who take up to carpentry, blacksmith and such other skilled or semi-skilled occupations. Those who depend on agricultural activities in interior villages, suffer on account of lack of contact with advanced areas in absence of infrastructural facilities. They are not able to improve their agricultural practices to the extent to which they would like. After independence, the axis of Valsad-Pardi-Vapi region has been fast growing as an industrial belt and quite a number of Dhodias have taken to industrial labour and other jobs as important means of livelihood.

The next advanced group of the tribals in Valsad district are Choudhari who are well dressed and advanced like Dhodias in their habits and style of life. They are distributed in the districts of Surat, Valsad, Bharuch and Dangs. However, they are mainly concentrated in the north-east sub-region of Surat district which has a common border with Valsad district. The Choudharis are plain-dwellers and live in settled villages. They are very industrious and their main occupation is agriculture. Since they do not have sufficient land per household, they have to supplement their earnings by working as agricultural labourers, construction workers, forest labourers, etc. during lean agricultural season. The literacy level among Choudharis was about 22 per cent which is quite good. On account of their close contacts with the advanced neighbouring people, there is a lot of influence of modernisation and industrialisation on the entire society of the Choudharis. They are undergoing rapid social change along with changes taking place around their habitat.[2]

The other groups of the tribals in Valsad district are Naikdas, Konkna, Kolgha, and Kolcha There are also some Kotwalias who are very backward. The main concentration of the Naikdas is in the Panchmahals, but they are also found in this district. They are poorer and backward although some of them are better off here than those living in the Panchmahals.

The group of Konknas are settled in the interior of the hilly tracks and depend on farming and landless labour for earning livelihood. They hardly do service, and if at all, they prefer to work as peons. They cultivate inferior variety of foodgrains called *Nagli*. The Kolgha tribals are largely landless. They earn their living as agricultural labourers. It was not possible for them to take to any other occupation and were treated as untouchables by other tribals. Many Kolghas earn their living by collecting minor forest produce. The Kolcha are similarly landless labourers. Only a few of them are engaged in farming of their own land.

The district of Dangs is predominantly a tribal district having 93.82 per cent concentration of the tribals called Dangi Bhils. There are 311 villages inhabited by tribals of various kinds. The Bhils, Kunbis and Warlis are predominant population in the district. The Kunbis were 45.3 per cent, Bhils 32.3 per cent and Warlis 14.4 per cent of the total tribal population. The rest are Gamits, Dhodias, Kathodi, Kotwalia and Naikas. The area of Dangs being a relatively thick forest area in the whole of Gujarat, the villages and the people living there were cut off from other developed areas. There were very few bus services connecting them with advanced people in the neighbouring villages. There is no doubt a narrow gauge railway line from Bilimora in the plains to Waghai in the Dangs. This facility was primarily used for transportation of valuable forest produce such as timber, fire-wood, etc. Most of the tribals here depend on forest labour and agriculture.

Impediments to Education and Training

The data on attendance of tribal boys and girls in primary schools and Ashram Shalas as supplied by the departments concerned have already been presented in the latter part of chapter eight. Here we shall deal with the subject in a detailed manner and shall try to throw light on the extent to which special groups of tribals in various districts either have taken to education or were lagging behind on account of various reasons.

(a) In the Danta taluk of district of Banaskantha, the Dungari Garasia Bhils were said to be backward. Among the boys, the education was about 5 per cent while among the girls, it was negligible. The schools were there but the children did not attend them to the extent to which it was desired. One of the reasons of lack of interest in education was that as soon as a boy was about ten years old, he was sent by the parents to the town of Ambaji to work in a hotel or shop in the main bazar. Some of them collected firewood, bark of the trees, *bor* fruit, timru leaves, etc. to sell them in the town of Ambaji. In the morning, they would start to jungles to collect minor forest produce and in the afternoon would go to the Ambaji bazar for selling them in the market. They hardly found time to go to schools. The other category of boys and girls were sent to marble mines for labour. They also found it difficult to go to attend schools.

One of the reasons of girls of Dungari Bhils not going to schools was that they were married by the age of 15. It was not considered necessary to educate girls who are at last going to be married away. The time and money spent on their education was, therefore as good as a mere waste. In the case of boys, it may be added that they were also engaged in looking after the cattle and agricultural activities in the family.

The other reason was that the school timings were fixed from 11.00 a.m. to 5.00 p.m. which were not convenient for the tribal children for various reasons and lack of habit formation. One of the respondents suggested that if the schools are run in morning times, it was likely that more boys and girls may attend. The boys who can afford to take education up to seventh standard would like to undertake further studies. However, since boarding facilities were not available for high school education, hardly 2 to 3 per cent of them were able to qualify themselves for admission to degree colleges.

The school teachers in general faced many problems while working in tribal areas. Some of the tribals doubted moral character of the teacher, and therefore, they were not able to establish intimate relationship with them. As a result, teachers in tribal villages found it difficult to get a house to live in. Moreover, there was also the difficulty of arranging food for teachers, if they have to spend long hours in tribal villages. The teacher was almost cut off from the tribal society in which he worked. He was also not able to educate his children if he took his family to tribal area. The facilities for communication was inadequate and he could not bring domestic requirements easily from distant places. When he is sick, he would not get adequate medical help and also there was a danger of theft in his house. Under such circumstances, he was not able to bring his family along with him to live in tribal areas.

In spite of reasonably good facilities for primary education, there was relatively less commitment for education on account of several reasons. As pointed out in earlier pages, here also, children instead of going to schools went after cattle for grazing. This was in spite of the fact that a number of schools had facilities for lodging and boarding for children. One of the requirements for attending schools was the availability of books and uniform with the children and it was this which only a few tribal parents were able to afford. The teachers in primary schools commuted from distant places.

To top all these difficulties, the teacher in recent times was asked to propagate family planning programmes among the tribals. The people kept away from him for this reason also and did not cooperate with him when they were asked to give information on the size of the family.

There was a general belief that Ashram Shalas if established in tribal area can be of great help in attracting students for education. If this was possible, the students would not have found it difficult tc have living accommodation there. And, poorer tribal children could not easily afford to educate themselves. There were also some problems of admission to Ashram Shalas where children of influential persons were given easy admission and others of the poorer households were left out. One of the subjects in Ashram

Shalas is teaching of agriculture. In some areas the students were reported to be misused by teachers who made them to work on their own lands. In spite of this, Ashram Shalas were preferred to general primary schools which as reported were poorly attended by the tribal children. There, the teachers have to go door to door collecting children for improving attendance. Inspite of these door to door campaigns undertaken by the teachers, hardly 30 per cent students were reported to attend primary schools.

(b) The situation in the Sabarkantha district was better with regard to primary and secondary school education. The difficulties of raising buildings for primary schools through popular contribution however created special problems. The Uttar Baniyadi schools imparted technical education from 8 to 12 standards and were not managed well by the local people. There were 27 Ashram Shalas in the district. There was a great demand for more of such schools to be started for the benefit of tribals. The government gave 95 per cent grants to voluntary organisations running these schools. The books were distributed free of cost to tribal students. But there were other problems reported with regard to inferior living conditions and unwholesome food in hostel; besides, lack of desired number of teachers, lack of full attendance of students etc. In some villages, overall conditions were so bad that the Ashram Shalas were run in the houses which were also used as cow-sheds at night.

Regarding the problems faced by teachers in the primary schools, it was reported that they were harassed by the tribals who were used to heavy drinking. Even some roudy elements demanded money for drinks from the teachers. It was difficult for them to keep their families with them on account of such adverse circumstances. The non-tribal teachers accepted departmental posting in tribal areas only for a short while, and as soon as they got an opportunity, they managed to get themselves transferred.

In case where tribal candidates were recruited as teachers with 35 per cent qualifying marks, for necessary incentive, they were said to be too weak in teaching. This was also one of the reasons why primary schools suffered in tribal areas. Some of the respondents felt that the appointed teachers should be those who were used to residing in the tribal areas. It was the duty of the management of the Ashram Shalas to see that if the teachers are not doing well, they should be changed. The maintenance allowance of Rs. 55 given to students admitted to Ashram Shalas was not sufficient and should be increased. In one of the earlier chapters we have already used data from correspondence throwing light on reasons of drop-outs in Ashram Shalas. Similar reasons of drop-outs were also reported here. The use of children in tending family cattle, household poverty, lack of hunger for education, etc. were the reasons of drop-outs in Ashram Shalas.

(c) In the district of Panchmahals, the tribals were relatively more advanced than elsewhere so far as education standards are concerned. Economically, however, some of them were very poor. There were 50 tribal boarding houses, 23 Balwadi and 17 Ashram Shalas managed and run by the voluntary organisations. The Bhil Seva Mandal runs the largest number of educational institutions in the district. The high schools were not many and the voluntary agencies were not much associated with these programmes. There was the general impression however that there was a great need of more Ashram Shalas with boarding houses for tribal children in the district.

According to one opinion, the Ashram Shalas and the hostels for the tribal students should be managed by enlightened leaders of their community. Even the voluntary organisations who were running educational institutions should have been put under the control of educated tribals. The government should see to it that this kind of change in the management takes place with the cooperation of voluntary organisations. One of the suggestions was that the officer in-charge of the social welfare committee at the District level should try to change the management of Ashram Shalas and Hostels by direct supervision.

Regarding science education, it was felt that there were hardly a few schools in this district where special room with equipment etc. were reserved for science education. This should be made possible at least for those schools with 5 to 7 standards for teaching. The problem of matching contribution for building school rooms should be relaxed because where the tribals were too poor to raise funds, they were not able to have the schools. It was reported that Hari Om Ashram Public Trust of Nadiad spent Rs. 2400 per room in recent times for building school rooms in several tribal villages.

There were quite a few interesting suggestions for improvement of education among the tribals in the district. These were, (i) one

Ashram Shala each be located at an interval of 5 miles; (ii) Instead of 120 students (boys and girls), as many as 200 students be admitted; (iii) syllabus of these schools should be altered so that it can be suited to forest based industries, agriculture, cottage industries etc.; (iv) every district should have at least one industrial training institute; (v) wherever schools are located, there should be arrangements for hostels, supply of books, uniform, etc. Some of these suggestions were reported to have already been made years age, but not much was done by the government.

(d) The situation regarding the tribal education in the district of Vadodara was probably as satisfactory, if not more, as in the Panchmahals. There were though many differences as may be seen from the account presented here. In primary schools for tribals up to 4th standard, there usually was only one teacher. In such schools, the teacher was the master of his own will. When he went to school, it was opened, otherwise it remained closed. One of the problems of lack of attendance of children in the schools was that the tribals lived in their huts scattered all over the fields. The children naturally lived with the parents and helped them in the manner they can. The economic poverty compelled some parents to send their children for labour and to look after cattle. These habits of not carrying for education of children sometimes got accentuated, because quite a number of educated boys and girls remained without jobs. This led to a lot of discouragement for sending children to schools. But the real problem was the total ignorance of the parents about great advantages that follow if the children were better educated even though they may work in tribal areas on land or in forests.

In most of the primary schools tribal children were admitted and their names were on the roll-calls, but they never attended classes regularly. Wherever, the mid-day meals programme was implemented, all the children remained in the school until meals were served. After taking meals all of them run away. The educated young tribals who should devoted time in educating children of their own backward groups would hardly prefer to stay in tribal villages. As soon as they educate themselves adequately, they tend to migrate to nearby towns for better services and jobs..

The tribal children who were kept in the primary schools from 11-00 a.m. to 5.00 p.m., were not able to earn a single paise to add to family income. This turned out to be a matter of great discouragement and barrier to sending children to primary schools.

As in some other districts, the teachers in primary schools of Vadodara had to go around collecting students from house to house to realise good attendance at the schools. The teachers taking all these troubles not only spent their valuable time but got too tired to be able to do primary role of teaching. Reportedly, this condition prevailed almost in the whole of tribal areas in the district. The education among girls was however, increasing as a result of which they no longer lived among their groups in villages. Education did not bring direct benefit to the parents of the educated girls in tribal villages.

In the village of Mankodi in Chhotaudepur taluka a Non-Formal Education Project was started for the students between 6 to 14 years. It was run jointly by the National Council of Education Research and Training, New Delhi and Gujarat Vidhyapith, Ahmedabad. The Zilla Panchayat, Vadodara provided active cooperation in initiating this programme. The classroom education was imparted to tribal children at night. The adult education programme was initiated in three talukas, and the organisers conducted 63 classes for the adults between the age of 15 to 25 years. The programme was enhanced by introduction of reading newspapers, literature and information material useful for increasing general knowledge. It was said that the programme helped in decreasing superstition and vices among the adults. Unless the teachers were well-versed in tribal dialects such as *Rathi* and *Bhily*, and were able to find out equivalent terms in Gujarati and the local dialects, they may not be able to impart education to adults.

The secondary education in tribal areas is required to be improved by providing new syllabus for teaching tribal students. It is not advisable to keep a common general syllabus for them. In order to remove language barrier to teachers, educated tribals with B.A. or B.Ed. qualifications be preferred for appointment in secondary schools.

The problems encountered by the Ashram Shalas and Uttar Buniyadi Shalas in the district were almost the same as elsewhere. A dull common daily routine of work from the beginning of every morning in Ashram Shalas proved to be tiresome to the students. A student had to get up at 5.30 a.m. in the morning and after making routine preparations, he had to start his programmes with the prayer meeting.

It was complained that programmes connected with the prayers as well as practical education in agriculture took away a substantiative time of the students. The time for teaching other subjects was greatly reduced. The government provided Rs. 55 stipend per month per student. In some Ashram Shalas they were ill-treated and kept half hungry. This created tension in their minds and ultimately after a month or so, they run away from the schools.

Notwithstanding this, it should be noted that the Central Government had instituted scholarships for bright as well as other pupils studying in 4 to 7 classes. Formerly, there were 9 scholarships of this type in three talukas of the Vadodara district which were later increased to 18 in order to give greater push to tribal education.

(e) The education among the tribals in the district of Bharuch was quite satisfactory so far as facilities in general were concerned. There was common dissatisfaction regarding education in one teacher primary schools. It was believed that this kind of schools did not impart effective education. But the situation was not so bleak as other categories of schools were also there.

In the taluka of Nandod, there were 209 schools of different kinds such as, (i) one teacher school — 90, (ii) two teacher schools — 46, and (iii) more than two teacher schools — 73. As mentioned earlier, one teacher schools were the main cause of slow spread of education in tribal area. The best solution for this was to form clusters of two to four villages and have jurisdiction of schools spread over 5 to 10 acres of land each on which agriculture, dairying, poultry, handicrafts, etc. can be taught. The other important measures for improving education among the tribals are: (a) school teachers should be dedicated and motivated for tribal education, (b) they should be given inservice training during vacations in order to upgrade their general as well as the subject-wise knowledge, (c) their residence should be within the premises of the schools so that they can function as sources of consultation for tribal population, (d) selected boys and girls should be sent to taluka level schools for further studies after selection on the basis of individual aptitudes.

The general impression given by non-officials was that female education which was almost nil in the past had been coming up gradually. This was on account of the increase in the number of Ashram Shalas where facilities for development were available. It was reported that 30 to 40 per cent of the female students attended schools. Some girls became even graduates.

As in the case of Banaskantha and Sabarkantha districts, situation of education in Bharuch was that there was demand for starting more Ashram Shalas in district. Most of the Ashram Shalas here were run by voluntary agencies and more or less managed by the educated tribals. In Panchmahals on the other hand, non-tribals were in the forefront of managing and running Ashram Shalas.

Some experienced persons observed that in the interest of good administration, not more than five Ashram Shalas be permitted to be managed by a voluntary agency. It was also felt that wherever Ashram Shalas were located, the local leaders should be delegated responsibility of management. The admission and recruitment to Ashram Shalas should be made on high standards of qualification, both for the teachers and students. The income derived from the demonstration work on agricultural plots attached to Ashram Shalas should be utilised for the benefit of the students who worked on them. There were quite a number of Ashram Shalas in the district that were run at a loss on account of weak managerial problems.

(f) In the district of Surat, the problem of running primary schools in remote tribal areas was serious. About 6000 primary school teachers were there, most of whom did not stay in the tribal villages on account of lack of adequate living accommodation. This was probably one of the reasons why teachers did not pay serious attention to teaching activities in schools. Poor school facilities was another problem. There were very few contractors prepared to undertake the responsibility of building schools in remote tribal areas. This was because the cost of school building was estimated to be Rs. 10,000 in all. The contributions collected were Rs. 7,000 from the government, Rs. 2,400 from Hari Om Ashram and Rs. 600 were expected to come as popular contribution in the form of voluntary labour for construction of school building. This total cost estimation was however inadequate and as a result, many villages remained without school buildings. Students had to sit in the verandah of some old buildings or in some huts for attending classes. Out of a total of 974 tribal villages, only 624 villages had schools. Whatever accommodation was there in schools, it was not up to the standard and so the attendance remained extremely poor.

One of the reasons of poor attendance at schools was, as in other districts, that the boys and girls had to work outside home for supplementing family income. Besides this, there was a strong feeling among the tribals that educated children do not either get jobs or have little chances to go for science subject which can really be helpful in enabling them to take jobs or higher studies. The education imparted in the subjects of Physics, Chemistry, Higher mathematics and English was so poor that many parents thought it useless to give them the so called higher education.

There were also problems of getting competent teachers who can seriously decide to come to tribal areas for improving the educational standards of the tribal children. Most of the well educated teachers preferred to go to non-tribal areas where facilities of living were satisfactory. The problems of management of boarding houses-cum-schools in the tribal areas were many. They were run by voluntary organisations with funds controlled by non-tribals and therefore there was little impact on getting the tribal children really involved in educational programmes. In some Uttar Buniyadi Schools, there were no doubt educated tribals who looked after the management, but on account of factionalism among them, the affairs of the management were rendered ineffective. In certain hostels of higher secondary schools, there were complaints of misappropriation of funds spent on food and other facilities for the students. There was wastage of grants from the government. The tribal parents who were keen to educate their children were very unhappy about the manner in which the Ashram Shalas were run and managed. As reported in the earlier case, there was also a great dissatisfaction against education of tribal children in Uttar Buniyadi schools, especially on account of lack of courses in Mathematics, English, Physics, Chemistry, etc. If the students are weak in these subjects, they cannot go for higher education as foundations for understanding of these subjects are not laid at the primary school level.

The taluka of Uchchhal, Nizar and Dharampur, boardering the state of Maharashtra required to be adequately covered by the effective educational programmes. All these three talukas not only require establishment of more primary schools, higher secondary schools, but also Ashram Shalas which alone can be of greater benefit to the tribal children.

(g) In the district of valsad, there were a number of specific groups of tribals most of whom did not take to education as desired. Among them Dhodias were however the most advanced. Both boys and girls were educated in this community and the level of literacy was relatively high. The percentage of literacy among the Dhodias was as high as 50 per cent and this can be understood by the statement of a non-official who said there were 300 Dhodia teachers in Pardi taluka alone. It was easy to find Dhodia graduates who were working as officers in the government and even a few of them had become Ministers on account of their education and leadership qualities. The female education among the Dhodias was also very high.

The next group of tribals with higher literacy was of the Choudhari. The literacy among them was reported to be about 22 per cent of their total population. Among the Konknas, there were two groups, one being relatively educated to some extent while the other being not so educated on account of their settlements located in interior of forests. There were two matriculates and even some graduates among the Konknas. Among the Naikdas, the literacy level was low. However, they were gradually reacting positively to the outside influence and had become conscious of giving education to younger generation. The literacy among the Dublas was only 13 per cent of their population. However, if Ashram Shalas were established in the area of their habitat they were likely to have sent children to schools. This was because they were living in contact with high caste people. Working closely in the domestic and agricultural spheres, they were influenced by a number of high caste values, habits and norms. The rest of the other groups of tribals were indeed very backward and literacy among most of them was negligible.

In spite of availability of school rooms or buildings for primary education, there was the lack of interest among the teachers who did not attend the schools regularly. In some areas, the attendance in primary schools was reported to be possible hardly for a week in a month. The few students who went to schools returned home after awaiting the arrival of their teacher. Wherever this kind of problems were encountered, it was wiser to close down the schools rather than waste limited resources. According to one opinion if schools were located at the interval of 7 to 8 miles, it was likely to contribute something concrete towards tribal education. It was estimated that on an average, one lakh rupees were spent every month on salaries of primary school teachers in a taluka. A heavy and wasteful expenditure of this type had to be rationalised and cut down properly.

Unless the teachers feel committed to tribal education, the problem of wastage of resources cannot easily be controlled. Grants to schools should be given on the basis of actual attendance of students and teachers and not simply on the basis of enrolment figures some of which were reported to be unrealistic. In the case of very backward tribal groups, there was a programme of giving incentives to the parents by contributing foodgrains free of cost to the households concerned. The text books were also given free of cost to the poor students of Kotwalia, Kolcha, etc., and as a result, attendance in some of the schools was reported to have increased. There was the provision of supplying school uniform free in certain areas. The posts of additional teachers for a primary school of standard 1 and 2 were also created by the government. In Dharampur taluka, there were about 20 villages where schools were run in the absence of buildings. Under these conditions, the teachers did not stay in the villages concerned. Both the school building and teachers' quarters were required to be built for improving primary education in Valsad area. In the district of Valsad, the teachers in Ashram Shalas sometimes did not get several benefits received by the primary school teachers run directly by the government. Sometimes, Ashram Shalas were not able to get enough grants from the government because they faced difficulty of having adequate attendance of students. According to a non-official, the Ashram Shalas were a must for improving tribal education. They should be managed instead of voluntary organisations by the government and established for a group of 4 to 5 villages. This kind of arrangement would be much better than having primary schools in relatively larger number where neither students nor teachers were found to go regularly.

The optimum number of students allowed per Ashram Shala was 120, but it is necessary that this norm was relaxed and 150 students were admitted in Ashram Shalas so that it becomes economically viable. Besides this, it would be useful to have 5 teachers per Ashram Shala instead of 4 at present. There were also some suggestions about the pay scales of the cooks in the kitchen of Ashram Shalas to be raised from Rs. 55 to 150 per month. The persons who worked as assistants in the kitchen should also get Rs. 100 p.m. instead of Rs. 50. Only if this kind of changes are made, it would be possible to retain good standard of food cooked in the kitchen for the benefits of the students. It was also suggested that the standard of scholarship be raised from Rs. 55 to 100 per student as was reported elsewhere.

(h) In the district of Dangs, predominantly inhabited by the tribals, literacy of total population was only 14.16 per cent. There were 336 primary schools in the district. Besides, there were 10 Ashram Shalas and 6 secondary schools. There was not a single college for higher education anywhere in the district. There were 12 villages having no primary schools at all, however, the children of these villages went to attend schools in neighbouring areas for education.

Of these ten Ashram Shalas, 9 were directly run by the government in which about 1200 students of Kunbi and Bhil tribals were studying. These 9 Ashram Shalas were located at the villages of Pipri, Rambag, Barpada, Malegaon, Chipli, Garpada, Gavan, Sigana and Mahal. There was only one Ashram Shala managed by a voluntary agency called 'Swaraj Ashram', established some years ago. The prescribed number of seats in Ashram Shalas were 80 for boys and 40 for girls. The problem of drop out in Ashram Shalas was as common as that reported from earlier districts. Out of the six secondary schools, four were being run by the government and two by the private agencies. Students from Kunbi and Warli communities were reported to be taking the greatest advantages of secondary education.

There were serious difficulties for students wanting to pursue higher studies after passing seventh standard. Unless hostel accommodations were also made possible for students taking secondary education, it would not be easy to raise the standard of education among tribal children. Wherever hostels were available, the admission for lodging and boarding was given only to the students residing within the radius of 5 kilometers. The distance of 5 kms. fixed for admission put those residing farther away at a great disadvantage. Even this limit of distance was most difficult to overcome by some students coming on foot or travelling by bus from nearby villages. It was, therefore, suggested that in order to prevent dropouts of students attending secondary schools, hostel accommodation must be made available to all the students admitted there. Wherever this facility was available, the quarters and hostel accommodation for students should be increased to prevent dropouts.

NOTE

1. Shri Amarsingh Chaudhari, former Chief Minister of Gujarat, a qualified

engineer comes from the Chaudhari group.

2. A comprehensive account of Chaudharis can be found in the recent Gujarati book of Arvind Bhatt, entitled *Gujaratna Chaudhario*, being a Ph. D. Thesis, published by Gujarat Vidyapith, Ahmedabad, 1985.

10

COMMUNICATION, MIGRATION, CHANGING OCCUPATIONS AND LEISURE

Introduction

In this Chapter we shall briefly deal with Communication facilities in remote tribal areas and then switch over to the patterns of migration, occupations and leisure time activities of tribals in the decade prior to 1981.

Communication

One of the most important factors which would bring about radical change in the life and labour of tribals will be better facilities of communication available to them in remote areas. For instance in a distant district town of Ahwa of the Dangs, there was a decade ago a passenger bus of the State Transport starting from Ahmedabad. There were hardly any other bus services available for visiting neighbouring areas. A narrow gauge railway line was running between the Bilimora in Valsad district and Waghai located in the Dangs. This was hardly adequate for communication facilities that the tribals could easily avail of because most of the trains were primarily goods trains used for transportation of minor forest produce and timber.

Leaving aside this special case of Dangs, it can be said confidently that after independence, many tribal talukas in other districts have been fairly well connected at least with bus routs, if not with train services to more advanced towns and cities of Gujarat. There were however, some remote areas and talukas such as Nizar, Uchchhal, Dharampur, etc. which were relatively cut off from easy communication facilities. In spite of this, a number of migrations of the tribals took place after monsoon season in particular indicating that transport facilities were available to tribals who wanted to earn their living outside their habitat. The common migration theory of push and pull factors advocated by the economists, however, are relevant to migratory habits of the tribals eager to take advantage of whatever means are available for physical mobility.[1] The information presented here after, throws ample light on migratory patterns of tribal life in contiguous and remote areas of their habitat. It is easy to conclude from the impressionistic review that rapid and wide-spread communication channels are gradually developing.

Many families in tribal areas in various places depend only on monsoon crops and have nothing to subsist upon in the next season. They have no alternative but to migrate for work. The basic reasons of tribal migrations are as follows:

(i) It takes place after monsoon when they have little work of agriculture,

(ii) It is a consequence of lack of employment opportunities in tribal habitat, and

(iii) It is spurred by draught and scarcity conditions due to inadequate rainfall. Thus, one or more members of the families of tribals migrate seasonally to places where they can get labour either in agriculture, road work, canal work, building and construction or any other work. They can get a variety of work in urban areas, ranging from domestic services to pulling hand-carts, rikshaws, etc.

Salient Features of Migration

The tribal areas of high concentration in Gujarat are situated on the eastern side of the State where there is a series of mountains, hills and hillocks. The soil is mostly rocky, barron or contain stones. The tribals have mostly to depend on monsoon crops. The wells are filled with water mostly in the monsoon. As there are rocks underground, inspite of boring operations, there is little hope to tap enough water. The tribals would hardly go for boring wells as the charges are too heavy to bear. In districts like Panchmahals, there were occasions when for years, it did not rain adequately and the area remained draught affected. The tribals depend on harvest from monsoon crops only, they remain in the acute need of relief works in times of scarcity. Even when monsoon is satisfactory, in view of their small holdings below 5 acres, a tribal family has to migrate to other areas where they take up work of any kind including labour in agriculture.

Since the principal means of livelihood of most tribals in normal times is agriculture, they have to try to use improved means of agriculture such as improved seeds, implements and fertilisers. In view of their unsound economic condition and indebtedness on account of burdensome social customs and other reasons of expenses at birth, death, illness, etc., they are unable to invest money for improved methods of agriculture. When they take a loan from a cooperative society, they are unable to repay the loans on account of little income during succeeding lean years or on account of damage to crops due to heavy rains. Thus their income from agriculture suffers gravely and they constantly remain in precarious condition of poverty, want and helplessness.

A micro level study of three villages of Dohad taluka of Panchmahals district was conducted by the Bureau of Economics and Statistics, Gujarat Government in 1971-72. The survey defined a "migrating household" as one, from which at least one member had migrated during the previous year, i.e. in 1970-71. It also observed that when the entire family migrates, the care of the cattle of the family is entrusted to another family. The migration is seasonal in order to raise supplementary income of the family.

The total number of sample households surveyed was 225. The survey revealed that the members from 86 per cent of the sample households in three villages migrated every year from January to May. Nearly more than half of the members of each household were found to have undertaken migration. Those who remained at home amounted to about 40 per cent members of the sample households. Regarding place of migration, the study revealed that highest number of migrants visited urban and rural areas in the district of Kaira. The rest of the migrants reported to be visiting rural areas of the district of Surat, Bharuch, Vadodara, Valsad and even Daman, and parts of Madhya Pradesh.

During the course of migration, the members of the household did not take any live-stock with them, but kept them in the custody of the members who were left behind to look after the households in villages. So far as the general occupation of agriculture was concerned it was revealed that 48 per cent of the households were engaged in agriculture, 50 per cent did non-agricultural labour and the rest two per cent worked as agricultural labourers and in miscellaneous services. It may be noted that of all the sample households 97 per cent had land up to 5 acres, one per cent more than 5 acres, and two per cent were landless.

The pattern of work at the place of migration was mostly confined to construction of roads and buildings. Taking an overall view of the period of migration in terms of number of days, the study revealed that: (i) 8 per cent households remained out for 16 to 30 days, (ii) 5 per cent for 31 to 45 days, (iii) 8 per cent for 46 to 60 days, (iv) 47 per cent for 61 to 90 days, (v) 26 per cent for 91 to 120 days.

The assessment of earnings of households based on the study indicated that (a) 3 per cent earned up to Rs. 50 per month, (b) 12 per cent earned between Rs. 51 to Rs. 100, (c) 45 per cent earned between Rs. 100 to 200, (d) 30 per cent earned between Rs. 201 to 350, (e) 3 per cent earned between Rs. 351 to 500, and (f) about 2 per cent of the migrants earned between Rs. 501 to 700. Sometimes the earnings of some households crossed the limit of Rs. 1000 per month.

Various findings of the studies of migration reported earlier indicated an amazing variety of pattern regarding the place of migration, wages earned and the conditions under which they worked. It is obvious therefore that no uniform information was available from which broad conclusions can be drawn.

Now, we shall start first with presenting the information derived from field interviews by project staff. It provides limited information from three districts viz. Panchmahals, Vadodara and Valsad. The migrations from the Panchmahals were reported to be fairly extensive. Some of the tribals were reported to be migrating to Vadodara, Kaira, Surendranagar and towns of neighbouring State e.g., Bhopal, Kotah, Ratlam and some parts of Saurashtra. Most of these tribal migrants were engaged in construction work on roads and highways. One of the reasons of their migrating to distant places for hard labour of this type was reported to be that tribals in Panchmahals had become greatly money-minded. This means that not only poor, but also well-to-do tribals took to seasonal migration. They suffered from being exploited in various kinds of jobs and were compelled to live in the open place without roof over head or other amenities. In the case of tribals of Vadodara district, a large number of them migrated to the city of Vadodara. On account of their migrations within the district, they were not facing serious problems of living accommodation, even though the problem of exploitation remained a great threat.

Migration of tribals from the district of Valsad were on account of demand for agricultural labour both within and outside the district. Some of the seasonal migrations were to take advantage of grass cutting seasons. It was reported from one village that as many as 75 per cent of the families migrated to Palghar for cutting the grass in grass lands of private parties.

Apart from migrating to larger towns and cities, there was a general trend among the tribals to migrate to nearby small and medium size towns located either in their own district or in contiguous districts. The variety of jobs they undertook at the place of migration may be listed as; cutting sugarcane, preparing cooking coal, harvesting wheat and other crops, picking cotton pods, collecting ground nuts and working in mines and quarries.

A study of seasonal migration of Bhils to Vadodara was conducted by the Zonal Director, Backward Class Welfare, Western Zone, Vadodara. Most of the Bhils migrating to Vadodara were reported to come from the district of Panchmahals in Gujarat, Kushalgadh taluka in Rajasthan and Jhabua district in Madhya Pradesh. All these contiguous regional areas are inhabited by the Bhils living on the borders of these three states. Before the study was conducted observations were made in the villages of Panchmahals from where Bhils had migrated. It was reported that the village huts and hamlets were found empty during migration season. Most of the migrant Bhils in the city of Vadodara were temporarily settled on the over-bridge area of Vishwamitri river, Railway Station areas, foot-paths of main roads, under-bridge areas and localities around Circuit House, Race Course, Chhani and Karelibaug areas.

In all, there were 51 families (out of about 650) interviewed during the course of study. It is interesting to note that the size of Bhil families who migrated to Vadodara varied at great length. The membership of 28 families each out of 50, varied between 2 to 7 members. On the other hand, there were about 22 families, the size of each ranged between 8 to 22 members. This information has led to the conclusion that larger the size of the family, greater the number of family members migrating from native villages. Majority of those who migrated had household land varying from 1 to 3 acres. Moreover, there was no surplus land in most of the villages to sustain all the people on land. The main reason for one such migration given by almost all migrant households was failure of maize crop followed by poor yield of wheat and other crops. It was more over reported that there was invariably a draught year once in every three years. Among many other causes, indebtedness was one of the contributory reasons why they would like to go outside to earn extra money. The average wages earned by the tribals in Vadodara ranged between Rs. 2 to 5 per day. Most of them worked for the whole day outside the place where they lodged in the open, and when they returned home, their meagre belongings remained safe and untouched by anyone in the area. Hardly were they found to be taking regular baths and washing their cloths. Almost all the families reported that they would not like to leave their village if they were able to have sufficient quantity of maize to maintain themselves throughout the year.

The respondents were asked to make suggestions which may help them give up seasonal migratory habits. Their suggestions are listed here: (i) more agricultural land should be distributed among them, (ii) vigorous developmental programmes required for better crops, (iii) provision for improved agricultural practices and inputs be guaranteed, (iv) irrigation facilities be improved, and (v) industries be established in nearby places where they can earn their spare time living. None of the above suggestions indicated that tribals were interested in diversifying their occupational pattern. However, there was an indirect suggestion of their willingness to be associated with industrial work.

The study of Vadodara indicated that the tribals migrating to towns and cities, should be taken special care by the local urban governments. They should be provided with adequate facilities of housing and minimum amenities such as water, light, latrines etc. In fact, it is this kind of migrants who carry the heavy burden of building residential and other accommodation in the cities and they certainly need affectionate care by the Municipal local governments. The report of the study bring out a few important suggestions such as: (a) Labour Contract Societies be organised with the help of the government and voluntary agencies at the native place of the migrant labour, (b) A taluka be considered as the centre of organising such labour societies, (c) Every tribal development block should keep a constant vigil over the trend of migration and factors responsible for the same, and (d) Prevention of migration to distant places be organised on long-term basis.

Areas of Seasonal Migration of Tribals

As far as possible, tribals prefer to get employment near their own places or in the neighbouring districts. If that is available, they would not go farther away. As mentioned before, the Bhils of Panchmahals were found to migrate mostly to rural areas of Kaira, Baroda and Surat districts. Some individuals who go to urban areas in Kaira were formerly found migrating in only the rural areas of Panchmahals, Valsad, Ahmedabad, Daman-Div and Madhya Pradesh. In the Bhiloda taluka of Sabarkantha, Dungari Garasia Bhils migrated after monsoon to neighbouring talukas of Himmatnagar, Idar and Modasa where they got agricultural labour, such as picking up cotton, collecting groundnut, thrashing wheat, doing earth work, etc. Tobacco growers in kaira district got work for watering and taking care of tobacco plants from the Bhils of Panchmahals. Tribals from Chhotaudepur migrated to internal regions of Kanam, Charotar and Khedbrahma, and got labour work for 8 months. Some went for picking groundnut and cotton in Sankheda and Dabhoi area and got work for about two months. In Jhagadia taluka, the Bhil Vasava in particular as well as other groups went to villages in Vagra taluka to get agricultural labour in harvesting, picking cotton, etc. Tribal males of 20 to 25 families from Chikda village were found going to Surat district to cut sugarcane, if monsoon at home was not favourable.

From villages in the Surat district and Umbergaon taluka, tribals were found going to Palgadh to cut grass and earn their living for 2 to 3 months. In times of need, the Palgadh labour contractors used to give loans to the Warlis of Malav in Umbergaon taluka to ensure continuance of their services of cutting grass for about five months in grass-lands. The Tribals of Sutharpada, a village on Maharashtra border of Nasik district, located in Dharampur taluka, is inhabited by Kolcha, Konkna and Warli. Some 20 families went to Nasik where males got employment in grape orchards and females cut grass. The work of Metal breaking and masonry in the neighbouring villages also attracted the Bhil migrants of the village Umber in Panchmahals.

Tribals were employed also for work on railway tracks as labourers. When Indian railways required labour for repairs or to lay-out new lines, tribals of the villages on the line were always at hand. Similarly the tribals got labour work on Highways, other roads, nalas, dams and canals where huge construction works were undertaken. There is a constant demand of labour for expansion and widening and repair of roads, which offered opportunity to the tribals for work.

The Forest Labour Cooperative Societies which replaced the private forest contractors gave labour to tribals within their area in cutting logs, removing stumps and in Charcoal making. The Forest Department also undertakes afforestation work, and the work of laying down forest boundaries by demarcating and erecting mile stones, walls, etc. This provided ample work to tribals.

The Bardoli Sugar Factory provided miscellaneous work to the tribals of Surat district. About 25 families from Kanjod, a village in Valod taluka were found going to Bardoli Sugar Factory after Diwali and earning livelihood for about 8 months. Nearly 15 to 20 tribals from village Umara of Mahuva taluka in Surat, went to Khedbrahma to prepare *gur* (molasses) from sugarcane. About 10 to 12 worked as tractor-drivers and went to the Bardoli area after Diwali to earn wages for 8 months. Quite a number of these tribals come from Dhodia and Konkna tribes

Although Panchmahals tribals were mostly migrating to rural areas of Kaira, Baroda and Surat districts, some individuals preferred to go to urban areas of Kaira. Dungar Garasias of Bhiloda taluka of Sabarkantha District went to villages in the talukas of Himatnagar, Idar and Modasa for agricultural labour. In the village Kothara of Chhotaudepur taluka, about 10 families were found to migrate to Kanam, Charotar and Khedbrahma regions and got wages for about 8 months. In the villages Mankodi and Nanupura of Chhotaudepur, 25 and 30 families respectively were found migrating to Sankheda and Dabhoi area to get agricultural labour for about 2 months. From a village called Dumala Haripura in Jhagadia taluka, 5 to 6 families were found to migrate to Vagra taluka of the same district for agricultural labour for 2 to 3 months. The Cooperative Sugarcane factory was another place where tribals of Kanjod village in Valod taluka migrated to earn their living for 8 months. About 25 families from Chikda village in Dediapada taluka were found to migrate to Surat district to cut sugarcane and got work for one and a half month. Tribals of Virpor in Valod taluka got employment for one month for grass-cutting in neighbouring grass land areas.

Palgadh is another centre where tribals for Malav village of Umbergaon taluka and from Dhamakhadi village of Mahuva taluka were migrating for cutting grass to earn their living for 2 to 3 months. They were paid at the rate of Rs. 8 for cutting 500 bundles of grass that took the work of two full days.

From Bhiloda taluka of Sabarkantha district, tribals of Dhandhas and Odhapada villagers went to neighbouring talukas of Himatnagar, Idar and Modasa. They earned Rs. 3 as wages per day with no meals for agricultural labour. In the case of village Odhapada, tribals got 6 seers bajri or maize or wheat in the place of Rs. 3 per day. For earth work, they were paid Rs. 4 to 7 to remove one cubic feet soil depending upon the distance of the place where it was taken.

In the coupes of forest cooperatives, etc. daily wages were paid at Rs. 5.50 per day. The work of cutting log of wood was given on piece meal basis. The work of planting trees was given on daily wage basis. In Ghantoli village of Dediapada taluka they got Rs. 4.50 daily for cutting wood.

In village Lakad-mal of taluka Dharampur, some boys and girls went for construction work of building under a mason in Valsad area; the monthly wages given to them was Rs. 100 per month. They earn this for a period of 8 months.

The tribals from the village of Titwa in Valod taluka of District Surat go to neighbouring villages for work. The males as well as females got Rs. 3 each without meals, tea, tobacco etc. They go for work in the morning and return to their village in the evening. This was of course not a case of seasonal migration. It gives an idea of the daily wages available in the area.

About 20 to 25 tribals called Bhil Wasava of the village of Haripura Dumala went to the Uchhal Cotton Seed Production Centre and Achhalia Seed Research Centre for nearly 8 months and got daily wages of Rs. 5.50. These villages were in the vicinity of the labour market. In distant villages of the same taluka, several cultivators took to growing bananas, and 21 to 25 tribals went there for labour. They got Rs. 1.25 and 2 seers of *jowar* as daily wages. The tribals were threatened and beaten up if they raised dispute regarding amount of wages paid to them.

The Bhils of Mahobatpura village in Naswadi taluka went to Indral Songir of (taluka Sankheda) which is at distance of 5 kilemeters, to quarry grinding stones, mortar, etc. Every year they got wages in the period of fair season. The wages received by them from the contractors could not be ascertained as none was available at the time of the visit.

The tribals who worked in grape orchards and on grass-lands got varying amount of wages. Males got Rs. 4 to 5 per day and females who cut grass got Rs. 1 to 2. Those who went to work in the areas of Valsad, Pardi, Dharampur for grass-cutting got Rs. 3 to 5 per day as labour charge.

So far as the seasonal migration continues, it should be ensured that the migrants must get full wages of Rs. 5.50 per day. Hardly any instances of payment of this amount had come to light. This was because, the tribals feared that they will lose even the meagre income from seasonal jobs if they insisted on full wages. They had to manage their life without essential needs of housing etc. The contractors engaging them on road building works gave them less amount as wages, so that their profits may remain high. This sort of exploitation should be put to an end, by carrying on suitable propaganda and taking legal action. The tribals on daily wages should also be provided with food and shelter by the contractors as the same is provided during relief works.

Tribals find it difficult to get, and later repay loans taken during lean months in view of vagaries of the monsoon. There should be a rational approach to advance loans and recover the same after harvesting the crops. This can help a great deal in preventing avoidable migrations. He must have sufficient to subsist upon at home. There was a suggestion that all loans to a tribal must flow from one source only. There is a lot of advantage in this, in as much as the total debt of a tribal can be known. All the credit giving government agencies and departments need not insist for recovery of loans from him every year. The tribal Sub-Plan project authorities should take a stock of his assets and liabilities while advancing money to him either as loan or as subsidy. It is fairly admitted that the benefits of Sub-Plans meant for tribals reach non-tribals in disguised form. Some tribals remained under the thumb of creditors and the seasonal income in kind or cash were cornered by the latter who utilised the benefits for personal end. Even the government quota of seeds, fertilisers, etc. were used in the fields of non-tribal creditors and not in the fields of the *bona fide* tribals.

Changing Occupations and Leisure Time Activity

Occupation is obviously an important subject of study for identification of change in tribal society and culture. The subject is overloaded with problems of value and perception of what is good and satisfying for a tribal to live upon. In bygone days, most of the tribals were said to be subsisting themselves by food-gathering, hunting and robbery. Agriculture seemed to have reached relatively later in the culture of the tribals as an important occupation for subsistence. Even scientific animal husbandry has been of recent innovation among the tribals. Today however, the large number of tribals are attracted towards agriculture as respectable occupation. However, on account of lack of adequate cultivable land, agricultural labour and other varieties of work in mines, factories, construction work, etc. have become common sources of livelihood.

(a) In the district of Banaskantha it was reported that sometimes the whole families left their villages after Diwali to earn living from labour and engaged themselves on construction of buildings and roads. Some of them go to jungles and cut wood and sell it in nearby bazars. In recent times, poultry farming, rearing of cows and buffaloes have come up as subsidiary occupations of the tribals. In any case, one thing was reported emphathetically that most of the tribals were able to maintain themselves without much difficulty in normal years. This was however not the case in the remote areas where they had to live without food for days together. On account of a variety of occupations available to them, they are now improving their economic conditions slowly and surely and some of them have even begun to own cycles, radios and transistors as means of entertainment and symbol of prestige.

Quite a number of tribals in Banaskantha worked in the mines of Gujarat Mineral Development Corporation. Some of them also worked in the mines of marble stone in the area. Those who succeeded in selling woods for domestic fuel paid visits to the Ambaji temple and bazar of the town. It may appear exaggeration, but some tribals households were reported to be earning every year Rs. 3000 to 4000 simply by selling wood at Ambaji. This is the main reason why the jungle areas in this part have been completely rendered barren. Some new types of occupations reported to be undertaken by the tribals of this area were jobs of bus conductors, drivers, clerk or peon in offices etc. The occupation of diamond cutting industry was also taken up by the tribal labourers. A person was able to earn Rs. 400 to 500 per month after having taken training in diamond cutting for six months only. In the town of Palanpur, 3000 to 4000 diamond cutting units were providing jobs to 30,000 to 40,000 workers. It was quite natural that some of the tribals prefered to engage in this occupation. The general reaction of some of the official and non-official respondents was that the tribals in general were negligent of time and careless about work assigned to them. They have to be taught to work hard, in time and sincerely. If money was given to them in cash, they had a tendency to squander away easily and again ask for help without any feeling of guilt.

As against this general observation, one of the officials reported that no tribal would like to earn his bread from the resources of Ambaji temple. Illustrating this point he indicated that in the times of draught, the temple opens kitchen from where food was served at a cheaper rate of only 25 paise per head. But hardly a few tribals took advantage of this facility. This is because their religious sentiments did not allow them to eat at the temple nearly free of cost.

(b) It was reported from the district of Sabarkantha that many tribals lived from hand to mouth because most of them were landless, illiterate and backward. There was a lot of unemployment reported among the tribals of this area. They were said to be greatly attached to land and considered other occupations including services in government or elsewhere as inferior categories of occupations. The extent of their attachment to land was expressed graphically in the local proverb which said that "The tribals have greatest pride in possession of women, rifle and land" (i.e. *Bayadi, Banduk* and *Bhony*). Other assets such as new skills, jobs, etc. were of little value.

(c) One of the most important characteristics of tribals can be judged from their attitude to work. A non-officials categorically reported that the tribals in general and Bhils of the Panchmahals in particular were not habituated to sit at one place and work. They preferred to spend laborious days in hot summer working on construction sites and repairs of roads. They would refrain from sitting in their homes and work on the spinning wheel. According to a respondent, the Bhil Seva Mandal at Dahod, has been working for many years to get the tribals accustomed to work at home on the spinning wheel and earn their living. It was unfortunately not of much success in getting the tribals rehabilitated to a work situation. It seems that nomadic life style is highly ingrained in the tribals.

A large number of activities in which Bhils were reported to be occupied in this district were associated with forest occupations. These occupations related to collection of minor forest produces such as Mahuda flowers, timru leaves, ceiling wax, gum, etc. They were also engaged in preparing Bidi, baskets and other items of cottage industry. As reported earlier, all these activities were fraught with opportunities of exploitation of the tribals by traders. Not only this, even the Forest Development Corporation was reported to be buying 20 kilograms of Mahuda flowers at the rate of Rs. 9 only. It was on the other hand sold by the Corporation at the rate of Rs. 30 per kilogram, a form of institutional exploitation. It was suggested that the monopoly of buying Mahuda flowers by the Corporation should be done away with so that the tribals were able to get better prices in the open market for Mahuda flowers collected by them.

The over-all improvement in the occupational problems of the tribals of this district can however be tackled through a number of developmental programmes about which mention has been made in earlier pages. In the first instance, irrigation facilities should be provided for which a block of fields occupied by different persons can be encouraged. The poultry farming, rearing of goats and cows, buffaloes, etc. have also to be encouraged to supplement their income from agricultural occupations. One of the outstanding suggestions for making more jobs available to unskilled tribals was to establish a loco-workshop at Dahod so that a number of tribals can easily be trained and occupied in various skilled and semi-skilled jobs in the railways. The other occupations suggested for the tribals were printing of textile, spinning ropes from cotton and nylon yarn and work in domestic industries.

(d) The work situations reported from Vadodara district indicated a considerable amount of diversification that is taking place among the tribals. There was however some general dissatisfaction about the lack of job opportunities for educated young tribal boys even after passing S.S.C. examinations. Even the expectation of getting loans for starting independent occupations seemed to remain unfulfilled in some cases. One of the informants indicated that educated young tribals should be employed in various kinds of government jobs such as clerk, peon, policemen, etc. They should also be able to go in for employment as teachers if suitable conditions were created.

In an interview with a group of 49 families in one taluka, it was revealed that they would be glad if they can get bamboo work for making various kinds of domestic utilities. But there were a few tribals who did not like to engage themselves in preparing baskets from bamboos and earn their living. Most of the parents were keen that their children were able to learn how to read and write and get better occupations rather than undertake handicrafts work. So far as young girls were concerned, preference for home industries for them was expressed. It was considered suitable for tribal girls to get engaged in preparing leaf-plates, leaf-cups, do sewing and rafoo work and other activities of stitching clothes, etc. Women were also considered suitable for collecting *timru* leaves, fire wood, gum, Mahuda flowers, *charodi* seeds etc. from the forest.

In some areas a large number of tribals undertook laborious work in stone quarries, almost for a large part of the year except during monsoon. The other occupations were of course related to agricultural labour which gave them opportunities to work in cotton fields, groundnut fields in various neighbouring areas where they migrated from time to time. It may be interesting to illustrate the types of work tribals were doing in two villages of Naswadi taluka of this district. From one village, 10 families migrated to Dabhoi and neighbouring areas for working in cotton fields for two months. One person was doing work as a tailor and another one was a teacher in a primary school. Other two persons were reported to be engaged in carpentry as well as masonry work. In another village, where Rathwas were predominant, three men and two women were working as teachers, two serving in the State Transport Services, one was working as a clerk, two were S.R.P. personnel, one was in the Police, two were working as bus conductors and one person was working as Security Guard. However, in addition to all these occupations in which some tribals were engaged, six people were reported to be employed in diamond cutting industries. This seems to be an exceptionally advanced village where tribals had taken up numerous occupations.

One of the non-officials indicated that the custom of working as bonded servants among tribals was prevalent in some parts of Vadodara district. This kind of contractual servant-master relationship was generally common in rural Gujarat. The farmers were constantly in need of a helping hand to look after various agricultural activities. The contractual services of this kind were fixed generally for 12 months and the servant was paid, at the end of the year, Rs. 600 cash, two suits of clothes, one pair of shoes, etc. He was also served morning tea, a meal at 11 a.m. and another one in the afternoon. The evening was free for him and he went away to spend the night with his family. In case additional person from the family of the servant was made to work in the fields, he was paid Rs. 3.50 per day and not Rs. 5.75 as prescribed by the authorities. This custom of undertaking the work as a bonded servant was prevalent among those tribal families who were not able to get-rid of their temporary or long term indebtedness. The good point about this master-servant relationship was that the tribal servant was not treated just as a slave. He can change his master any time he liked and if his relationships were good, the master even undertook the responsibility of meeting the expenditure for marrying sons and daughters of such a bonded servant.

(e) The occupational situation among the tribals in Bharuch district was favourably as advanced as in the Vadodara district. Some of the educated tribals were of course unemployed. There were some who worked as teachers, nurses, clerks, etc. According to a non-official, many a tribals had taken to carpentry and tailoring work. They had come to realise that mere agricultural labour would not bring job satisfaction and money required for improving their living standards. However, those whose main occupation remained agriculture, did side business and resorted to illicit distillation of liquor to increase family income in lean months. The main occupation of the Bhil Vasava of this district was agriculture. However on account of insufficient land for self-cultivation, many of them worked as agricultural labourers. They also worked as labourers in timber industries and sale of minor forest produce including honey for which they undertook bee keeping occupation.

In a village called Haripura, many a tribals had undertaken bonded services with landlords. This kind of services may be fixed for a whole year or for six months. The servant was paid Rs. 250 for 12 months plus two suits of clothes two big towels, one pair of shoes, etc. Moreover, the servant got every month one and half to two *maund* of Jowar, 5 kilos of onion, half kilo chillies, and some quantity of tobacco and tea every day. The servant also got a full meal from the landlords on festival days. The servant spent the night with his family. Most of the tribals were reported to be habituated to take liquor but did not indulge in gambling through a widespread den called *Warli Matka*. However, they enjoyed dancing, eating and merry-making during fairs and festivals. A special groups of tribals called Gowalias in this area were in fact landless Bhils turned cow-herds. They were as poor as the Kotwalias who had primitive habits and subsisted themselves on daily food received from tending the cattle of others.

(f) Most of the tribal areas in Surat district were effected by the influence of educated and advanced people in the district. This created a conducive climate for the tribals to educate themselves formally or informally and get interested in more than one occupations for earning livelihood. The Dublas were mainly engaged in agricultural labour because they were more or less landless. They were politically conscious but due to economic backwardness and lack of education, they had undertaken a number of new white-collar or semi-skilled jobs. The most advanced group of tribals in the district were Dhodias who were progressively giving up agriculture, in which they are well-versed as compared to other tribals. The occupations of teachers, clerks and various categories of industrial labour were taken up by them without any hesitation. Beyond agricultural occupations and industrial labour, there were a number of inferior variety of occupations, such as basket making, broom making, fishing, collecting minor forest produce, etc. were the main stay of large number of tribals in this district. It was quite natural that many a tribals therefore worked under unfavourable circumstances either in the native place or in the places of their seasonal migration. However, those who had given up nomadic life were engaged as bonded servants with well to do landlords and other masters with whom they worked more or less under similar terms and conditions reported about in the contractual relationships referred to in previous two points.

(g) The situation regarding tribal occupations in the district of Valsad seemed to be more fluid than probably in Vadodara, Bharuch and Surat districts. This is because Valsad district is sandwiched between Bombay metropolls and Surat city and also because of the fact that a number of industries are coming up in some of its talukas through which the broadgauge railway line is passing ever since the times of the Britishers in this area. A number of tribals were said to be engaged in pressing-grass from the grass lands in the Umbergaon taluka of this district. Many more, however, were engaged in cutting-grass for a few months every year. Some areas of the district were also famous for orchards of mango, chiku, etc. where tribals worked. A number of tribals were also engaged in collecting fruit, looking after fruit trees, sorting and packing fruit for export etc. In the peak mango season, a number of migrant tribals came to this area even from bordering State of Maharashtra and worked here from March to June every year. After the onset of monsoon, most of these tribals as well as others from the neighbouring areas went back to their villages.

In spite of great demand for labour in industry, agriculture, orchards, quarrying, etc. it was reported that hardly anybody gave the minimum wage of Rs. 5.50 to a tribal. All the masters with whom these tribals worked were non-tribals such as Parsis, Patel, Desai, etc. A number of tribals also migrated from the district to Maharashtra, and specially to the place like Vasai, Thana etc., in the vicinity of Bombay. It seems that the tribals of this district were largely on the move because they were landless and therefore helpless.

(h) The occupational structure of the tribals in the district of Dangs reported by an official was as follows. Of the total population of the tribals, 67.46 per cent were cultivators in which males and females were almost equal partners. The agricultural labourers were 20.15 per cent in which female participation was relatively greater than that of the males. The other categories of occupations in which some of the Dangi Bhil tribals were engaged comprised 12.39 per cent of total population. In this miscellaneous category of occupations, the proportion of female workers to males was 1:3.

The largest sources of household income in the Dangs however, was not from agriculture, but from the jungles. According to a non-official, the income from the jungles in Dangs amounted to Rs. 3.5 crores per annum. The number of tribals were naturally engaged in forest labour cooperatives. Some of those who belonged to the educated group of Kunbi and Bhil were also reported to be engaged in teaching, clerical jobs, nursing, casual service etc. Some of the Gamit and Warli tribals were reported to be working in the government as well as in army. Although the recruitments in army was negligible, some Bhils were reported to have joined military and police force.

In the end, we may throw some light on leisure time activities of the tribals in the whole of Gujarat. The cinema and stage dramas as well as Bhavai are common sources of entertainment among the tribals. They were also fond of getting recreation from traditional dances on festive occasions such as Divaso in Surat district and several other special festivals connected with Holi, Diwali, Pithora worship, ancestor worship etc. in other districts. In recent times, radios and portable transistors have added to traditional recreation facilities for the tribals. This facilities may be found even in remotest tribal villages. In some areas use of bicycle has also been reported as an item of communication and recreation for the tribals. This seems to be an objective interpretation of what a bicycle means to a tribal, who might not be accustomed to use it for the purpose of travelling long distances.

NOTE

1. To migrate, according to Oxford dictionary, means to move from one place (country, town, college, house, etc.) to another; so far as birds or fishes are concerned, it means to come and go with the seasons or to move under natural forces. One who moves from one place to another is a migrant, whether it is an individual or it is a family.

11

CULTURE CHANGE, ETHICS, MORALITY AND HEALTH

Introduction

As it is well-known, culture is a nebulone concept and it includes among many things ethics, religion, morality and even health as related to values, attitudes and behaviour. It is important, therefore, to understand tribals in the light of their life style and world view. The composite subject covered by the title of this chapter has many dimensions which deserve treatment in depth. What is attempted here is only a bird-eye view of broad aspects of the sub-titles in which the chapter is divided. The land reform measures and their impact on tribal development can be felt to some extent in the changes taking place in tribal life and culture in Gujarat after independence. This can serve as a comparative material to understand the changing scenario after 1980 to date in Gujarat. Moreover, the facts and interpretations can be used by interested readers in making basic comparison of relative conditions and development of tribal groups and their cultures in other states of India also. To that extent we should look upon this analysis of certain issues of the Gujarat tribals as a gross macro material providing a perspective of inter-regional situation of the tribal culture obtained in the country.

Customs, Dress, Housing and Food Habits

In this section we shall describe in general the changes taking place in socio-economic and material culture of the Gujarati tribal life. The information was collected with the specified purpose of indicating some trend of change among tribals. It throws considerable light on the level of general cultural development of tribals in various districts. The customs and ceremonies of marriage, birth and death appears to have been less effected by changing conditions of tribal life. The other areas of tribal material culture connected with dress, food-habits, etc. are undergoing relatively more rapid change. We shall deal with all these aspects under each broad title describing changes that had taken place both at specific group level and at the level of districts and talukas of tribal Gujarat.

(a) *Marriage Customs*

In the district of Banaskantha, the ceremony of betrothal takes place at the tender age of five years both in the case of boys and girls. As soon as a girl reaches the age of 10 years, she is sent to her in-laws' family even though formal marriage ceremony may not be over. This kind of freedom is taken in general before formal marriage is celebrated. When the couple comes of age, become self-sufficient to run the households and is economically better off, they are ritually married sometimes late in life. At times they might have given birth to a few children. In some extreme cases, marriageable or married children get an opportunity to set their parents or even their grands parents getting formally married in their presence. On such rare occasions, the marriages were celebrated in groups which may include parents as couples as well as the children and their spouses. The group marriages cost about Rs. 5000 to Rs. 7000 and therefore only the well-off tribals went in for this kind of marriages.

The folk festivals and fairs are the occasions when most of the tribals enjoy full life in dancing and merry-making. On such occasions, it is customary for a boy to elope with a girl of his choice. For the ultimate marriage settlement after elopement, the father of the son had to pay Rs. 1000 to the father of the girl. The regular marriage was celebrated after the birth of the first child and specially when they were able to spend money independently for the marriage ceremony. Usually, the groom's party would take 100 to 200 members to the in-laws village for marriage. The members of the party were fed with the hotch-potch of Makai by the family of the bride. The ceremony was performed by a tribal priest called *Pujaro* from among themselves. High caste Brahmin priest was not required. The bride was gifted a cow, a goat, and a pair of clothes at the time when she is sent to her husband's family. The customs regarding this event varied a great deal and there were no fixed rules and regulations which required specific treatment of the groom's party by the bride's party or the gifts given by the parents of the bride on such marriages. In some areas, the father of the bride offered a special kind of sweet jelly called *Sheero* to 30 to 35 members of the groom's party.

If the person was without a son, he married his daughter to a younger man who agreed to stay and work with him as member of family. Such a married person is called *Khandhalio* or *Ghar Jamai.* This man stays with the father-in-law until the latter's the death. As soon as the father-in-law dies, he has to leave his wife and the children. This is because the land is not transferred to him as the regular son-in-law. The land of the deceased person went entirely to the agnatic relations of the clan or lineage. Only the cattle left by the deceased father were owned by the daughter. In case there was no separation between the husband and the wife, all that was given to the daughter, excepting ancestral land, went alongwith the man whom she had married.

There is also the custom of re-marriage common among the tribals. The widow's father would get Rs. 500 from the groom's party at the time of her re-marriage. The sons of the widow by her previous husband would stay with the family of the genitor. The normal marital relationships among some tribal communities suffer from disharmony on account of possible suspicion of extramarital relationship on the part of women. Most tribals live in the huts built on their fields and are not to be found living at one place in a nucleated cluster of hutments. If anybody visited their huts located at isolated places, they become doubtful about the character of their wives. This is one of the reasons why they do not leave their women alone as far as possible. When they went out of the village they took their wives alongwith them.

In the district of Sabarkantha, the situation regarding the marriage custom remained more or less the same. However, in some groups, the bride's party had to offer liquor to the party of the groom when they visited their place. Not only this, the bride's party would accept bride-price called *Dapu* to be paid by the groom's party in cash. This was the reason why some families borrowed money from private money-lenders after mortgaging their land, sometimes at the exorbitant rate of 36 to 60 per cent interest. This was reported from Khedbrahma taluka.

There were cases where the groom's party while visiting the bridge's place for marriage carried with them cooked breads of wheat weighing 10 mounds or so. This used to become such a heavy drain on their stock of food that for the rest of the year, the family of the groom had to live eating inferior variety of grains such as Kodra, Maize, and so on.

Even the simplest marriage would cost Rs. 2000 and more on behalf of the groom's party. The indebted father of the married son would expect the latter to get separated from the family so that all the debt incurred on his marriage be paid by him alone. Nevertheless, the son was given about half an acre of land if the father was well-off. The newly married son and his wife had to maintain themselves on the food-grains produced on this piece of land. They were required also to pay-up the debt which might have taken place on the occasion of marriage.

The earlier accounts of marriage customs showed that the institution of marriage was at different stages of stabilization among tribal communities. It all depended on the development of social system of various groups of tribals. We shall now take a hurried view of some of the outstanding differences and variations in the customs of marriage among tribals.

In the district of Panchmahals, Vadodara, etc. some advanced tribals who can afford to have marriage ceremonies done with the help of a Brahmin would no doubt prefer to do so. But there were large number of socially and educationally backward tribals who preferred to get children married according to their own traditional customs. In some cases, it was the brother-in-law of the bride and groom who took leading role in settling marriage by lifting the prospective groom on shoulder and express joy through dancing on the occasion. Among some tribes, the wives of the brothers of the bride and those of the groom's brothers took initiative in solemnising marriage. Although in general, it was the groom's party that went out for marriage to the bride's family among some tribal communities in Surat and Valsad, it was the bride's party that went to the groom's party for the purpose of marriage. There were a variety of customs on determining as to who feeds the members of the marriage party. Sometimes the members of the marriage party went for marriage after taking their meals at home, but they were at times offered another meal by the groom's party.

The custom of dowry was slowly entering into the marriage institutions of tribals. Sometimes, the bride's parents had to give groom's father the gift of Rs. 850 in cash, two pairs of clothes, a lot of food-grains and liquor to drink. Among some advanced and educated tribal groups, there was a tendency to get old marriage customs *sanscriticised* to the extent possible.[1] On the other hand, there were groups of tribals whose grown-up boys and the girls begin to live together as man and woman without marriage. In course of time after the birth of a few children they get married as per the custom. Among some communities, marriage of the children cannot be solemnised until the parents themselves had completed ceremony of their marriage. In such cases, married children would fully enjoy group-dancing at the late marriage of their own parents.

So for as *Khandhalia* marriage was concerned, one found varying conditions in actual practice. An unmarried man can be adopted as *Khandhalia* by the girl's party if her brothers and sisters were too young to look after parental property and land. The custom of polygamy was prevalent among some tribal communities. It was prestigious for a man to have more wives. In one case, it was reported that a rich tribal had as many as 8 wives.

The separation or divorce between married couples takes place on the outskirts of the village of one of the party. The settlement of divorce was negotiated by the relatives and intermediaries on both sides. At the end, the leaders of the village are treated with liquor, food and refreshments.

The role of local tribal Panchayat was however very important specially at the time of marriage. Among some backward communities, the groom's father had to pay an amount of Rs. 500 to Rs. 800 for taking the bride to this house in anticipation of marriage. This custom was referred to as taking the bride on credit (*Udhadi*). As reported earlier, the marriage for a young man or a woman was a must among all the tribals, irrespective of whether they celebrated it at the initial stage of marriage or after the birth of a few children. In any case, poor tribals incur debt to meet marriage expenses, as they are mostly short of money.

Among the tribals of the Dangs, expenditure at marriage ceremonies was relatively very low. In recent times, the government was reported to be advancing loans for the purpose of marriage from the Dangs Loan Funds. This has helped many tribals from avoiding debt of a private money-lender.

(b) *Death Ceremonies*

The information on birth ceremonies among the tribals collected during the field work was not adequate and so we shall deal here only with some salient features of death ceremonies in general. The 12th day after the death of a person is generally an important occasion on which death ceremonies are performed by most of the tribals. In some areas 13th day after the death of a person was considered important for conducting mortuary rites helpful in "stabilising the soul" of the dead person, either in the form of an idol or an effigy. The relations of the dead person who come on such occasions from distant places carried with them food-grains from which meals were prepared for all the members of congregation. In some areas, the mourners did not stay over night with the family of the dead person. In the event of accidental death of a married woman, if her parents were not informed in time, they asked her husband's family to pay a fine to them. It amounted to giving a compensation to the parents of the girl for her death at her husband's place. This however, does not make out a rule that the husband's family was accused of having killed her. On such occasions also, a poor tribal family had to incur debt for payment of such customary fines in the manner in which they spent money for getting their son married.

In some areas, it was possible for the family of a dead person to avoid performing death ceremonies on 12th day after the death. There was freedom to celebrate such a ceremony after 4th, 8th or even after 12th month, depending on the convenience of the family to be able to spare about Rs. 1000 required for death ceremony. In certain cases of poor households, blood relatives of the dead person contributed at the rate of Re. 1 to Rs. 2 in order to help bereaved persons to fulfil customary obligation toward the deceased. Reform movements were spread among tribals to help them in giving up such expensive customs altogether. The practical compromise suggested the completion of such ceremonies within the expenditure of Rs. 500 only.

The dead person in general is creamated provided the family can afford to have the fire-wood required for the purpose. In case, this kind of expenditure was not within the reach of the bereaved family, the dead was buried, and it was customary to plant sapling of a tree on that spot. There was also the custom of organising religious songs specially on the 13th day of the death of a person. Among some groups of tribals, there was the custom of presenting pieces of clothes by the relatives to the deceased and later on it was gifted away to the sisters or her children. There was also a custom of putting drops of liquor, tobacco etc. in the mouth of the dead person. In some cases before putting the pyre on fire, it was recited, "If you take re-birth, you should be borne a Bhil, but not a Baniya, otherwise in next birth you will have to die holding the scales in your hand." This indicated hostile attitude of tribals toward the life style of a Bania. The deceased was also advised that "you should meet all the previous blood relatives and live with them peacefully and give all your support and cooperation to them". There are many more finer customs around death among some groups such as burning a sacred lamp and dancing of unmarried young girls to appease the spirit of the dead.

In some areas of Surat district, the death ceremony was performed on the 3rd day, right on the cremation ground. The family members of the dead person carried cooked food to the cremation ground and left it there alongwith a pot of water. On the 8th day, they performed a special ceremony for establishing a foundation and image of dead person in the form of idol or effigy called *Khatrun* (singular). On this event, a stone was brought and a figure of a person was drawn with the colour of red powder called *Sindur*. This piece of stone representing the dead person was offered food and later on taken to the side of the river and placed on one spot. On the top of this figure, they put an elaborately decorated dome of backed clay which looks like a small shrine.

There were many variations of worship. Some did not feed the blood relatives on such occasions because they could not afford the expenditure. In some groups of tribals, there was a custom of preparing effigy of grass on the 3rd day of the death of a person. On this event, the relatives would go to the cremation ground and leave there 8 to 9 cups of leaf filled with cooked food as an offering to the dead person. This again was followed by the ceremony of establishing foundation of the dead in the form of an idol called *Khatrun*.

As indicated earlier, there had been stages of evolution and development of tribal life and culture. Various Hindu customs have made inroads and got incorporated in the life of some of the advanced tribal groups. For instance, the tribals called Dhodias who are relatively more educated than many other tribals have taken up Hindu customs not only in the field of marriage, but also with respect to death ceremonies. The process of *sancritisation* affects tribal life and customs right from birth through marriage and death. However, it all depends upon as to what were the stages of development of a specific group of tribals, or sometimes of a few families in touch with Hindus. Many latent and manifest events occur in the process of social reform movements that tend to absorb changes from generations to generations.

(c) *Dress and Ornaments*

The dress and ornaments among the tribals have undergone considerable change due to their coming in contact with the outside world and improvement in socio-economic conditions.

Formerly, the well to do males in tribal communities in the Banaskantha and Sabarkantha areas used to wear short *dhoti* and *angarkha* and *bandi* (sleeveless jacket) made of hand woven cloth. They would also put on a piece of cloth called *faria* on the head. The *angarkha* worn by some advanced tribal groups was generally of black colour with machine embroidery work. In place of short *dhoti,* a small cloth was worn round the waistline of the body. The *faria* consists of a very short piece of cloth almost of the size of a small towel.

In the interior of Panchmahals, Vadodara, Bharuch, Surat, Dangs and Valsad districts, most tribals used to wear *langoti* or loin-cloth of the cheapest cotton cloth. The females wore petti-coat called *ghaghra* which was a piece of cloth wound on the back side of the body and tucked there. For upper garments women wore *kabja* and *odhani.* The *odhani* was just a small piece of cloth hanging from the head. In Surat district, it was found that the tribal women wore two dresses only, viz., a *kabja/choli* and simple *sari* called *salla* worn in the style of loin-cloth called *Kachhota*.

During the previous decades, the dress of the tribals had undergone many changes. The advanced tribal males would use full *dhoti, paheran* or shirt or *bandi* on the lower and upper part of body, and on the head they would wind a towel or put on a cap. In Surat, Dangs and Valsad districts some of the tribals such as Warlis wear half-pants instead of *dhoti.* The new dress is generally from textile mill-made cloth. The tribal youths and boys are found wearing pant or half-pant and shirt. The females have gradually adopted as lower garment, full hanging *ghaghra,* keeping it loose and flowing, instead of making a *kachhota.* They also wear *blouses* and *sari* either made from coarse textile cloth or of medium and fine variety. In the interior areas of tribal districts the elderly males and females did not change their style of dress to a great extent.

In some interior parts of Chhotaudepur taluka in Vadodara district, tribals were seen still wearing *langoti* and long shirt to cover the body, and a *faria* or a towel or a small piece of cloth on the head.

So far as ornaments are concerned, tribal females previously wore necklace called *hansli* of brass or silver bead-work, etc. around their neck. The bead work consists of both multicolour beads called *manka* of glass and lac. On their legs, they wore brass anklets called *kallas.* On arms they wore silver or *rupa* (an alloy of silver) bangles. In the Panchmahals, they wore ornaments prepared from mixed metal of tin, lead and *rupa.* In the Sabarkantha area, they used bangles of lac, wood, rubber and glass along with many other variety of ornaments prepared from aluminium or silver. In Dangs, the females used to wear a necklace made of small and big currency coins. Sometimes the old coins of Queen Victoria along with bead work, aluminium bangles, etc. are worn by women. In Surat district, the females wore ornaments prepared from brass, *rupa,* nickel and lac beads called *manka.*

Recently, the tribal women began to wear glass, rubber or plastic bangles along with necklaces prepared either from silver or lac beads (*manka*) or those made from rolled-gold. In the Bharuch district, it was learnt that women wore *hansli* (around the neck) and girdle ornament around the waist made from steel. Those who can afford, wore light-weight necklace called *doro* made from gold or silver. The gold-earrings were also worn by women where their economic conditions permitted.

(d) *Housing and Building Material*

Formerly, the tribals used locally available building materials for housing purposes. These consisted of bamboo and/or wood, leaves of palm and *khajuri* trees, grass, etc. found in the areas in which they lived. They also used to make use of straw, hey or grass of paddy, *jowar* or *tuver* stalks, etc. which were available after the crops are harvested. They erected the walls and roofs of their huts or houses with the help of wooden logs and bamboos. The roof of the house was thatched with palm leaves, grass of paddy, *khajuri* leaves etc. Where bamboos were not available, the walls were made of stalks of the plants of cotton, *tuver* etc. The walls were then smeared with plaster of mud and cowdung mixed together. In recent times the use of backed earthen tiles was found to be used increasingly for roofing.

The old style of housing has undergone a marked change at some places. New houses are now built with better material and are generally covered with country made of manglore tiles. Backed bricks are now freely used along with stone where convenient. Cement concrete pucca houses are built wherever financial position permits. Many of those who cannot afford, continue to build houses on the old pattern, with mud walls and thatched roofs.

(e) *Utensils, Furniture, etc.*

Formerly the tribals would use various earthen vessels for cooking food. Some who could afford, used brass and aluminium utensils also. In view of changes in their economic condition and environmental and living style, quite a few were able to purchase brass and copper utensils. The well-to-do tribals have begun to use even utensils of stainless steel, though in a limited way.

The use of furniture was rather poor in tribal households. The service class tribals and those who were holding offices as Surpanch, Police Patel, those working in Co-operative Societies, etc., own one or more chairs or raised wooden plank called *bankada* and *pat.* Generally one would sit on a cot also used for sleeping, outside the hut at any time of the day or night.

On account of service in private firm, business or government departments and other new occupations in towns, tribals faced problems of commuting. The facilities of public buses, cycles, etc. were used by tribals for communication purpose. It was noticed that the tribals engaged in services and other occupations with better income were able to purchase radios, transistors, etc. for entertainment, news and instructions on improving agriculture, animal husbandry, and so on.

(f) *Food Habits*

The tribals raised coarse millets and cereals such as *maize, jowar, bajari, nagli, bavto, kuri, banti, morio* and pulses like tuver, val, gram, math, etc. Paddy was sometimes grown in kyari lands. They were used to eat porridge of maize, jowar, bajari, etc. Similarly they used to eat loaves prepared from a variety of coarse grains. The pulses like *mug, tur, urad, chana* were also used to prepare curry and meals. The vegetables called *valor* etc. easily grown in courtyards and fields were used with meals. In times of scarcity, tribals were accustomed to eat roots of trees called *kalia kand.* These were dug and taken from the forest and used as food after boiling. Since these roots are poisonous, they were kept in running water overnight in order to make them edible.

With the change of times, many improvements had taken place in their food habits. The costly food-grains such as wheat, rice, etc. and fresh vegetables were incorporated in their diet. They had begun to make frequent use of costly pulses, rice, breads, modern snacks, biscuits, etc. Vegetable cultivation which was hardly practiced earlier, had become favourite practice where irrigation facilities were available. The vegetables like onions, brinjals, chillies etc. were freely grown both for selling and domestic use. In the rice-growing areas of Surat and Valsad districts, rice had remained the staple food of tribals. They had begun using spices and oil in the preparation of vegetables, curry, etc. and thereby improved the test and value of their diet.

Ethics, Superstition and Morality

The information on the above topics collected during the field interviews is not complete in many ways. However, it tries to throw significant light on certain ethical and religious practices which continued to persist and dominate tribal culture in spite of changes felt in other walks of tribal life. Religious institutions as such have not been well developed among the tribals because of their primitive beliefs in spirits and ghosts even though some of them had come under the influence of Hindus, Muslims, Parsis, Christians or people of other religions.

Reference may be made here to illustrate the influence of a popular Hindu sect called *Moksh Marg* on which a note is presented in *Appendix*-V. The influence of this sect was reported to be prominant in the districts of South Gujarat. Secondly there was a sect called Sati Pati Panth which was secular in nature having overtones of indigenous ethical tribal values. Thirdly there was a great influence of Ambaji Mata among the tribals and non-tribals of the Sabarkantha and Banaskantha districts.

Fourthly, there was a sect based on truth as ultimate reality. Truth is the only path to salvation, i.e., *Sat Keval Panth* was a unique sect popular among the tribals of South Gujarat. The village called Sarsa in Kaira District of Anand Taluka is said to be the centre of this sect. There are about 100 tribal families in Chhotaudepur area under its influence. The devotees take vows to lead virtuous life and not to drink liquar, eat meat and commit theft. The Tribal followers of *Sat Keval Panth* had greatly benefited by refraiming from indulging in vices which were burdensome to them on account of their poor economic conditions.

These and other religious influences have, however, not been institutionalised among the tribals of Gujarat. This is a subject which requires special attention and unless intensive studies are made, nothing concrete can be said on the religious undercurrents among the tribals of Gujarat.

Hereafter we shall deal with the subject of tribal ethics and morality in a very general way and try to understand the socio-economic and cultural aspects of values, attitude and behaviour, demonstrated in the day-to-day lives of the tribals. Since religion and ethics are intertwined and interrelated with superstition and morality they are all treated in combination with one another to highlight cultural dimensions of tribal life. Some features of this highly complex subject are presented districtwise in the following points.

(a) It was reported from the district of Banaskantha that in the case of serious dispute, theft or murder, the proof of allegation and settlement of the dispute were resolved at the temple of Ambaji. The person suspected of the crime of any kind was made to take bath and was asked to stand in front of Amba Mata temple with a pot full of water along with a coconut. The guilty person thus presented to the goddess had to say, "I have not committed the crime and if I am speaking a lie, the goddess will punish me". After this event, if anybody including men or cattle in his household was not caught up, in a couple of days, by serious disease, he was believed to be an innocent person.

That was how the tribals of this area tried to solve their problems of crime and to establish higher ethical standards in their attitude and behaviour in life. During festive occasions, people assembled at the temple of Ambaji for worship and enjoyed themselves performing dances before the goddess. The material offerings given to the goddess consisted of coconut, goat or hen. In recent times, this practice of live sacrifice at the temple is said to be declining.

At the time of reaping new crops such as wheat, maize, *bajari*, etc. they would first make offerings before use to the goddess Ambaji. Moreover, at the time of initiation of a new borne baby, worship by a new couple or for blessing to a barren couple, tribals would pay visits to the goddess so that she may protect them against evil forces. One of the non-officials indicated that although tribals were illiterate, they are very faithful to the people who come to their help in times of need. A person called Motilal Tejawat had fought for their cause some 40 to 45 years ago. He was not only respected but more or less worshipped like God after his death. They went as far as offering money and coconut at his shrine to acknowledge his obligations.

The tribals are generally superstitious. Sometimes father and son would suspect each other of black-magic and would not stay together. In the case of contacting disease, they would generally believe in the influence of evil spirits. It was common for a tribal first to go to a Bhuva (medium man) for treatment. Mostly this led to aggravation of a disease. And later they would go to the hospital. One of the non-officials reported that tribals normally are addicted to drinking, but recently this habit had become rampant. The liquor was said to be distilled in almost all tribal homes for business. It was easy to find liquor on the high-way leading to Ambaji temple. There were certain old practices such as killing the buffaloes or oxen in order to celebrate the occasion called *Lokai* during which they would offer ieast of meat to the people of their group or sub-group. At this time, they also distributed clothes among close blood relatives to appease spirits of ancestors.

The incidences of dispute over women were common in this district and that is why there were many chapter cases recorded by the police. These chapter cases result in exploitation on account of corrupt practices of intermediaries and sometimes the police. The number of chapter cases recorded in 1976-77 were 378-Banaskantha, 614-Sabarkantha, 1638- Panchmahals, 865-Vadodara, 1492-Bharuch, 2116-Surat, 949-Valsad and 53-Dangs. Table 11.1 gives exact figures of crimes recorded among the tribals on account of various reasons. The total number of cases in every district however did not explain whether these incidences were higher in one district than the other, unless total size of population was compared. The information in the tables was received from official sources and is therefore reliable. Wherever the figures are blank, the information was not supplied by the officers concerned. No information was received from Surat and Dangs districts.

TABLE 11.1: The Crimes by Tribals Recorded During Three Calendar Years 1975 to 1977

Name of the District **	Calendar Years	Number of crimes committed by tribals on account of disputes relating to								Total
		Land including field boundaries and encroachments	Elopement, Martial disharmoney or infidelity	Right to take water, fishing, etc	Property other than land	Family quarrels	Jealousy, revenge or suspicion	Excitement, fatigue and drunkenness	Accusation of witchcraft and sorcery	
Banaskantha	1975	2	9	—	2	—	9	4	—	26
	1976	1	6	—	—	—	4	1	—	12
	1977	—	16	—	4	—	7	5	—	32
Sabarkantha	1975	33	12	1	47	4	12	13	1	123
	1976	27	12	2	30	1	22	16	—	110
	1977	25	11	—	42	7	16	11	—	112
Panchmahals	1975	49	38	2	8	38	26	62	12	235
	1976	74	52	3	10	94	38	40	12	323
	1977	70	49	4	6	91	22	69	26	337
Vadodara	1975	13	4	—	11	7	25	24	2	86
	1976	30	10	—	11	24	38	5	2	120
	1977	35	2	—	22	5	31	39	3	137
Bharuch	1975	2	6	1	12	10	5	2	—	38
	1976	10	1	6	7	11	3	3	—	41
	1977	2	12	—	10	6	5	1	1	37
Surat	1975-77	NA	NA	NA	NA	NA	NA	NA	NA	NA
Valsad	1975	5	7	2	3	2	2	10	—	31
	1976	4	4	3	2	3	1	19	1	37
	1977	3	6	—	2	4	3	13	—	31
Dangs	1975-77	NA	NA	NA	NA	NA	NA	NA	NA	NA
Grand Total		385	257	24	229	307	269	337	60	1868
Average Per Year		128	86	8	76	103	90	112	20	623

** The information was not supplied for Surat and Dangs Districts by the authorities concerned.

One of the non-officials mentioned that the intermediaries among the tribals who were sometimes the members of Village Panchayats were constantly in contact with police department and were able to bring amicable settlement between fighting groups of people. However, as intermediaries, they sometimes played a dangerous role in exploiting both the parties in dispute. Their power and influence in the community was sometimes so great that they behaved like feudal lords and dictated terms for settlement. They coax both the parties to exchange molassis in order to sweeten their mouths and forget the cause of dispute and give up revengeful attitude. In olden times however, most tribals including their leaders were truthful and maintained high standard of morality of solving serious disputes among themselves. Not only this, if a stranger visited a tribal household, they would receive him very courteously and offer food and resting facilities. Sometimes, a tribal host would go as far as remaining hungry in order to offer a square meal to a guest.

(b) The information from the district of Sabarkantha was unique. Here we had valuable information from volunteers. The non-official concerned reported that liquor was being drunk by the tribals in almost all the villages. It was just not possible to get rid of this habit because the police department itself was benefited on account of violation of prohibition. The tribals distill liquor and sell, and when they were caught by the police, they paid to police Rs. 50 to 100 and got themselves released. It was reported that most of the police constables were used to drink liquor themselves.

One of the serious weaknesses from which the tribals of this area suffered was a strong sense of avenging the wrongs done by the enemy and adversary. Even a small dispute may lead to serious clashes between two parties or sub-castes of the main tribal group. The Parmar and the Gamar sub-groups of the same tribe of Bhils were reported to be indulging in blood feudes. If a person was beaten or killed by one group, the other group would raid the whole village and plunder whatever things were available including cattle, foodgrains etc. Some of the disputes became so intense and notorious that the whole family of an accused person had to leave the village for good. If a group approached policemen during such incidence, they had to pay them bribe and get exploited. In the case of mutual settlements, Rs. 7 to 10,000 were paid to the family of an aggrieved party, depending on the seriousness of the dispute. However, lion's share from such amounts was taken by the intermediaries named 'Bhanjgadia'. Such incidences inflicted heavy drain on the resources of the families who were sometimes ruined.

(c) It was reported from the district of Panchmahals that prohibition had not created any impact on the habits of the tribals. Even though the police department was aware of free use of liquor among the tribals, they did not stop it on account of corrupt practices employed to exploit the victims. It was believed that to stop drinking habits among the tribals was extremely difficult. However, if the government was able to take strong and effective measures some degree of success in the programme of prohibition was likely to be achieved.

(d) In the village of Rangpur in the district of Vadodara, a voluntary organisation running Anand Niketan Ashram tried to help tribals in many ways. It is more a secular institution than religious, but it imparts certain values of good behaviour among the tribals in order to reduce cases of quarrel, crime, lechery, theft, etc. among them. The main goal of the voluntary institution is to give education. However, medical help and other technical education such as training for mechanics, motor drivers, etc. was also undertaken by the Ashram.

In the field of agriculture, irrigation etc. Anand Niketan helped the tribals a lot. The influence of this institution was reported to be in the radius of 10 miles around Rangpur. Apart from other benefits derived from the services of the Ashram, the tribals had given up drinking, meat-eating, etc. Instead of wearing only loin-clothes and remaining half naked, they had adopted clean habits, hygiene, decent clothes, and so on.

(e) In the district of Bharuch, the tribals were reported to be quite inclined towards religious beliefs and practice. At the time of harvest, they would offer foodgrains to the Gods before using the same for domestic purpose. There were some tribals who believed in a sect called Sat Keval Panth, the main temple of which is located in a place called Sarsa. Another sect called Sati Pati Panth has also influences in a few villages in the area. This is more a religious sect with political over-tones claiming traditional sovereignty of the tribals over the land and forests. The believers of this sect claim that they were the rulers of the area and so it was not obligatory for them to accept the authority of the government functionaries. The currency note of the government of any denomination was looked upon by them not as a currency note, but only a promise by the government to pay equivalent value for exchange of goods and services. In brief, the tribals of this area were not only superstitious but also suspicious of other people working and living in the area. Under this kind of normlessness and disrespect for government authority, the selling of illicit liquor, warli matka gambling, etc. was practiced freely and without restraint by the tribals.

(f) In the district of Surat, one finds a large number of tribals of different types following a variety of sects and religions. However, the Sati Pati Panth was in great vogue in at least 10 villages around Valod and Dahegam. In other villages of the district, the influence of the sect was negligible. As indicated earlier, the followers of the sect look down upon the authority of government functionaries. They believed that all the land belonged to them as were held by their ancestors and there was on need of paying revenue or any other taxes and dues to the government. They actually did not bother to pay government dues and instigated people of neighbouring villages to do the same. Even when they received Tagavi loans from the government in times of scarcity or draught, they hardly bothered to pay the fixed instalments in course of time. When the notice was served by the Officers of the Revenue Department, they refused to accept it and returned it with some illegible writings by way of challenging the authority of the government. The Centre of activities of this sect was located in the Katswan village of Vyara taluka. The leader of this movement was one Keshri Singh Tetia Singh. The network of his leadership was also to be found at Taluka levels in the area.

(g) In the district of Valsad, there was a considerable influence of *Moksh Marg* to which reference has been made earlier. The followers of this sect were largely Konkna and Dhodia tribes. They did not take their food without taking bath and did not touch liquor and abstained from non-vegetarian food. The non-officials favourably reflected on this religion and felt that prohibition can be easily implemented through such religious sects rather than expensive government machinery and programme of prohibition.

Some of the tribals such as Kolcha and Warli were reported to be distilling liquor of Mahuda and Molasses to a considerable extent. They were reported to be indulging in these practices not only to earn their living but also because some of the tribals were highly addicted to drinking. They can do without a square meal rather than liquor. This however had a bad impact on their ability to look after agriculture, because due to drinking habit they were not able to become punctual in conducting various agricultural operations that can improve crop yield.

Belief in witch-craft, sorcery and superstition was also common in some parts of the district. Pestilence in the crops and animals were attributed to supernatural causes. That was why they first went to the medium men Bhuva and Bhagat in order to find out the remedy ot such mishaps, rather than make use of insecticides, medicines and preventive measures. Sometime, they went to the extent of believing that this kind of scourge was on account of witch-craft. In case a son dies at a particular place or residence, they would give up living in that place for good in order to keep away from the influence of evil spirits. In some border areas of the district, about 75 per cent of the people were reported to be addicted to drinking. If one visited somebody's house in the evening, he was likely to be in the danger of a serious quarrel with a drunken person.

In some parts, the corruption had become so rampant that no one was able to control or do away with it. The social workers in particular were said to be not only liers but also bad characters. They would have even kept a women from the tribals. Such a pathetic situation was found in the area where 30 years ago Godawari Parulekar launched the movement of spreading social reforms and education among the tribals. Since, Parulekar was known as leftist political worker, a counter movement was started by another social worker, Mohanlal Mehta to wean away tribals from the leftist movement. Mehta had to help the tribals in trying to get rid of slavery imposed upon them by the Parsi landlords who were said to have enslaved most of the tribals by offering free liquor and toddy for drinking.

(h) In the district of Dangs, a considerable influence of Christian missionaries was reported. According to a non-official, there were about 7000 tribals who were the followers of Christianity in the district. However, so far as other cultural aspects of the tribals of this area were concerned, it was alleged that the district of Dangs was infested by bad elements. The people of tribal origin were the worst victims of thieves from outside. The social workers of this area were accused to be as dangerous mafia robbers as those of Chicago in United States of America. In order to illustrate this habit of thieving by outsiders through clandestine use of local tribals, it was reported that every year, goods worth Rs. 6 lakhs were stolen from the Dangs Saw-mill.

Health Problems of Tribals

The modern concept of health is not known to the tribals in general.

However, quite a few tribal leaders and educated youths have come intimately in contact with urban life and have begun to realise the need of public health and other programmes of curative and preventive medicine for the improvement of health of their communities. But that may not be considered a real change in the perspective and attitude of tribals towards health problems. A very large number of tribals are illiterate and live in far flung and remote areas in the State. The problem of health also includes that of hygiene, hospitalisation, etc. and we have here a variety of information that throws light on the health situation in most of the tribal areas of Gujarat about ten years ago.

(a) In the district of Banaskantha, there were many tribal areas where Primary Health Centres and maternity and child welfare centres were started by the state department of health. In some of the inaccessible areas, it was reported that the stock of medicine, medical staff, etc. were not available most of the time. A few staff members who were posted in the P.H. centres did not prefer to live in nearby towns and neglected their official duties. Some of the medical officers of heath were reported to be taking more interest in private practices which was prohibited under the government rules. In fact, they were given non-practicing allowances. When a serious patient was to be hospitalised, the tribal custom required that some of the kith and kins also accompanied the patient in the hospital. This kind of custom sometimes created a lot of problem for the hospital staff. However, it was necessary that the medical officers concerned treat them with a sense of difference, keeping in mind their cultural values, and give them human treatment. If the patient and the relatives were not treated with due regard by the hospital staff, it is likely that even after admitting the patient, they might run away on the second or the third day along with the patient. If things like this happened once, it spread bad-rumours which went against the interest of running Primary Health Centres. The other tribal patients and visitors would stop paying visits to such centres. This means that the health centre staff should give psychological treatment not only to the patients, but also to the kith and kins who accompany the patients. Regarding administering of the medicine, it was reported that most of the tribals preferred injections as compared to taking oral tablets or liquid medicine. When a visiting patient was given tablets and liquid medicine to carry home there had been cases where without caring for the cost of the medicine, it was thrown away by tribal patients.

It seems that the acceptance of the real knowledge of preventive medicine will take many years for adoption. It may take at least a generation to be adequately accepted and retained among the tribals. In this district, the incidence of T.B. was reported to be quite common. The next was deadly sexual diseases of Syphilis and Gonoria. The skin diseases such as scabies, boils etc. were common not only in this area, but elsewhere also. There is a leprosy treatment community centre in Danta taluka at Ambaji.

According to general observations of the officials, as well as non-officials, the standard of sexual character among the tribals in this area had gone down considerably. This may be because of their poverty. It can lead to spread of contagious venerial diseases which have proved to be deadly not only to them, but also to others on account of illicit sexual relationships. Quite a few tribals were reported to be suffering from urinary track infection. It may be noted that extra-marital sexual freedom enjoyed by a daughter or a sister of tribal household was not taken too seriously. But if the wife or a husband had illicit relationship, it led to immediate separation and divorce. Whatever may be other problems connected with lechery, it was reported that pilgrims to Ambaji temple were responsible for spreading venerial diseases in Gujarat. An element of exaggeration in the statement can not be ruled out.

The age old traditional practices of treating a patient by taking him to the medicine-men called Bhagat for diagnosis and treatment continued to persist in some parts of tribal area. This means that in the first instance, rather than going to a hospital, they would go to the medicine-men for treatment of witchcraft under the belief that the person is suffering on account of black magic, evil spirit, wrath of ancestors, etc. They also try herbal medicines of indigenous nature. When a person becomes extremely serious in spite of sorcery and witchcraft treatment, they would go to get him treated in a hospital as a matter of last resort.

Many tribals are so poor that they have no money even to travel by bus and carry the patient to the hospital. When a person is hospitalised, doctors sometimes find that he is suffering from multiple diseases such as typhoid, malaria, tuberculosis, etc. Even when they approach a doctor, they continue to believe in superstition, and out of ignorance, give up modern treatment before complete recovery. Even if his relations may be prepared to take necessary medical facilities to help the patient, he will not give necessary cooperation in taking medicine, and so on.

The tribals did not have full faith in family planning programmes.

Most of the parents had 7 to 8 children. This was probably because they believed that birth of a baby is the gift of God and a person is born with his or her own luck. The government or parents can not do anything special about the life of a baby. Death is also a gift of God. They believe that absence of food is not the main cause of death. Here is a reference to a belief that if at all people die, natural calamities such as scarcity, accident, divine wrath, etc. are responsible. No man is responsible for causing end to life, because it just happens. "More number of children does not necessarily mean that scarcities, diseases and draughts will follow, and lead to death." This is a part of tribal belief system and world view. The family planning functionaries were laughed at and sarcastically dubbed as those who come to turn people impotent. If a woman has to be operated for termination of pregnancy, it is necessary that her kinsmen are also consulted by the in-laws. The families of both the husband and the wife have rights and obligations towards the life of the woman and the baby to be born. It is a fact that generally the maternal in-laws of a woman will not permit her to be tubectomised. This is one of the reasons why family planning programme was not to be quite successful among the tribals. Other reasons of their dislike for operations for family planning were that some of them had suffered physically because they were not able to take anti-infection precautions and care after the operation. Specially in the case of women, they believed that after operation, a woman was not able to lift heavy weight or do laborious jobs. In some cases kinsmen of a woman were reported to have gone and attacked the affinal in-laws and even killed some persons for having compelled the married daughter to go in for family planning operations. In some cases, even the family planning motivators and workers were beaten up by the tribals in villages.

According to a non-official, some of the tribals preferred to take medicine from Ayurvedic medical practitioners. Sometime, they themselves were expert in herbal medicine which can be effective on special kinds of diseases. Indigenous herbal doctors were not reported to divulge their secrets to others. The tendency to go back and forth from allopathic to home treatment, medicine man was quite common. For instance, the Sarpanch of Jodhsar village suffered from Cancer and the doctor had advised him to undergo an operation. He went to Ahmedabad for this purpose, but was not convinced about the operation advised in the hospital and returned to his place. He then went to a person of his own community who was administering home-medicine to patients. After examining him, the so called doctor, stamped a hot piece of iron on his neck which relieved him of the problem of cancer. Whatever may be reason behind the efficacy of such a treatment, it continuous to appeal to many a tribals. The modern medical treatment will need more time and education for acceptance.

(b) In the district of Sabarkantha, the problems of health of the tribals were more or less of similar nature as those reported from Banaskantha. One of the reasons of spread of disease among the tribals according to a non-official, was excessive indulgence in sex play by the tribals in absence of any other means of entertainment. He, therefore, felt that there should be some diversion offered to the tribals to engage themselves in other activities of entertainment so that they can maintain good health. However, the general problem as reported earlier was the real and serious problem of malnutrition. Malnutrition leads to anaemia, scabies and even serious diseases of deadly nature such as T.B., cancer, etc. The general impression though was encouraging that the tribals from this area had become medicine minded although some of them went to their own out-moded practice of consulting traditional medicine man.

Regarding the impression of medical facilities through Primary Health Centres, and sub-centres, there were complaints of lack of medicine and good treatment. There were several suggestions regarding improvement of services through primary health centres. It was reported that the Primary Health Centre at Vijaynagar was upgraded to 30 bedded hospital. Similarly, there was a 25 bedded hospital at Isri. The situation in sub-centres was not satisfactory everywhere and therefore it was suggested that they should be upgraded to class-II dispensaries so that better medicine and health facilities can be made available to the tribals. Moreover, there was a demand for operation theatre for minor ailments at places called Kheradi and Poshina. There was a need for availability of staff quarters at the sub-centres, some of which did not have their own buildings.

The training of medical and paramedical personnel was in progress, and the mid-wives locally called *Dai* were given one month training along with Rs. 300 stipend for this purpose. This amount of stipend was the same routine facility for those working in non-tribal areas. It was most necessary that some more incentives be given to *Dais* and nurses working in tribal areas.

It was suggested that an integrated multi-purpose health

programme should be developed so that both male and female medical and para-medical personnel can be trained to propagate the need of family planning among tribals. There was also the need of community health workers chosen from amongst the tribals themselves. They should be given training in public health practices so that they become more effective due to trust and acceptability among the local people. There were reported to be four special nutrition programme centres for six-year old children. The expectant and nursing mothers were also helped through this programme operated through Taluka Panchayat. The scheme of maternal and child health received better acceptance than the Applied Nutrition Programme introduced in some talukas of this district.

(c) The health problems among the tribals in the district of Panchmahals were quite different than those reported from earlier two districts. No doubt, here also people suffered from a variety of diseases specially on account of poverty leading to mal-nutrition and unhygienic living conditions. The special categories of diseases reported here were water-borne diseases such as thread worm, hook worm, dysentery, etc. The diseases such as elephantises pot-belley, venerial diseases were also reported from this district. The V.D. in particular was reported to be quite prevalent. However, hardly a few cases of this were reported to the primary health centres. There were also cases of T.B. and cancer among the tribals. But it was encouraging that the patients were said to visit primary health centres for medical advice and help.

It was reported that more primary health centres were required to be established in this district so that people can save themselves from becoming victims of various diseases. Wherever primary health centres existed, it was reported that sometimes medicines were not in stock. In spite of this, it was necessary that people were made aware of health needs and preventive medicines. This is because quite a number of tribals from this district were still taking recourse to the traditional medicineman called *Bhuva* or *Bhagat*. If more educational programmes through demonstration and audiovisual media were developed, there was the possibility of creating awakening among the tribals about health care. Cinema and T.V. as special medium should be extensively used for medical education as people were impressed by pictures, and would easily respond to this kind of mass media programmes.

(d) In the district of Vadodara only 25 per cent of the tribals paid visits to primary health centres for treatment of diseases. In the case of chicken-pox and such other contagious diseases, they hardly went for medical treatment, because they believed that like small-pox, this kind of diseases come on account of anger and wrath of divine powers governing the fate of people. Hardly any tribal would come forward for innoculation of the children against these diseases. There was a doubt among some tribals that the programme of innoculation was meant for killing children. Such misconceptions were based on their utter ignorance of modern medicine.

Among the variety of diseases reported in this district, T.B., Asthama, V.D., dysentery, hook worm, anaemia, etc. were common. Some of the diseases were no doubt on account of mal-nutrition. Anaemia in particular was found to be more prevalent among tribal women. As suggested earlier, 75 per cent of the tribals went to medicine-man and worshipped them and gave them costly offerings to get rid of diseases.

So far as family planning programmes were concerned, operations were somehow accepted as a means of family planning. The tribals in general did not go for family planning operations except when they were in need of money offered to them as incentive. A couple on an average had 5 to 8 children. At the time of delivery, only 20 per cent of the cases were brought to the Primary Health Centres because of complications or failure of the traditional mid-wives to get the babies delivered successfully. The spread of V.D. is reported to be quite high on account of promisquity among the people. No one objected adultry on behalf of ones daughter or sister, but in case his wife was caught or suspected, she was likely to be killed.

In general, most of the tribals liked to get injections for getting quickly cured rather than take tablets or liquid medicines. They hardly take full medical treatment according to the advice of the Doctor. Whatever course of action they might have decided at home before visiting the doctor, they would stick to it. Doctor's advice may not be of much avail. Even in the case of deep wounds, they refused to take stitches and tetanus injections. They would just be happy with massaging ointment and bandages for injuries of physical assault or fall. As in certain backward areas, the tribals here were not against medical treatment in general. Therefore, there was demand for doctors for the primary health centres which remained under-staffed on account of unlawful private practices. It was suggested that not only doctors, but also nurses be trained as special category of tribal medical practitioners so that they can win the confidence of the people.

(e) There was a marked distinction in the attitude and behaviour of the tribals towards medical treatment in the district of Bharuch. Formerly, they used to get deliveries of children done with the help of untrained mid-wives. That had later changed radically and there were trained mid-wives among tribals who had taken up the services successfully.

Earlier they were used to take herbal medicine and refrained from going to hospitals. This had changed a great deal and even for family planning programmes, tribal women were reported to be taking active role in adopting practices and spreading new message among the people. Only a few tribals were reported to depend upon traditional medicine-man to get rid of diseases. There was also a considerable progress in keeping clean environment among the tribals. Earlier they used to drink water from any open source, but later they resorted to well-water. Not only this, they would now use water for ablution which they hardly used to practice before. In Dediapada taluka of this district, there was one Primary Health Centre and three sub-centres. However, there was a demand for sub-centres also at Malsamot and Piplod villages.

(f) In the district of Surat, there were 19 Primary Health Centres of which 17 were under the control of village Panchayats and two run by the State Government. Each Primary Health Centre had three sub-centres called 'Rural Family Planning Centres', each having other three smaller sub-centres. Inspite of these facilities, the tribals were suffering from a number of common diseases which were reported earlier in the case of other districts. One of the persons reported that V.D. was not so prevalent here. However, T.B., malaria and skin diseases were common. Many tribals suffered from Vitamin 'A' and sodium deficiencies which led to eye trouble and gout. Eating of fish by some tribals had also resulted in certain kinds of diseases, added to other water borne diseases. The family planning programmes were well received except perhaps by the Dubla tribals and the Scheduled Castes in certain areas. Tribals here gave less importance to the birth of a son than of a daughter. This was one of the reasons why there was less antegonism among tribals towards family planning programmes. There was also a belief in the efficacy of indigenous herbal medicine as well as the treatment through medicine-man. The beliefs in witchcraft had recently led to burning alive of a "witch" women suspected of causing harm to cattle, crops, and people.

(g) In the district of Valsad, many tribals were reported to be suffering from skin diseases, dysentery, gastroenteritis, round-worm, elephantices, etc. Tuberculosis was also reported to be quite common. The spread of V.D. was not so rampant elsewhere as it was in the Umbergaon taluka of this district. In general, all the tribals of this area had not become medicine minded and, still some of them who were backward, went to Bhuva and Bhagat. Some of the tribals were so poor that they did not have money to purchase medicines prescribed by doctors.

The Primary Health Centres do not get enough grant as a result of which stocks of medicines for distribution among the patients were not readily available. The government was keen to see that the doctors went to Primary Health Centres located in the tribal areas. However, nobody has studied fully the difficulties of qualified doctors working in remote tribal areas. Some of the difficulties of doctors reported were that they had no residential accommodation and other facilities of latest medical magazines or books helpful in keeping them up to date. There were also no facilities of laboratory to test blood, urine etc. as a result of which diagnosis remained inadequate. It was also reported that political workers sometimes created trouble for the doctors who needed protection from the government in case of victimisation and political interference.

(h) In the district of Dangs, the diseases reported to be common were malaria, dysentery, diarrhea, cholera and respiratory diseases. Leprosy was also reported to be prevalent in some parts of the district. Family planning operations were being accepted by the poorer tribals of this area under the temptation of getting money by way of compensation. It was reported that 50 per cent of the eligible couples in the district had undergone family planning operations.

NOTE

1. There is a tendency among the tribals to accept high caste Hindus as reference group and emulate their Brahminical rites, rituals and social customs, dress, etc. This process of socio-cultural change has been identified by Prof. M.N. Srinivas as Sancritisation, and it carries varying frames of references in Indian society.

12

SUMMARY FINDINGS, RECOMMENDATIONS AND SUGGESTIONS

Introduction

In this concluding chapter, we present summary, recommendations, suggestions and findings of the study. The section one tries to analyse loopholes in land system and the protective measures preventing alienation of tribal land effected from the historical past todate. Secondly, the next section presents recommendations and suggestions on land system and measures for land reforms as compared with those in most other states of Indian Union. The third section deals with suggestions and findings of some aspects of tribal development as related to tribal area sub-plan administration and Panchayati Raj programmes. One of the factors of emphasis on tribal development is stepping up education among children and youths of tribal communities in Gujarat. In last one decade, i.e. from 1980 onwards, massive efforts have been made by the State Government on all fronts including education for tribal development. The recommendations and suggestions made here may not be applicable to various tribal sub-plan areas taken separately, but collectively they are more or less relevant to tribal situation in Gujarat.

ANALYSIS OF LOOPHOLES IN LAND SYSTEMS AND REFORM MEASURES

Land reforms have been in Gujarat a continuous process. By the end of the nineteenth century, steps were taken for survey and settlement of land revenue in the areas directly governed by the British. Wherever scarcity and draught conditions prevailed, farmers in general and the tribals in particular found it extremely difficult to maintain themselves in absence of other sources of livelihood to supplement income. The scarcity-hit people, both non-tribals and tribals were not able to pay land revenue in such hard days, and even when the assessment was revised to a lower level by the government, they were unable to meet the situation as no efforts were made to develop their potential.

With a view to safeguard the land of such unfortunate persons in backward areas, the British Government passed an amendment bill in the Bombay Land Revenue Code in 1901, introducing a new Section 73 imposing a ban on transfer of lands without the permission of the Collector in such backward villages where survey and settlement was not introduced. Government had acquired powers to take action on violations by issuing a notification. And also possibly to exclude or exempt such class of persons as were considered necessary from the operation of the Section 73.

It should be noted that there already existed Section 68, under which an occupant of agricultural land was entitled to the use and occupation of his land for the period of which his tenure was limited. If the tenure was unlimited or a survey settlement was extended to the land, he was so entitled in perpetuity, though conditionally, on payment of amounts of land revenue for the same and on fulfilment of any other terms or conditions lawfully annexed to his tenure. The lands to which survey and settlement was extended were thus considered liable to land revenue and as no terms and conditions were annexed to the tenure, these lands enjoyed the status of old tenure and were alienable and partible.

There was a provision inserted in the year 1901 in Section 68, that when unoccupied and unalienated (Government waste) land happened to be granted to any person, non-tribal or tribal, the District Collector could impose the conditions restricting alienation and partition of land subject to Rules made by the Government. Lands granted by the Collector on these conditions were termed as new tenure lands.

In 1901, Section 73 was substituted for the first time and it provided that all occupancies subject to conditions lawfully annexed to the tenure shall be heritable and transferable. The 'New' or 'Restricted' tenure came into being by insertion of Proviso to Section 68 and enactment of a new Section 73A.

In the state of Gujarat, the legal provisions existing at present for prohibiting alienation of tribal lands and for restoring tribal lands unauthorisedly occupied are contained in Sections 73A and 79A respectively, inserted in the erstwhile Bombay State. These sections read as under;

Power to Restrict Right to Transfer

"73A (1). Notwithstanding anything in the foregoing Section, in any tract or village to which the State Government may, by notification published before the introduction therein of an original survey settlement under Section 103, declare the provisions of this section applicable, occupancies shall not after the date of such notification be transferable without the previous sanction of the Collector."

"73A (2). The State Government may, by notification in the official Gazette, from time to time exempt any part of such tract or village or any person or class of persons from the operation of this section."

Summary Eviction of Person Unauthorisedly Occupying Land

"79A. Any person unauthorisedly occupying, or wrongfully in possession of any land (a) to the use or occupation of which by reason of any of the provisions of this Act he is not entitled or has ceased to be entitled or (b) which is not transferable without previous sanction under Section 73A or by virtue of any condition lawfully annexed to the tenure under the provisions of Section 62, 67, or 68, may be summarily evicted by the Collector."

Section 73A as it stands at present, prohibits alienation of tribal lands in areas (1) where original survey and settlement has not been introduced and (2) where the State Government by notification makes the provisions of this section applicable. Thus the tribal lands in surveyed and settled areas were totally saved and there was no restriction on alienation of tribal lands in these areas.

Out of 32 tribal Talukas covered under Tribal Area Sub-Plan, lands in about 16 Talukas were treated as surveyed and settled and so tribal lands of about half the area of Tribal Area Sub-Plan were without any restriction on alienation, and the tribals freely alienated their lands under pressure of circumstances or due to underhand dealings of the interested parties. There was no legal provision what-so-ever to prohibit alienation of tribal land in these 16 Talukas.

So far as unsurveyed and unsettled areas were concerned, publication of Government notification was a condition precedent to application of Section 73A. These areas were those which were governed mostly by the ex-princely States which were merged and integrated with other territories of Indian Union in the year 1948. There was practically no restriction on alienation of tribal lands during the period of more than 12 years from 1948 to 1961, until Government of Gujarat issued notification applying Section 73A in ex-Princely State areas covering 16 Talukas.

During this vacuum period of 12 years, there was no such restriction and alienations of tribal lands freely took place, and there was no legal remedy to revert consideration of cases of such alienations for want of notification.

Thus it becomes most significant to note that until the year 1961, there was practically no restriction on alienation of tribals land in all the 32 Tribal Talukas covered under the Tribal Area Sub-Plan.

After 1961, the 16 Tribal Talukas (covered by Ex-princely States) were brought under purview of Section 73A by issue of Government notification. But the trend of alienation of the tribal lands which had already set in, continued unchecked, because the administrative machinery to detect alienation was strengthened only in 1977 by appointment of LND 5 Units (headed by Deputy Collectors) under the Tribal Area Sub-Plan.

Incidentally it may be mentioned that the Government notification of 1961 was applied to Vansda Taluka as it was taken for granted that the villages there were unsurveyed and unsettled. However, the Hon. Gujarat High Court in Special Civil Application No. 1191 of 1974 declared on 2-2-1978 that the survey and settlement in the villages of Vansda Taluka done during the period of ex-Vansda princely State must be deemed to have been effected under the Bombay Land Revenue Code and application of Section 73A would not, therefore, be feasible. Thus no action could be taken by LND 5 Unit for detecting alienation of tribal lands in Vansda Taluka of ex-Princely State even after 1961. Such a position may arise in respect of other ex-princely States where survey and settlement was carried out during the regime of the ex-princely States concerned.[1]

Next to land alienation there are five major land reform measures of tribal land system, viz., tenancy, ceiling on land, fragmentation and consolidation of land, forest land and indebtedness and money-lending. We shall now present summary recommendations, suggestions and findings of our study on all these six topics and then conclude this chapter by throwing some light on tribal development problems and Panchayati Raj in general.

RECOMMENDATIONS AND SUGGESTIONS ON LAND REFORM MEASURES

Alienation Abolition Act

The loopholes mentioned in the preceding sections both legal and otherwise resulted in continuing alienation of tribal lands unfettered. It was, therefore, felt that the Gujarat Government may consider to undertake a special and independent legislation covering the following special features for prohibiting alienation of tribal lands and for restoration of all categories of alienated lands. Steps taken by other States in the case of specific points are briefly listed at the end.

(1) Alienation of tribal lands should be strictly prohibited for all tribal lands wherever situated in the State i.e. whether the areas are surveyed and settled or not, whether the areas are scheduled areas or not, and whether the lands are in Tribal Talukas and Tribal Pockets or not. The condition or necessity of issuing a Government notification should be dispensed with.

(2) Alienation of tribal lands may be allowed only for genuine public purposes like construction of school buildings, libraries, hospitals, extension works, dispensaries, etc.

(3) Provision should be made for restoration of tribal lands irrespective of the period during which they were alienated by removing bar of any limitation keeping in view provision made in respective Acts by other State Governments.

(*Vide*: (i) In Bihar State, the Bihar Scheduled Areas Regulation, 1969 made provision of limitation period of 30 years in respect of immovable property belonging to a member of the scheduled tribe, (ii) In Kerala State, the Kerala Scheduled Tribes (Restriction on Transfer of lands and Restoration of Alienated lands) Act, 1975 provides that the transfers of immovable properties possessed, enjoyed or owned by a member of S.T. effected on or after 1-1-1960 are deemed to be invalid, (iii) The Maharashtra Restoration of Lands to Scheduled Tribes Act, 1974 provides for restoration to a tribal his land gone into the hands of a non-tribal between the period from 1-4-57 to 6-7-74. For transfers arising after this period, the Maharashtra L.R. Code and Tenancy Laws (Amendment) Act, 1974 was enacted, (iv) The Orissa Regulation II of 1956 was amended making provision for enhancing the limitation from 12 years to 30 years for restoration of tribal lands, (v) The West Bengal Restoration of Alienated Land, 1973 provides for effecting restoration of land alienated after 1967 due to distress or for the maintenance of the family or for meeting the cost of cultivation. This Act provides for restoration of land to small cultivators including tribals).

(4) Besides the application by the concerned tribal for restoration of his lands, there should be provision in law for *suo moto* action by the competent authority, so that cases of alienation by poor and ignorant tribals may not go unnoticed.

(5) The jurisdiction of the Civil Court in respect of cases of alienation and restoration of tribal lands to non-tribals should be barred. It calls for inserting Section 73 AA in this matter.

(6) Provision requires to be made for treating admission of the tribals against their own interest as inadmissible in evidence in any proceedings regarding tribal lands. Such provisions exist in the enactments of the government.

(*Vide*: (i) Bihar Scheduled Areas Regulation, 1969, in Bihar State, (ii) Regulation II of 1956 as amended in Orissa State, (iii) The Maharashtra Land Revenue Code and Tenancy laws (Amendment) Act, 1974 and the Maharashtra Restoration of Lands to Scheduled Tribes Act, 1974).

(7) In proceedings relating to tribal lands, provision should be made for an officer of the rank not below that of the Mamlatdar to be joined as a party on behalf of tribals, so that rights of tribals can be safeguarded.

(*Vide*: The provision made by the Bihar State in the Bihar Scheduled Areas Regulation Act, 1969 for appointing Deputy Commissioner as a party).

(8) Provision for imposing penalty on non-tribal by way of imprisonment and fine may be made if the non-tribal gets occupation of tribal land in contravention of legal provisions made in this behalf.

(*Vide*: (i) The Orissa State Regulation No. II of 1956, amended in 1975 to provide for rigorous imprisonment and fine for unauthorised occupation of tribal land, (ii) In Bihar State, provision has been made in Chotanagpur Tenancy Act, 1908 for imprisonment and/or fine for unlawful transfer of tribal land and in case of continuous offence, a further fine not exceeding Rs. 50 each day).

(9) In case of tribal lands alienated to non-tribals, if the transferee has constructed a substantial structure on the land before the proposed enactment, provision may be made to validate the transfer if the transferee either makes available to the transferer an alternative holding of the equivalent value in the vicinity or pays adequate compensation for rehabilitation of the transferer.

(*Vide*: The provision made in Bihar State in the Chhotanagpur area referred to earlier).

(10) In proceedings regarding restoration of possession of tribal lands instituted by a tribal, provision may be made to the effect that no magistrate shall have jurisdiction under Criminal Procedure Code, 1973 in respect of dispute between that person and any other person claiming to be in possession or enjoyment in respect of the said land.

(*Vide*: The provision made by Kerala State in the Kerala Scheduled Tribes–Restriction of Transfer of Lands and Restoration of Alienated Lands Act, 1975).

(11) Provision may be made for prohibiting the attachment and sale of tribal lands in execution of the money-decree against a member of the Scheduled tribe.

(*Vide*: (i) The provision made in Orissa State in (a) Orissa Land Reforms Act, 1960 and in (b) Regulation II of 1956; and (ii) in Lakshadweep Union Territory in the Regulation of 1964).

(12) If the tribal does not agree to take back possession of the tribal land for any reason whatsoever (influence and pressure by others, or his honesty etc). provision may be made that such land should be vested in State Government and subsequently may be allotted to a landless tribal or tribal with marginal landholding.

(13) Any document regarding transfer of tribal land should not be accepted for registration by the Registrar/Sub-registrar except in cases in which specific permission is given by the State Government or authority authorised by State Government.

(*Vide*: (i) The provision in the Orissa State in the Orissa Land Reforms Act, 1960, and (ii) The provision in Kerala State in the Kerala Scheduled Tribes–Restriction of Transfer of Lands and Restoration of Alienated Lands Act, 1975).

(14) In Tribal areas covered by Tribal Talukas and Tribal Pockets, if a non-tribal wants to sell his land, it can be sold only to landless tribal or tribal having a marginal holding.

(15) For Tribal areas covered by Tribal Talukas and Tribal Pockets provision should be made that unless the contrary is proved, if a non-tribal is found in possession of a tribal land, it should be restored to the tribal under the presumption that he or his predecessor had acquired that land through transfer from tribal landholders. A provision such as this will be helpful in detecting concealed cases of transactions.

(16) For transaction of transfer of tribal land between tribal transferor and non-tribal transferee which have taken place before the coming into force of the proposed enactment regarding restoration of tribal lands, which transactions are not otherwise invalid under any law in force then, provision may be made for restoration of the land to the tribal transferer on payment of an amount equal to multiples of assessment as may be fixed or the amount of consideration paid by the non-tribal transferee, whichever is less plus the value of improvements.

(*Vide*: The Maharashtra Restoration of Lands to Scheduled Tribes Act, 1974, according to which multiple of assessment is fixed at 48 times of the revenue assessed).

(17) Provision may be made that for transfer of tribal land which become invalid after the coming into force of the proposed enactment prohibiting alienation of tribal land, the consideration money paid by the non-tribal transferee to the tribal transferer should not be refunded.

(*Vide*: The Land Regulation, 1956 amended in 1975 in the Orissa State where such provision is made).

(18) Provision may be made for alienation of tribal lands from tribal to tribal in some special circumstances and sanction may be given only by the State Government. The special circumstances, other than cases of transfer due to heirship and partition, in general may be: (i) In case the tribal family wants to give up forever the agricultural occupation and desires to

settle elsewhere for non-agricultural occupation including trade, service etc.; (ii) In case there is no direct heir to the tribal who desires to transfer his land by sale, gift etc.; (iii) in case the tribal is old, infirm and unable to pursue agriculture and there is none in his family who can lookafter his land; and (iv) The tribal purchaser should not be rich and well-to-do, and must be personally engaged in agricultural occupation or agricultural labour. Moreover, the holding after the said transfer should not exceed the holding prescribed for a small farmer.

Tenancy Legislation

The following two amendments were made by the Gujarat State in the Bombay Tenancy and Agricultural Lands Act, 1948. It is hereinafter referred to as Gujarat Tenancy Act V of 1973 which came into force with effect from 9-3-1973 :

(a) In no case shall a tenancy be terminated for personal cultivation and non-agricultural use by the landlord, if the tenant is a member of the Scheduled Caste or Scheduled Tribe. [Section 31B(4)].

(b) Surrender of tenancy rights in favour of landlords have been barred. All surrenders can be made only in favour of the State Government and such land will vest with the State Government free from all encumbrances for disposal according to the provisions of the Act in accordance with the priority list.

Before the above 2 amendments came into force, the landlords had right to terminate the tenancy of tribal tenants on the ground of personal cultivation or non-agricultural use of land up to a specified period. Similarly landlords were also able to get the land voluntarily surrendered by a tribal tenant up to a specified period. During this period, tactful and intelligent landlords of tribal tenants availed of the legal provisions in getting back the land from the tribal tenants on the ground of personal cultivation or by voluntary surrender. The tribal tenants who made voluntary surrender have done so on account of poverty, illiteracy, indebtedness and influence of landlords. Some of these surrenders might be fictitious and fake.

The departmental information (presented in Table 4.1 of Chapter 4) shows the figures of lands lost by tribal tenants for personal cultivation by landlords and lands surrendered in favour of landlords in respect of only 14 tribal talukas and one tribal pocket. In all 3317 tribals voluntarily surrendered 3203 hectares of land and 1450 tribals lost legal right over 2095 hectares of land for personal cultivation by landlords. Thus a total of 4767 tribal tenants lost 5298 hectares of land on the above two counts and thus they were deprived of becoming deemed purchasers.

The above two amendments which could have protected tribals were made at a very late stage. It is likely that the figures of tribal tenants and the lands lost by them as revealed from the limited departmental data on the above two counts, if studied in detail in all 32 talukas and 15 pockets, would go much higher.

From the above, it can be observed that the tribal tenants' lack of knowledge about their legal rights in land and their inferior social and financial status as compared to their non-tribal landlords were among the main handicaps and reasons which virtually nullified their rights under the vital provisions of the law. It seems reasonable to make following suggestions to overcome some of these problems.

(1) In a proposed legislation, a provision should be made for restoration of the lands from the non-tribals who got back the lands from the tribals on the above two counts by relaxing the period of the time limitation. When this is done, tribals can be made deemed purchasers and conferred occupancy rights when the lands are restored to them as tenants.

(2) There is a provision in Section 70(b) of the Tenancy Act, allowing a person to apply to the Mamlatdar whether he is or was a tenant. This requirement for obtaining the decision of the Mamlatdar, that a tribal is or was not a tenant of his land, has been taken advantage of by intelligent and tactful landlords using fair and foul means and got possession of tribal lands. Also, there were cases in which mutation entries in Village Forms were effected, indicating that a tribal was not a tenant on the land and thereby his name as tenant was deleted, and such entries were certified with the result that a tribal could not become a deemed purchaser.

In all such cases of doubtful alienations, provision should be made in the proposed Act for Restoration of Tribal lands so that in such cases, the lands should be restored to the tribals concerned, and they may be subsequently conferred occupancy rights as deemed purchasers.

(3) One of the hurdles of restoration of the tribal land is that the names of non-tribals, probably those from whom tribals had borrowed money, were entered as tenants in the village records and subsequently they (non-tribals) became occupants of the land as deemed purchasers. Under the existing law, it is not possible to restore possession of such lands to the tribals in tribal areas which were treated as surveyed and settled, and where Section 73A of the Land Revenue Code was not applicable.

Maharashtra State made provision in Section 4 of the Maharashtra Restoration of Lands to Scheduled Tribes Act, 1974 to restore lands to tribals from non-tribals who have purchased or who were deemed to have purchased tribal lands in accordance with the provisions of the relevant Tenancy Law. Gujarat State may consider making suitable enactment to cover such cases.

(4) There were some tribals who became occupants, as deemed purchasers under Tenancy Law, but they had not as yet been able to pay the instalments of purchase price to their previous landlords. (Reference is invited here to the aforesaid Table 4.1 in Chapter 4).

Maharashtra Government made a scheme in 1977 under the Tribal Sub-Plan for granting to the tribal tenant purchasers residing in the specified tribal areas, subsidy and interest-free loans to enable them pay the purchase price in respect of their lands. Under this scheme, the financial assistance was sanctioned as follows:

(a) Subsidy equal to purchase price minus six times the assessment; and
(b) interest-free loan recoverable in 12 annual instalments equal to remaining amount of purchase price, i.e. equal to six times the assessment.

The amount of financial assistance was sanctioned to cover purchase price of the land up to five acres.

It may be possible for the Gujarat Government to consider introduction of such a scheme under the Tribal Area Sub-Plan in tribal areas concerned.

Land Ceiling Act

The study of the Land Ceiling Act and its implementation brings out the following points for serious consideration by the Gujarat Government.

(1) The Gujarat Agricultural Lands Ceiling Act, 1960 has made provision that a person belonging to a Scheduled Tribe shall have precedence over other persons for the allotment of land declared surplus. The occupancy price to be charged from the allottee is equal to the amount of compensation to be paid to the landholder whose land is declared surplus. The amount of compensation of cultivated land ranges from 80 to 200 times the assessment of the land. Due to the extremely poor financial condition of the Tribals, it is very difficult for them to pay such heavy price. It is, therefore, suggested that the concessional occupancy price at the rate of six times the assessment should be charged to the tribal allottee and the remaining amount of the difference between the full and the concessional occupancy price should be met with, as subsidy to the concerned tribal from the Tribal Area Sub-Plan. The concessional occupancy price at six times the assessment may be given as interest-free loan to be recovered in 12 annual equal instalments from the Tribal Area Sub-Plan.

(2) To evade the provisions of the Ceiling Law, the following devices were reported to have been adopted by tactful and intelligent landlords so that their land in excess of the ceiling limit may not be declared surplus.

(a) Partitioning of land among family members by unregistered ante-dated documents,

(b) creating rights of tenants in the names of persons who were acquainted or related to them and thus enabling them to become deemed purchasers under the Tenancy Law. Cases are also reported where such landlords had taken money in advance and then given tenancy rights to others who became occupants as deemed purchasers under the Tenancy Law and thus they also got the purchase price in addition to advance money. Thus they were able to get the full value of their land by adopting such tactful methods, on account of unforeseen loopholes by makers of law.

Prevention of Fragmentation and Consolidation of Holdings Act

(a) *Prevention of Fragmentation of Land*

Different parcels of lands held by a tribal landholder in a village, are generally situated at different places. For instance, some are on rocky and hilly areas while a few others in somewhat plain area. The fertility of each parcel of land is naturally different. And so, each and every heir of a deceased landholder prefers to have his share by subdividing each parcel of land with differences in the fertility of the soil. This results in smaller and uneconomic fragments, and at times of the size below standard area prescribed by the above Act. However, in the Record of Rights, the names of all the heirs of a deceased are shown against each parcel of land under joint possession, though the position on the ground is different, as indicated above. In the Record of Rights, therefore, there appears no fragments, while fragments do exist in the land cultivated by the heirs of a tribal ancestor.

The only reasonable solution that can be suggested to correct the situation is to pursuade different heirs of an ancestor to manage the cultivation of such lands jointly and to share the expenditure involved and divide the total produce of harvested crops among themselves. This is the only way in which the illegal position at the ground level, and in the records, can be allowed to persist without suffering from the evil of fragmentation.

(b) *Consolidation of Land-holdings*

1. Out of 54 villages selected for field survey (39 of Tribal Talukas and 15 of Tribal Pockets) consolidation scheme was applied to and completed in only 13 villages. The findings of these cases are as under:

(i) possession of fragments and parcels were exchanged for the purpose of forming compact Blocks in 7 villages, (ii) in the second group of 3 villages, possession according to the Block scheme had taken place partially, and (iii) lastly in 3 villages possession had been fully exchanged as revealed from the survey.

In the second and third category, where lands were partially or fully exchanged, most of the lands belonged to non-tribals. Out of these 6 villages, 4 villages were from Pocket areas and 2 villages from

Tribal Talukas. Thus out of 13 villages, the consolidation scheme was not successful in 10 villages shown in Categories (i) and (ii) above.

In the 'Report on Consolidation of the Holdings Gujarat State' by H.K.L. Kapoor Committee, it was pointed out that the areas having one or more of the following characterisations, were unsuitable for implementation of the consolidation scheme:

(1) Areas having undulating and hilly terrain;
(2) Areas having disproportionately large varieties of soil;
(3) Areas where there is an insignificant problem of scatteredness; and
(4) Areas having a large percentage of Adivasi population or other inhabitants who are socially backward.

Firstly, the above 10 villages where the consolidation scheme were successful, might have been taken up before the preparation of the Kapoor Committee's report and one or more of the above characterisations might have effected the results. The above characterisations may be kept in view when the question of taking up tribal villages for introduction of the consolidation scheme arises in future. The feasibility of the scheme, the willingness of the landholders for implementation etc. must be thoroughly examined while taking up a tribal village for the implementation of this scheme.

Secondly, the Record of Rights (in these 10 villages) has been rewritten according to the consolidation scheme as if the possessions have all been exchanged according to the formation of land Blocks, and as such, Block Nos. are shown in place of survey numbers and for sub-divisions of Survey numbers. However, the position on the ground was different in cases in which the landholders have not exchanged their possession.

This resulted in a lot of difficulties for the village officers concerned in doing crop inspection and keeping notes of the crops in the Block numbers in the village records. Since possession was not according to Blocks, in such cases, serious administrative difficulties were faced in day-to-day working of the village officers.

In principle, the Record of Rights is the Record of possession of land by an occupant. This was not observed under these conditions. The Vital statistics of crops collected at various levels were also affected.

In the end, it seems appropriate to suggest that the Record of

Rights in villages in which the consolidation schemes were not successfully implemented be brought in conformity with the possession on the ground.

Record of Rights

The tribal people are bound to their land by many an intimate ties. It is, •therefore, necessary that the Record of Rights of Tribal lands should be upto date and maintained correctly. The work of preparing the Record of Rights as far as the Tribals are concerned requires utmost care and vigilance as the tribals are illiterate and ignorant of the implications of various entries and enactments. The approach to keeping land records should be a humane one rather than legalistic and should take full cognizance of tribal custom and tradition.

The Record of Rights in tribal areas were found to be not up-to-date due to the following factors:

(1) During the times of ex-Princely states, there was a practice of taking forced labour commonly known as 'Veth' from every land-holder called *Khatedar*. In order that a *Khatedar* may not have to supply more persons to the state for forced labour, he preferred to keep all his land in one *Khata* (land-holding) only. This was one of many reasons why all tribal lands were entered in the name of the eldest male heir of the family. The practice of demanding forced labour is obviously out-dated and does not at all exist at present. However, the custom of primogeniture persists and the heirs of a dead person maintain a joint *Khata* in the name of the eldest brother, while separately cultivating their parcels of land for personal benefit. This is one of the reasons why the Record of Rights cannot be up to-date in tribal villages.

(2) On account of varying fertility of soil in parcels of inherited land and the anticipated breach of Fragmentation Act referred to earlier, the names of all heirs are shown jointly against each piece of land, which is actually sub-divided for the purpose of cultivation. Thus the position in the Record and that on the ground differs.

(3) On account of the compulsions of incurring debts for social ceremonies, maintenance in times of scarcity and draught and in lean periods, many a tribals had no alternative but to

alienate his land to a money-lender. However, due to ban on land alienation, he tends to enter into concealed transaction with his creditor. Such transactions were not brought to the notice of revenue authorities and so land alienations of this kind were not reflected in the Record of Rights.

(4) The programmes of resurvey, as well as revision survey were undertaken in tribal areas. However, the survey staff had to ignore the existing partitions of parcels of land separately cultivated by each heir, and set aside the provision of the Prevention of Fragmentation Act.

(5) In villages where consolidation scheme was implemented, tribals mostly did not exchange lands as required for consolidation of land Blocks. This created an anomaly in the situation as the Record of Rights was prepared according to Block Scheme prescribed by the government. This point has been discussed earlier in detail. As mentioned before, it seems appropriate to suggest that suitable steps should be taken to ensure that the Record of Rights actually reflects the position of landholdings on the ground.

Compulsory Acquisition of Tribal Lands for Public Purpose

In all the large-scale irrigation projects, tribals in Gujarat were the losers of their lands as these projects are generally located in hilly and rocky tribal tracts. The tribal lands for dams are compulsorily acquired and they are rendered almost landless and homeless. The fruits of irrigation go to the people living in downstream areas in the plains, and they are usually the non-tribals.

In order to compensate the loss of land to the tribals to the fullest extent, the following points call for serious consideration:

(1) In the first instance, a tribal should be allotted equal land in exchange of the land compulsorily acquired, instead of giving him compensation in cash.

(2) The loss of living accommodation and facility in house/hut and breakable household materials which cannot be shifted should be fully compensated for rehabilitation.

(3) The amount of award price paid to him in cash was so nominal that he was not able to purchase adequate land for his living. He should, therefore, be given land in exchange, so that

chances of his losing in the bargain on account of time lag in notification of acquisition and actually getting the award money may not arise.

(4) On account of restrictions on alienation of tribal lands under Section 73A of the Land Revenue Code, it was almost impossible to make correct valuation of his land. In absence of any reliable method for this purpose, his lands were valued at very low rate. It will be appropriate therefore, that the statistics of sale of old tenure lands in the neighbouring villages or tracts may be utilised as satisfactory yard-sticks for working out fair compensation.

(5) Again, because of restriction on alienation of tribal lands (which is in his interest), his lands were not valued as old tenure lands and thus he was put to grievous loss when his land was compulsorily acquired from him by the Government.

It will be in the fitness of things, therefore, that his ancestral land is valued as old tenure land. Tribal lands which are granted as new tenure lands may in fact be valued as such.

FOREST LAND AND FORESTS, MONEY-LENDING, CREDIT AND INDEBTEDNESS

Tribal Rights in Forest Land and Forests

The forests were opened up for exploitation by non-tribals. There was onrush of timber contractors permitted by forest department to cut trees and/or prepare charcoal. The demand for timber at higher prices was a temptation for individual tribals to cut wood indiscriminately and sell to timber merchants and others. In course of time, however, their age-old rights to cultivate forest land and to cut trees were restricted. Hunting could no more give them games to live by, and the changed circumstances compelled them to resort to illicit cutting of trees and seek new avenues of labour outside their habitat to sustain their families after monsoon. The problems connected with the occupancy and use of forest land and trees by the tribals in general, are complex, as revealed from the following points.

(1) In the district of Dangs, Government of Gujarat issued orders in 1970 conferring occupancy rights only on Dangis and not on

any outsider who had obtained leases of certain lands either from Dangis Rajas or from forest department. This step was quite proper in the interest of the tribals who were the original occupants of the Dangs. The Government had not placed any restriction on the extent of leased area for which occupancy rights could be conferred. This resulted in inequitable distribution of conferment of occupancy rights among Dangis. A person holding a big area of leased land became the occupant of larger areas, while a person holding a small area became occupant of smaller areas. Had the Government put some ceiling limit on this, it would have become possible for most of the Dangi tribals to take advantage of having their own land-holdings. It has become difficult to correct the situation at this point of time. It is, therefore, recommended to help these land-less tribals by giving them first preference in distribution of jobs in forest department, forest cooperatives, and so on.

(2) In order to regulate authorised farming and to curb unauthorised cultivation of forest lands in all areas other than Dangs, the Government of Gujarat issues various orders from time to time. The original orders issued in 1961 and 1964 were to grant occupancy rights of forest lands to the backward class persons whether cultivating forest land authorisedly or unauthorisedly. Non-backward classes were given occupancy rights of forest lands provided they cultivated authorisedly, however, they had no claim on forest lands if cultivated unauthorisedly.

(3) According to the orders issued in 1972, the forest lands cultivated authorisedly or unauthorisedly by cultivators prior to 31-12-1967 were permanently granted holdings up to 8 acres including other lands which might have been occupied as per the rules. This order treated tribals and non-tribals on an equal footing and so it allowed the latter also to become occupants of forest lands cultivated unauthorisedly by them.

The above mentioned concession to non-tribals resulted in depriving the needy landless tribals of the chances to own forest land. It is high time the Government stop giving such concessions to non-tribals especially in respect of forest lands over which the tribals have fundamental claim of occupation.

(4) After merger of the ex-Princely states and on application of

the Bombay Merged Territories and Areas (Jagir Abolition) Act, 1953, the forest areas remained as private forests of the Jagirdars. The Gujarat State enacted the Gujarat Private Forests (Acquisition) Act, 1972 for acquisition of private forests. During the intervening period, the Jagirdars wantonly permitted indiscriminate cutting of trees in private forests and allowed unauthorised cultivation of forest lands to tribals and non-tribals alike. This resulted in a huge loss of trees, making the forests barren. The only way to make good the losses of these rich forests, is to take up intensive afforestation work without any time-lag in planting saplings and rearing trees in the ex-private forest areas. The tribals should be encouraged to take up afforestation and solve their unemployment problem at least on short term bases.

(5) A large number of intermediaries, contractors etc. in the forest areas are replaced by Forest Labour Cooperative Societies. These cooperative societies developed vested interests when they were governed by non-tribals and/or rich tribals working as office-bearers, as secretaries etc. Unless the bye-laws of forest cooperative societies are changed or modified suitably in order to eliminate non-tribals and rich tribals from becoming members and holding positions of power, the tribal members cannot be protected from exploitation.

(6) To increase forest wealth, Village Forest scheme in general should be introduced wherever feasible. Also, *gobar gas* plants should be widely propagated and encouraged so that forest trees may not be cut and burnt as fuel for domestic purposes. The subsidy for construction of *gobar gas* plants should be raised to 85 per cent from the tribal Area Sub-Plan. The remaining amount may be given as interest-free loan.

(7) In order to prevent illicit cutting and misuse of forest wealth by unscrupulous tribals or non-tribals, it is essential to introduce sound management and constant patrolling of forest areas. In addition to this, the process of introducing diversification of occupations among the tribals would create alternative sources of income. Such measures may prevent tribals from illicit cutting of forest trees.

(8) The Village Panchayats specially in forest areas have a special role to play towards protection of trees and development of

the forest. A special Forest Committee in Village Panchayat can help in giving concrete shape to the idea of village forestry.

Money-lending, Credit and Indebtedness

The tribal by and large is compelled to incur debts to solve his immediate and pressing economic demands arising out of marriage, illness, social obligations, daily necessities, etc. For such needs he requires credits in cash on the spot to solve the problems. Sometimes relatives and the well-to-do tribals come to his help, but such cases are few and far between. He is able to get necessary credits promptly from private money-lenders and traders who exploit him. It is therefore, necessary that adequate institutional credit facilities with simple formality are made available to them. The usual arrangement of advancing loans to the tribals are through Government agencies and other Banking institutions and Cooperative Societies. However, this is limited only for the use in land development, buying seeds, fertilisers, agricultural implements, bullocks, livestock, poultry, etc. This arrangement does not cover loans required for social purpose, e.g., daily events like marriage, death etc. These are considered as non-productive items of credit for which the tribal has to tap private sources where he is exploited due to usurious practices of the creditor.

(1) To save him from the clutches of money-lenders, traders, etc. credit facilities even for social purpose through institutional means should be made easily available to him even on personal security basis.

(2) The landless tribals who depend entirely on labour, are not treated as creditworthy persons. For the purpose of advancing loans to them especially for social purposes, the factor of uncreditworthiness should not come in their way of getting credits from institutional finances.

(3) The village shops belonging to Bohras, Memons, Banias Marwaris, Ghanchi, Luhana etc. situated in Tribal villages should be completely removed. This is the only way to put an end to the exploitation of the tribals. In the placc of these, multi-purpose shopping centres and their branches should be opened in these areas through Cooperatives. These shopping

centres may also serve as centres of exchange of goods and commodities, like sale-purchase marketing miniature yards in tribal areas.

(4) There are pedestrian traders such as Pathan, Sindhi muslims, etc., who trade in bullocks for tribals. They sell bullocks at exhorbitant rates to tribals with the condition to receive payment in instalments. First instalment of one third of the price is recovered at the very time of transaction. The remaining amount is taken on a prescribed date once in an year (2nd day of the bright half of Phalgun). If the remaining amount is not paid on the prescribed date, the bullock is just taken back by the trader and the money previously paid is forfeited.

This kind of exploitation should be stopped by appointing vigilante officers of the Cooperative Department. The entry of such traders into tribal areas for this purpose should be banned. Arrangements for advancing loans for bullocks in one instalment should be made through suitable institutional means.

(5) In certain tribal Talukas and Pockets, very few or no applications for abolition of debt under the Gujarat Rural Debtors' Relief Act, 1976 were received. The time limits to send applications may be extended and wide publicity should be made in the Tribal villages for sending applications through reliable leaders.

(6) The Debt Settlement Officers appointed for the disposal of applications, normally fixed hearings at Taluka places or at other important centres in a taluka. Non-tribal money-lenders usually manage to see that the tribals remain absent at the time of hearing of the case. As an alternative, they try to strike a favourable compromise with the tribals under pressure of temptation or influence. In order to overcome such a situation, the hearings of cases should as far as possible be kept at the villages from where applications were received so that complainant was able to have a congenial atmosphere for him to explain his case without pressure or temptation by the non-tribals. Besides, the cases should not be decided ex-parte, but opportunities created such that presence of complainant and his say in the cases are guaranteed.

PANCHAYATI RAJ AND DEVELOPMENT PROGRAMMES

As discussed earlier at length, the development programmes for tribal areas are implemented through Village Panchayats. The Project Administrators of Tribal Area Sub-Plans play key role in the whole programmes which encountered many hurdles right from the problem of communication facilities to poor quality of land, water, draught conditions, lack of facilities for training manpower and education. We present here the few important issues and related suggestions based on the findings of this study.[2]

(1) One of the bottle-necks in the development of tribal areas is the absence of communication facilities. Village functionaries find it quite difficult to keep in touch with tribal population or make adequate living condition for them as a result of which development programmes suffer a great deal.

(2) The expectations of collecting matching funds from the tribal communities to help specific development programmes have remained unfulfilled and so this policy should not be pursued rigidly. Most of the funds for development should flow from tribal area sub-plan allocations.

(3) The rate of water supply through irrigation facilities should be fixed at a very low level per unit so that more tribal landholders can take advantage of this facility and improve their agricultural practices e.g., cropping pattern yield, etc.

(4) A special functional classification of tribal economy varying from area to area and to sub-areas should be worked out before planning and implementing development programmes.

(5) The staff of various development departments and the funds under various heads earmarked for expenditure should be put at the disposal of the Project Administrator of Tribal Area Sub-Plan. Not only this, the project administration be strengthened by more man-power to discharge its new and varied responsibilities fully.

(6) In certain tribal areas of extreme backwardness, special schemes should be prepared to help individual tribal households so that they can become economically self-sufficient and independent in course of time.

(7) In special water works such as Meshvo Dam project, the betterment levy collected by the government for use in Dash

Koshi villages was unfair because this kind of advantage accrued due to sacrifices of sub-merged valuable land of the villages of Bhiloda area and not of Dash Koshi area.

(8) The tribals believed that it was sufficient to send only one child to the school and engage the remaining children to look after cattle, agriculture and other subsidiary activities of the household.

(9) In the draught-prone areas, the poorer tribals be given more than 50 per cent subsidy for various agricultural activities. Under such extreme circumstances, special arrangements for dispersal of subsidy even up to 75 per cent be provided through the Tribal Development Corporation.

(10) The dispersed villages in tribal areas may be given independent Village Panchayats. The villagers should make their own decisions as to how their resources can be utilized and amenities made available for welfare and development. It is not advisable to think of converting them into nucleated villages where farmers are normally deprived of opportunity of direct work in fields and supervision facility of crops. Such vigilance is possible only when they build their huts right in the fields located in difficult terrain.

(11) The entire structure of the Village Panchayat for the tribal area should be reformulated so that village development and panchayati structure can easily function in an integrated manner. This is possible only if group panchayats in some parts of tribal areas are reconstituted eliminating village/villages of mixed population and having independent village sites.

(12) With regard to decentralisation of powers and functions of the tribal Village Panchayats, it was felt that there was no use giving more powers to the Sarpanch or Panchayat Committee because, on account of illiteracy, the people were not able to take the full advantage of such provisions.

(13) One of the important mechanisms to attract tribal children to attend schools was to provide mid-day meals, so that it supplements nutrition needs of tribal children in general and boosts up school attendance.

(14) In certain areas, there is a great unemployment problem among the tribals and this calls for serious thinking on how to introduce the Right to Work and Food for Work Programme

for tribals, both educated as well as illiterate.

(15) With all the pros and cons, the Ashram Shalas were more liked by the people than the Primary Schools in tribal areas. Thc provision of food, clothing and residential facilities for students, if properly provided and managed, these Shalas are bound to improve prospects of spreading education among tribals.

(16) The Employment Exchange services of the South Gujarat University in Surat was a better venue through which applications of tribal candidates for employment in various jobs were received. It is likely that the actual registration in the rest of the universities in the state was poor either because tribal students were unaware of these facilities at the universities or that the latter did not make wide publicity to inform tribal households.[3]

(17) The total number of tribal candidates employed in government jobs in 1976-77 were 2257. This amounted to 73.02 per cent of the total number of educated tribals employed in services through State Employment Exchanges. Employment of educated tribals in other sectors was comparatively poor.

(18) The official data revealed that the programme of Industrial Training Institutes if implemented through the Tribal Area Sub-Plan, it was likely to get better response for enrolment of the tribal students.

EDUCATIONAL FACILITIES

Dropout in Primary Schools

The following factors were said to be responsible for dropout in the primary schools.

(a) Inability of parents to spend for books, clothes, uniforms, etc.
(b) Need of children to lookafter cattle when the parents are away to earn daily bread.
(c) Need of children to lookafter young babies when parents are away for work.
(d) Lack of hunger for education.
(e) Unemployment of young educated tribals.
(f) Unsuitability of timings of the school from 11.00 a.m. to 5.00

p.m. There was a suggestion that morning and evening times will be suitable, so that more boys and girls would be able to attend schools.

(g) Inability of teachers to know the local tribal dialects through which tribal children can easily be taught.

Difficulties of Primary School Teachers

(a) The teachers experienced difficulties of residential accommodation as there were no quarters for teachers. The houses of tribals were not found suitable for teachers' family members to live in.

(b) The teachers in villages experienced difficulties of giving higher education to their own grown up children.

(c) Lack of communication facilities to bring domestic requirements easily from market towns.

(d) Lack of satisfactory arrangements of medical facilities for family members of teachers.

(e) Danger of threat and theft in certain tribal areas.

(f) Lack of socio-cultural assimilation of the teachers' family members and those of tribal families.

(g) Difficulties of getting sufficient number of children in the school inspite of visiting house to house, in different *falias* scattered in a large area. In view of the above difficulties the teachers temporarily accept postings in tribal areas but manage to get transfer to non-tribal areas as soon as possible.

(h) Teachers at some places feel harassed due to drinking habits of tribals who pick up quarrels and show roudy habits.

(i) Wherever there was no possibility of constructing a pucca building for school for want of popular contribution the schools were housed in privately-owned huts of some well-to-do tribals.

(j) There were generally one teacher schools up to 4 Std. in tribal villages located in the interior. The teacher working in such a school found difficulties in getting casual leave during emergency. But when he remained absent, the school remains closed. It was, therefore, demanded that the primary school should have at least 2 teachers, so that at least one can keep it going.

(k) Tribal teachers may be preferred for postings in tribal areas, as they know the tribal dialect and can easily mix and create confidence among the local people.

(l) The grant-in-aid for running primary schools be given on the basis of actual attendance of tribal students and not simply on enrolment figures which were likely to be false or unrealistic.

Preference of Ashram Shalas vis-a-vis Primary Schools

(a) The tribal students got free lodging and boarding facilities in Ashram Shalas and so there was no burden on the parents.

(b) The students living in Ashram Shala had no botheration to do any household work and had not to take care of younger siblings and cattle.

(c) The teachers in most cases had facilities both for adequate school buildings and residential quarters, so that they can concentrate on teaching and lookingafter students.

(d) Teachers did not experience any difficulty in securing presence of sufficient number of students who were given residential and boarding facilities right there.

(e) The students got congenial atmosphere for spending school hours and spare time usefully in the Ashram Shalas. There is a good scope for community living with other students and sharing in day-to-day activities like cleaning, kitchen gardening, agriculture work, etc.

(f) The difficulties of some of the primary school teachers who had own land to lookafter, generally managed to get postings as teachers in nearly areas. During peak period of agriculture season, they remained irregular in attending the schools. In one-teacher schools, the premises remain closed for days and the students went home frustrated. Such difficulties did not arise in Ashram Shalas.

Suggestions for Improving the Working of Ashram Shalas

(a) The optimum limit of admission to Ashram Shalas be raised from 120 to 200 students.

(b) The number of Ashram Shalas be increased such that there may be at least one in the radius of 5 kilometers and can replace a primary school in that area.

(c) The government grant at the rate of Rs. 55 per p.m. per

student was insufficient for the diet of tribal students. This may be raised to the extent that tribal students get adequate and nourishing meals.

(d) One voluntary organisation may not be allowed to run more than 5 Ashram Shalas in a district. An often repeated suggestion was that, for efficient working, Ashram Shalas should be run by the Government as in Dangs.

(e) Voluntary organisations depend on government grants and so they are not able to pay timely salaries to teachers, cooks and *gruh-mata* adequately. This was because as compared to pay scales of teachers in Primary Schools their salaries were lower. It was natural therefore, that efficient and competent teachers were not available for Ashram Shalas.

(f) Income from the activities of demonstration-farms, gardening, horticulture units, etc. in Ashram Shalas was credited to the funds of Voluntary Organisation incharge of management. Instead, the produce of farms etc. should be locally utilised for the benefit of students directly as they who work for the same.

(g) The syllabus of Ashram Shalas especially in Uttar Buniadi classes was very tight and tribal students found it very difficult to cope with the situation. It was suggested to change it such that basic requirements of tribal students to equip themselves for work in industries, agriculture, cottage-industries etc. were adequately met.

(h) The teachers of the Ashram Shalas be given inservice training from time to time as similar facilities were offered to teachers in other categories of government schools.

Secondary Schools in Tribal Areas

(a) There were no hostel facilities for tribal students in secondary schools and in institutions imparting technical training courses. These students in general had to travel long distances to attend the courses. Unless hostel facilities were provided to them at the place of learning, they cannot take full advantage of these institutions.

(b) Secondary schools in tribal areas, suffered due to lack of good and efficient teachers to teach subjects such as English, higher Mathematics and Science. These subjects were so very essential for admission to higher technical courses like medicine, engineering, etc. that without strong background of them, the tribal students cannot do well in the institutions of higher learning, where seats are reserved for them.

MIGRATION, HEALTH AND CRIME

Migration

(a) The tribals generally migrated to cities and towns during off agricultural season. They have no adequate facilities for housing where they went to work. They have no minimum amenities like clean water, light at night, latrines, etc. Local bodies such as Panchayats, notified areas, municipalities, and corporations who benefit indirectly from their hard labour should provide such facilities and amenities to tribal migrants.

(b) Except from the government works, the tribals did not get full wages at the place of migration. It was necessary that suitable measures were taken by the government and local bodies that this kind of exploitation was eliminated.

(c) There was a suggestion from Panchmahals district that for making more jobs available to unskilled tribals, the Railway loco-workshop at Dahod be expanded so that a large number of tribals can be trained and employed in various skilled and semi-skilled jobs in the Railways.

(d) The following new occupations of long-term standing were suggested to prevent short-term out-migration of tribals:

(i) printing of textiles; (ii) spinning ropes from cotton, nylon etc.; (iii) preparation of leaf-plates, leaf-cups (*patarala-padia*), by tribal women; (iv) stitching and repairing clothes by tribal women; and (v) handloom and cottage industries for both tribal men and women.

Health and Medicine

(a) In some tribal areas, the Primary Health Centre staff was not reported to be taking keen interest in serving the tribals. Many of them preferred to live and work in nearby towns and paid only casual visits to the health centre.

(b) Some medical doctors in particular were said to be interested in private practice which in fact was not allowed according to the rules of the department, and in its place special non-practicing allowance given to them.

(c) There were a number of medico-legal cases which took place in the tribal areas on account of serious fights involving land and women. The doctors were reported to avoid treating wounded persons who can otherwise be saved.

(d) In some tribal areas, sexual relationship among tribals were reported to be loose. This gave rise to V.D. that was reported to be spreading in the whole of Gujarat. However, exaggerated, the problem calls for immediate attention of doctors.

(e) The variety of diseases prevalent in tribal areas were skin infection, including syphilis, scabies, etc. as well as typhoid, malaria, cancer and T.B. A tribal reported to have one type of disease was found to be suffering from multiple diseases by the medical doctors in urban hospitals.

(f) The tribals were against family planning operations because they feared that it led to impotancy. The tubectomy operations among women were greatly resented specially by her parents' family members who went sometimes as far as to attack her in-laws for taking decisions without consulting them.

(g) Most of the tribals had begun to prefer taking injections in the time of sickness rather than take oral tablets or liquid medicine. This calls for educating tribals on medicine and health practices.

(h) There was among the tribals an age-old custom to invite as many as close relations as possible to pay visits when a sick person is admitted into a hospital. The hospital staff has to put up with this, as it may have beneficial impact on recovery of patients.

(i) It was considered appropriate to give not only medical but also psychological treatment to tribal patients by permitting the relatives to come to the hospital and even stay there shortly if required.

Court Cases and Crime

(a) Ignorance, jealousy, superstition, etc. are some of the causes of crime among the tribals. However, the disputes over land and elopement of married women add very serious dimensions to the crime situation among the tribals.

(b) Most of the crimes including chapter cases and/or cases of murder, etc. lead to mutual compromises among aggrieved parties. Such compromises are struck either in the court of law or outside by tempering with evidences. In both these categories of compromises, the leaders from either group took the leading role. Such go-betweens were tribal or non-tribal leaders and are called *Bhanjgadias* who may be sometimes influential leaders. They were said to be exploiting the tendency and weakness for crime among the tribals susceptible to misunderstanding, speculation or rumours.

(c) Sometimes the poorer tribals tend to be exploited by knowledgeable and interfering people among themselves. It is necessary therefore, that Free Legal Aid programmes are instituted where the rate of crime is higher in tribal areas. The Free Legal Aid programme can be helpful in preventing and mitigating tribal crimes on account of quarrels on land, women or other kind of disputes.

NOTE

1. Reference is invited here to the findings of National Seminar on Land Alienation and Restoration in Tribal Areas in India, held at the Tata Institute of Social Sciences, Bombay, in mid-1976. The editors of the published report have correctly identified main policy issues such as: (i) total ban on the transfer of tribal lands, (ii) transfer of land between tribals, and (iii) retrospective application of legislation for restoration of lands alienated to non-tribals. It is, however, difficult to know as to how they have considered "Lack of clear understanding and perspective on this subject" as a policy issue. (*Land Alienation and Restoration in Tribal Communities in India*, S.N. Dubey and R. Murdia, Eds., Himayala, Bombay, 1976, pp. 206-207).
2. The status of a Project Administrator at district level be raised to that of an Additional Collector who can pay immediate attention not only to developmental but also legal-rational problems of the tribals.
3. Recently established North Gujarat University can provide Employment Exchange facilities especially for the tribal students of North and East Gujarat tribal areas.

APPENDICES

APPENDIX-I

GOVERNMENT NOTIFICATION ON APPLICATION OF LAND REVENUE CODE SECTIONS 73-A

Presented below is a Government of Gujarat Notification No. LND-3961/41509-G, dated 4-4-1961 imposing restriction on tribal land alienation in the villages in seven Scheduled Areas in the State. A list of villages accompanies the notification.

"In exercise of the powers conferred by Section 73-A of the Bombay Land Revenue Code, 1879 (Bombay V of 1879) the Government of Gujarat hereby :

(1) declares that the provisions of the said Section 73-A shall be applicable to all those villages in the Scheduled areas in the State of Gujarat in which survey settlement under the said Code has not been introduced, and to which the provisions of the said Section 73-A have not been made applicable before the issue of the notification; and

(2) exempts from the operation of the said Section 73-A, all persons not being members of a Scheduled Tribe, holding lands in the villages to which the said Section 73-A is declared to be applicable by this notification."

Seven Scheduled areas declared in Gujarat under para (1) of Schedule 6 of the Constitution of India.

Sl. No.	District Taluka	Scheduled area Mahal or Taluka	Area to which Section 73-A is applicable	
1	2	3	4	
1.	Dangs District	Dangs Taluka	------------	
2.	Surat District	1. Uchchhal Mahal 2. Vyara Taluka 3. Vankal Tappa Nanchhal area of Mangrol Taluka	(A) *35 Villages of Nizar Taluka* (1) Khadade (2) Khorade (3) Torade (4) Nevale	(5) Balabe (6) Bej (7) Birde (8) Borathe

Contd.

1	2	3	4
		4. Songadh Taluka Certain portion of Nizar Mahal	(9) Meghpur (21) Lakhanikhed (10) Modale (22) Lekarwadi (11) Rajpur (23) Vadali (12) Vesgam (24) Sale (13) Kherve Tarfe Dhanare (25) Akkal Uttar (26) Ashapur (27) Chhokhi Amli (14) Gamathi (28) Ziribeda (15) Tapikhad Kale (29) Zumakati (30) Dabari Khaba (16) Nasarpur (31) Panibara (17) Bhilbhwali (32) Borikuva (18) Bhiljaboli (33) Morabe (19) Raygadh (34) Vadpada (20) Ranikhad Kale (35) Harduli (B) *32 Villages of Uchchhal Mahal* (1) Uchchhal (17) Nurabad (2) Sundarpur (18) Thuti (3) Manekpur (19) Jamane (4) Kayali (20) Pethapur (5) Bhutkhurd (21) Nanchhal (6) Vadapatal (22) Parchuvi (7) Bhintbudrk (23) Chacharbundh (8) Hirpur (24) Chhapati (9) Narayanpur (25) Babarghant (10) Bhadbhuja (26) Khabada (11) Jamadi (27) Kamlapur (12) Vadade Khud (28) Selud (29) Anandpur (13) Sankarda (30) Pankhari (14) Sasa (31) Mirkot (15) Kataswan (32) Zaranpada (16) Dhaj
3.	Valsad District	1. Umargam 2. Dharampur Ta. 3. Vansda Taluka	(1) Vansda Taluka
4.	Bharuch District	1. Nandod 2. Jhagadia 3. Dedipada 4. Valia Mahal 5. Sagbara Mahal	Area of former Rajpipla State.
5.	Vadodara	1. Villges of Gadh-Boriad Estate of Naswadi 2. Chhotandepur	Chhotaudepur taluka, villages of former Ghadboriad State in which Naswadi taluka is included.*

Contd.

1	2	3	4
6.	Panchmahal	1. Devgadhboriad 2. Limkheda 3. Village of Santrampur State which are included in Jhalod taluka.*	(1) Devgadhbaria (2) Limkheda (3) Santrampur (4) Jhalod
7.	Sabarkantha	1. Vijaynagar 2. Khedbrahma 3. Bhiloda 4. Meghraj	(1) Vijaynagar (2) Khedbrahma (3) Bhiloda (4) Meghraj

* The contents of this table are translated from the Gujarati version supplied along with the Government Notification referred to before.

APPENDIX-II

EXCERPTS FROM A NOTE ON PRESENT POSITION OF LAND RECORDS IN TRIBAL VILLAGES OF GUJARAT AND PROGRAMME OF ACTION*

A. Existing Situation

Tribal Area Sub-Plan of Gujarat State comprise of 32 Talukas in 7 Districts. The Scheme of (i) Resurvey and a Revision Survey of the Tribal Area Villages, (ii) Rewriting and Reconstruction of Torn Land Records of Tribal Area Villages and (iii) Introduction of village site Survey of the Tribal Area Villages was sanctioned by Government in the Fifth Five Year Plan for the Tribal Area Sub-Plan of the State initially. The said schemes works are continued as spillover in Sixth Five Year Plan also.

Resurvey

The Tribal Area Villages are surveyed and their survey records are available, but as the Survey of the villages was carried out long before i.e. 80 to 90 years ago, and position having much changed on the spot, and with a view to up-to-dating the Village Records as on the spot, it was decided to undertake Resurvey.

As per Rules, a Resurvey is generally done at an interval of 30 years, which has not been done so far. The Resurvey of these lands are, therefore, keenly awaited. Besides, it was observed that the Maintenance of Boundary marks was intact, stereotyping the boundaries of the fields as per Survey, was also neglected during the years of Second World War and thereafter, the survey records have ceased to reflect the position on the spot. In addition to this, several changes which have taken place, during the long spell of time gone unnoticed, has rendered the Survey out of date. This is much so that, if due care is not taken in-time, the Survey will cease to meet its

* This note is based on the information supplied on 12-12-1979 by the Settlement Commissioner and Director of Land Records, Gujarat State, Ahmedabad.

requirements. Before the survey records become also late as explained above, it was necessary that it should be brought up-to-date by undertaking resurvey, whenever necessary. It was, therefore, proposed that the resurvey or Revision Survey of the Tribal Area Villages be taken up under this Scheme, and is in progress. If the changes exceed 25 per cent of the Survey Numbers checked, a resurvey is undertaken and if the changes are up to 25 per cent, a Revision Survey is taken up. The cost is recoverable on completion of work done under Section 135 of Government Land Revenue Code (G.L.R. Code).

Rewriting of Torn Land Records

Similarly, out of the total villages of Tribal Area, certain villages are of the ex-States area villages. They were Surveyed during ex-State regimes long back. The said Survey was treated as Scientifically Surveyed and the Survey Records were continued to remain in force even after the merger of the States. The old Survey and Classification records of these Villages which were prepared 80-90 years ago, have become torn and papers there of are in brittle condition. Due to the effect of time and due to handling of the papers often, these useful survey records have become brittle or are in torn condition. These important Records are required to be recopied/reconstructed immediately before they are destroyed or lost. The work was, therefore, proposed to be taken-up and the said work is in progress under the Tribal Area Sub-Plan Scheme.

Village Site Survey of Tribal Area Villages

The work of introduction of Village Site Survey of the important tribal area villages have been taken up to protect the Rights of Tribals. These records are also much useful for development activities of these villages and maintenance of Records of Rights of the concerned property-holders.

The Survey of all the Villages of the State, is completed, but it was done before 80 to 90 years ago and hence Resurvey is necessary. Settlement under Chapter VIII-A Land Revenue Code was done only in the talukas of 5 districts of the Pre-reorganised Ex-Bombay State Area Villages and in the rest of the areas ad hoc rates of Land Revenue Assessment have been fixed. Regular settlement is not carried out in most of the areas of the State. The question for undertaking regular settlement operations in the State was under examination of the Taxation Enquiry Commission.

B. Proposed Action

The Scheme of Resurvey and Revision Survey of the villages of the Tribal Area was commenced under the Tribal Area Sub-Plan as an advance action and the said work was in progress in the subsequent annual plans also. The target was fixed to complete the Resurvey work of 400 Tribal Area Village in the Fifth Five Year Plan at an estimated cost of Rs. 40 lacs. The target of 450 villages at an estimated cost of Rs. 106 lacs is proposed to be fixed in the Sixth Five Year Plan in Tribal Area Sub-Plan to complete the work as spillover scheme.

During the year 1974-75, preliminary advance action work was commenced for imparting training to the staff. The training was imparted to 200 Scheduled Caste and Scheduled Tribe candidates and on completion of training, they were switched over to regular scheme work during the year 1975-76. The regular scheme work had commenced.

C. Resurvey of Villages in Tribal Area Sub-Plan

Out of 4956 Tribal Area Sub-Plan villages, 310 villages were Resurveyed in Fifth Five Year Plan period (For 4 years 1977-78) under the Tribal Area Sub-Plan of the State, 450 villages were proposed in Sixth Five Year Plan at a cost of Rs. 106 lacs. The work of the remaining villages will be completed in the next plan period.

Looking to the urgent need and possibility of the implementation of the scheme, 450 villages were proposed to be completed under this Scheme at an estimated cost of Rs. 106 lacs, and the work was in progress in Sixth Five Year Plan in Tribal Area Sub-Plan period. Looking to the actual increasing cost of the establishment, i.e. pay, D.A., etc. and due to Revising of prices of the Survey Instruments, stationery etc. and consequence pay scales, the estimated amount of Rs. 106 lacs will remain short. The resurvey is required to be done physically on spot and manual labour of the staff personnel is necessary. They have to do the work as per prescribed diary scaled and so it is a time consuming scheme. The work of the rest of the two schemes will be completed by the end of Sixth Five Year Plan period.

Progress of Work Done for Land Record Schemes in T.A. Sub-Plan

(i) Resurvey and Revision Survey work done in Tribal Area Sub-Plan, under special scheme.

Year	Target		Achievement	
	Financial Rs. lacs	Physical-villages	Financial Rs. lacs	Physical-villages
(A) Fifth Five Year Plan				
1974-75	1-16	Advances action of training.	0-79	Advance action
1975-76	8-00	80 Villages	10-79	*Resurvey* 22 Villages completed 23 Villages in progress *Revision Survey* 43 Villages completed Total 88 villages
1976-77	10-00	100 Villages	17-32	*Resurvey* 68 Villages completed. *Revision Survey* 44 Villages completed. Total 112 villages
1977-78	16-80	105 Villages	15-98	*Resurvey* 120 Villages completed
(B) Sixth Five Year Plan				
1978-79	18-00	115 Villages	18-51	117 Villages
1979-80	19-50	90 Villages		Current year work in progress
1980-81	25-00	90 Villages	—	—

(ii) The work done in State Plan Scheme in Tribal Area Sub-Plan is also as under:

1976-77	8-12	50 Villages	9-54	*Revision Survey* 44 Villages completed *Resurvey* 36 Villages completed
1977-78	4-00	50 Villages	7-22	69 Villages completed

(iii) The work of rewriting and reconstruction of torn Land Records, has been completed by 1976-77 as a Tribal Area Sub-plan Special Scheme. The details of work done is as under:

Year	Target		Total work done by the end of 1979-80		
	Financial Rs. lacs	Achievement Units	Financial Rs. lacs	Physical Units	No. of pages (in lacs)
1974-75	0-90	Advance Action work	0-70	0-47	0-45
1975-76	4-00	3-20 Lakhs Units	4-44	3-75	1-05
1976-77	0-99	1-30 Lakhs Units	0-80	0-83	0-06 T.A. Sub-Plan
1977-78	—	—	—	—	Out of Plan

(iv) The work of Rewriting and Reconstruction of Torn Land Records of Tribal Area Villages done under the State Plan Scheme in Tribal Area Sub-Plan as under:

Year	Target			Total work done by the end of 1978-79		
	Financial Rs. lacs	Physical		Financial Rs. lacs	Physical	
		Units	Pages		Units	Pages
Fifth Five Year Plan						
1976-77	3-50	2-00	1-00	4-94	5-20	0-71
1977-78	5-00	2-50	1-00	3-76	14-84	0-80
		4-50	2-00			
Sixth Five Year Plan						
1978-79	4-00	6-00	1-00	4-56	6-22	0-93
1979-80	6-00	7-00	1-00	Work in Progress		
1980-81	6-00	5-00	1-00	—	—	

APPENDIX-III

QUESTIONNAIRE – GUIDE LINE

The Tribal Land Systems Study Project

I. Land Revenue Laws and Rules

The land system in Gujarat is the outcome of a long process of evolution. At no time, the system remained static for long. It underwent practically continuous changes under the different ruling dynasties (Hindu, Muslim and Maratha) and acquired the present pattern and shape under the British administration. The exigencies of administration determined the rates, the pitch, the term of settlement and the exemption from payment of land revenue. The relations among the tiller of the soil, the intermediary and the Government were settled on the basis of the past practices. In Gujarat, the *Ryotwari* system of land revenue was introduced by the British enjoining upon the holder of land to pay land revenue directly to Government. These practices and precedents were codified into the law called the Bombay Land Revenue Code, 1879. The holdings or occupancies were made heritable and transferable. But on account of ignorance and improvidence of the backward and hilly tribes, the lands held by them were made non-transferable without the permission of the Collector by the amendment Act of 1901... (Section 73-A). This amendment was made consequent upon many transfers of agricultural lands to non-agriculturists and under severe economic distress caused by the plague of 1898 and the famine of 1900. The object was to safeguard the land revenue payable to Government. Except these restrictions on transfer (New Tenure), there seems no other protective or preventive provision made in the Land Revenue Code. Since more than seven decades have passed and the tribals have undergone social and economic metamorphosis under various measures of land reforms and forest policy. Five Year Plans, abolition of tribal debts and bonded labour, the impact of these measures on the tribal life and livelihood needs to be studied in depth.

1. Survey And Settlement

(a) Are the tribal areas surveyed and settled? If so, was any concession given in the settlement of land revenue assessment for the tribal lands at the time of the original settlement and subsequent revisions of land revenue?

(b) If no concession was given, what concessions are necessary for smooth realization of land revenue from tribals?

(c) What special factors should be taken into account in fixing assessment for the tribal areas?

2. Rights in Land

(a) What are the traditional or customary rights of tribals in the lands?

(b) Are they recognised and accepted in the L.R. Code and Rules?

(c) Are any special rights conferred by law? Whether Govt. granted occupancy right to tribals in respect of lands under their cultivation for generations? Whether any concession was given in the amount of occupancy price payable to Govt.? If so, whether any conditions or restrictions were imposed? If so, what are they?

(d) Generally, tribals hold lands on restricted tenure as a protection against transfers or alienations to non-tribals (vide Section 73-A)

Despite these restrictions, many alienations are made by tribals to non-tribals. Have you any suggestions to make for plugging the legal loopholes and preventing transfers, benami or otherwise, in future?

3. Realization of Land Revenue

(a) Are tribals able to pay land revenue in normal years? If not, what are the reasons? How do they discharge their liability of L.R. to Govt.? Are they driven to money-lenders for payment of land revenue?

(b) In the event of natural calamities such as drought, floods, frost, etc., are tribals given suspension and remission of land revenue?
Are these suspensions and remissions on a par with non-tribals or is any differential treatment given to the tribals in realization of land revenue?

(c) Tribals live from hand to mouth and have hardly anything to fall back upon. For recovery of land revenue, are coercive measures taken against the tribal defaulters? If so with what results?

4. Alienations of Tribal Lands

Despite legal provisions against transfer of tribal lands to non-tribals, there are many cases of alienations to non-tribals.

(a) What are the causes of such alienations?

(b) Are there distress sales or alienations? Please suggest measures, legal and otherwise, for preventing such transfers.

(c) Are there any provisions for restoration of alienated tribal lands to their original tribal holders? If so, does Govt. give any assistance, financial or otherwise to tribals in restoration? If there is no provision, what suggestions have you to make in this respect?

(d) After issue of orders of restoration of land, whether physical possession on the spot has been given to the tribal?

5. **Administration**

(a) Is the staff appointed for administration of land revenue (Talati, Patel Circle Inspector, etc.) adequate?

(b) Do they stay at the tribal village and perform their duties or occasionally appear at the village, during the visits of the superiors or in the event of a very urgent matter?

(c) If they do not stay at the village, what hardships they have to undergo for obtaining tagavi subsidy, other agricultural inputs or disposal of their applications for grant of lands, house-sites, copies of village records, etc.?

(d) Is the village revenue staff sympathetic to the tribals or biased in favour of the non-tribals. Who are lording over the tribal areas?

(e) Have you any suggestions to make Revenue and Panchayat administration more responsive to the needs and aspirations of the tribals?

II. Land Reforms

Land reforms programmes have been undertaken with the twin objectives of:

(1) removing the impediments which come in the way of increase in agricultural production as arise from the agrarian structure inherited from the past and,

(2) eliminating all elements of exploitation and social injustice within the agrarian system by providing security of tenure to the tiller of the soil and equality of status and opportunity to all sections of the rural population.

The land reforms consist of:

(a) abolition of intermediaries between the Govt. and the tiller of the soil,

(b) tenancy reforms, i.e. regulation of rent, security of tenure and conferment of ownership rights on the tenants,

(c) ceiling on land-holdings,

(d) agrarian reorganisation including consolidation of holdings and prevention of fragmentation of holdings,

(e) conferment of house-sites.

1. Abolition of Intermediaries

(a) What were the special Inam and non-ryotwari tenures (Talukdari, Bhagdari, Narwadari, Matadari Jagiri, etc.) in the tribal areas?

(b) Are they abolished by special legislation? If so, what tribal rights in land are recognised? What fresh rights in land have been conferred on the tribals?

(c) Whether any special rights have been provided for tribals in regard to regrant or grant of lands and the occupancy price (purchase price) payable? If so, please give details. Are they deprived of customary facilities which they got from them?

(d) What is the reaction of the tribals to the abolition of intermediaries?

(e) How are these Abolition Acts implemented? Is the implementation done in favour of the tribals or weighted in favour of land-lords, money-lenders and others?
What is the attitude of administrators in implementation? Is it biased against the tribals?

(f) Whether the elements of exploitation are removed from the tribal areas?

2. Tenancy Reforms

(a) Are tribals given security of tenure, right of purchase of lands under their cultivation, house-sites, etc.? If so, give details.

(b) Are they given differential treatment in regulation of rent? If so, what is the quantum of rent fixed for them?

(c) Are they given permanent, heritable and transferable rights in the land under their cultivation? If not, why and what restrictions are placed on their right of transfer? What is the effect of the restrictions? Have they operated adversely on the tribal life and living?

3. Ceiling on Land-holdings

(a) What are the special provisions made in the ceiling law for the tribals in regard to:
   (i) allotment of surplus lands.
   (ii) payment of purchase price or compensation payable for surplus lands allotted.
   (iii) any other provisions for tribals.

(b) Are tribals allotted lands from the surplus lands? If so, what is the extent of the area allotted and the number of tribals benefited thereby?

(c) What is the state of implementation of the law? Was it bogged down in litigation? If so, how did it affect tribals?

4. Prevention of Fragmentation and Consolidation of Holdings

(a) Whether this reform has been introduced in the tribal areas? If not, what are the reasons?

(b) Whether this reform is acceptable to the tribals? If not, what is their reaction?

(c) If it is introduced, what is the attitude of the officers implementing the law? Is it biased against the tribals and is in favour of the non-tribal land-holders?

General

(a) What is the general impact of the land reform programme on the life and livelihood of the tribals?

(b) Are impediments to increase in agricultural production and elements of exploitation and social injustice removed from the agrarian structure as envisaged in the Five Year Plans? If not, what are your suggestions for making the land reforms more effective for the welfare of the tribals?

(c) What is the general attitude of tribals towards the land reform programme? Are they acceptable to them? If not, what are the reasons?

III. Forests

To most of the tribals, the forest is their beloved home, their livelihood and their very existence. They were the original inhabitants of the forests which they cleared and brought the lands under their cultivation. They maintained themselves by gathering forest produce and cultivation of patches in forests.

The forests are administered for the public benefit. But the conservation of forests involves regulation of rights and restrictions on the privileges of users in the forest area. As a result, restrictions are placed on the tribals on their use of forest lands and produce. Occupancy rights are generally given to tribals in protected forests. No such rights are given in the reserved forests.

(a) What are the customary rights of tribals enjoyed and recognised by Govt. in the Forest Manual?

(b) Has the Forest Department conceded ownership (occupancy) rights to tribals in respect of the forest lands under their cultivation for generations? If not, what are their objections? Are the objections valid or reasonable?

(c) In the competing claims of the Forest Department (conservation of the forests and cultivating rights of the tribals), what is to be preferred?

(d) If the tribal rights in the cultivated lands are to be preferred, what restrictions or safeguards do you suggest for conservation of the forests?

(e) What is the impact of forest laws on the life and livelihood of the tribals?

(f) Tribals have many complaints and grievances against the Forest officers in regard to the implementation of various welfare schemes for the tribals. What are your suggestions for remedying the situation?

IV. Tribal Debts and Bonded Labour

Land alienation and money-lending are the two most important economic problems of tribals.

The tribal debts form part of the general rural indebtedness. Liquidation of such debts is connected with:

(a) abolition of bonded labour;
(b) implementation of the Minimum Wages Act.
(c) provision of house-sites and
(d) distribution of surplus lands among the landless tribals.

Alongwith liquidation of debts, structural changes are essential such as prevention of alienation of tribal lands to non-tribals, complete stoppage of unauthorised money-lending and creation of a wide network of banking services. Peculiar social structure and age-old interclass relationships camouflage much of the tribal indebtedness.

The system of bonded labour has developed from dependence of the vast bulk of the poor tribals on landlords and big farmers. It is the result of less income, much unproductive expenditure and improvidence on the part of the tribals.

(a) What are the causes and extent of the tribal debts?
(b) What measures have been taken to prevent, reduce or liquidate tribal debts?
(c) What is the effect of the Money Lending Act of 1946 as amended from time to time?
(d) What steps have been taken for restoration of the mortgaged lands of the tribals?
(e) What is the extent of the restored lands and how many tribals have been benefited?
(f) What are the operational effects of

the laws or executive orders on the tribals? Are they freed from the debts?

Bonded Labour

(a) How is the bonded labour connected with tribal debts?
(b) What are the incidents of bonded labour?
(c) To what extent are the tribals involved in bonded labour?
(d) What measures have been taken by Govt. for abolition of the bonded labour?
(e) What are the operational effects of the implementation of the Bonded Labour Systems (Abolition) Act, 1976? Are the tribals benefited?
(f) What measures have been taken to rehabilitate the freed bonded labourers? Is alternative credit provided after abolition of debts?
(g) What are the reactions of the bonded labourers? Are they happy to be free or feel the loss of security enjoyed by them?

V. The Five Year Plans

The Five Year Plans aim at growth with social justice and economic equality. They need to be considered, so far as they help strengthen the tribal economy, remove the ecological isolation of tribals, increase education and literacy among the tribals and provide gainful employment.

(a) What schemes have been undertaken affecting the tribal land such as soil conservation, consolidation of holdings, prevention of fragmentation, provision of irrigation facilities and supply of agricultural inputs? To what extent have the tribals taken advantage of those schemes? Do they feel that the schemes are for their economic betterment?

(b) What are socio-economic changes taking place in the life-style of the tribals and their farming methods and allied agricultural activities?

(c) Whether the funds sanctioned and allotted for tribal development were fully utilized? If not, the reasons thereof?

(d) What are the difficulties in implementation of tribal schemes? How far lack of adequate infrastructure, trained administrative cadre, general apathy of the bureaucrats to field work in the difficult tribal habitat and the failure of Govt. to enlist co-operation of the voluntary agencies in the execution of the various projects are responsible for delay or inadequate execution of the tribal schemes?

VI. Panchayati Raj

In order to increase participation of the people in the planning process, the Panchayati Raj was introduced in the State in April 1963, after enacting the Gujarat Panchayats Act, 1961. Under the Act, certain powers and functions of Govt. have been delegated to the Panchayati Raj bodies under the Bombay Land Revenue Code and other laws. The development schemes including the schemes in the tribal areas are implemented by these bodies as agency of Government.

(a) What are the special provisions regarding land use and management of tribal lands in the Gujarat

Panchayats Act, 1961?

(b) What powers and functions have been delegated to the Panchayati Raj institutions under the provisions of Bombay Land Revenue Code, the Bombay Tenancy and Agricultural Lands Act, the Prevention of Fragmentation and Consolidation of Holdings Act, 1947, the Bombay Court Fees Act, etc.?

How are the tribal lands administered under the delegated powers and functions?

(c) Whether a certain percentage of funds is earmarked for the Scheduled Tribes;

(d) Whether any concessions are given to tribals in grant of loans, subsidy for agricultural schemes and land improvement schemes (seeds, manures, pesticides, technical guidance, implements, etc.)

(e) Give details of the schemes implemented for improvement of live-stock, poultry farming, fishing and dairy farming to tribals? Whether the schemes are acceptable to tribals?

(f) Is there a key village scheme in operation in the area? If so, how are the tribals benefited?

(g) Are Tribals given preference in the village housing schemes?

(h) Whether mid-day meals are provided to the children of the Scheduled Tribes in schools?

(i) Whether preference is given to tribes in locating Rural Works programme?

(j) Whether in deserving cases of tribals, the percentage of popular contribution is reduced or waived?

(k) What is the attitude of the non-tribals to the schemes for the welfare of tribals? Do they show traditional apathy or bias against the tribal schemes?

(l) Whether there is adequate decentralisation of powers and functions to the Panchayati Raj bodies? If not, what are the reasons?

(m) What is the provision for coordination of the activities of the Project administrator and the Panchayati Raj institutions, so far as the Tribal Area Sub-Plan schemes are concerned?

(n) How are the tribal schemes implemented through the Panchayati Raj institutions? Are there any bottlenecks (i.e. lack of coordination and cooperation)?

APPENDIX-IV

CASE MATERIALS ON LAND ALIENATION

Introduction

As it is clear from the accounts in Chapter 4, the heart of the problem of tribal land system lies in unprecedented alienation of tribal lands. The Government of Gujarat has taken steps to implement Section 73-A of the Bombay L.R. Code 1879 in order to prevent unauthorised alienation of tribal lands. It has encountered unforeseen hurdles and problems having administrative, socio-economic and cultural dimensions. This can be discerned in the following two cases from the Deputy Collectors teams named LND-5, specially appointed to detect case of tribal land alienation, concealed or otherwise. These cases in the form of official communications were addressed to a District Collector and to the Director of this project respectively. They represent dilemmas of decision-making and provide excellent case materials on the subject. Obviously, they are short of being full case studies in the strict sense of the term. The original names of places and people are not revealed in the text.

Case Material No. 1

Presented below is a brief letter from a Deputy Collector LND-5 who was kind enough to respond to the request of the Director of this Tribal Land Systems (TLS) Study Project for sending copies of the Government letters in connection with the cases of land alienation detected by him, alongwith the stay orders of the High Court to the appeal of a non-tribal involved in a case.

The LND-5 Unit for detecting the cases of land alienation of the tribals consisted of 1 - Deputy Collector, 2 - Dy. Mamlatdars, 4 - Circle Inspectors and 1 - assistant who started work on 28.2.1978. The Unit worked in five talukas of a predominantly tribal district. Section 73-A introduced from 4-4-61 was said to have been applicable only to one taluka 'N' of the five. The Unit therefore, tried to detect alienation of tribal land in this taluka alone. The

Government had issued a circular one month before the starting of this Unit, that if the land alienation has taken place between two tribals or voluntary agencies, no orders should be passed until further notice from the Government in this regard. This is the reason why orders were issued for restoration of land in the cases of tribal land transfer to non-tribals as per Section 79-A and Section 202. The cases connected with this orders were referred to the Gujarat High Court who gave the ruling that since Section 73-A was not applicable to taluka 'N', all the cases detected by the Unit and orders issued in this regard stand null and void. Letter of Deputy Collector, LND-5 Unit with minor modification throws further light on the subject.

Dear Shri

With reference to your D.O. letter No. T.L.S. 5 (III) dated 8-3-1978, I am sending herewith the copies of following Government Notification Resolution and circular for your guidance.

(i) Government Agricultural & Lands Deptts. Notification No. 3961/41509 G. dated 4-4-61.
(ii) Government Agricultural & Lands Deptts. Resolution No. even dated 4-4-61.
(iii) Government Revenue Department Vernacular No. ADJ-1077-M.R. 3041-2 dated 6-1-78.

2. Before publication of Government notification dated 4-4-61, the villages of A, B, C, and D talukas of M district, being already surveyed and settled under Land Revenue Code, the said notification is not applicable to those schedule area. While the said notification is applicable to the villages of N taluka as per orders given in G.R. dated 5-4-61, as the survey settlement introduced during Ex-State regime is not considered under Chapter VIII A of the Bombay Land Revenue Code 1879. This unit has therefore, done the field work and detected total 1039 case of breaches of Section 73-A of L.R.C.

3. In the year 1964 one Non-Adivasi purchased lands of Adivasi of P village of N taluka, without obtaining the previous permission of Collector under Section 73-A of L.R.C. After hearing the parties, the Collector of M declared the sale void in the year 1973. The purchaser filed an appeal before Special Secretary who confirmed the order of

Collector and rejected the request of applicant. The purchaser thereafter filed special civil application No. 1191 of 1974 against the order of Collector and Special Secretary under article 226 of Constitution of India, in the Hon. High Court and obtained stay order on 26-7-74 for not executing the order of Collector and Special Secretary, pending final hearing and further order of the High Court. The Hon. High Court issued final judgement in Special Civil Application No. 1191 of 1974 on 2-2-78 and declared that :

"The original survey settlement in the villages of N taluka is done in the year 1923 by ex-State. The merger took place on 10-6-48 and the land Revenue Code and other Acts of the Bombay State made applicable with effect from 28-7-48 to the merged territories. 'The Government of Bombay in its Revenue Deptt. has issued a notification No. Revenue Department 1611-B/219 dated 6-2-52 recognising very clearly;' the survey settlement in the merged area would however remain unaffected and they must be deemed to have been effected under the Bombay L.R.C., application of Section 73-A would not therefore be feasible where survey settlement have already been introduced".

"It is too late in the day now for the State of Gujarat to say in the year 1961, that those survey settlement cannot be deemed to have been made under the :and Revenue Code".

"In above view of the matter, the stand taken by the Government was ex-facie bad. The notification in question, therefore did not apply to these lands and consequently the petition therefore succeeds, the impugned orders are hereby set aside. Rule accordingly made obsolete".

4. In view of the above decision of High Court, Section 73-A of L.R.C. is not applicable in the villages of N taluka and hence we cannot take any action in 1039 cases which have been detected by my unit.

5. However the Collector M has submitted the copy of the Judgement of High Court to Government in R.D. vide his letter No. dated 23-2-78 requesting the Government to issue necessary instructions in the matter and whether the Government desire to file an appeal in this case. The instructions from the Government are awaited.

6. I am not in a position to send the copy of High Court Judgement of the above case. If it is necessary for your study the

same may kindly be obtained from Collector M.

With kind regards

Yours Sincerely,
Dy. Collector LND-5
(N. Taluka)

Case Material No. 2

This is a fairly long communication from a Deputy Collector LND-5, to the Collector of his district, under whose jurisdiction he worked and conducted searching operations to detect tribal land alienation with the help of a team of the revenue staff. The matter is suitably modified.

Sir,

In continuation of my previous report data 16-7-77 No. LND-5-77, I herewith submit my further report to government for orders for the early solution of practical difficulties in implementation of Section 73-A of the Bombay L.R.C. 1979 in 280 villages of X Taluka, as well as in 129 villages of Y Taluka.

2. As reported earlier, since the publication of government notification No. LND/3961/41509/G, dated 4-4-61, I have completed the survey of transfer of land of tribals without previous permission of the Collector and located instances of transfer as under:

Name of Taluka	No. of Village	Total cases of aliena-tion	Sale to Adivasis	Sale to Non-Adivasis	Partition among the Adivasis families	Breach of condition other than 73-A
X	280	6,319	2,996	405	2,817	101
Y	129	895	421	161	309	4
		7,214	3,467	566	3,126	105

3. Now, I have started to dispose of cases under L.R. Code 1879

for restoration of possession to the original occupant and I experience following difficulties in implementation of 73-A as under.

4. As per above government notification dated 4-4-61 issued under a Section 73-A, following conditions are to be fulfilled.

(1) Section 73-A is to be applied before introduction of original survey and settlement.
(2) It should be applied to the scheduled area.
(3) It should be applied to the land held by scheduled tribe occupants.
(4) After issue of the above notification tribal occupant can transfer his land only with the permission of competent authority, i.e. Collector.

I submit herewith facts prevailing in X and Y talukas on the above points as under:

Before issue of the above notification, I have verified from the available process file of the office of Mamlatdar on this issue that the Bombay Land Revenue Code of 1879 was applied to the concerned Princely State in 1909 and survey and settlement was introduced under the signature of notification issued by the than ruler. In these notification no section of Land Revenue Code was quoted, but the L.R.C. was in force in the state and these notifications were issued under the provisions of L.R.C. 1879. These original notifications were submitted by the Mamlatdar to the Government of Bombay through the Collector under his letter No. LND, dated 17-7-1950.

5. Subsequently, Mamlatdar has reported under his letter No. LND dated: 24-3-1952 stating that survey and settlement is done in "X" taluka before merge of the Princely State except 8 villages for which Mamlatdar has proposed to apply Section 73-A of the Bombay Land Revenue Code.

Process file of government notification dated 4-4-61 ends at the office of the Mamlatdar. From the above letter of Mamlatdar dated 24-3-1952 what decision was taken by the State Government on the above reference is not known. However, it is presumed that government might not have considered the scientific survey and the settlement carried out by the Princely State within the meaning of Section 103 of the Bombay Land Revenue Code, though it was applied since 1909 in this State. But this point does not give any indication of clarification in the above government notification dated 4-4-1961. Not only that, but also it does not give any specification about area of X and Y talukas. It gives the idea about scheduled area and unsurveyed and unsettled area.

6. Besides this, there has been never any recovery or revision survey carried out in "X" taluka after merger of the state. As such, it is very difficult to rule out the argument put by the parties that land of this taluka was unsurveyed and unsettled without specific clarification received from the government regarding the last report of the Mamlatdar as stated above on the date 24-3-1952.

7. In view of the above facts on this point, it is proposed that the process file underlying above government notification dated 4-4-1961 may be traced out and decision of government on the above report of Mamlatdar may be obtained to rule out the argument of survey and settlement in the state.

Second point of notification is that it should be applied to the scheduled area defined under the Constitution of India. On this point, it may be excused to bring out the fact that the government notification dated 4-4-1961 has remained unnoticed till 1974 at the district level for the execution in the village records at the village level. Only after the Collector's notification of 1973, dated 19-1-1974, the names of villages were notified where Section 73-A is being applied. On what basis these villages X or Y, were notified under Section 73-A is not known from the process file from the office of the Mamlatdar. But it is presumed that the villages covered under the scheduled area, and areas under the management of native state are notified by the Collector under his notification dated 14-4-1961 in general applied to all scheduled area of the state without specifying districtwise such area. From the survey of the village records and process file of the office of Mamlatdar, it is seen that taluka office and village officers i.e. talaties were unaware of the applicability of Section 73-A of the Land Revenue Code in this taluka till the date of the issue of the notification of the Collector dated 19-1-1974. So all taluka level officers went on certifying the entry of the transaction of the land occupied by the scheduled tribal people till that date. As such there is one argument from the parties that they were not only ignorant of the provisions of the applicability of Section 73-A but local authorities were also unaware of this provisions and they have already certified the entry of such transactions, such transactions as state above must not be less than 80 per cent of the total cases traced out, i.e. about 5000 cases where mutation entries of the transaction are certified by the local officers. So in such cases it is a question whatever "mutation entry certifying officer" should be made a party to it or not. It is suggested that these legal provision is not kept out of the litigation to the civil court and as a safe measure, "mutation entry certifying officer" may be made a party for avoiding any mistake in the proceedings of the case.

8. Third point of the notification under consideration is that it is applied to the land held by scheduled tribal occupants only. In this district and particularly in X taluka, very controversial point having very vital effect is about "Rathwa Koli". As per constitution, Rathwa is a notified sub-caste of the scheduled tribes recognised by the government. As per village records most of the occupants are registered as either Koli or Rathwa Koli and they are not recognised as scheduled tribes while preparing the cases under Section 73-A. It is noticed that they give the statement as either Rathwa or Rathwa Koli.

9. Moreover, after issue of the above notification dated 19-1-1974 by the Collector, Mamlatdar have issued circular to the village officer i.e. *talaties* to register entry in the village record of right covering all occupants and the land to which Section 73-A is applied and in these entries, they have been written as 'Rathwas' though in their *Khatas* i.e., V.F. No. 8-A & VII/XII, it is written as 'Koli' or 'Rathwa Koli'. As such there is a contradiction in village record itself which creates complication and controversy in finalisation of cases. As I understand, Ex-Collector has already reported since long to the government of Gujarat, Education and Labour Departments suggesting that "Rathwa Koli" should be considered as scheduled tribes, considering their socio-economic condition. As there is no difference between Rathwa and Rathwa Koli, their Social and Religious customs are the same. Their economic condition is almost equal. However, it is not known whether any decision is taken by the government on this point. As such there is very crucial point for dispersal of above cases for uncertainty of sub-caste of the tribal people. If we insist to obtain caste certificate from Mamlatdar or Taluka Development Officer, it will add one more harassment to the tribes and delay in disposal of cases. Apart from this there is not a sound proof for issue of the caste certificates with these officers,

except affidavit of an applicant and recommendation letter of Village Panchayat as most of the adult tribals of this taluka are illiterate. In addition to this, there the seller is challenged to be non-tribal whether caste certificate from the above officer to be called or not is also a point that requires to be clarified, as Mamlatdar is of the impression that he is authorised only to certify tribes and he is advised by the collectorate that he has no authority to issue caste certificate other than backward class. It is a fact that in a welfare and development of the weaker section of society due care is being taken with a view that real benefit goes to the real beneficiary, and for that necessity of caste certificate is admitted as an essential evidence in almost all schemes of welfare activities and as such local officers are authorised to issue caste certificate of scheduled tribes.

10. Section 73-A of the Land Revenue Code Restricts the right of Scheduled tribe occupants without prior permission in comparison with non-tribes. The end of this provision is safeguarding the occupancy of the tribel occupants from easily falling their lands in the hands of non-tribes and money-lenders. In other words, scheduled tribe agriculturists are saved from the exploitation of local money-lenders taking away their lands for nominal price consideration.

11. However, it will be seen from the surveyed figures mentioned in above para 2 that most of the transfers without prior permission are among the tribals and hence now, there is a strong feeling developed, among the *adivasis* that this provision is operated against their interest in the name of their safeguards from non-tribes. As such, their main demand is to exclude transactions among the tribes which is not provided in the present provision of Section 73-A. Not only that but also there is no positive indication of permitting them for partition among the family members and remote relatives during the life time of an occupant. From the above figures, it will be seen that of about 50 per cent, most of the located cases are only partition cases and most of the partition cases are made during the life time of the occupant to avoid the quarrel among the co-shares after the death of occupants and remaining cases are only partitioned without mutation and heirship formalities after the death of the occupant, as most of the tribes yet have no sense of necessity to get mutation entries registered in the record of rights and hence there are some instances that since three to four generations, no mutation entry is

registered in the record of rights. In such cases only they get co-sharers' name registered in the form of VII/XII, and with that proof they get their claim served for getting loan, subsidy, etc. In other cases, they get loans and subsidies in the name of oldest heir and divide their individual shares.

12. Besides this, there is no provision under Section 73-A to regularise the transactions retrospectively and hence they take shelter of the provisions of other land reform Laws, like Bombay Tenancy and Agricultural Lands Act and Prevention of Fragmentation Act. There cannot be tenant on the land covered under Section 73-A after 4-4-1961. However, as stated above, Government notification dated 4-4-1961 lost the sight of the local authorities and there are number of cases numbering thousands that have been decided by the Agricultural Land Tribunals in this taluka. The parties remained silent as they have been successful to avoid one restriction with the help of legal authorities, and possession regularised with the fine to the purchaser.

13. Moreover, Section 73-A does not give power to the competent authority to regularise the transaction or to forfeit the land to the Government in case of denial by the original occupant to take over possession, so there is a strong feeling among the tribes that this restriction is working against the interest of tribe purchasers and also against the natural justice, as land is to be restored without any compensation to the purchasers. Consequently, one trend very fastly developing in this area is that tribe and non-tribe purchasers are trying to certify the sellers as non-tribe with the help of documentary evidence of the village record itself as stated above. There is likelihood of developing unrest and litigation among the poor tribes for small piece of lands against local authorities. Their very genuine point is that the local authorities were not aware of the provision of Section 73-A for years together and they went on certifying transactions and *mutation* entries, than how can poor illiterate tribes know this restriction. So, they argue that all the certifying officers who have certified mutation entries may be made parties.

14. Considering the point of justice and equity, it is suggested that out of above 7,214 (see point 2) transactions 3,126 transactions are the partitions only and they should be confirmed. I have learnt from Panchmahals district that LND-5 Unit is directly sending the case papers to the concerned Mamlatdars for registration and certification

of mutation entries in such partition cases. Secondly, out of remaining 4088 cases there are 3467 transactions among the tribals and these are sales mostly among the remote relatives, so, their demand is to regularise the sales of land which is not going out of possession of tribals. I believe this demand is from almost all the districts of the State where Section 73-A is applied.

15. In this connection attention is invited to the minutes of the meeting of the Collectors of three districts. Abstracts of the minutes on this point is as under:

> "The details of transfers by tribals to tribals and tribals to non-tribals should be separately reported. It was represented that transfers between tribals also are invalid as per present instructions. It is necessary that such transfers are allowed to be regularised. Keeping in view that tribals themselves do not start cornering lands of economically weaker tribals. The Collectors are requested to send proposals with details so that Government can consider the issue".

16. In view of the above, it is presumed that Government is of the view of consideration for regularising transactions among tribal to tribal, provided there should be the proviso in Section 73-A itself or Government may issue special Notification adding the proviso in original notification dated 4-4-1961. So Government may kindly be moved showing above details with reference to the above minutes of the meeting of the Collectors. If these points of partition among the tribal families and sale among tribals are considered to be regularised, there will remain only 566 cases of sale to non-tribals out of these cases as per my knowledge, 119 cases are already decided by project officer, and 20 cases are decided by this office. Then only 427 cases remain to decided.

17. Out of above 427 cases, it is presumed about one fourth must be sale of land for residential and non-agricultural use. So it will be very difficult to evict the buyers from their residential buildings. As per present provision of Section 73-A there is no provision to exempt the land put to non-agricultural use and as such after breach of provision of Section 73-A, there is a breach of provision of Prevention of Fragmentation Act, and further non-agricultural use without permission. As such, there is a series of breach of provisions

under Land Revenue and Land Reform Laws. In such cases it will be very difficult to evict present occupant under Section 79-A as subsequent breach of provisions of Land Revenue Code and Prevention of Fragmentation Act provides provision of regularisation. Not only that but in case, if original tribal occupant is not willing to take the possession of Land in question, it will be difficult for local authority to settle the issue finally, and there will be no up-to-date record of right as construed under Land Scheme No. 5, as there is no ban on the Jurisdiction of Civil Courts, and poor tribals will be involved in landless Civil Court litigation. Besides this, out of 427 cases 'zeable number of cases are sale to the Government departments, Panchayat authorities, Cooperative Societies and Voluntary Social Service Institutions, viz. Vadodara District Backward Class Seva Sangh, etc. for the development activities of tribals themselves. These sales were made for construction of Ashram Schools, Ashram School buildings, Primary Health Centres, Godowns for Cooperative Societies, etc. It is surprising that Government Departments and Public Service Institutions have failed to seek prior permission of the Collector before entering into sale contract of land belonging to tribals. This is the main argument put forth by the private buyers that Government Departments failed to seek prior permission, then to what extent Government expect individual illiterate tribals to seek the prior permission before the transaction. In view of the above facts, it is suggested that all such sales to Government Departments Panchayats, Social Service Institutions and Cooperative Societies be regularised as Government policy, as they can be considered *bona fide* sales without any element of exploitation. If this proposal is considered favourably by the Government, then there will be hardly 300 cases of sale to non-tribals in both the talukas out of which 161 cases are only of Y taluka and remaining will be of X taluka.

18. I may submit herewith that the main survey of the work is over, case preparation work is about 30 per cent completed and according to the present speed of the work with the present staff, it will be over before December 1977, and if Government agrees to drop the cases of partition among the family members, it will be over by end of October. If Government agrees to the above proposal, there will be very small case work, and X taluka is very light so far its normal revenue workload is concerned. So it will be difficult to

dispose of these cases by the regular Prant Officer incharge of the taluka. As such, Government may be moved to discontinue the post of Dy. Collector. At the most one Dy. Mamlatdar and one Circle Inspector may be given to regular Prant Officer to look after the execution of the orders of the Prant Officer. I may mention here that after 1974, there is hardly any sales transaction notice to the non-tribal, and in almost all villages mutation entries, for the land covered under Section 73-A are registered by the *talatis*. Provision of Section 73-A is now more or less popular in the villages and particularly among non-tribal people. As such, it is suggested that for such small work, big establishment headed by the Dy. Collector is not necessary. This establishment may be under the Plan Scheme for strengthening the land records of the tribal occupants and as such this is totally establishment oriented scheme without giving any tangible material benefit to the tribals. In view of the above facts, it is suggested that instead of maintaining such big establishment, there should be proper custody of the village record of Scheduled area at talukas level in possession of one or two assistants, namely, Dy. Mamlatdar and Circle Inspector, as for the present, mostly all *talatis* are keeping this record where they are staying, and mostly they stay in taluka headquarters.

19. I may submit herewith that during my survey, I have found following main reasons for breach of the provisions of Land Revenue Code and Rules and various Land Reforms in Tribal areas.

(1) Having no necessity felt by the Tribal Occupants for heirship mutation after the death of head of family.

(2) Non-attendance of such changes by the *talatis* for a long time, though occupant approach them in time.

(3) In spite of repeated instructions from taluka Officer, *talatis* are making change in V.F.No. VII-XII without mutation and they do not report to the Mamlatdars, such change in possession.

20. Above defects can hardly be solved till village records are kept in the possession of *talati*, and are kept at the places of their sweet will without any security of the same. So I suggest to keep a permanent arrangements for proper custody of the record at taluka level and regular system of review of the possession of the land with

the actual position at site by the officer not below the rank of Mamlatdar and any change in possession and any mutation entry must be passed through such officer and there should be total checking of *pahani patrak* of every survey number in such scheduled area by the Mamlatdar, and annual certificate there of should be obtained from such Mamlatdar. The occupants will be saved from unauthorised entries made by the *talaties* in *Pahani Patraks* and Government will be saved from time to time creating big establishments of Record of Right Team Survey now and then.

21. Lastly I submit that Section 73-A puts only restriction of previous permission of the Collector before transfer and this huge task has come up before us only due to non-attendance of the provisions by the local officers in time, so big number of transactions are carried out. Now considering general principles of contract act, these transactions with economic prices in absence of element of exploitation, are worth considering with the consent of seller for regularisation. So it is requested to move the Government for consideration and early decision on the above points. As seems today, a big problem likely to affect law and order situation can be solved permanently and finally. If it is deemed fit henceforth, Section 73-A may be made more beneficial to the tribals to save them from costly litigations.

Dy. Collector LND-5
(X Taluka)

APPENDIX-V

INFLUENCE OF MOKSHA MARGA HINDU SECT ON TRIBALS

Introduction

For obvious reasons, we shall first throw light on the basic tenants and influence of this popular Hindu Sect on the tribals of South Gujarat and then give some information on the origin and development of the Sect.

In the districts of Surat, Valsad and the Dangs, one comes across tribals, who, along with other non-tribals follow the teachings of Moksha Marga which literally means "Path to Salvation". The devotees put a secterian mark on their forehead. It is in red colour powder and resembles U shape. This symbolic mark is originally of Vaishnavite Sect. The mark carries three vertical dots in the middle of U shape. The Moksha Margis worship premordial sound of Pranava Mantra OM, which is a manifestation of Brahma. The devotees follow pious life and observe sacred codes of conduct as laid down in Hindu Shastras. They take no liquor in any form, and avoid taking even *nira* or *nira-gur* (made from the bark of Palm tree), abstain from eating meat and do not keep sexual contacts with persons other than married partner. They aspire for a higher spiritual life, ethical worldly existence and ultimate salvation after death.

Philosophy of Moksha Marga

Moksha Marga is based on the Hindu concept of Sanatana Dharma propounded in the Hindu Scriptures. It says that the whole world is one family and that all creatures have but one soul. The aim of life is to realise the Supreme Reality enshrined in the Pranava Mantra OM. The supreme being is full of love, knowledge, yoga and devotion. These divine elements of the eternal vedic relation should be resorted to throughout one's life. One should get *Diksha* dedication through a guru who is disinterested and well versed in the knowledge of Moksha Marga. Even while accepting the duties and functions of the physical body, one should follow the path of service to humanity and practice universal brotherhood in the spirit of self-control self-abstinance and follow the rules and regulations of moral code of conduct as laid down in Dharma Shashtras (treatise on religious duty). The essence of life is Dharma (duty) and goal of Dharma is Moksha (Salvation).

Background of the Founder

The founder of this sect was one Vallabhram Suryaram Vyas, born on the 8th day of dark half of the month of Shravan at 12-00 midnight in Vikram era 1901. The time and date of his birth was said to be the same as those of Lord Shri Krishna.

Shri Vallabhram hailed from Ahmedabad and even today his descendants are living in the city. He was a Mevada Brahmin by birth. His father was a professional narrator and singer called *Kathakar* of Hindu religious stories in prose and verse. In his early life Vallabhram had reportedly realised the vision of the Supreme Reality in the essence of the word OM under the blessings of his spiritual guru Vishveswara Narayana. He was said to have passed through many births, lives and mission in life. He was ordained and destined by god to give *Diksha* (baptism) and spiritual knowledge to those who aspire initiation in the sect of Moksha Marga.

He wrote commentaries on *Mahabharata* in prose and in verse and travelled from place to place among the masses in South Gujarat and neighbouring areas. He dissuaded people from petty crimes, quarrels, meat eating, amassing wealth by *Adharma* or corrupt means, drinking liquor, etc., and persuaded them to follow Moksha Marga, i.e., the path of liberation from the cycle of birth and death. He advocated that salvation was the ultimate aim of human life. One can attain it by meditation and becoming one with the soul of the Sadguru and God Narayan.

Vallabhram established the Omkareshwar Mandir at Ahmedabad in Vikram Samvat 1959, after installing Siddhi Yantra therein. The site of the temple was enclosed later on by walls, and the Statue of Omkar was installed. Inexplicable visions of god and experience of spirituality were reported to be experienced by the follower of Moksha Marga who offered their prayers in the temple. The sect of Moksha Marga is open to all men and women irrespective of caste, colour or creed.

Shri Vallabhram gave special attention to the poor, depressed, illiterate or uneducated and preached in simple Gujarati language, so that all can understand and follow his teachings. He denigrated hypocrisy in the name of religion and insisted on the path of truthfulness, righteousness, compassion, forbearance, non-violence, purity, joviality, fraternity and love for all. At the time of his appointment to the *Gadi* (throne) of the Moksha Marga, Vallabhram declared that the ultimate Guru is Parabrahma, and that he gave the knowledge to others as he was inspired by God Vishweshwara Narayana.

The Moksha Margis, both non-tribals and tribals were to be found in the villages of Surat, Valsad and the Dangs districts. Other tribal districts were not influence by the Sect. In the Mahuva Taluka, there were 5 to 10 households of Moksha Margis in every tribal village. They congregate alternatively in any one village in Karchelia area on the 11th day of the bright half of every month for worship, chanting *Bhajans* and listening to religious discourses. At Anaval village, they observe the occasions of religious festivity called *Utsavas* on the death anniversary of Vallabhram, the founder of the Sect and his successor son Ramji Lal. The day of death anniversary of both was the fifteenth day of the bright half of the month of *Chaitra*, i.e. *Gurupurnima* or teacher's full moon day. Most of the followers of Moksha Marga assemble every year on Janmastami day at Ahmedabad, the birth place of both the Gurus.

At Anaval temple of Moksha Marga, provision is made for a lecture hall, residential accommodation and other modern facilities for the pilgrims and visitors. The work was undertaken on a large scale for which donations from the followers and well-wishers of Moksha Marga were collected.

Impact of Moksha Marga on Tribals

The followers of Moksha Marga carry on indoctrination work with the help of musical instruments, microphones and loudspeakers from village to village. In the interior of areas such as the Vyara taluka of Surat district, there were 575 followers distributed in 23 villages. Local followers of Vyara town itself meet weekly at a place of worship and have a programme of chanting and exchange of religious thoughts through *Satsang, Bhajan, Kirtan*, etc. In the villages also programmes of *Satsang* by religious preachers was arranged for the benefit of members. In Uchchhal taluka of Surat district, there were about 2500 tribal followers of this Sect spread over 13 villages. In Vansda taluka of Valsad district, the followers were to be found in practically all villages, with a concertation of sizeable number of followers in 21 villages. Some devotees from Naswadi, Gandevi and Bilimora give religious discourses and hold discussions with the villagers for spreading the message of the Sect. In Umbergaon taluka of Valsad district, about 1000 tribals and about 300 non-tribals in 20 villages were the followers of Moksha Marga. The religious discourses resulted in economic, social and religious transformation of the tribals and non-tribals. It was reported that this Sect had following even outside Gujarat and India. More than 1000 followers were said to have been listed from foreign countries e.g., America, United Kingdom and Muslim countries also.

The Impact of Moksha Marga on Tribal Life and Culture

As mentioned earlier, a devotee of Moksha Marga has to lead a pure life, give up drinking liquor, including *nira* (toddy juice). They have also to give up eating meat, nira-gur, eggs, fish and all other vices. There has been positive influence of Moksha Marga on the economic conditions of poor tribals. The savings from abstinence have enabled them to maintain themselves and their families within limited income. They were able to purchase necessities of life and to lead a peaceful life and set an example to others in the society. One can predict that in course of time they would raise their level of living in tune with non-tribals who are also the followers of Moksha Marga, and can get merged with the mainstream of life.

It is to the credit of Moksha Marga that a religious climate and desirable ethical standard was created that would finally wean away tribals from hard drinks and other inmoral vices. The significant impact of the Moksha Marga was thus on the moral behaviour of the tribals leading to their economic batterment. Where the legal measures of prohibition and the services of Gandhian social workers could not succeed, this sect surprisingly succeeded in checking the evil of drinks and other vices among the tribals.

APPENDIX-VI

PROCEEDINGS OF THE SEMINAR ON THE REPORT ON TRIBAL LAND SYSTEMS STUDY

Introduction

The Seminar on the Report of Tribal Land Systems in Gujarat was held under the auspices of the Indian Institute of Public Administration, Gujarat State Regional Branch, Ahmedabad, in the Committee Room of the Indian Chamber of Commerce and Industries, on 6th April, 1980 at 10.00 a.m. to 12 noon. The Seminar formed a part of the celebrations of the Silver Jubilee Year of the IIPA, which commenced on the previous day when the Final Report was presented to Her Excellency Smt. Sharda Mukherjee, the then Governor of Gujarat.

The Seminar was presided over by Shri Chinubhai Chimanbhai, Chairman of IIPA, Ahmedabad. The discussions at the Seminar were conducted under the Chairmanship of Dr. T.B. Naik, Director, Tribal Research and Training Institute, Gujarat Vidyapith, Ahmedabad.

Participants at the Seminar

Besides Shri Chinubhai and Dr. Naik, those present at the Seminar were Sarvashri P.N. Mittal and S.R. Modi, Hon. Secretary and Treasurer respectively of IIPA, Ahmedabad, Mrs. Swaranalata Varma, IAS, a member of Regional Executive Board was also present. Members of the T.L.S. Project research team present at the Seminar were, Sarvashri G.O. Parikh, Shri T.S. Shah and Shri R.G. Bhatt. Invited participants attending the Seminar were Prof. V.R. Gaekwad, Prof. Pravin Pathak, Dr.Siddharaj Solanki, Sarvashri R.B. Lal, Shri Gaurishankar Pandya, Shri M.I. Masavi, Shri K.D. Makwana, Shri Dilip Dave, Shri C.M. Patel, Shri S.P. Patel Shri J.N. Rathod, Shri G.D. Patel, Shri S.D. Vashi, Shri C.M. Chaudhary, Shri C.B. Upadhyaya, and Shri B.S. Patel, and others. The findings of the report were presented by Dr. H.R. Trivedi, the project director. Welcoming the participants, Shri Chinubhai first introduced Dr. T.B. Naik, Chairman of the Seminar. He expressed happiness that a noted anthropologists of his stature had agreed to spare his valuable time and chair the Seminar. He further said that we should try to take the greatest advantage of the efforts made by the research workers on such difficult subjects and felt that the report on which the Seminar is held today will not be forgotten in future either by the Government to whom it is submitted or the scholars interested in this subject. He further said that tribal land system is an interesting, but a difficult subject on which valuable discussions should take place because of the gravity of the problem of tribal land alienation. He was glad that IIPA State Branch had undertaken this important study and a good work was completed. He then invited Dr. H.R. Trivedi to present the salient features of the report, a summary of which was circulated among participants. At the outset, however, he expressed keen desire to know as to what were the methods used for collection of data from various sources. He was happy to learn that a variety of standard research methods including case study and survey research were used with questionnaires and guidelines.

He remarked that it is necessary that the research worker must carefully choose methods of collecting data keeping in mind what he is trying to study. If his methods are not appropriate, it is very likely that what he intends to study may not be properly reflected in the nature of the data. He then invited the members of the audience to raise relevant points for discussion on the subject. The participants who took active part in the seminar were: Prof. V.R. Gaekwad of Indian Institute of Management, Dr. Pravin Pathak of Sardar Patel Institute of Economic and Social Research, Dr. S.S. Solanki, Mr. R.B. Lal and Mr. M. Masavi, Mr. Chaudhary of the Tribal Research and Training Institute, Gujarat Vidyapith, Mr. P.N. Mittal and Mrs. S.K. Verma (IAS) of IIPA State Branch.

Salient Features of the Discussions

On the issue of differentiation between tribal and non-tribals communities for the purpose of the study of land as well as other aspects, Dr. Trivedi indicated that the leaders at national level and the policy-makers have considered it important to distinguish between these two groups of people after independence, for development programmes. Besides, from the point of view of differentiation of various kinds existing between two cultures, there was nothing wrong in making such for categories for practical consideration. It is needless to say that our Constitution itself has already provided legal status and privileges for development of Scheduled Tribes in the country. So far as the concept of tribal land is concerned, it is not the same as the non-tribal might have thought about, because the very concept of property as such among the tribals is very much different than that among the non-tribals on account of great variations in the two cultures. So far as the definition of tribal land is concerned, it is more or less the same as defined in the Land Revenue Code of Government of Gujarat. Nevertheless, in olden times, most of the tribals reportedly looked upon that whole areas of the forest land including trees, covering an extensive area of a village boundary as the land on which they had rights. Dr. Naik felt that it is doubtful whether any government in the past were able to understand the manner in which the lands were occupied by the tribals for multiple use of ancestor worship, earning livelihood by food-gathering, cultivation, etc. The problem of alienation of tribal land in the present context is possibly associated with how differently the tribals and the government look upon the occupancy rights based on clan or collective ownership of land by the households defined by the norms of family composition of the literate and educated people.

It was further highlighted that the restrictive measures on alienating tribal land are provided under Section 73-A of the Bombay LRC. This Section of the Land Revenue Code was enacted in the British times in 1901 in order to help highly distressed families of poorer tribals so that they may not lose their land under stress and strain of draught and scarcity conditions. Section 73-A stipulated that the Collector of a district will study every proposed case of alienation of the land of a poorer tribal, in the notified area and on the merit of each case will allow the land-holder to sell, mortgage or transfer his land. This Section became a preventive measure against alienation of the land of the Scheduled Tribe (either among themselves or with non-tribals) irrespective of unforeseen conditions of economic stress and strain experienced by a marginal or a small tribal land-holder.

This kind of work in general has not been done in any other state except in our progressive State of Gujarat. This is revealed from the presentation of the contents of the summary of the report. Dr. S.S. Solanki said that the Editorial Committee of *Adivasi Gujarat,* the Journal of TRTI would seriously think of publishing this summary in one of the issues of the journal. He deplored as to what had happened in the past with regard to land alienation of tribals. Many tribals were more or less forced to give up their land in favour of non-tribals. He gave an illustration of a muslim shop-keeper who started his shop in a tribal area, occupying only 10 gunthas of land got as initial help from a tribal, but later on, he the managed to become the occupant of in all 20 acres of land. Giving another illustration, he said that in one tribal village 95 per cent of the total land amounting to 400 acres was in the possession of only 3 non-tribals. Such problems and instances of glaring usurption of tribal land usually happened as the result of loop-holes in law.

One of the participants raised several points of irregularities in the manner in which the tribal land is treated by the government. The greatest injustice is however done to a tribal when his land is acquired by the government on account of public works programmes such as building of irrigation dams etc. A person who lost about 50 acres of land sunk by water in the project of an irrigation dam in the past was compensated in exchanges of only 4 acres of alternate land by the government at another place. Under such circumstances, the number of living descendants of the original tribal land-holder would get nearly next to nothing as a share in the land-holding of the remote ancestor. Many tribals wish to retain the original land-holdings with the eldest male member of the joint family because the amount of land held by a family is related to the social status of the family concerned. In any case, the recent happenings have created a number of problems in which the tribal is loser even when he had taken loans from financial institution. There were cases where the banks have almost come to the point of auctioning the land of the tribals who were not able to repay the loan advanced to them within the stipulated period of time.

Replying to some of the points raised, Dr. Trivedi indicated that so far as attachment and sale of tribal land are concerned, the study team have made a recommendation that it should not be done in the case of needy and poor tribals. This was presented in point 11 of the summary of the report which says, "Provision may be made for prohibiting the attachment and sale of tribal land in execution of the money-decree against a member of the Scheduled Tribe". It was further indicated that the original report has discussed in detail the number of loop-holes in the law and the attitude of the lower functionaries such as the Talati towards land records in tribal areas. The report has also taken the note of a great disadvantage to which the tribals are put when their land is acquired by the government for development of irrigation dams and such other schemes. The money given for compensation to the tribal is so meagre that they are not at all able to get the same size of the land in return. It takes many years to complete the proceedings to enable him to get the full amount of compensation. It is also indicated in the report that the developmental programmes including irrigation dams, etc. in tribals areas mostly benefit the people in the down-stream areas and in the planes the maximum advantage is taken by the non-tribals rather than the tribals.

There were several points raised indicating that improvements had taken place in the treatment of land, in the areas where tribals were in close contact with non-tribals. The situation in the tribal pockets in particular had shown some advantage to the tribal land-holders. The alienation of land of a poor tribal for the purpose of better utilisation of land may be allowed temporarily to a non-tribal. The main emphasis of allowing a tribal to alienate his land on such exchanges should however be permitted between two tribals rather than a tribal and a non-tribal.

One of the participants felt that a lot of land remains unutilised because of its falling within the jurisdiction of railway department in rural areas. It is necessary that the problems of bringing such lands under plough may be studied so that a lot of land which goes waste can be put to better use for the purpose of agriculture either in tribal or non-tribal areas. It was also indicated that the problem of industrialisation in the rural areas has recently been so aggressive that it is difficult to solve the problem of alienation of land of restoration of the same to those who might have already taken up other kinds of subsidiary occupations. The process of industrialisation can certainly be helpful in creating supporting occupation of various kinds for the tribals whose land is sometimes lost without substantiative return to them.

The Chairman of the Seminar Dr. T.B. Naik in his summing up of the discussions expressed happiness at the outcome of the Seminar discussions. He congratulated the IIPA State Branch and Dr. Trivedi for presenting a good report on the subject of tribal land system. In the end Shri Mittal, Hon. Secretary of IIPA thanked Dr. T.B. Naik and the participants for sparing valuable time and contributing their mite in the discussions at the Seminar so as to make them stimulating and meaningful.

BIBLIOGRAPHY

Listed with priority to the year of publication

Bombay Government Records, No. XXIII, Bombay, 1956.

Records of Bombay Government, No. XXVI, New Series, 1956.

Bombay Land Revenue Code, Section 3(4), Bombay, 1879.

J.M. Campbell, *The Gazetteer of Bombay Presidency*, Vol. III, Kaira and Panchmahals, Bombay, 1879.

J.M. Campbell, *Gazetteer of Bombay Presidency*, Vol. V, Bombay, 1880.

J.H. Parmar, *The Revakantha Directory*, Vol. I, Rajkot, 1903.

F.S. Master, *Palanpur Agency Directory*, Vol. I, Rajkot, 1908.

F.S. Master, *The Mahikantha Directory*, Vol. I, Rajkot, 1922.

Gazetteer of Bombay Presidency, Vol. VI-B, Rewa Kantha, Cambay and Surat Agency, Bombay, 1927.

Annual Administration Report of the Idar State, Rajkot, 1930-31.

Administration Report of the Sanjeli State, Rajkot, 1936-37.

Report on the Administration of Sant State, Rajkot, 1940-41.

Administration Report of the Dharampur State, Rajkot, 1940-41.

Report on the Administration of Baria State, Rajkot, 1942-43.

Rajpipala State Administration Report, Rajkot, 1942-43.

Baroda Administration Report, Baroda, 1944-45.

Administration Report of Vansda State, Rajkot, 1944-45.

Administration Report of Chhotandepur State, Rajkot, 1945-46.

G.D. Patel, *The Report of Alienation Enquiry Officer on Idar State*, (unpublished), 1951.

G.D. Patel, *Land Alienation Report of Danta State* (unpublished), 1951.

G.D. Patel, *The Land Problem of Reorganised Bombay State*, Bombay, 1957.

Report of the Scheduled Areas and Scheduled Tribes Commission, Government of India, New Delhi, 1960-61.

U.N. Dhebar, *Report of Scheduled Areas and Scheduled Tribes Commission*, Government of Gujarat, Ahmedabad, 1961.

Gujarat State Gazetteers: Bharuch District, Ahmedabad, 1961.

Land Revenue Rules, 1921, Government Press, Baroda, 1961.

Process Report of Land Reform, Government of India, Planning Commission, Delhi, 1963.

Report of the Study Team on Tribal Development Programmes, P. Shilu, A Committee on Plan Projects, Planning Commission, New Delhi, 1969.

Gujarat State Gazetteer: Dangs District, Ahmedabad, 1971.

Gujarat State Gazetteers: Panchmahals District, Ahmedabad, 1972.

Gujarat State Gazetteers: Sabarkantha District, Ahmedabad, 1974.

P.C. Joshi, *Land Reforms in India*, Allied Publishers, Bombay, 1975.

Report of the National Commission on Agriculture, Part XV, Agrarian Reforms, New Delhi, 1976.

Harshad R. Trivedi, "The Evalution of National Policy for Tribal Development", in *Micro-social Studies in Development and Change*, Chugh Publications, Allahabad, 1977.

G.P. Misra, *Some Aspects of Change in Agrarian Structure*, Sterling Publishers, New Delhi, 1977.

S.N. Dubey and R. Murdia, Eds., *Land Alienation and Restoration of Tribal Communities in India*, Himalaya, Bombay, 1977.

Tribal Area Sub-Plan (Revised), Government of Gujarat, Gandhinagar, 1979.

Tribal Sonvenier, Adim Jati Sevak Sangh, Delhi, 1979.

Arvind Bhatt, *Gujaratana Chudario* (in Gujarati), Gujarat Vidyapith, Ahmedabad, 1985.

INDEX